Charity Accounting and Taxation

Charity Accounting and Taxation

Fifth Edition

The Buzzacott Charity Team

Contributors
Philippa Booth
Edward Finch
Amanda Francis
Katherine Patel
Luke Savvas

Bloomsbury Professional

2010

Bloomsbury Professional Limited, Maxwelton House, 41–43 Boltro Road, Haywards Heath, West Sussex, RH16 1BJ

© Bloomsbury Professional Limited 2010
Previously published by Tottel Publishing Ltd

A CIP Catalogue record for this book is available from the British Library.

ISBN for the complete set of volumes 978 1 84766 267 5

Typeset by Phoenix Photosetting, Chatham, Kent
Printed in the United Kingdom by Hobbs the Printers Ltd, Totton, Hampshire

Preface

This is the fifth edition of Charity Accounting and Taxation and follows the format of earlier editions, namely it is a mixture of textbook information and critical comment interspersed with illustrative examples taken from the published accounts of over 70 charities. It incorporates all relevant legislation affecting charity accounting and taxation as at 31 December 2010.

The purpose of this book is to act as a companion to other textbooks, helping the reader to understand some of the more difficult issues that have been posed by recent developments in charity accounting. Liberal use has been made of references to the Charities SORP and we are grateful to the Charity Commission for allowing us to reproduce many sections throughout the text of this book.

We have updated this book to incorporate information concerning changes arising out of the 2005 version of the Charities SORP and changes in the law affecting the charity sector as a result of the Charities Act 2006.

The later chapters dealing with taxation issues have been largely rewritten to take account of the changes introduced in the Finance Acts passed in the seven years.

We are grateful to the hundreds of charities who have so willingly sent us copies of their reports and accounts. The examples drawn from these are really the backbone of this book.

Our thanks are due to those who have helped us put this edition together, particularly members of the Buzzacott Charity Team.

Amanda Francis
Katharine Patel
Edward Finch

December 2009

About the Authors

Philippa Booth Prior to moving to France, Philippa Booth was the Buzzacott Charity Team VAT Manager. She advised many of the firm's charity clients on matters such as the VAT implications of major capital projects and the impact of contracting on charities' VAT status. She worked with many of the firm's religious clients using her rare ability of presenting a complex issue in a way and manner that non-VAT experts could understand with ease. She has written and lectured widely on VAT.

Amanda Francis is a Partner of the firm and head of the Charity & Not-for-Profit team. Amanda works with a wide range of charity and not-for-profit clients, providing audit, accounting and advisory services. Her particular interests lie with religious, welfare and service charities. Amanda is a Governor of the Royal Star & Garter Homes and a trustee of the Buzzacott Stuart Defries Memorial Fund, and received a Papal Knighthood in 2008 being made a Dame of the Order of St Sylvester.

Edward Finch is a Partner of the firm and works in the Charity & Not-for-Profit team. He works with a broad range of charity and not-for-profit organisations and has particular interests in overseas development and social enterprise.

Katharine Patel is a Partner of the firm and works in the Charity & Not-for-Profit team. She has particular responsibility for the provision of audit, financial accounting and regulatory compliance services to a portfolio of charity clients.

Luke Savvas is a Partner of the firm and works across various teams including Business Services and the Charity & Not-for-Profit team. He regularly lectures and writes articles on charity taxation matters and advises numerous charity clients.

Contents

Preface		v
About the Authors		vi
Table of statutes		xiii
Table of SORPs		xvii

1 Charity — **1**
1 Definition — 1
2 Charitable purposes — 2
3 Public benefit — 4
4 Advantages of charitable status — 7
5 Constitution — 8
6 Charity Commission — 14

2 Trustees' responsibilities — **19**
1 Trustees' legal responsibilities — 19
2 Scope of responsibility — 24
3 Management structure — 26
4 Constitution — 27
5 Trustees' insurance — 28
6 Reporting duties — 29
7 Remuneration of trustees — 30

3 Accounting requirements — **32**
1 Charities Act 1993 — 32
2 Companies Act 2006 — 34
3 Statement of recommended practice – SORP — 45
4 Summary information return — 48

4 Trustees' report — **50**
1 Duty to prepare a trustees' annual report — 50
2 Reference and administrative details of the charity, its trustees and advisers — 52
3 Narrative information — 54

5 Accounting policies and accounts structure — **66**
1 Guidelines — 66
2 Accounting policies — 68
3 Accounting for separate funds — 72
4 Branches — 79
5 Connected charities — 81
6 Consolidation — 83
7 Associates, joint ventures and joint arrangements — 84

Contents

6   Statement of Financial Activities   87
   1   Purpose   87
   2   The basic construction   90
   3   Reconciliation of funds   98
   4   Adaptation of formats   100
   5   Summary income and expenditure account   101
   6   Discontinued and acquired operations   110

7   Incoming resources   111
   1   Guidelines   111
   2   Recognition – basic principles   114
   3   Grants and donations receivable – recognition of incoming
      resources subject to restrictions and conditions   115
   4   Contractual arrangements   121
   5   Voluntary income   123

8   Resources expended   141
   1   Introduction   141
   2   Analysis of expenditure   142
   3   Recognition – basic principles   145
   4   Costs of generating funds   146
   5   Charitable activities   152
   6   Grant-making   155
   7   Governance costs   160
   8   Support costs   161
   9   Accounting for contractual arrangements and grants payable 166
   10   VAT   168

9   Balance sheet presentation   170
   1   Guidelines   170
   2   Grouping of funds   174
   3   Fixed assets   185
   4   Current assets   186
   5   Liabilities   187

10   Fixed assets, valuations and depreciation   188
   1   Overview of fixed assets   188
   2   Relevant accounting standards   189
   3   Recognition and initial valuation of fixed assets for the
      charity's own use   191
   4   Heritage assets   192
   5   Revaluations of fixed assets, other than investments   194
   6   Depreciation of fixed assets (other than investments)   197
   7   Calculation of depreciation charge and impairment of fixed
      assets   198
   8   Fixed assets – investments   200

11   Current assets, liabilities and reserves   204
   1   Current assets   204
   2   Debtors and accrued income   204

	3	Liabilities	206
	4	Commitments	207
	5	Loan liabilities/guarantees	210

12	**Cash flow statements**	**211**
	1	The requirement for a cash flow statement	211
	2	The object and nature of the cash flow statement and the disclosure requirements	212
	3	Definition of cash	214
	4	Problem areas specific to charities	214

13	**Notes and disclosures**	**219**
	1	Introduction	219
	2	Accounting policies	219
	3	Funds' structure and movements	227
	4	Connected charities	228
	5	Subsidiary undertakings	229
	6	Netting off	231
	7	Income from charity shops	232
	8	Detail of income and expenditure	234
	9	Grants payable	237
	10	Concessionary loans	245
	11	Support costs	245
	12	Transactions with trustees and related persons	250
	13	Indemnity insurance	256
	14	Emoluments of employees	256
	15	Auditors' and independent examiners' remuneration	258
	16	Pensions	258
	17	Ex gratia payments	263
	18	Fixed assets	264
	19	Provisions and commitments	266
	20	Guarantees	266
	21	Contingent assets and liabilities	267
	22	Loan liabilities	268

14	**Summarised accounts**	**270**
	1	Introduction	270
	2	SORP and legislative requirements	271
	3	How the information is shown	272

15	**Scottish, Irish and exempt charities**	**288**
	1	Introduction	288
	2	Exempt charities	289
	3	Scottish charities	290
	4	Irish charities	295
	5	Common Investment Funds	297

16	**Audit and other external scrutiny**	**298**
	1	Introduction	298
	2	Auditing standards	311

Contents

3   'Whistle blowing'   313
4   Contractual requirements of the auditor   314
5   Comments and conclusions   316

17   Tax exemptions and charities   **317**
1   General   317
2   Income tax and corporation tax   317
3   Capital gains tax   324
4   Application for charitable purposes   325
5   Non-charitable expenditure – the restriction of tax exemptions 331
6   Value Added Tax   335
7   Inheritance tax   335
8   Business rates and council tax   336
9   Benefits-in-kind, stamp duty, betting duty   337
10   Landfill tax   337
11   Community amateur sports clubs   338

18   Tax and trading activities of charities   **339**
1   General principles   339
2   The trading exemption   339
3   Small traders   341
4   Trading subsidiary   342
5   Profit-shedding   343
6   Payments by a company to a charity under Gift Aid   344
7   VAT implications   345
8   Sponsorship   345

19   Tax incentives to donors   **349**
1   General proposition   349
2   Deeds of covenant   349
3   Donations to charity: Gift Aid   350
4   Payroll giving   357
5   Business gifts   358
6   Employee secondments and donated salaries   359
7   Interest-free loans   360
8   Gifts of capital assets   360
9   Gifts of securities and shares and land   360
10   Inheritance tax   361

20   Charities and VAT   **362**
1   General framework   362
2   VAT recovery   365
3   Property   374
4   Specific reliefs – zero-rating   385
5   Exemptions   387
6   Other supplies   394
7   Administration of VAT   397
8   Miscellaneous   403
9   Conclusion   404

Appendix 1   Useful addresses   405
Appendix 2   Charity Commission Publications   409
Appendix 3   Charity Commission definition of gross income and
    total expenditure   413
Appendix 4   Stages of an audit   415
Appendix 5   Auditors ceasing office   417
Appendix 6   The duty of auditors to report matters of material
    significance to the Charity Commission and OSCR   419
Appendix 7   Model Gift Aid declaration   424
Appendix 8   Sponsorship and Gift Aid declaration   425
Appendix 9   Trust and estate charities form   426
Appendix 10   Company tax return form: charity supplementary
    pages   428

Index   **433**

Table of statutes

Charities Act (NI) 2008 . . 15.51, 15.52
  ss 6–11 . . . . 15.53
  Sch 1 . . . . 15.53

Charities Act 1992
  s 58 . . . . 18.40
  59 . . . . 18.40

Charities Act 1993 . . . . 1.6, 2.38,
     3.1, 3.14, 5.10, 8.1,
     14.1, 14.11, 13.5,
     16.6, 16.14, 16.16,
     16.24, 16.38, 17.40,
     App 6
  s 8 . . . . App 6
  16 . . . . 1.34, 1.53, 17.38
  17 . . . . 1.53
  18 . . . . App 6
  34(2) . . . . App 5
  34(3) . . . . App 5
  41–49 . . . . 3.3, 3.4
  43 . . . . 16.25
  44 . . . . 16.25
  43(2) . . . . App 5
  43(3) . . . . App 5
  43A(2) . . . . App 5
  43A(3)(a) . . . . App 5
  44 . . . . 16.65, App 6
  45 . . . . 2.46
  72A 2.51
  73F 2.42
  97(1) 2.3
  Sch 2 . . . . 1.75, 15.14, 15.6, 15.8
    5A . . . . App 5

Charities Act 2006 . . . . 1.4, 1.11,
    1.14, 1.27, 1.37,
    1.49, 1.60, 1.63,
    1.64, 1.73, 1.75,
    1.8, 2.51, 2.52, 3.2,
    3.3, 3.4, 3.8, 3.14,
    15.5, 15.6, 15.12,
    16.6, 16.11, 16.14,
    16.18, 16.19, 16.22,
    16.65, App 56
  s 1C 1.65
  3(2) 1.14
  11 . . . . 15.8

Charities Act 2006 – *contd*
  28 . . . . 3.4

Charities Act 2009 . . . . . 2.24, 15.46,
    15.49

Charities and Trustee
  Investment (Scotland) Act
  2005 . . . . 15.34, 16.6,
    16.11, 16.20, 16.22,
    16.23, 16.24, 16.38,
    16.43
  s 7 . . . . 15.43, 15.44
  7(4) 15.40
  28 . . . . App 6
  30 . . . . App 6
  31 . . . . App 6
  44(1)(c) 16.43
  46 . . . . 16.65, App 6

Companies Act 1985 . . . . . 2.38, 3.1,
    13.5, 13.12, 15.21,
    16.43
  s 30(4) 1.48
  230 . . . . 13.12

Companies Act 2006 . . . . 3.5, 3.6, 3.8,
    4.8, 6.40, 6.41,
    6.42, 16.3, 16.6,
    16.7, 16.11, 16.17,
    16.24, 16.38, 16.43
  s 386 . . . . 3.8
  396 . . . . 3.8
  414 . . . . 3.8
  426 . . . . 3.8
  435 . . . . 14.88
  441 . . . . 3.8
  477 . . . . 16.19
  498(2) 3.8
  498(3) 3.8
  ss 519–525 . . . . App 5
  s 1211 . . . . 16.25
  1212 . . . . 16.43

Corporation Tax Act 2009
  s 70 . . . . 19.42
  s 105 . . . . 19.41
  1300 . . . . 19.40

Finance Act 1989
s 59 . . . .   19.4

Finance Act 1996 . . . . 17.11, 17.58

Finance Act 2000 . . . . . .   17.2, 18.12,
                               18.19, 18.28,
                               19.2, 19.4,
                               19.8, 19.10
s 40 . . . . 18.27, 19.14
  40(7) 18.27
  41 . . . . 18.14, 18.27
  46 . . . . 17.11, 17.12,
                               17.14, 18.11

Finance Act 2002 . . . .   19.41
s 58 . . . .   17.94
  97 . . . .   19.52
Sch 18. . . . .   17.94
Sch 29. . . . .   18.39

Finance Act 2006 . . . . 17.11, 18.29,
                               19.17
s 56 . . . .   18.9
  57 . . . .   18.27

Gambling Act 2005
Sch 11 . . . . 17.11, 17.91

Income and Corporation Taxes
  Act 1988. . . . .   17.4, 17.41,
                               18.2, 18.3, 18.4
s 56(3)(c) 17.27
  209(2)(b) 18.29
  505. . . . . 13.12, 17.4,
                               17.14, 17.15,
                          17.18, 17.28, 17.34,
                               17.39, 17.56,
                               17.62
  505(1) 17.58, 17.70, 17.72
  505(1)(a) 17.22, 17.23
  505(2) 17.58
  505(3) 17.68
  506(3) 17.42
ss 506A–506C 17.48
  510. . . . .   18.13
  531. . . . .   17.23
  601(4) 17.27
  703. . . . .   17.33
  715(1)(d) 17.27
  776. . . . . 17.23, 17.30
  839. . . . .   17.49
Sch 20. . . . . 17.41, 17.44, 17.45,
                               17.71, 18.15,
                               18.17

Income Tax (Trading and Other
  Income) Act 2005. . . 17.11, 17.21,
                               19.40
s 47 . . . .   19.40
  70 . . . .   19.42
  108. . . . .   19.41
  624. . . . .   19.45

Income Tax Act 2007 . . . .   17.15, 18.2,
                               18.3, 18.4
s 420. . . . .   19.4
  424 . . . .   19.12
  505(1)(c)(iic) 17.22
ss 520–537 . . . .   17.4
s 521(4) 17.64
  524 . . . . 17.34, 17.18,
                               17.39
  526. . . . .   17.11
  527 . . . . 17.11, 18.12
  529. . . . .   17.24
  531. . . . .   17.22
  531(1) 17.11
  531(2) 17.11
  533. . . . .   17.11
  534. . . . .   17.27
  536. . . . .   17.21
ss 539–542 . . . .   17.62
s 540. . . . .   17.62
  540(3) 17.64
  542. . . . .   17.62
ss 549–557 . . . .   17.48
s 543. . . . .   17.41
  547. . . . . 17.41, 17.42
  558. . . . . 17.41, 18.15
  561. . . . .   17.41
  645. . . . .   17.27
  755. . . . .   17.23
  993. . . . .   17.49

Industrial and Provident
  Societies Act 1965 . . . . . .   1.58

Inheritance Tax Act 1984
s 23(4) 19.53
  58(1)(a) 17.79

Law Reform (Miscellaneous
  Provisions) (Scotland) Act
  1990 . . . .   15.20

National Trust Act 1907 . . . . . .   1.59

National Trust Act 1937 . . . . . .   1.59

National Trust Act 1939 . . . . . .   1.59

National Trust Act 1953 . . . . . .   1.59

National Trust Act 1971 . . . . . .   1.59

Rating (Charity Shops) Act
    1976 . . . .   17.82

RSPCA Act 1932 . . . .   1.59

Statute of Charitable Uses in
    1601 . . . .   1.7

Taxation of Chargeable Gains
    Act 1992
    s 256 . . . . 17.39, 17.72
    256(1) 17.70
    256(2) 17.36
    257 . . . .   19.46

Trustee Act 1925 . . . .   2.9

Trustee Act 2000 . . . .   2.6, 2.17, 2.18,
                            2.19, 2.20

Trustee Investment (Scotland)
    Act 2005 . . . .   15.18
    s 44 . . . .   15.19

Trustee Investments Act 1961 . .   2.18,
                            17.44

Value Added Tax Act 1994 . . . .   20.12,
                            20.26
    Sch 6 . . . .   20.96
    10 . . . . 20.94, 20.95,
                            20.98

Table of SORP 'Accounting and reporting by charities' references

SORP 1995 . . . . 1.61

SORP 2000. . . . . 6.14, 7.49, 8.5, 10.32

SORP 2005. . . . . . 2.48, 3.2, 3.8, 3.10,
                     3.11, 3,12, 3,14,
                     3.15, 3,19, 3.20,
                     4,3, 4.9, 4.17, 5.10,
                     5.31, 5.34, 6.15,
                     6.16, 7.9, 7.24,
                     7.27, 7.42, 7.43,
                     7.49, 7.51, 7.57,
                     7.80, 7.81, 8.5, 8.6,
                     8.16, 8.32, 8.44,
                     8.47, 8.49, 8.50,
                     8.53, 10.1, 10.2,
                     10.9, 10.13, 10.14,
                     10.21, 10.22, 10.24,
                     10.27, 10.29, 10.32,
                     10.34, 11.16, 12.7,
                     13.1, 12.20, 13.9,
                     14.8, 15.22, 16.32,
                     16.36, 17.9
para 3 . . . . 3.17
     5 . . . . 3.17
     8 . . . . 15.47
     10 . . . . 3.16
     15 . . . . 3.16, 4.1
     16 . . . . 4.1, 7.3
     21 . . . . 3.13
     26 . . . . 2.46
     27 . . . . 2.46
     28 . . . . 2.46
     29 . . . . 2.46
     30 . . . . 2.46
     30(a) 7.1
     31 . . . . 2.46
     32 . . . . 2.46
     35 . . . . 4.2
     37 . . . . 4.6
     41 . . . . 1.62, 3.18, 4.10,
                      4.13
     42 . . . . 3.18
     43 . . . . 3.18
     44 . . . . 2.28, 3.18, 4.15,
                      4.16, 4.18, 4.29,
                      4.30, 4.31, 13,18,
                      13.20

SORP 2005 – *contd*
para 45 . . . . 3.18, 4.15, 4.16,
                  4.18, 4.29, 4.30,
                  4.31
     46 . . . . 3.18, 4.15, 4.16,
                  4.18, 4.29, 4.30,
                  4.31
     47 . . . . 3.18, 4.15, 4.16,
                  4.29, 4.30, 4.31
     48 . . . . 3.18, 4.15, 4.16,
                  4.29, 4.30, 4.31
     49 . . . . 3.18, 4.15, 4.16,
                  4.29, 4.30, 4.31
     50 . . . . 3.18, 4.15, 4.16,
                  4.29, 4.30, 4.31
     51 . . . . 3.18, 4.15, 4.16,
                  4.29, 4.30
     52 . . . . 3.18, 4.15, 4.16,
                  4.29, 4.30
     53 . . . . 3.18, 4.15, 4.16,
                  4.24, 4.29, 4.30
     54 . . . . 3.18, 4.15, 4.16,
                  4.29, 4.30
     55 . . . . 3.18, 4.15, 4.16,
                  4.29, 4.30
     56 . . . . 3.18, 4.15, 4.16,
                  4.29, 4.30
     57 . . . . 3.18, 4.15, 4.16,
                  4.27, 4.29, 4.30
     58 . . . . 3.18, 4.15, 4.16,
                  4.29, 4.30
     59 . . . . 3.18, 4.15, 4.16,
                  4.28, 4.29, 4.30
     60 . . . . 3.18, 5.2
     61 . . . . 3.18, 5.2
     62 . . . . 3.18, 5.2
     63 . . . . 3.18, 5.2
     64 . . . . 3.18, 5.2
     65 . . . . 3.18, 5.11, 5.17,
                  9.12, 13.12, 13.13
     66 . . . . 3.18, 5.17, 9.12,
                  13.12
     67 . . . . 3.18, 5.17, 9.12
     68 . . . . 3.18, 5.17, 9.12,
                  13.123
     69 . . . . 3.18, 5.17, 9.12
     70 . . . . 3.18, 5.17, 9.12
     71 . . . . 3.18, 5.17, 9.12

Table of SORP 'Accounting and reporting by charities' references

SORP 2005 – *contd*

para 72	3.18, 5.17, 9.12
73	3.18, 5.17, 9.12
74	3.18, 5.17, 5.19, 6.28, 9.12
75	3.18, 5.17, 9.12, 9.13, 13,14
75(c)	9.16
76	3.18, 5.17, 9.12
77	3.18, 5.30
78	3.18, 5.26, 5.30
79	3.1, 5.24, 5.30
80	3.18, 5.30
81	3.18, 5.30
82	6.2
paras 82–243	3.18
para 86	6.31
88	6.32
89	6.9, 6.31
90	6.27, 6.46
94	7.7, 11.7, 11.11
95	7.7, 13.26
96	7.7
97	7.7, 7.8
103	7.29, 11.8
104	11.5
105	7.14, 11.5
106	11.5
107	11.5, 11.9
108	7.18, 7.19, 11.5
109	11.5
110	11.5
111	7.23, 7.45, 7.47, 11.5
116	7.11, 7.13
117	7.23, 7.47
121	7.3
122	7.3
123	7.3, 7.37, 7.41
124	7.3, 7.37, 7.41
125	7.3, 7.37, 7.41
126	7.3, 7.37, 7.41
127	7.3, 7.37, 7.41
128	7.3, 7.37, 7.41
129	7.3, 7.45, 7.46, 13.31
130	7.3, 7.45, 7.46
131	7.3, 7.45, 7.46
132	7.3, 7.45, 7.46
133	7.3, 7.48
134	7.3, 7.48, 7.50
135	7.3, 7.48
136	7.48
137	7.3, 7.56, 13.31
138	7.3, 13.31, 13.38

SORP 2005 – *contd*

para 139	7.3, 7.73, 13.33
140	7.3
141	7.3
142	7.3, 7.61
143	7.3
144	7.3
145	7.3, 7.65
146	7.3
147	7.3
148	8.7
150	8.55
151	8.55, 8.57
152	8.55
153	8.55
154	8.55, 11.16
155	8.55, 11.16
156	8.55, 11.16
157	8.55, 8.62, 11.16
158	8.55, 11.16
159	8.55, 11.16
160	8.55, 11.16, 13.60
161	11.16
162	11.16
163	11.16, 13.73
164	8.45, 13,53
165	8.45, 13,53
167	8.46, 13,54
177	8.2, 8.4
178	8.4
179	8.4
180	8.4
181	8.4, 8.13
182	8.4
183	8.4, 8.14
184	8.4
185	8.4, 8.17
186	8.4
187	8.4
188	8.4, 8.22
189	8.4
190	8.4, 10.16
191	8.4, 8.23, 10.16
192	8.4, 8.25, 10.16
193	8.4, 10.16
194	8.4, 10.16
195	8.4, 10.16, 10.18
196	8.4, 10.16
197	8.4
198	8.4, 10.16
199	8.4, 10.16, 10.52
200	8.4, 10.16
201	8.4, 10.16
202	8.4, 10.16

SORP 2005 – *contd*

para 203	8.33, 8.4
204	8.4
205	8.4
206	8.4, 8.36, 13.44
207	8.4, 8.36, 10.40, 13.44
208	8.4
209	8.4
210	8.4, 8.42
211	8.4, 8.42
212	8.4
213	8.4
214	6.18
218	10.38
218(b)	7.78
219	7.79
224	10.55
225	10.55, 13.72
226	10.55
227	10.55, 13.73
228	10.55
229	10.55, 13.73, 13.74
231	13.73
232	10.62, 13.73
233	13.73
235	13.73, 13.85
236	13.87
237	13.87
238	13.118
244	3.18, 9.1
245	3.18, 9.1, 9.2, 9.5, 9.9
246	3.18, 9.1
247	3.18, 9.1, 9.3, 9.11
248	3.18, 9.1
249	3.18, 9.1, 9.6
249	3.18, 9.27
250	3.18, 9.1
251	3.18, 9.1, 9.15, 9.17
paras 252–312	9.22
para 252	9.3
253	9.3
254	9.3
255	9.3, 13.28
256	9.3
257	9.3, 9.25
258	9.3, 10.43
259	9.3, 10.53
260	9.3, 13.124
261	9.3, 10.20
262	9.3, 10.35
263	9.3, 10.35, 10.36
264	9.3, 10.35, 10.36

SORP 2005 – *contd*

para 265	9.3, 10.35, 10.37, 10.38
266	9.3, 10.35
267	9.3, 10.10
268	9.3, 10.10, 10.56
269	9.3, 10.10
270	9.3, 10.10
271	9.3, 10.10
272	9.3, 10.10, 10.57
273	9.3, 13.112
274	9.3, 13.112
275	9.3, 13.112
276	9.3, 13.112
277	9.3, 13.112
278	9.3, 13.112, 13.114
279	10.23, 10.26
280	10.23
281	10.23
282	10.23
283	10.23
284	10.23, 10.28
285	10.23
286	10.23
287	10.23
288	10.23
289	10.23
290	10.23
291	10.23
292	10.23
293	10.23, 10.25
294	10.23, 10.31
295	9.3, 9.26, 12.26
296	9.3, 10.60, 11.1, 11.3
297	9.3, 10.63
298	9.3
299	10.65
299	9.3
300	9.3, 10.65
301	9.3, 10.65, 13.117
302	9.3, 10.65
303	7.61, 9.3, 10.65, 13.73
304	9.3, 10.65
305	9.3, 10.65
306	10.65, 13.119
307	9.3, 10.65, 10.69
308	9.3, 10.65
309	9.3, 10.65
310	9.3, 10.65
311	9.3, 10.65
312	9.3, 10.65
313	9.3, 11.1

Table of SORP 'Accounting and reporting by charities' references

SORP 2005 – *contd*

paras 313–350 .... 3.18
para 314 .... 9.3, 11.4
315 .... 9.3
316 .... 9.3
317 .... 9.3, 11.18
318 .... 9.3, 9.29, 11.12,
                           11.18
319 .... 9.3, 11.18
320 .... 9.3, 11.18
321 .... 9.3, 11.18
322 .... 9.3, 11.18
323 .... 9.3, 11.18
324 .... 9.3, 11.18
325 .... 9.3, 11.18
326 .... 9.3, 11.18, 13.121
327 .... 9.3, 11.18
328 .... 9.3, 11.18, 13.123
329 .... 9.3, 11.18
330 .... 9.3, 9.3
332 .... 9.3
333 .... 9.3
334 .... 9.3
335 .... 9.3
341 .... 11.21
345 .... 11.22
346 .... 11.22, 13.129
347 .... 11.22
348 .... 11.22
349 .... 11.23, 13.132
350 .... 11.23
351 .... 3.18
352 .... 3.18
353 .... 3.18
354 .... 3.18, 12.30
355 .... 3.18
356 .... 3.18, 5.1, 5.9,
                           13.4
357 .... 3.18, 5.9
358 .... 3.18, 5.9, 13.5
359 .... 3.18, 5.9, 13.6
360 .... 3.18, 5.9
361 .... 3.18, 5.9, 13.7
362 .... 3.18, 5.9, 13.7
363 .... 3.18, 5.9, 13.7
364 .... 3.18, 5.9, 13.7
365 .... 3.18, 5.9, 13.7
366 .... 3.18, 5.9, 13.7
367 .... 3.18, 5.9, 13.7
368 .... 3.18, 5.9, 13.7
369 .... 3.18, 5.9, 13.7
370 .... 3.18, 5.9, 13.7
371 .... 3.18
372 .... 3.18
373 .... 3.18

SORP 2005 – *contd*

para 374 .... 3.18
375 .... 3.18
376 .... 3.18
377 .... 3.18, 14.9
378 .... 3.18, 14.9
379 .... 3.18, 14.9
381 .... 3.18, 5.35, 13.23
382 .... 3.18, 5.35
383 .... 3.18, 5.35
383(d) 5.33, 13.22
384 .... 3.18, 5.35, 13.22
385 .... 3.18, 5.35
386 .... 3.18, 5.35
387 .... 3.18, 5.35
388 .... 3.18, 5.35
389 .... 3.18, 5.35
390 .... 3.18, 5.35
391 .... 3.18, 5.35
392 .... 3.18, 5.35
393 .... 3.18, 5.35
394 .... 3.18, 5.35
395 .... 3.18, 5.35, 5.42
396 .... 3.18, 5.35
397 .... 13.12
398 .... 13.24
399 .... 13.24
400 .... 13.24
401 .... 13.24
402 .... 13.24
403 .... 13.24
404 .... 13.24
405 .... 5.43, 13.25
407 .... 3.18, 5.44
408 .... 3.18, 5.44
409 .... 3.18, 5.44
410 .... 3.18, 5.44
411 .... 3.18, 5.44
412 .... 3.18, 5.44
413 .... 3.18, 5.44
414 .... 3.18, 5.44, 5.47
415 .... 3.18, 5.44
416 .... 3.18, 5.44
417 .... 3.18, 5.44
418 .... 3.18, 5.44
419 .... 3.18
420 .... 3.18
421 .... 3.18
422 .... 3.18
423 .... 3.18
424 .... 3.18
425 .... 3.18, 6.43
426 .... 3.18
427 .... 3.18
428 .... 3.18

SORP 2005 – *contd*

para 429 . . . .   3.18
430 . . . .   3.18
431 . . . . 3.18, 13.104
432 . . . . 3.18, 13,99
433 . . . .   3.18
434 . . . .   3.18
435 . . . .   3.18
436 . . . .   3.18
437 . . . . 3.18, 13.102
438 . . . . 3.18, 13.102
439 . . . . 3.18, 13.102
440 . . . . 3.18, 13.102
441 . . . . 3.18, 13.102
442 . . . . 3.18, 13.102
443 . . . .   3.18
444 . . . . 3.18, 13.103
445 . . . . 3.18, 13.103
446 . . . . 3.18, 13.103
447 . . . . 3.18, 13.103
448 . . . . 3.18, 13.103
449 . . . .   3.18

SORP 2005 – *contd*

para 450 . . . .   3.18
451 . . . .   3.18
Appendix 1
GL9 . . . .   13.19
GL10 . . . .   8.7
GL13 . . . .   8.11
GL26 . . . .   8.11
GL28 . . . .   8.41
GL29 . . . .   8.29
GL30 . . . .   7.25
GL38 . . . .   8.21
GL45 . . . .   7.28
GL47 . . . .   10.70
GL52 . . . .   8.1
GL55 . . . .   8.1
GL61 . . . . 7.35, 8.11
Appendix 3
GL4(b) 9.17
Table 3 . . . . 7.3, 7.4
Table 7 . . . . 9.1, 9.3
Table 10 . . . .   14.6

Chapter 1

Charity

1 Definition

1.1   Traditionally, charity has been synonymous with love. It is an attitude of mind; an emotion; a virtue. It is also an activity; it is not something that can simply be contemplated, it needs to be done.

1.2   So what activities are loving and charitable? It is often said that charity begins at home. The love and care shown by the members of a family to each other are clear examples of charitable activity. In his first epistle to the Corinthians, St Paul said that love 'suffereth long, and is kind; love envieth not; love vaunteth not itself, is not puffed up, … beareth all things, believeth all things, hopeth all things, endureth all things'.

1.3   While it is helpful and important to bear in mind that these are the characteristics of charity, we have to be a little more precise in the way in which we use the word for the purposes of this book. While it may be true that charity begins at home, it is equally true that it does not stop there but extends into a variety of activities. A few of the most obvious of these are the relief of suffering and poverty, the advancement of humanity and the protection of the environment. These activities demonstrate a care for friends, neighbours and the public generally.

1.4   It is this concept of benefiting the public which is central to the legal definition of charity and this has now been enshrined in the definition of charitable purpose contained within the Charities Act 2006. This is examined more fully at **1.8** ff below.

1.5   The organisations which have been set up to carry out activities for the benefit of the public are commonly called charities. These are the organisations to which the advantages of charitable status should be accorded. Charitable activity at home is to be thoroughly encouraged but as it is normally for the benefit of the family rather than the public it does not bring any tax relief!

1.6   Essentially, therefore, we are dealing in this book with those organisations which have been established for charitable purposes and which, in the main, will be registered under the Charities Act 1993 with the Charity Commission.

2   Charitable purposes

1.7   Charitable purposes have been described in many eloquent ways, including St Paul's letter to the Corinthians and the preamble to the Statute of Charitable Uses in 1601, to name but two. While St Paul concentrated on the generosity of spirit behind the action, the Statute of Charitable Uses 1601 was more concerned with describing the types of activity that were regarded for the public benefit. Apart from curing the sick, giving alms to the poor, providing shelter for the homeless and similar compassionate activities, the Act included the building of sea walls, highways, the building of houses of correction and the provision of soldiers. Doing things, therefore, for the public benefit includes improving communications, defence, maintaining law and order and caring for the environment. Most of these activities are now undertaken chiefly by the government, but it is important to remember that, if undertaken privately, they may well qualify as charitable activities provided that there is seen to be a measurable benefit to the public.

1.8   Most readers will be familiar with the classification of charitable activities included in Lord McNaghten's judgment in *Income Tax Special Purposes Comrs v Pemsel* (1891) 3 TC 53 HL. This consisted of the relief of poverty, the advancement of education, the advancement of religion and other purposes beneficial to the community not falling under any of the preceding heads. This 1891 classification remained the leading legal authority on what activities could be said to be carried on for charitable purposes until the new definition of charitable purpose introduced by the Charities Act 2006 and the Regulations thereto.

1.9   The question, therefore, is why change a definition which has helped define charitable purpose for the past few hundred years and which has enabled the definition to evolve in line with demographic trends and other changes in society?

1.10   There are two main reasons. Firstly, the number of charities being registered under the fourth head has increased markedly in comparison to the first three heads. Secondly, there was growing disquiet that whereas there was a presumption of public benefit for the first three heads, no such presumption existed for fourth head charities. It has been claimed, therefore, that there had developed two classes of charity – those that must prove they were charitable and those which did not have to prove this. Indeed it was claimed by certain sections of the media that those charities within the fourth head provided more benefit to the public than those which fell within the first three heads. Government and the Charity Commission saw a need to increase public understanding of charities and correct this misconception.

1.11   The Charities Act 2006, therefore, removes the presumption of public benefit and:

1.   gives the Charity Commission an objective to promote awareness and understanding of the operation of the public benefit requirement;

2.   requires the Charity Commission to publish guidance to help meet its public benefit objectives;

3.   requires the Commission to carry out consultation before issuing guidance; and

4.   provides that trustees must have regard to the guidance when they exercise their powers or duties.

However, the real change is that it provides for the first time a statutory definition of 'charitable purpose'.

1.12   Following the government's consideration of the 'Private Action, Public Benefit' recommendations during 2003 and considerable discussion and debate, under the Charities Act 2006, for the purposes of the law of England and Wales, 'charity' means an institution which:

(a)   is established for charitable purposes only; and

(b)   falls to be subject to the control of the High Court in the exercise of its jurisdiction with respect to charities.

1.13   The meaning of 'charitable purpose' has been expanded from the four purposes contained within the 1891 classification and now means a purpose which falls within any of the following 13 purposes:

- the prevention or relief of poverty;

- the advancement of education;

- the advancement of religion (to include a religion which involves the belief in more than one god and a religion which involves the belief in no god);

- the advancement of health or the saving of lives (where the advancement of health includes the prevention or relief of sickness, disease or human suffering);

- the advancement of citizenship or community development (to include rural or urban regeneration and the promotion of civic responsibility, volunteering, the voluntary sector or the effectiveness or efficiency of charities);

- the advancement of arts, heritage, culture or science;

- the advancement of amateur sport (where 'sport' means sports or games which promote health by involving physical or mental skill or exertion);

- the advancement of human rights, conflict resolution or reconciliation or the promotion of religious or racial harmony or equality and diversity;

- the advancement of environmental protection or improvement;

- the relief of those in need by reason of youth, age, ill-health, disability, financial hardship or other disadvantage;

- the advancement of animal welfare;

- the promotion of the efficiency of the armed forces of the Crown, or of the efficiency of the police, fire and rescue services or ambulance services; and

- other purposes beneficial to the community.

1.14   The Charities Act 2006 requires a two-stage test for new registrations as charities. First, that the proposed purposes for which the charity is established fall within one or more of the above 13 heads above and, secondly, that the purposes are for the public benefit. Section 3(2) of the Charities Act 2006 states categorically that it will no longer be presumed that a particular purpose is for the public benefit.

1.15   The concept of public benefit is discussed in more detail in section 3 of this chapter. There are many organisations which may claim that they carry on an activity that is for the public benefit but they will not all achieve charitable status. This is because the objectives of a charity must be solely for charitable purposes. Clubs and trades unions normally exist for the benefit of their members and so, while much of their work may in their view be for the benefit of the public, a large part of it is also for their mutual benefit. Similarly, many businesses may argue that they exist to provide a service to members of the public, nevertheless they do so in order to make a profit for themselves. The crucial difference, therefore, between these organisations and charities is that the latter exist solely for the benefit of their beneficiaries.

1.16   It not infrequently happens that a charity strays into some activity which is not regarded as charitable and the tax effects of this are considered in Chapter 17. Where it is a relatively minor infringement, there may be no serious repercussions. Particular care, however, needs to be taken to avoid crossing the narrow lines of legality affecting:

(a)   trading activities; and

(b)   political lobbying.

1.17   Despite significant public support for it, the government rejected the proposal to allow charities to carry out substantial trading activities outside their primary purpose. On the other hand, the government has shown sympathy for the wish of charities to have greater latitude in campaigning for their objectives. The line between this and political lobbying has hitherto been drawn very tightly. These items are considered further in Chapter 18.

3   Public benefit

1.18   The term 'public benefit' is not defined in legislation. Instead as noted in **1.11** above it is the responsibility of the Charity Commission to provide guidance on the matter following public consultation. In its general guidance (available to download from its website) the Charity Commission sets out two key principles both of which must be met in order to show that an organisation's aims are for the public benefit. Within each principle there are a number of factors that must be considered in all cases. These are:

THE PRINCIPLES OF PUBLIC BENEFIT

1.   There must be identifiable benefit or benefits:

    (a)   it must be clear what the benefits are;

    (b)   the benefits must be related to the charity's aims;

    (c)   benefits must be balanced against any detriment or harm.

2.   Benefit must be to the public, or a section of the public:

    (a)   the beneficiaries must be appropriate to the aims;

    (b)   where benefit is to a section of the public, the opportunity to benefit must not be unreasonably restricted:

        (i)   by geographical or other restrictions; or

        (ii)   by ability to pay any fees charged;

    (c)   people in poverty must not be excluded from the opportunity to benefit;

    (d)   any private benefits must be incidental.

1.19   Principal 1(a) states that it must be clear what benefits to the public arise from carrying out a charity's aims. Examples of different sorts of benefit include providing housing for the homeless or giving medical care to the sick. The Commission requires charities to identify and describe the benefits provided although that does not mean that they must be able to be quantified or measured. Many benefits will be self evident but in some cases the Charity Commission will ask for evidence of independent, expert opinion from someone suitably qualified. It is for the trustees to provide evidence that their organisation's aims are for the public benefit.

1.20   Principal 1(b) requires that the benefits be related to the charity's aims, so benefits which arise from the charity's work that are not related to its aims will not be taken into account. Where a charity has more than one aim, each of those aims has to meet the public benefit requirement – ie it will not be sufficient for only some to do so.

1.21   Principal 1(c) states that the benefits must be balanced against any detriment or harm which arises. Examples of detriment or harm cited by the Charity Commission that could arise include something that is damaging to the environment or mental or physical health or encourages hatred towards others. The Commission will require to see 'real evidence' that a detriment occurs – it will not just assume it.

1.22   Principal 2(a) recognises the link between an organisation's aims and those who are able to benefit. Sometimes a charity's aims are intended to benefit the public generally and sometimes a section of it. The Charity Commission states that it is not simply a matter of numbers – although the number who can potentially benefit must not be insignificant. The number of people able to benefit at any one time can be quite small as long as anyone who could qualify for benefit is able. The example given by the Charity Commission is a care home that offers only a small number of bed spaces but where anyone eligible to apply can be considered for those limited spaces.

1.23   Principal 2(b) makes it clear that any restriction on potential beneficiaries must not be too restrictive. However, some restrictions will be permitted – for example, those based on charitable need such as poverty, age or ill-health, and those based on personal characteristics such as gender, race or religion. The important issue is that a restriction should not be such that the charity is seen as an 'exclusive club' that only a few may join.

1.24   Many charities do charge for their services but Principal 2(b) also makes it clear that such charges need to be reasonable and necessary if the charity is to carry out its aims. Where a charge is such that it restricts those who may benefit to those who can afford to pay then this may be a problem.

1.25   Ability to pay is the issue addressed by Principal 2(c) which states clearly that where an organisation excludes people from the opportunity to benefit because they cannot pay the fees charged, then its aims would not be deemed to be for the public benefit. This does not mean that charities have to offer services for free or offer concessions on fees (although this would help) but means that thought needs to be given to other ways in which people on low incomes might benefit. For example, an independent school may work in collaboration with a local state school; an arts charity might broadcast concerts on local radio, and so on.

1.26   Finally, Principal 2(d) states that where people benefit from the charity, other than as a beneficiary, the 'private' benefits must be incidental to or a by-product of carrying out the charity's aims.

1.27   Under the Charities Act 2006 all organisations wishing to be recognised as a charity must demonstrate explicitly that their aims are for the public benefit. The responsibilities of charity trustees with regard to public benefit and the requirement to report on public benefit are discussed further in Chapters 2 and 4.

1.28   The decision as to whether or not a charity is fulfilling the public benefit test is the responsibility of the Charity Commission. The Commission will base its decisions on current case law and will apply and interpret that law in the light of changing social and economic conditions. In most cases, this will involve using an evidence based approach. What is clear is that the Commission will not allow public opinion to decide what is or is not charitable or for the public benefit. The Charity Commission does not anticipate that a significant number of charities will fail the public benefit test. What seems likely, however, in the first few years of the test being considered is that fee charging charities will be targeted.

1.29   Decisions of the Charity Commission with regard to public benefit may be challenged. In the first instance this should be by discussing the decision with the Commission by using its internal decision review procedures. Guidance on these procedures is available on the Commission's website.

1.30   If, after this process, a person or organisation is dissatisfied, they can appeal to the Charity Tribunal. If the Tribunal disagrees with the Commission's decision, it may decide to quash the decision and replace it with its own decision. Alternatively, it may direct the Charity Commission to look at the decision again. The Tribunal can award costs in certain circumstances but it will not be able to award compensation.

1.31   Finally, a decision can be appealed to the High Court provided the person or organisation has first obtained the permission of the Charity Tribunal or the High Court itself. Appeals against the Charity Tribunal can only be made on the grounds that the Tribunal has made a mistake in law and not because it has made a mistake as to facts.

Comment

1.32   It remains to be seen how the public benefit test will be policed in practice. However, it is clear that this is an aspect that no charitable organisation can afford to be complacent over. Charity trustees need to ensure that they are familiar with the requirements. The aims of the charity need to be thought about to ensure they are consistent with the objects of the charity set out in its governing document. In addition, care is needed to ensure that the aims are communicated in a consistent manner through different types of media such as the charity's publications, its website and its annual report. It is certain that fee paying charities such as schools, independent hospitals, arts charities and care establishments will be targeted in the first few years and it may not be too long before a case is brought before the Charity Tribunal.

4 Advantages of charitable status

1.33   The biggest single advantage of charitable status is the exemption from most forms of direct taxation and a certain amount of relief from indirect taxation. This aspect is considered in detail in Chapter 18.

1.34   Other benefits of charitable status include certain legal advantages. For example, charitable trusts cannot fail for uncertainty, they can be written in perpetuity and, if their original purposes cease to exist, application can be made to the Charity Commissioners for a scheme whereby they can be reconstituted for another similar purpose. For instance, a charity established with an endowment to provide water troughs for horses in Liverpool eventually found itself with little or no demand for its services but with some assets. Under ordinary Trust Law, such assets would eventually have passed indirectly to the Treasury via the Duchy of Cornwall as *bona vacantia*. Under Charity Law, however, the trustees were able to apply for a scheme under what is now s 16 of the Charities Act 1993 to enable the charity to continue with wider charitable objects. This is done by making application to the Charity Commissioners, proposing the additional objects sought. The Charity Commissioners then have the task of considering the application in the light of the cy-pres doctrine, which means they have to decide what is the next best objective to the original. In this case it might have been to help the animal protection societies in Liverpool or perhaps a national society connected with the care of horses. Either way, the charity did not die.

1.35   Although registration with the Charity Commission subjects the trustees of the charity to the supervision of the Charity Commission, this can also be an advantage as the Charity Commission's job is not simply that of registrar and overseer; it is also there to give assistance to charity trustees in matters relating to the administration of their trust (see **1.63** ff).

1.36   A further advantage of charitable status is the additional credibility that it gives to any organisation appealing for donations. Not only is this desirable when appealing for funds from the public, it is essential if seeking support from charitable trusts. They have to ensure that they apply their funds for charitable purposes only and are very reluctant to give money to organisations which are not themselves charities for fear that it can or may be used for a non-charitable purpose. That could endanger their own status.

1.37   There are no discernible disadvantages attaching to charitable status, although some would argue that the cost of compliance may make it less desirable for small organisations. At present, any organisation claiming to be a charity with an annual income in excess of £5,000 must be registered. The Charities Act 2006 insists that all charities with incomes above this level be registered with the Charity Commission.

5   Constitution

1.38   A charity need not have any special constitution provided that there is sufficient evidence of its objects and internal regulations. For most charities, it is usual to have some formal constitution usually drawn up with the help of a solicitor. The following are the most normal forms of constitution.

Trust

1.39   Charitable trusts are unique to English legal culture and have been used for many, many years to facilitate and safeguard gifts. Such a trust arises where a donor agrees with the trustees to put into their hands a sum of money or other property to be used exclusively for the charitable objects specified by the donor.

1.40   Although technically a trust can be created by word of mouth, the Charity Commission requires written evidence of the existence of the trust and the nature of its activities so that it is clear whether or not it is for charitable purposes.

1.41   Nowadays very few charities are constituted by a declaration of trust. It is an ideal form for charities which have very simple objects or narrow objects which do not require the trustees to enter into onerous contracts with third parties. The trust is not a legal entity in its own right and as such the trustees enjoy no limited liability. Hence, third parties such as bankers, employees, customers, etc who deal with the trust are at law dealing with the charity's individual trustees. As such the trustees are personally liable to third parties for the charity's contractual and tortious acts.

1.42   However, it still remains a serious option for grant-making charities where questions of trustees' personal liability may not be so important.

1.43   A simple declaration of trust, stating that the trustees hold the property so settled on charitable trusts, will normally suffice provided it is quite clear that the funds cannot be used for any other purpose. Some such trusts are drawn up with very wide charitable objects while others are more specific to reflect the wishes of the settlor. In many cases, the initial amount settled is a nominal sum to which greater sums are added later by the settlor or others through donations, etc.

1.44   In some cases, the initial settlement into the trust is substantial, such as a house left by will to be held as a capital asset for the benefit of the charity and not to be spent. In such cases, the initial asset is considered to be a 'permanent endowment' and there are particular accounting requirements concerning permanent endowments, as is explained in Chapter 5 and further referred to in Chapter 6.

SISTERS OF THE HOLY FAMILY OF BORDEAUX CHARITABLE TRUST: 31 DECEMBER 2008

Introduction

The Sisters of the Holy Family of Bordeaux (the Institute) is a Roman Catholic Religious Institute founded in France in 1820. Its Generalate is now located in Rome. The Institute is governed by its own constitution.

The accounts accompanying this report are the accounts of the charitable trust on which the assets of the Institute in Great Britain and Ireland are held. The charity is governed by a trust deed dated 4 April 1961, and is registered under the Charities Act 1993, Charity Registration Number 232633.

Company limited by guarantee

1.45   A company limited by guarantee has a legal identity separate from those who run it. As such it has its own rights and duties and holds its own assets (including property) rather than through trustees. A charity formed as a company limited by guarantee will be set up as a company first of all with a memorandum and articles of association as its governing documents and then registered with the Charity Commission. It will need to comply with the requirements of company law in addition to those of charity law. In particular, its directors or trustees will also be under a duty not to continue to operate if the company is insolvent.

1.46   A charity formed as a company limited by guarantee has the advantage that the trustees, or directors to give them their proper title, are afforded the protection of limited liability as regards the debts of the company and their own responsibilities are as defined in the Companies Acts. As the legal responsibilities of trustees can be very considerable, and potentially very costly to themselves, it is more common to constitute large charities as limited companies. Major charities, such as OXFAM, Barnardos, the Save the Children Fund, Help the Aged and the British Heart Foundation are all constituted in this manner.

1.47   There is the additional advantage that the company structure is familiar to most people who have dealings with the commercial world. The memorandum and articles of association, the powers and duties of the directors, the holding of annual general meetings and the appointment of auditors are all familiar matters which are included in the constitution. The titles are sometimes changed from director to trustee or member of council. Otherwise, the structure is the same as any other company except for the fact that there is no share capital, only the nominal personal guarantees given by subscribers.

1.48   The disadvantage of a company limited by guarantee has been the need to comply with two regulators' requirements – those of the Charity Commission and the Registrar of Companies – and to comply with both charity and company law.

GIRLS FRIENDLY SOCIETY: 30 SEPTEMBER 2008

Governance

Girls Friendly Society in England and Wales is a company limited by guarantee (Company Registration No 3172713) and is registered under the Charities Act 1993 (Charity Registration No 1054310). A statutory declaration in accordance with the provisions of Section 30 (4) of the Companies Act 1985, whereby the company is exempt from the use of 'Limited' in its name, has been filed with the Registrar of Companies.

The reporting and accounting requirements are the same as for other companies and these are discussed in Chapter 3.

Charitable incorporated organisation (CIO)

1.49   The CIO is the new corporate structure introduced by the Charities Act 2006. The CIO will be a corporate body with limited liability, coming into existence only on registration with the Charity Commission. It can either be used to establish a new charity or to convert an existing charity with another legal form into a CIO.

1.50 The CIO embodies most of the advantages of being a company limited by guarantee with none of the administrative issues associated with having to register as a company.

1.51 The CIO must be a body corporate with a constitution, a principal office in England or Wales, with one or more members who will either have no liability on the winding up of the organisation or a liability limited to an amount specified in the constitution.

1.52 A CIO has a constitution rather than a memorandum and articles. It has a principal office rather than a registered office and those who control it are referred to as charity trustees. However, as with companies limited by guarantee, the members and trustees are distinct although, in practice, they may be the same people. There will, in time, be further requirements yet to be set out in regulations.

Scheme of the Charity Commission

1.53 Several charities, particularly those whose original trusts have become out of date or unworkable for some reason, are governed by a 'scheme' made by the Charity Commission under Charities Act 1993 ss 16 or 17.

NIGHTINGALE HOUSE: 30 SEPTEMBER 2008

Governance

Nightingale House is governed by a scheme made by the Charity Commission on 29 May 2002, and is registered as a charity under the Charities Act 1993. The Charity Registration Number is 207316.

The scheme dated 29 May 2002 replaced a previous scheme dated 24 March 1961.

EDITH CAVELL AND NATIONS FUND FOR NURSES: 31 DECEMBER 2008

Constitution

Edith Cavell Fund for Nurses is an unincorporated body which, during the year to 31 December 2008, was governed by a Scheme of the Charity Commission dated 2 March 2007 which supersedes all previous Governing Schemes. It is registered under the Charities Act 1993 – Charity Registration No 210571.

The Charity uses the working name of NurseAid.

Unincorporated association

1.54 This is appropriate for small charities only in reality and traditionally has been used for membership organisations where the relationship between the members is determined by the form of the constitution. A committee (ie the trustees) is usually elected to run the organisation on behalf of the members.

1.55 It is very simple to operate provided the terms of the governing document are clear and workable in practice. In particular, the constitution must make it clear where control lies.

1.56 The unincorporated association is not a legal person in its own right separate from its trustees. As such its trustees may, in certain circumstances, be personally liable to third parties. In the event of an unincorporated association being unable to pay its debts, members tend to 'disappear' leaving the committee members or trustees to pick up the tab for the association's creditors.

1.57 Many local charities, such as Women's Institutes or Parent Teacher Associations and similar charities that are dependent on a membership governed by a management committee, will produce a rule book or constitution which is their governing instrument. For many such organisations, model constitutions are available from their national coordinating body. The National Council for Voluntary Organisations also produces model constitutions to suit various charities. Their address is given in Appendix 1.

THE ATTINGHAM TRUST: 30 SEPTEMBER 2008

Introduction

The charitable objectives of the Trust are as follows:

- To examine the architectural and social history of historic houses and collections and their gardens and landscape setting.

- To study the contents of these houses – their paintings, sculpture, furniture, ceramics, silver, textiles and other applied arts, as well as the planning and decorative treatment of the interiors.

- To stimulate discussion on the problems involved in the conservation and presentation of country houses and collections.

- To provide scholarship assistance for those who wish to engage in the foregoing.

Governance, structure and management

The Attingham Trust is governed by Rules adopted on 13 December 1982 as subsequently amended, and is registered under the Charities Act 1993 – Charity Registration No 262819.

Industrial and provident or friendly society

1.58   Some charities, particularly registered social landlords or housing associations as they used to be called, are incorporated under the Industrial and Provident Societies Act 1965 and these enjoy substantially the same benefits as those incorporated under the Companies Acts. Friendly societies are perhaps less familiar to people in ordinary commercial life, although there are many non-charitable organisations which are incorporated in this manner such as trades unions. While the accounting requirements for both industrial and provident or friendly societies are very similar to those of limited companies, special care must be taken in the case of registered social landlords to comply with the very detailed and complex accounting requirements issued by the Housing Corporation under the Housing Acts.

Other constitutions

1.59   Although the foregoing are the most common constitutions for charities, there are some older and larger charities which have been constituted by Royal Charter. These include the Royal National Lifeboat Institution (RNLI), the Imperial Cancer Research Fund, the Red Cross, the Royal Society for the Protection of Birds (RSPB), and the British and Foreign Bible Society. Some charities are formed under their own special Acts of Parliament such as the National Trust Acts 1907 to 1971 and the RSPCA Act 1932. In all of these cases, their constitutions will be governed by their own charter or special Act. In the future, there may arise the Charitable Incorporated Institution as an alternative to the Company limited by guarantee (see comment at end of **3.8**).

1.60   As stated above, in an effort to bring more uniformity to the regulation and governance of charities, the Charities Act 2006 has introduced provisions to enable charities to be constituted as 'Charitable Incorporated Organisations' (CIOs). This will pave the way for all charities eventually to be governed chiefly by the Charities Acts.

THE CORPORATION OF THE HALL OF ARTS AND SCIENCES: 31 DECEMBER 2008

Constitution

The Corporation was incorporated under a Royal Charter dated 8 April 1867 which has been supplemented by two further supplemental Charters and no less than four Acts of Parliament and with a membership comprising owners of seats in the Hall. The constitution is now primarily set out in the Royal Albert Hall Act 1966. The Corporation is a registered charity (Charity Registration No 254543).

Comment

1.61   It is surprising how many published accounts of charities used to give no indication of the charity's constitution. In many cases, it was only apparent from the terms of the auditors' report, which stated that the accounts complied with this or that Act. Following the publication in 1995 of the first Charity SORP (Accounting by Charities, Statement of Recommended Practice) the position has improved immensely.

1.62   Most charities now include these details in their annual report and accounts. One of the recommendations in the SORP published in March 2005 detailed in paragraph 41 what further reference and administrative information should be shown in the annual report. In summary, these are:

(a)   the name of the charity – including the name by which it is registered and any other name by which the charity makes itself known;

(b)   the charity registration number (in Scotland the Scottish Charity Number) and, if applicable, the company registration number;

(c)   the address of the principal office of the charity and, in the case of a charitable company, its registered office;

(d)   the names of trustees and the method of their appointment;

(e)   the name of the Chief Executive or other senior staff members;

(f)   the names and addresses of other relevant organisations or persons. This should include the names and addresses of those acting as bankers, solicitors, auditors and investment or other principal advisers;

This is examined in detail in Chapter 4.

6   Charity Commission

1.63   The Charity Commission has four offices, one each in London, Liverpool, Taunton and Newport. The structure of the Commission has changed as a result of the Charities Act 2006 from one which had comprised a Chief Charity Commissioner and four other non-executive commissioners to a more corporate structure. Today the governance responsibilities for strategy and future direction of the Commission lie with its Board of non-executive members. Corporate decision making that affects the day-to-day operation of the Commission is delegated to an Executive Group. This group is chaired by the Chief Executive of the Charity Commission and includes four Directors and the key Heads of Functions. The four Directors are responsible for Charity and Legal Services, Policy and Effectiveness, Corporate Services and Charity Information. The Directors' duties include implementing the programmes and policies arising from the Board and ensuring effective service delivery. The Directors are each supported by committees comprising their own senior staff together with representatives of other key parts of the organisation.

1.64   Under the Charities Act 2006 the Commission's objectives include the following:

1. To increase public trust and confidence in charities.

2. To promote awareness and understanding of the operation of the public benefit requirement.

3. To promote compliance by charity trustees with their legal obligations in exercising control and management.

4. To promote the effective use of charitable resources; and

5. To enhance the public accountability of charities to donors, beneficiaries and the general public.

1.65 Under s 1C of the Charities Act 2006, the general functions of the Charity Commission are:

1. Determining whether institutions are or are not charities.

2. Encouraging and facilitating the better administration of charities.

3. Identifying and investigating apparent misconduct or mismanagement in the administration of charities and taking remedial or protective action in connection with misconduct or mismanagement therein.

4. Determining whether public collections certificates should be issued, and remain in force, in respect of public charitable collections.

5. Obtaining, evaluating and disseminating information in connection with the performance of any of the Commission's functions or meeting any of its objectives.

6. Giving information or advice, or making proposals, to any Minister of the Crown on matters relating to any of the Commission's functions or meeting any of its objectives.

1.66 The Commission has powers to institute inquiries, call for documents, order audits and exchange information with a wide range of public bodies, including the police and HM Revenue & Customs. In extreme cases, it can suspend or replace trustees or even appoint receivers to protect or salvage charity assets. The Commission is, however, forbidden by law from acting itself as an administrator of any charity. That is the responsibility of the duly appointed charity trustees.

1.67 The Charity Commission maintains the Central Register of Charities which contains legal, financial and operational details of about 190,000 charities. The Register can be viewed online by going to the Charity Commission's website or at any of the Commission's offices, which are listed in Appendix 1.

1.68 Charities are classified by reference to:

- their field of activity (eg medical, environment, welfare);

- the identity of their beneficiaries (eg children, young people, the elderly); or

- their method of operation (eg sponsors or research undertaken).

The Charity Commission also keeps copies of charities' constitutions and latest submitted accounts – the latter documents now being available to view or download from the Charity Commission's website.

A significant part of the Charity Commission's time is taken up with registration of new charities, considering schemes for alteration of existing charities and dealing with legal complexities. It is unusual for the Charity Commission to interfere directly in the affairs of any charity unless its suspicions have been aroused by its own monitoring activities or by members of the public, by the media or by the auditors or independent examiner. It will, however, respond to calls for help from charity trustees.

1.69   The monitoring role of the Charity Commission had been rudimentary up to 1990 but has improved enormously since, largely as a result of the computerisation of the Register and additional investment in resources. All charities on the Register now automatically receive notification that their Annual Return forms are due for completion and reminders if they are ignored. Annual Returns may be completed online or on paper if a charity wishes. Annual accounts are demanded along with the annual returns and these accounts are selectively scrutinised by Charity Commission staff. Whereas in 1988, less than 10% of charities were filing accounts, 20 years later over 95% of large charities and nearly 90% of small charities were doing so.

1.70   The Official Custodian for Charities is a 'corporation sole' set up by Parliament to hold property in trust for charities and provide certain services for them free of charge. His office is a division of the Charity Commission. He may hold land or personal property on behalf of charity trustees. Up to 1991, the Official Custodian also held stocks and shares on behalf of charity trustees, collecting dividends and recovering income tax and accounting to each charity free of charge.

1.71   During 1990, the Official Custodian handled £85 million worth of capital transactions and received £94 million worth of dividends and interest on behalf of 41,000 charities.

1.72   Between 1992 and 1995 the investment holding function of the Official Custodian was phased out, largely as a cost-saving exercise. This considerable task was accomplished most efficiently and all the stocks, shares and cash were transferred to the trustees of the charities concerned who, thenceforward, have had to make other arrangements for the collection of dividends and recovery of tax.

1.73   In order to mollify the effects of this divestment by the Official Custodian, the Charity Commission encouraged charities to consider using Common Investment Funds (CIFs), especially charities which are unable to afford the services of professional financial advisers. These funds are created by schemes made by the Charity Commission in accordance with the Charities Act 2006. They operate in a similar way to unit trusts and used to be able to invest in a wider manner than individual charities. (But see Trustee Act 2000; **2.6** ff.) Moreover, charities can register units in the name of the charity rather than individual trustees, thus avoiding the problems associated with changes in the board of trustees. As CIFs are exclusively for charities, the managers ensure that all dividends and interest are remitted gross.

1.74   In a document published in 2005 setting out the way forward for 2005–2007 'Charity Working at the Heart of Society', the Charity Commission set out the following guiding principles that would shape its priorities and actions:

'● Build on the progress of recent years and become a modern regulator.

● Be independent and enabling, working both with, and for, the charitable sector.

● Place a new vision and strategic purpose at the heart of our activities. This will be shared with both charities and the public so that everyone knows what we do and the guiding principles that support our actions.

● Be accessible, accountable and transparent: encouraging greater dialogue with charities and trustees, becoming better listeners and being more collaborative, outcome-focussed and proactive.

● Be accurate, consistent and timely when asked for advice, based on well-publicised performance standards.

● Concentrate our engagement with charities on where it is most needed. Small charities will be regulated in a way which is appropriate for their size; but we will have greater expectations of larger charities due to their size and impact. Where trustees have made honest mistakes we will respond flexibly; deliberate wrong-doing will be dealt with rigorously.

● Support the improved performance of charities by working much more in partnership, particularly with umbrella groups, "signposting" other sources of expertise and introducing wider networks of communication and influence to help them.

● Deepen our knowledge of the sector through the information submitted to us by charities and gained from our own casework. We will share this knowledge widely across the sector, helping to define best practice and make charities aware of the standards to which they should aspire.

● Engage more actively with politicians and government in influencing the policy formulation process for the sector as a whole.

● Promote the work of trustees and volunteers and the contributions charitable activity makes to society.'

1.75   The jurisdiction of the Charity Commission is limited to England and Wales. The Charities Act lists those charities in England and Wales which are exempt from the jurisdiction of the Charity Commission. Exempt charities have not to date been regulated by the Charity Commission often on the grounds that they are regulated in other ways by government or public authorities. Exempt charities include several universities and their colleges, voluntary aided schools, certain museums and galleries and two independent schools – Eton College and Winchester. Excepted charities have often been excepted from registration by order of the Commission because they have umbrella organisations which have some form of regulatory role. Examples would include Scouts, Guides, and some religious organisations. It has been felt for some time that the existence of exempt and excepted charities has led to anomalies in the way charities are regulated. The 2006 Act provides for the removal of exempt or excepted status from many charities entirely in the longer term. Accountability is to be tightened up for those that retain exempt status and for those that remain excepted in the short term. Every charity must now register with the Charity Commission except those with gross income of less than £5,000 per annum or which remain exempt or excepted. The list of exempt charities as set out in Sch 2 to the Charities Act 1993 has been reduced. Those exempt charities which have been removed from the list will be re-designated excepted charities in due course. Charities that will be affected by this include the Church Commissioners, Industrial and Provident Societies, Friendly Societies, Oxford and Cambridge University Colleges and Eton and Winchester Schools.

Comment

1.76   Since the publication of Sir Philip Woodfield's 'Efficiency Scrutiny of the Supervision of Charities' in 1987, which disclosed many shortcomings and made 46 recommendations for improvement, the Charity Commission has made huge strides forward. It is now an effective regulator and an accessible source of advice and assistance. Its continuing effectiveness will depend upon matching resources to the needs of charities and liaising with the technical groups and umbrella bodies within the charity sector.

Chapter 2

Trustees' responsibilities

1 Trustees' legal responsibilities

2.1 It is often said that accepting the role of trustee of a charity is one of the most onerous responsibilities a person can accept. Certainly in today's world where there is greater emphasis on charities demonstrating that they are transparent and accountable, it is important that trustees can demonstrate that they understand their responsibilities and can be seen to be carrying them out.

2.2 Charity trustees come from all walks of life, and are often united by their wish to create positive change in society. Most people are eligible to serve as trustees. The work of a trustee should be rewarding and enjoyable, and an opportunity to serve the community whilst learning new skills.

2.3 Charity trustees are the people who are ultimately responsible for the general control, management and administration of the charity (Charities Act 1993 s 97(1)) – including its strategy, its policies, its activities and achievements. They are the individuals charged with the overall stewardship of the charity's assets and resources. Their appointment is made by the governing instrument.

2.4 The responsibilities of trustees can be divided neatly into four areas: the overall responsibility, compliance, a duty to act prudently at all times, and a duty to act with care.

Overall responsibility

2.5 The trustees have the ultimate responsibility for directing the affairs of the charity, and ensuring it is solvent, well run and delivering the charitable outcomes it was set up to achieve. This responsibility will include also the need to ensure that at all times the charity's aims are for the public benefit (see Chapter 1).

2.6 Whilst trustees can generally delegate certain powers to agents or employees of the charity, they will always retain the ultimate responsibility for running the charity. The powers that they can delegate will be defined in the charity's governing document and legislation such as the Trustee Act 2000 which states that trustees can delegate:

- carrying out a decision that the trustees have taken;

- the investment of assets; and

- raising funds for the charity.

However, someone acting as a delegate or agent of the trustees should always make it clear in dealings with third parties that they are acting in that capacity. When delegating to employees, trustees should ensure that the scope of the authority is laid down in writing and there is a defined means by which employees should report back to trustees. This can be done through written policies and procedures. For further discussion regarding trustees' ability to delegate their powers see **2.23** ff .

Duty of compliance

2.7   There are four aspects to the duty to ensure compliance with all aspects of law and regulation:

2.8   First, trustees must ensure that the charity complies with charity law, and with the requirements of the Charity Commission as regulator; in particular, they must ensure that the charity prepares trustees' reports, annual returns and accounts as required by law. They must also ensure compliance with charity fundraising laws and regulations. Where any fundraising is done either directly or on the charity's behalf:

- monies must be accounted for properly and all funds collected;

- monies must be paid in to the charity's bank account before deduction of expenses;

- literature should explain clearly what donations from the public will be used for;

- professional fundraisers must be used only once a legal contract has been drawn up;

- trustees should approve fundraising methods and literature;

- trustees should be open and honest about the costs of fundraising appeals;

- trustees should explain in their annual report the effectiveness of the fundraising efforts.

2.9   Secondly, the trustees must ensure that the charity does not breach any of the requirements or rules set out in its governing document and remains true to the charitable purpose and objects set out there. The Trustee Act 1925 provides that all trustees have an absolute duty to carry out the terms of their trust and not to commit or allow any breach of that trust. Where this is not possible the trustees may need to apply for a Scheme from the Charity Commission to amend the objects. Otherwise, they may find themselves personally liable for any loss suffered by the beneficiaries of the trust if they fail in this primary obligation through wilful default or neglect.

2.10   Thirdly, trustees must comply with the requirements of other legislation and regulators which may impact on the charity. For example:

(a)   company law;

(b)   employment law;

(c)   health & safety;

(d)   racial equality, disability discrimination, equal opportunities;

(e)   Care Quality Commission;

(f)   when working with vulnerable adults and children – the range of legislation protecting such people.

2.11   Lastly, trustees must act with integrity and avoid any personal conflicts of interest or misuse of charitable funds or assets. It is for this reason that most trustees are unpaid and must not benefit in any way from their connection with the charity, although expenses can be reimbursed if reasonable and necessary.

Duty of prudence

2.12   This has four aspects. Trustees:

- should ensure that the charity is and will remain solvent;

- should use the charity's assets wisely and only in furtherance of the charity's objects;

- must avoid undertaking activities that might place the charity's funds, assets or reputation at undue risk; and

- must take special care when investing the charity's funds or borrowing monies for it to use.

2.13   The overriding principle here is that trustees must act reasonably and prudently in all matters relating to the charity and must always bear in mind that their prime concern is the charity's interests. Income and property must be applied for the purposes set out in the charity's governing document.

2.14   Generally speaking charities may not accumulate income and it must be applied for charitable purposes within a reasonable time of receipt.

2.15   Charity trustees must take care to avoid conflicts of interest. This can be done by:

- making a declaration at each meeting;

- completing an annual form to confirm connected parties, etc.

2.16   As custodians of the trust property, the trustees are responsible for the proper maintenance of real property, investment of cash and care of all other assets, including prompt collection of debts, tax recoverable and the like.

2.17   *Trustees' responsibilities*

These responsibilities are similar to those of a company director, but the standard of care may be more exacting for trustees. In particular, for example, trustees should have regard to the following areas:

- land and buildings – trustees should know what they are worth and ensure that they are covered by adequate and appropriate insurance;

- cash management – surplus cash should be held in interest earning accounts or invested;

- bank accounts – ideally at least two trustees should be signatories on all bank accounts;

- endowments – trustees should ensure that their value is safeguarded.

2.17   With regard to investments, the Trustee Act 2000 allows trustees to place funds in any kind of investment as though they were the absolute owners of those funds; subject, however, to any restrictions and exclusions in the governing document.

2.18   The Trustee Act 2000 largely replaced the Trustee Investments Act 1961 which defined the classes of investment open to trustees. Broadly speaking, the 1961 Act required trustees, unless their governing instrument gave them wider powers, to invest at least 25% of their funds in cash deposits or fixed interest Government securities and not more than 75% in equities. In selecting equities, trustees could only choose companies which had paid dividends in each of the past five years, thus precluding privatisation issues, new technology stocks and other opportunities.

2.19   Under the provisions of the Trustee Act 2000, trustees are given the same powers as an absolute owner to invest in any investments subject to an overriding duty of care to:

(a)   show such skill and care as is reasonable, making allowance for his or her knowledge, experience or professional status;

(b)   consider the need for diversification and the suitability of investments;

(c)   obtain and consider proper advice where appropriate;

(d)   consider the size and risk of the investment;

(e)   consider the need to produce a balance between income and capital growth;

(f)   consider ethical implications.

2.20   The Trustee Act 2000 also empowers trustees to delegate their investment management to professional investment managers, subject to their overriding responsibility to review the management regularly. Included in their delegation is the power to appoint nominees or custodians to hold investments on behalf of the trustees.

Duty of care

2.21   There are three aspects to this:

- Trustees should use reasonable care and skill using any personal experience.

- 'Reasonable' is taken as meaning having regard to any special knowledge or experience a trustee may have. Professional trustees (ie those trustees that have professional qualifications or specialist knowledge because of the skills and qualifications they have) are deemed to have a higher level of knowledge and hence owe a greater duty of care.

- Trustees should use expert professional advice when needed.

Comment

2.22   The unprecedented volatility in world investment markets seen in the months following September 2008 demonstrates the need for trustees to regard investment of charity funds as a long-term decision and one where proper professional advice needs to be sought. It will be interesting to see how investments fare over the next three to five years and how trustees amend their investment policies in the light of the 2008/09 experience.

Delegation of powers

2.23   In practice, trustees often have to operate by delegating their tasks to full-time employees and these, in turn, may employ professional advisers to assist on such matters as fundraising, money management and investment advice. Care should be taken to ensure that the governing instrument allows trustees to delegate their powers. In many cases, particularly those regarding investment management, the trustees will remain legally responsible for the investment management even though a reputable firm of managers has been appointed to act. In general, trustees will be protected against any claim made against them for breach of trust or other failure caused by an employee or agent if they can show that they exercised due care in appointing that person and continued to exercise reasonable control over him or her through reporting procedures, etc.

2.24   Part 3 of the Charities Acts 2006 defines further the responsibilities of charity trustees, particularly in connection with their public accountability and compliance with fundraising regulations.

2.25   The Charity Commission (see **1.63** ff) has responsibility for the general supervision of charities in England and Wales, other than those which are currently specifically exempted from registration. Their leaflets give detailed guidance to charity trustees on a variety of issues and these are listed in Appendix 2. In particular, reference should be made to leaflet CC3 'The Essential Trustee: What you need to know'. For exempt charities or those operating from Scotland, Northern Ireland and the Republic of Ireland, an indication of the trustees' legal responsibilities is given in Chapter 15.

2   Scope of responsibility

2.26   The governing instrument must define precisely the limits of the trustees' responsibilities and, in case of doubt, the trustees themselves should record their understanding of their responsibilities in the trustees' minute book.

2.27   It is of paramount importance that there should be no confusion over what matters are within the responsibilities of the trustees and what matters are outside. The old tradition of 'beating the bounds' of a parish whereby the councillors and parish clerk solemnly walked round the perimeter of the parish once a year is, perhaps, a good image for trustees to bear in mind when considering the content of their annual report and accounts.

2.28   Paragraph 44 of SORP asks trustees to include within their annual report, after the explanation of the nature of the governing document and details about the appointment, training and induction of trustees, the following:

(a)   The organisational structure of the charity and how decisions are made. For example, which types of decisions are taken by the charity trustees and which are delegated to staff.

(b)   Where the charity is part of a much wider network (for example charities affiliated within an umbrella group) then the relationship involved should also be explained where this impacts on the operating policies adopted by the charity.

(c)   The relationships between the charity and related parties, including its subsidiaries and with any other charities and organisations with which it cooperates in the pursuit of its own charitable objectives.

2.29   Questions to be considered, therefore, will include the following:

(a)   Is the charity part of a wider network?

(b)   If so, what is its relationship – a branch, a holding company, an autonomous body under an umbrella organisation? (The Glossary in Appendix 1 of the SORP defines the relationships.)

(c)   What is the charity's relationship with other organisations with which it cooperates in pursuit of its charitable objectives – does it have a participating interest, eg 20% share in a trading company?

(d)   Does the charity share administration with another charity? If so, which, if either, controls the other?

2.30   Having established the way in which the charity is organised, the trustees are in a position to mark out the scope of their legal responsibilities and, therefore, the extent of their accountability.

THE BRITISH RED CROSS: 31 DECEMBER 2007

Organisation

The board of trustees comprises nine trustees elected from the four UK Territories and up to eight trustees co-opted by the board itself (in 2007 there were seven co-opted trustees on the board).

Newly elected and appointed trustees join the board at the start of the calendar year in most instances. Their terms of office last for three years, and they can serve two consecutive three-year terms, after which they must stand down from the board for at least one year.

A nominations group is convened to oversee trustee recruitment. Where the recruitment is for elected trustees, Volunteer Council chairs form electoral colleges to elect their respective Territory trustees; the board of trustees ratifies the election result. When recruiting co-opted trustees, the nominations group interviews short-listed applicants and presents its recommendation for appointment to the board of trustees.

The board has appointed a finance committee to oversee its financial transactions, including investments. This committee, which also acts as the audit committee, has been given specific responsibilities and makes relevant recommendations to the board. While the approval of policy is a matter for the board, that body works closely with the chief executive and his colleagues on the senior management team, which is charged with the implementation of policy.

Based in London, the UK Office of the British Red Cross houses the offices of the chairman, the chief executive and central staff. The main functions of the staff are to lead the implementation of the policies laid down by the board and to support the work of local volunteers and staff in the UK and overseas. The UK Office staff perform operational activities in the areas of UK services, international operations, income generation, communications, human resources, finance and strategy.

There are four Territory teams in the UK: Northern England; Scotland, Northern Ireland and the Isle of Man; London and South Eastern England; and Wales and Western England. These teams support the work of volunteers and staff in 21 British Red Cross Areas. There are a further eight Branches in British Overseas Territories. Since 2006, the financial results of these Overseas Branches have been included in the consolidated financial statements. Previously they were excluded on the grounds of non-materiality.

A wholly-owned trading subsidiary, Britcross Limited, supports the fundraising activities of the British Red Cross. The assets, liabilities and trading results of this company, which is incorporated in the UK, are consolidated into the financial statements. As its activities are integral to the British Red Cross, the commentary on fundraising on [page 16] also covers the activities of this subsidiary.

[*continued on next page*]

> *The British Red Cross, continued*
>
> The British Red Cross is a prominent member of the International Red Cross and Red Crescent Movement, with volunteers and staff contributing to a number of initiatives within both the International Federation of Red Cross and Red Crescent Societies (Federation) and the International Committee of the Red Cross (ICRC).

2.31   From the foregoing paragraphs, it is self-evident that the charity accountant must at the outset have a written memorandum setting out all areas of trustee responsibility and all other areas relevant to the accounts which are outside that responsibility. The trustees' report will summarise this in the description of the charity's organisation and the notes to the accounts will include the accounting policies which will explain what is included and how, and what is excluded and why. (See Chapter 5.)

3   Management structure

2.32   Consideration of the scope of the responsibilities of the trustees will dictate the type of management structure that will be most suitable to the organisation. It does not matter what the objects of the charity are; it is purely a question of the size and complexity of the organisation and its management requirements. It is dangerous, therefore, to generalise. The charity should examine its own needs for effective management and control, consult its own advisers and look upon itself as unique. That said, there are certain guidelines that are common to all organisations to which trustees should pay heed.

2.33   Trustees are normally non-executive and unpaid, though possibly very active, members of a charity. While being legally responsible for the actions of the charity, they will very often delegate the tasks for the day-to-day running of the charity to full-time executives. Typically, the charity will have a governing board of trustees which will appoint a chief executive who will be responsible for managing the charity's affairs through departments and branches staffed partly by fully paid personnel and partly by volunteers.

2.34   It is the chief executive's responsibility to install an appropriate internal control system, office procedures, an accounting system and a management reporting system to enable him or her to control the business of the charity, and to report periodically to the board of trustees.

2.35   In a very small charity which consists virtually of a single crusader, that person may be both the trustee and the chief executive having to do everything, with the help of a few volunteers. While allowances may be made in such circumstances, if substantial monies are involved, that person must have very strong regard for their trustee position and ensure that they can account not only for the money received but also for their actions in dealing with it. It is no good pleading lack of resources when things go wrong; it is up to the instigator to ensure that there are adequate control procedures to fit the circumstances.

2.36   For a larger charity, the trustees must ensure that they have a chief executive who is properly qualified for the work that he or she may be asked to do. They must be satisfied that the structure is efficient and properly matched to the tasks of the charity. If there is a divisional or branch structure, there should be proper lines of communication which are well tested and operate effectively. This becomes even more important if the charity is operating internationally.

4   Constitution

2.37   However the charity is constituted, the trustees should consider, in the light of their responsibilities and management structure, whether the constitution is suitable to the nature and scale of the charity's operations. Circumstances will change as the charity's activities develop and the original constitution may no longer be appropriate. The following checklist may be helpful.

(a)   Does the charity enter into significant contracts of employment or for the supply of services, premises, equipment and the like? If so, perhaps a corporate structure with limited liability should be considered.

(b)   Is the charity grant-making from an invested endowment fund? If so, a simple declaration of trust or trusts should be sufficient.

(c)   Is there a membership base to the charity? If so, beware giving each member a vote in the affairs of the charity. It can become politically divisive, cumbersome and expensive to administer. Better to restrict votes to members of an elected council.

(d)   Is there a branch structure? Should each branch be a separate autonomous charity or should it be under the control of the 'head office'?

(e)   Is the trustee body self-perpetuating? Would it be beneficial to instil some compulsory change?

2.38   In general, simple charities with few employees, few contractual obligations and one centre of operation should be constituted by a trust deed. This will limit the degree of statutory compliance to the Charities Act 1993 as far as accountability is concerned. More complicated charities may find it preferable to be constituted under the Companies Act 1985 as a company limited by guarantee or, in the future, as a charitable incorporated organisation (CIO). These have two major benefits.

(a)   In the event of the charity becoming insolvent, the trustees will be protected by the limited liability of the company or CIO. Any unpaid creditor wishing to claim against a trustee would have to prove wilful default or negligence on the part of the trustee under the Insolvency Act 1986. In the case of an unincorporated charity becoming insolvent, the boot is on the other foot. If the trustees are unable to meet the liabilities of the charity, they must justify the position to the creditors or possibly to the Charity Commission or to any receiver or administrator or liquidator who may be appointed.

(b)   Most people are familiar with the structure and working of a company and, therefore, if there are a large number of employees and contractors to the charity, a corporate structure with corporate procedures is likely to be more understandable and acceptable than an unincorporated body. Whilst this will in due course be true of a CIO it may not be the case in the first few years during which such entities exist.

5 Trustees' insurance

2.39   In view of their responsibilities and potential liabilities, it may be prudent to consider insuring against some or all of the inherent risks.

2.40   There are basically two classes of risk: those which will affect the assets of the charity and those which will affect the trustees personally. Clearly, trustees should ensure that the assets of the charity are safeguarded and, to the extent that their own actions or inactions put them at risk, they may consider taking out insurance, the cost of which can be borne by the charity. Such risks will be losses arising from bona fide decisions taken by the trustees in the ordinary course of carrying out their duties.

2.41   Trustee indemnity insurance covers trustees from having to personally pay out when legal claims are made against them for a breach of trust, or a breach of duty or negligence, committed by them in their capacity as trustees. Provided trustees have the necessary legal authority, they are entitled to be insured against claims that may arise as a result of their legitimate actions as trustees, and will be covered against liability as long as they have acted honestly and reasonably. In most cases, this authority will be provided by the new statutory power introduced by the Charities Act 2006.

2.42   Trustee indemnity insurance directly protects an individual trustee, rather than the charity itself. For this reason, it is regarded as a form of 'personal benefit', needing a proper legal authority before the charity can purchase it. Many charities have long had this type of authority in their governing documents, but where a charity does not, s 73F of the 1993 Act now provides a general power to buy such insurance using charity funds. The cost must be reasonable and trustees must be clear that trustee indemnity insurance is in the best interests of their charity.

2.43   Care must be taken to ensure that a charity's governing document does not explicitly forbid the purchase of trustee indemnity insurance. If this is the case, the charity will need to go to the Charity Commission for authority to purchase such a policy.

2.44   Cover cannot be obtained to protect trustees personally against claims for wilful default or neglect.

2.45   The following is an example of a typical note in a set of accounts dealing with this aspect.

SLG CHARITABLE TRUST LIMITED: 31 DECEMBER 2008

Indemnity insurance

The charity has purchased insurance to protect the charity from any loss arising from negligent acts, errors or omissions on the part of the members of the Board of Management, employees or agents and to indemnify the members of the Board of Management or other officers against the consequences of any neglect or default on their part. The insurance premium paid by the charity during the year totalled £998 (2007 – £1,018) and provides cover of up to a maximum of £250,000 (2007 – £250,000).

---

6   Reporting duties

2.46   The Charities Act 1993 s 45 requires all charity trustees, other than those who are exempt or excepted from such obligation, to prepare an annual report and this, together with the accounts – audited or independently examined as appropriate – should be filed with the Charity Commission within ten months of the accounting year end. This applies to all charities with incomes in excess of £10,000 a year, incorporated and unincorporated alike.

2.47   The annual report or trustees' report must comply with the requirements of regulation 40 of the Charities (Accounts and Reports) Regulations 2008 and paragraphs 26–32 of SORP. These are considered in Chapter 4.

2.48   The accounts of the charity which accompany the annual report will comply with the appropriate governing statute (see Chapter 3). Most will comply either with the requirements of the Charities (Accounts and Reports) Regulations 2008 or those of the regulations made under the Companies Act 2006. In either case, they will be expected to comply with the requirements of SORP and consist of:

- a statement of financial activities;
- a balance sheet;
- a cash flow statement (if required by Financial Reporting Standards);
- a summary income and expenditure account (if required by charity with endowment); and
- notes to the accounts.

2.49   The trustees are responsible for selecting and applying consistently appropriate accounting policies and for the preparation of the accounts. In practice, they may delegate this function to the charity accountant, but just as they must be involved in defining the scope of their responsibilities and, therefore, their accountability, so they must take an active part in approving the accounting policies upon which their accounts are based.

7 Remuneration of trustees

2.50   The general rule of law is that trustees must not make a profit out of their position of trust or put themselves in a position where their duties and responsibilities as trustees might conflict with their own personal interests. This is taken to mean that a trustee cannot be paid for holding the office of trustee per se. It has, however, been common practice for trust deeds to contain a 'charging clause', allowing professional trustees, such as solicitors or accountants, to be paid for their services.

2.51   The position with regard to the payment of trustees generally who provide services to the charity has been relaxed somewhat by the Charities Act 2006. The Act has inserted a new s 73A into the Charities Act 1993 which allows trustees and people connected to them to receive payment or a benefit for services (as distinct from carrying out their trustee duties) provided the following conditions are met:

(a)   the amount of the payment must be reasonable and set out in a written agreement between the person and the charity;

(b)   the charity trustees must be satisfied that it is in the best interests of the charity for the person to provide those services in exchange for the payment;

(c)   only a minority of trustees receive payment from the charity at any time; and

(d)   the charity's constitution does not contain any express clause prohibiting trustee benefits.

2.52   Whilst the 2006 Act has relaxed the rules, it is important to stress that it still does not allow trustees to be paid for carrying out their duties as trustees.

2.53   Legitimate payments which a trustee has had to meet personally in order to carry out his or her trustee duties may be refunded by the charity. As is best practice with all expense claims, expenses being reclaimed from the charity by a trustee should normally be supported by bills or receipts. Most typically such expenses will be the cost of travelling to trustee meetings or charity events.

2.54   Further guidance on the refund of expenses and on the payment of trustees may be found in the Charity Commission publication CC11 'Trustee expenses and payments'.

Comment

2.55   There is still a large body of opinion that suggests that this rule is too restrictive. In the case of some larger charities, the amount of time demanded of trustees is often so onerous that it is doubtful if suitable candidates for the office can continually be found without some monetary compensation. This is particularly the case when trustee meetings and related committee meetings are held during the working day and trustees may be required to forfeit salary in order to attend them. This view needs to be contrasted with the view that payment of trustees would introduce personal conflicts and hinder the objectivity and independence required in charity trustees. The concept of unpaid trusteeship has been one of the defining characteristics of the charitable sector and contributed greatly to public trust and confidence in charities. It is essential that this is maintained.

Chapter 3

Accounting requirements

3.1   All charities are obliged to give an account of their stewardship, but to whom and in what form is not always clear. The key lies in the document constituting the charity and this in turn leads to the authorities that regulate its activities. Most, but certainly not all, charities in England and Wales are subject to the supervision of the Charity Commission and the requirements of the Charities Act 1993. Many charities are incorporated as limited liability companies and must, therefore, also comply with the requirements of the Companies Act.

3.2   The purpose of this chapter is to cover the main statutory accounting requirements that are likely to affect most charities and outline the charity SORP (Statement of Recommended Practice (Accounting and Reporting by Charities)), which gives guidance on the practical application of accounting norms in a way that will satisfy all of those requirements.

The Charities Act 2006 strengthens the accounting regime for charities and has removed a number of the inconsistencies in the requirements for non-company charities and company charities. In particular, the 2006 Act has simplified the thresholds for both accounting and audit requirements.

1   Charities Act 1993

3.3   The accounting requirements for those charities which are not companies are set out in Part VI of the Charities Act 1993 and are contained in ss 41–49 of the Act with additional detail given by the Charities (Accounts and Reports) Regulations 2005 and the Charities (Accounts and Reports) Regulations 2008. The 2006 Act has adjusted the existing thresholds.

Charity accounts, reports and returns – summary of the Charities Act 1993

3.4   The following is a summary of the main requirements of the 1993 Act as amended by the Charities Act 2006.

Section 41   Keep accounting records sufficient to show and explain all the charity's transactions, and which are such as to:

(a)   disclose at any time, with reasonable accuracy, the financial position of the charity at that time, and

(b)   enable the trustees to prepare accounts which comply with the requirements of the regulations under s 42.

Section 42   Prepare annually a statement of accounts complying with regulations.

(a)   Charities with incoming resources up to £100,000 pa may produce a receipts and payments account, and a statement showing their assets and liabilities. They may alternatively opt to produce full accrual accounts with a balance sheet.

(b)   Charities with incoming resources of over £100,000 pa must provide full accounts on the accruals basis, in accordance with the requirements of regulation 8 of the Charities (Accounts and Reports) Regulations 2008. These require the trustees to prepare:

  (i)   a Statement of Financial Activities (SOFA) analysing the total incoming resources and the application of resources and any other movements in the total resources in a way most appropriate to the charity's operations;

  (ii)   a balance sheet;

  (iii) notes amplifying, explaining and disclosing items included in the accounts.

The principles upon which the accounts should be prepared are contained within the 2005 and 2008 Regulations. **Section 43 as amended by section 28 of the 2006 Act** Charities must have their accounts audited if:

(a)   The charity's gross income exceeds £500,000 in the year in question; or

(b)   The charity's gross income exceeds the accounts threshold (ie £100,000) and at the year end the aggregate assets of the charity before deduction of liabilities exceed £2.8 million.

A charity's expenditure level is no longer taken into account in deciding whether or not an audit is needed and there is no need any longer to consider the financial position of the charity in the preceding financial year.

If the charity's accounts are such that neither of the above conditions are satisfied but the charity's gross income for the year exceeds £10,000 then the accounts must be either professionally audited or independently examined.

The duties of the auditor or independent examiner are set out in the regulations and are discussed further in Chapter 16.

Section 44   The Secretary of State to make regulations conferring powers on the auditor or independent examiner to have access to all necessary information. These are contained in regulation 8 of the 2005 Regulations.

Section 45   Trustees to prepare and file, for charities over the £10,000 threshold, an annual report in accordance with regulation 10. This will give legal and administrative details about the charity, explain the objects, policies and organisation, and give a narrative report on its activities, achievements and developments, commenting on the financial position in relation to all of these in the context of the long-term objects of the charity. This is dealt with more fully in Chapter 4.

Section 46   Special provisions for exempt and excepted charities:

(a)   exempt charities to keep 'proper books of account' and, if not otherwise regulated, to prepare annual accounts under this Act consisting of an income and expenditure account and balance sheet;

(b)   excepted charities need not submit accounts, unless they have elected to register. They must however prepare accounts and they must also submit an annual report with accounts if requested to do so by the Charity Commissioners.

Section 47   Annual reports and accounts lodged with the Charity Commission are open to public inspection.

Section 48   Trustees to lodge an annual return for any charity with a gross income or total expenditure in excess of £10,000.

Section 49   Criminal liability of persons persistently in default in relation to accounting requirements.

2   Companies Act 2006

3.5   The Companies Act 2006 and the regulations made under the Act set out the requirements for the preparation of company accounts, which will include all charities incorporated or registered under the Companies Act. The following are the main points covered:

(a)   the format of the accounts;

(b)   the content of the accounts; and

(c)   the rules for determining amounts included in the accounts.

3.6   There is a fundamental requirement for accounts to show a true and fair view and many trustees and charity accountants consider this to be a major point when deciding whether or not to follow precisely the rules laid down in the Act. Bearing in mind that the authors of the Companies Act probably did not have charitable companies in the forefront of their minds when drafting the regulations, it is likely that certain aspects will not suit the reporting requirements of a charity. It should, however, be a rarity that this section has to be invoked by a charity. In general, corporate charities must abide by the accounting provisions of the Companies Act 2006.

3.7   In the past, some charities have considered it necessary to depart from these requirements on the basis that the accounts would not otherwise give a true and fair view. With SORP, which applies equally to incorporated and unincorporated charities, this is likely to become even rarer.

Preparing company accounts

3.8   The following is a summary of the accounts provisions contained in the Act which have been extracted from *Preparing Company Accounts – Small Companies Accounting Under the Companies Act 2006*, by Ray Mayes, a consultant of Buzzacott, published by CCH (17th edition 2009/10). Some items, especially those relating to shares, are not applicable to charitable companies, but they are left in for the sake of completeness.

Introduction

The Companies Act 2006 lays down provisions relating to:

● prescriptive formats of accounts;

● the content of accounts; and

● principles and rules for determining amounts included in the accounts.

This section summarises accounts provisions of Companies Act 2006, insofar as they relate to accounts ('individual accounts') of 'small' companies that are prepared in accordance with Companies Act 2006 s 394. A company is treated as 'small' if it does not exceed more than one of the following criteria: Turnover of £6.5 million; balance sheet total of £3.26 million and average number of employees (on a monthly basis) of 50.

Accounts

Full accounts prepared for shareholders must be prepared for all companies, irrespective of size.

The full accounts of a 'small' company, however, are less detailed with reduced disclosure requirements. A small company may also take advantage of the FRSSE.

A company qualifying as 'small' or 'medium-sized' may, in addition, prepare 'abbreviated' accounts for filing with the Registrar of Companies.

Depending on certain size criteria, small companies may be exempt from the requirement for audit. Dormant companies may also take advantage of audit exemption.

Company accounts are produced from the company's underlying financial records ('proper accounting records') as explained below.

TABLE: INDIVIDUAL ACCOUNTS (COMPANIES ACT 2006 SECTION 396)

Each financial year, the directors must prepare individual accounts comprising:

● a balance sheet, and

● a profit and loss account   [*continued on next page*]

Table: individual accounts (Companies Act 2006 section 396), continued

Showing true and fair view of:

- the state of affairs at the year end, and

- the profit or loss for the financial year
    Complying (as to form, content and notes) with the provision of:

- Small Companies and Groups (Accounts and Directors' Report) Regulations 2008 (SI 2008/409)

- any additional information (or departure from requirement) necessary to show a true and fair view.

Comment

It should be noted that a charitable company which is 'small' will still be required to comply with the charity SORP and this may mean disclosing more information than is required under the Companies Act or the FRSSE.

True and fair view

There is a fundamental requirement for full accounts (individual accounts or group accounts) to show a 'true and fair' view. The directors of a company must not approve accounts unless they are satisfied that they give a true and fair view of the company's assets, liabilities, financial position and profit or loss.

The requirement for full accounts to show a 'true and fair' view applies irrespective of whether or not the accounts are subject to audit. Any decision concerning the method of accounting or means of disclosing information must take this basic requirement into account.

The basic accounting principle is that annual accounts should show a 'true and fair' view, a term that has never been defined in statute or case law.

In essence, accounts are deemed to present a 'true and fair view' if they:

- comply with any relevant legislation or regulatory requirement;

- comply with accounting standards and generally recognised practice (GAAP);

- comply with recognised and accepted industry based practice;

- provide an unbiased (fair and reasonable) presentation;

- are compiled with sufficient accuracy within the bounds of materiality; and

- faithfully represent the underlying commercial activity (the concept of 'substance over legal form').

The requirement for accounts to give a 'true and fair' view is also embodied within European Accounting Directives. In the case of IAS accounts, there is a requirement under international accounting standards that such accounts much achieve a 'fair presentation'.

'True and fair view accounts' (not a statutory term or specifically defined but used in this book for convenience) are financial statements intended to give a true and fair view of the financial position and profit and loss (or income and expenditure) of an entity.

A 'true and fair view' is required to be given of the state of affairs of the company (and/or consolidated undertakings) as at the end of the financial year and of the profit and loss of the company (and/or consolidated undertakings so far as concerns members of the parent company) for the financial year.

Where compliance with the provisions of CA 2006 as to the matters to be included in 'annual accounts' ('individual accounts' or 'group accounts') or the notes would not be sufficient to give a true and fair view, the necessary additional information must be given in the accounts or in a note to them.

If in *special circumstances* such compliance is inconsistent with the requirements to show a 'true and fair view', the directors must depart from the relevant provision of CA 2006 to the extent necessary to show a 'true and fair view' and must explain such departure in a note to the accounts (the true and fair 'override' principle).

The 'true and fair view' has the ultimate legal override; an entity may override accounting standards only to give a 'true and fair view' and this would be only in exceptional circumstances. A departure from an accounting standard must be justified and explained.

Format of accounts

The form and content of accounts is covered by regulations made under the Companies Act 2006.

The form and content of Companies Act individual accounts is determined in accordance with:

- the Small Companies and Groups (Accounts and Directors' Report) Regulations 2008 (SI 2008/409) for small companies
- the Large and Medium-sized Companies and Groups (Accounts and Directors' Report) Regulations 2008 (SI 2008/410) for medium-sized companies and large companies.

Schedules within SI 2008/409 and SI 2008/410 prescribe the required formats from which companies may choose for Companies Act individual and group accounts.

Once a format has been adopted, the company must use the same format for subsequent years unless, in the directors' opinion, there are special reasons for changing; these must be disclosed in the year of change.

Every balance sheet and profit and loss account must show the items listed in the adopted format if, of course, they apply either in the financial year or the preceding year.

Adopting a particular format is not as restricting as it may seem, as there are a variety of options, for example:

37

- departure is allowed if it is made to ensure a true and fair view (see above);

- certain headings may be combined (provided combination is disclosed);

- immaterial items may be disregarded;

- information can be given in greater detail than prescribed and items not listed in a format may be included, if directors so wish; and

- certain information may be given in notes instead of on the face of the accounts.

A company's accounts may include other items not listed in the various formats but there are three specific items which may not be treated as assets in a company's balance sheet:

(a)   preliminary expenses;

(b)   expenses of, and commissions on, any issue of shares or debentures; and

(c)   costs of research.

Where there is no amount to be shown for a format item for the financial year, a heading or sub-heading corresponding to the item must not be included, unless an amount can be shown for the item in question for the immediately preceding financial year under the relevant format heading or sub-heading.

For every balance sheet or profit and loss account item, the corresponding amount for the immediately preceding financial year must also be shown. Where the corresponding preceding year amount is not comparable, the current year amount may be adjusted, but particulars of the non-comparability and of any adjustment must be disclosed in a note to the accounts.

Every profit and loss account must show the amount of a company's profit or loss on ordinary activities before taxation.

Accounting principles

Company accounts are required to be prepared in accordance with the principles set out in:

- Schedule 1 of SI 2008/409 – small companies

- Schedule 6 of SI 2008/409 – small company groups

- Schedule 1 of SI 2008/410 – medium-sized (and large) companies

- Schedule 6 of SI 2008/410 – medium-sized (and large company) groups

These principles are the fundamental accounting concepts that underlie accounts and are also incorporated within accounting standards (FRSs and SSAPs) generally, and (for small companies adopting it) the FRSSE.

The basic statutory accounting principles are as follows:

- *Going concern* – The company or reporting entity is to be presumed to be carrying on business as a going concern.

- *Consistency* – Accounting policies must be applied consistently within the same accounts and from one financial year to the next.

- *Prudence* – The amount of any item must be determined on a prudent basis and in particular:

  (a) only profits realised at the balance sheet date should be included in the profit and loss account; and

  (b) all liabilities having arisen in respect of the financial year (or preceding financial year) should be taken into account (including those liabilities becoming apparent up to the date of approval of the accounts (in accordance with the Companies Act 2006 s 414)).

- *Accruals* – All income and charges relating to the financial year to which the accounts relate must be taken into account, without regard to the date of receipt or payment.

- *Individual determination* – In determining the aggregate amount of any item, the amount of each individual asset or liability that is taken into account should be determined separately.

- *Netting* – Amounts in respect of items representing assets or income must not be set off against amounts in respect of item representing liabilities or expenditure (as the case may be), or vice versa.

- *Substance of transactions* – In determining how amounts are presented within the accounts, regard should be had to the substance of the reported transaction or arrangement in accordance with GAAP.

If it appears to the company's directors that there are special reasons for departing from any of the accounting principles in preparing the company's accounts in respect of any financial year they may do so. Particulars of the departure, the reasons for it and its effect must be given in a note to the accounts.

Accounting standards (FRSs generally) enhance the above principles by determining that accounting policies adopted should be relevant, reliable, comparable and understandable.

For fixed assets, stocks, investments and goodwill, rules regarding valuation, accounting and disclosure are laid down.

Historical cost principles are stated as the normal method of accounting but alternative bases (eg revaluation and current cost) are allowed provided that details and related historical cost figures are disclosed.

Only 'realised' profits can be included in the profit and loss account.

In determining for accounting purposes 'realised profits' (and 'realised losses'), such profits or losses mean profits or losses of the company that fall to be treated as realised in accordance with principles generally accepted at the time when the accounts are prepared, unless the Companies Act specifies some other treatment.

Comment

This causes one of the main difficulties when trying to fit the Companies Act requirements within the Statement of Financial Activities recommended by the SORP (see Chapter 6 which requires the inclusion of 'unrealised' investment gains).

Notes to Accounts – disclosures

For small companies, Schedule 1 of SI 2008/09 Small Companies and Groups (Accounts and Directors' Report) Regulations 2008 sets out the information required to be disclosed in a small company's accounts, covering the following heads:

- reserves and dividends;
- disclosure of accounting policies;
- share capital and redeemable shares;
- fixed assets;
- financial instruments valued at fair value;
- investment property and living animals and plants at fair value;
- reserves and provisions;
- details of indebtedness (including payments by instalments and nature of security);
- guarantees and other financial commitments;
- particulars (analysis) of turnover;
- preceding year items included in the profit and loss account – effect of inclusion;
- exceptional items – the effect of transactions (within ordinary activities) that are exceptional by size or incidence; and
- sums denominated in foreign currencies – basis of translation into sterling; and
- dormant companies acting as agent.

The enhanced disclosures for medium-sized companies are contained in SI 2008/410 The Large and Medium-sized Companies and Groups (Accounts and Directors' Report) Regulations 2008.

Directors' report – contents and requirements

The directors of a company are required to prepare directors' report for each financial year of the company.

Where the company is a parent company, and the directors of the company prepare group accounts, the directors' report must be a consolidated report (a group directors' report) covering all undertakings included in the consolidation.

A group directors' report may, where appropriate, give greater emphasis to matters that are significant to the undertakings included in the consolidation, taken as a whole.

Small companies, however, are permitted to prepare a directors' report that is much reduced in content, omitting much of the information otherwise required to be included in the directors' report of a medium-sized or large company.

Basically, the directors of larger companies are required to prepare a directors' report complying with CA 2006 provisions as follows:

- general matters (s 416) including SI 2008/410 disclosures;

- business review (s 417);

- matters covering company and subsidiaries (SI 2008/410) (parent company preparing group accounts); and

- statement as to disclosure of information to auditors (audited accounts) (s 418).

Quoted companies are also required to prepare:

- a directors' remuneration report (s 421), covering aspects of directors' remuneration such as remuneration details, company policy, service contracts, share options and pension disclosures, and

- operating and financial review (OFR).

Group accounts

A parent company (other than a small parent company) which has 'subsidiary undertakings' is required (with certain exceptions) to prepare group accounts in the form of consolidated accounts of the company and its subsidiary undertakings, as if they were a single company. Consolidation is not restricted to subsidiaries which are companies.

Group accounts (when prepared) are required to comply with the provisions of the Companies Act 2006 as to form and content of consolidated accounts and additional information to be given. Regulations under the Companies Act 2006 provided SI 2008/409 Schedules 6 and 3 (Small companies) and SI 2008/410 Schedules 6, 4 and 5 (large and medium-sized companies), require *inter alia* the following accounting for consolidations:

- elimination of group transactions;

- provisions for acquisition and merger accounting;

- treatment and disclosure of 'minority interests';

- non-consolidated subsidiary undertakings;

- joint ventures and associated undertakings; and

- preparation 'as if' the group were a single company

A subsidiary may be excluded from consolidation on the grounds of immateriality and *must* be excluded in the following circumstances:

- severe long-term restrictions;

- temporary control – holding with a view to subsequent resale.

Audit reports

Full statutory accounts (together with an audit report, if appropriate) are required for shareholders for all companies.

For companies other than those applying the provisions for companies subject to the small companies regime, the availability or otherwise of audit exemption will determine whether the accounts should be accompanied by an auditors' report.

The auditors must consider whether the information given in the directors' report is consistent with the accounts and must state that fact in their report. There is no requirement to state in what respect it is inconsistent.

Where abbreviated accounts are prepared (under 'small' and 'medium-sized' company filing provisions), a special auditors' report is required stating that in the auditors' opinion:

- the company is entitled to deliver abbreviated accounts; and

- the abbreviated accounts have been properly prepared.

Adequate accounting records

Companies are required to keep 'adequate accounting records' (previously referred to as 'proper accounting records') in accordance with the Companies Act 2006 s 386. Company accounts are produced from these underlying financial records.

Companies Act 2006 s 386 is summarised in the following table.

ADEQUATE ACCOUNTING RECORDS

A company is required to keep accounting records ('adequate accounting records') which are sufficient to show and explain the company's transactions. The accounting records must:

- Disclose with reasonable accuracy, *at any time*, the financial position of the company *at that time*;

- Enable the directors to ensure that any accounts required to be prepared comply with the requirements of Companies Act 2006 (and where applicable, of Article 4 of the IAS Regulation) and, for example, that the balance sheet and profit and loss accounts comply in form and content;

- Contain entries from day to day receipts and expenditure (with sufficient identifying detail); and

- Contain a record of company assets and liabilities.

[*continued on next page*]

Adequate accounting records, continued

If the company deals in goods, the accounting records must also contain statements of:

- Stock held at the year end;

- Stocktaking (records and procedures) underlying the year end stock; and

- All goods sold and purchased (except for retail sales), in sufficient detail to identify the goods and the buyers and sellers.

A parent company must ensure that any subsidiary undertaking keeps such accounting records as ensure compliance with the Companies Act 2006 or IAS.

Comment:

Directors should be constantly aware of the company's financial position and progress. The exact nature and extent of the accounting systems and management information needed to exercise adequate control will depend on the nature and extent of the company's business.

Adequate control over records and transactions involves monitoring:

- Cash;

- Debtors and creditors;

- Stock and work in progress;

- Capital expenditure;

- Contractual arrangement; and

- Plans and budgets.

Approval and signature of accounts

The directors' report, statutory accounts and the auditors' report all require appropriate approval and signature.

A company's annual accounts must be approved by the board of directors and signed on behalf of the board by a director of the company. The signature must be on the company's individual balance sheet and the name of the signatory must be stated.

The directors' report must also be approved by the board of directors and signed on their behalf by a director *or* the secretary of the company; the name of the signatory must be similarly stated.

The auditors' report must state the names of the auditors and be signed and dated. Where the auditor is a firm, the report must be signed by the senior statutory auditor in his own name, for and on behalf of the firm of auditors.

The above requirements also apply to the approval and directors' signature of abbreviated accounts.

The balance sheet and directors' report of a small company which have been prepared in accordance with the special provisions for companies subject to the small companies regime and must each contain a statement by the directors to that effect in a prominent position above the signature.

If the accounts are prepared in accordance with the provisions applicable to companies subject to the small companies regime, the balance sheet must contain a statement to that effect in a prominent position above the signature.

Publication of non-statutory accounts

If a company publishes any of its statutory accounts (as required under s 441) (other than a summary financial statement under s 426), they must be accompanied by the auditor's report on those accounts (unless the company is exempt from audit and the directors have taken advantage of that exemption). A company that prepares statutory group accounts for a financial year must not publish its statutory individual accounts for that year without also publishing with them its statutory group accounts.

If a company publishes non-statutory accounts, it must publish with them a statement indicating:

●   that they are not the company's statutory accounts;

●   whether statutory accounts dealing with any financial year with which the non-statutory accounts purport to deal have been delivered to the registrar; and

●   whether an auditor's report has been made on the company's statutory accounts for any such financial year, and if so whether the report:

   (a)   was qualified or unqualified, or included a reference to any matters to which the auditor drew attention by way of emphasis without qualifying the report; or

   (b)   contained a statement under the Companies Act 2006 s 498(2) (accounting records or returns inadequate or accounts or directors' remuneration report (where applicable) not agreeing with records and returns), or the Companies Act 2006 s 498(3) (failure to obtain necessary information and explanations).

A company must not publish with any non-statutory accounts the auditor's report on the company's statutory accounts.

'Non-statutory accounts' are accounts or other published financial information that are not the company's statutory accounts. Simplified accounting information, abridged accounts, announcements of company results to employees or the press, might be classified non-statutory accounts.

This completes the extract from 'Preparing Company Accounts', by Ray Mayes of Buzzacott, published by CCH (17th edition, 2009/10).

Comment

During the debate on the Charities Bill in 1992, an undertaking was given by the government to review the accounting requirements under company legislation as they affect charitable companies, with a view to bringing these into line with the accounting requirements under the Charities Act. This undertaking is hopefully being fulfilled. The Charities Act 2006 includes this form of incorporation for charities and allow existing corporate charities to convert to CIO status, thus removing them from company law regulation as regards reporting and accounting and placing them instead under the Charities Acts' regulations.

3   Statement of recommended practice – SORP

3.9   Whilst the Accounting Standards Board takes responsibility for setting accounting standards which have general application, such as Financial Reporting Standards (FRSs) and Statements of Standard Accounting Practice (SSAPs), they have delegated responsibility for Statements of Recommended Practice (SORPs) to the regulatory authority responsible for the industry or sector concerned.

3.10   Thus, the SORP 'Accounting and Reporting by Charities' was issued in its revised form in March 2005 by the Charity Commission and applies to all accounting periods beginning on or after 1 April 2005.

3.11   The status of the SORP is that of recommendation rather than requirement. However, to conclude that this leaves it as optional whether to follow the recommendations or not is a dangerous presumption. In the preamble to the SORP, there is a statement by the Accounting Standards Board which includes the following.

> 'On the basis of its review, the ASB has concluded that the SORP has been developed in accordance with the ASB's code of practice and does not appear to contain any fundamental points of principle that are unacceptable in the context of present accounting practice or to conflict with an accounting standard or the ASB's plans for future standards.'

3.12   This is colloquially referred to as 'negative franking' and effectively elevates the SORP to the status of current best practice. Therefore, any charity which chooses not to follow or to ignore a recommendation must be able to justify its decision.

3.13   Paragraph 21 of SORP contains the following statement in this respect.

> 'Trustees may occasionally find that following a recommendation is incompatible with the obligation to give a true and fair view. They should then use the alternative accounting treatment which gives a true and fair view and provide particulars within the accounting policy notes (in accordance with paragraph 359) of any material departure from the recommendations in this SORP. A departure is not justified simply because it gives the reader a more appealing picture of the financial position or results of the charity.'

3.14   *Accounting requirements*

3.14   The Charities (Accounts and Reports) Regulations 1995, 2000 and 2008 issued under Charities Acts 1993 and 2006, lend further weight to the SORP. Paragraph 3 of Part III of Sch 1 to the Charities Act 1993 specifically requires that the values of assets and liabilities in a charity's accounts should be determined in accordance with the principles set out in the SORP.

3.15   The recommendations in the SORP as best practice should therefore always be followed by charities producing accounts which are required to show a true and fair view, except in two cases:

(a)   if the recommendation is incompatible with the obligation to give a true and fair view; or

(b)   if the recommendation is incompatible with statutory accounting requirements imposed on the charity (in this case, the recommendation should be adapted to meet the special circumstances as nearly as possible).

Summary of the SORP

3.16   The purpose of a charity's annual report and accounts

'The purpose of preparing a trustees' annual report and accounts is to discharge the charity trustees' duty of public accountability and stewardship.' (para 10)

'The trustees' annual report and accounts should therefore:

(a)   provide timely and regular information on the charity and its funds;

(b)   enable the reader to gain an understanding of the charity's objectives, structure, activities and achievements;

(c)   enable the reader to gain a full and proper appreciation of the charity's financial transactions during the year and of the position of its funds at the end of the year.' (para 15)

3.17   Scope

'The accounting recommendations of this SORP apply to all charities in the United Kingdom that prepare accounts on the accruals basis to give a true and fair view of a charity's financial activities and financial position regardless of their size. Constitution or complexity.' (para 3)

'Where a separate SORP exists for a particular class or charities (eg SORPs applicable to Registered Social Landlords and to Further and Higher Education Institutions), the charity trustees of charities in that class should adhere to that SORP and any reporting requirements placed on such charities by charity law.' (para 5)

3.18   Content

(a)   Trustees' annual report   – This should include:

    (i)   reference and administrative details of the charity, its trustees and advisers;

    (ii)   narrative information on:

      – structure, governance and management;

      – objectives and activities;

      – achievements and performance;

      – financial review;

      – plans for future periods; and

      – funds held as custodian trustee on behalf of others.

(paras 41–59)

(b)   General accounting principles   – This defines what should be included in the accounts and how:

    (i)   Fundamental accounting concepts;

    (ii)   Accounting standards;

    (iii)   Accounting for separate funds:

      Unrestricted income funds (including designated funds);

      Restricted – income and capital (endowments);

      Endowments – permanent and expendable;

    (iv)   Accounting for gains and losses;

    (v)   Reconciliation of funds;

    (vi)   Particulars of individual funds and notes to the accounts;

    (vii)   Branches.

(paras 60–81)

(c)   Statement of financial activities   – This shows the total incoming and total outgoing resources of the charity including capital gains and losses

   – It gives an analysis of both incoming and outgoing resources

   – It separates restricted funds from unrestricted funds

   – It shows for each class of fund whether there is a net inflow or outflow of funds

   – It provides a reconciliation of all movements in the charity's funds

   – Detailed guidance is given on all relevant issues.

(paras 82–243)

(d)   Balance sheet   – This shows all the assets and liabilities of the charity

   – It represents the resources available to the charity and how they are deployed

		– Details of heritage assets and contingent liabilities may be contained in notes rather than on the face of the balance sheet.	
			(paras 244–350)
(e)	Cash flow statement	– Application and disclosure.	(paras 351–355)
(f)	Accounting policies	– This includes recognition of incoming resources such as legacies and grants	
		– It deals with deferred income, life memberships etc	
		– Expenditure policies include costs of generating funds, management and administration, as well as direct charitable expenditure	
		– Recognition of liabilities especially in relation to grants payable is considered.	
			(paras 356–370)
(g)	Summary financial information and statements	– General principles and contrasting characteristics of summarised financial statements and information	(paras 371–379)
(h)	Special sections	– Consolidation of Subsidiary Undertakings	(paras 381–406)
		– Accounting for Associates, Joint Ventures and Joint Arrangements	(paras 407–418)
		– Charitable Companies	(paras 419–429)
		– Accounting for Retirement Benefits	(paras 430–448)
		– Accounting for Common Investment Funds and Investment Pooling Schemes	(paras 449–451)

Comment

3.19   The SORP applies to all charities (both incorporated and unincorporated) except registered housing associations (now registered social landlords), universities and common investment funds, all of which have their own SORP.

3.20   While it is important to comply with the statutory requirements governing the accounts of the charity, which are set out in this chapter, it is equally important to do so in accordance with the recommendations of the SORP, which are considered in detail in the following chapters. In general, compliance with the SORP will ensure compliance with the statutory requirements.

4   Summary information return

3.21   One of the recommendations of the Private Action, Public Benefit report was that those charities which are large enough to require an audit should (in addition to submitting their report and accounts to the Charity Commission each year) also file a Summary Information Return. This would detail a range of qualitative and quantitative information about the charity, focusing on the charity's impact, how it measures its performance against its aims and how it intends to improve its performance. This now forms Part C of the Annual Return to be submitted to the Charity Commission.

Comment

3.22   The object of the Summary Information Return is to provide comparable information on the impact that the activities of charities are having and their performance generally.

Chapter 4

Trustees' report

1 Duty to prepare a trustees' annual report

4.1   Paragraph 15 of SORP summarises the purpose of the trustees' annual report and accounts of a charity and states that they should:

'a)   Provide timely and regular information on the charity and its funds;

b)   Enable the reader to understand the charity's objectives, structure, activities and achievements; and

c)   Enable the reader to gain a full and proper appreciation of the charity's financial transactions during the year and the position of its funds at the end of the year.' (Para 16)

4.2   Paragraph 35 of SORP makes it clear that the accounts alone will not meet all the information needs of users.

'Accounts themselves also have inherent limitations in terms of their ability to reflect the full impact of transactions or activities undertaken and do not provide information on matters such as structures, governance and management arrangements adopted by the charity. The accounts of a charity cannot alone easily portray what the charity has done (its outputs) or achieved (its outcomes) or what difference it has made (its impact). This is mainly because many of these areas cannot be measured in monetary terms: indeed some areas are difficult to measure with any numbers at all. The trustees' annual report provides the opportunity for charity trustees to explain the areas that the accounts do not explain.'

4.3   As a result the SORP requires charity accounts to be accompanied by information to be contained in a trustees' annual report. The trustees' annual report needs to be a coherent document explaining what the charity is trying to do and how it is going about it. Ideally, it will assist the reader in understanding what progress the charity has made against objectives set and in understanding the charity's future plans. A good report will also explain the charity's governance and management structure and hence give insight into the ways in which trustees and management communicate, how decisions are made and how they are implemented and monitored.

4.4   The basic concept of the trustees' report is one of communication – communication of what the charity does, how it benefits its members and society generally, its financial position and what it hopes to do in the future in the context of those future plans.

4.5 The obvious way for charities to improve accountability and transparency and meet stakeholders' expectations is to give greater importance to their annual report. It is the obvious way to communicate information to everyone interested about the financial position and performance of a particular charity, the deployment of its resources, organisational structure, policies, priorities, activities and achievements. A good annual report:

- demonstrates that resources are being used wisely and for the stated purpose;

- shows that the charity is being organised and managed properly;

- demonstrates that the charity is carrying out its activities efficiently and effectively; and

- attracts new resources to enable the charity to continue its activities.

4.6 The responsibility for the preparation of the trustees' annual report lies with the trustees. As the report provides important information about the charity and its accounts, paragraph 37 of SORP requires that the report should always be attached to the accounts whenever a full set of accounts is distributed or otherwise made available.

4.7 The SORP sets out the basic requirements for a trustees' annual report but does not preclude a charity from including other information – for example, a chairman's report, environmental information, impact assessments, etc if the trustees so wish. On the other hand, the production of annual reviews, newsletters and website information should not be regarded by trustees as a substitute for the trustees' annual report.

4.8 Charitable companies must prepare a directors' report in order to meet the requirements of the regulations made under the Companies Act2006. Charitable companies should not prepare two reports – a directors' report and a trustees' annual report – but should ensure that the statutory directors' report contains all the information required to be provided in the trustees' annual report.

4.9 SORP 2005 divides the contents of the annual report into a number of distinct categories:

- reference and administrative details of the charity, its trustees and advisers;

- structure, governance and management;

- objectives and activities;

- achievements and performance;

- financial review;

- plans for future periods; and

- funds held as custodian trustee on behalf of others.

2 Reference and administrative details of the charity, its trustees and advisers

4.10   Paragraph 41 of SORP sets out the requirements regarding the disclosure of the reference and administrative details of a charity, its trustees and advisers.

'The report should provide the following reference and administrative information about the charity, its trustees and advisers:

(a)   the name of the charity, which in the case of a registered charity means the name by which it is registered. Any other name by which the charity makes itself known should also be provided;

(b)   the charity registration number (in Scotland the Scottish Charity Number) and, if applicable, company registration number;

(c)   the address of the principal office of the charity and in the case of a charitable company the address of its registered office;

(d)   the names of all those who were the charity's trustees or a trustee for the charity on the date the report was approved. Where there are more than 50 charity trustees, the names of at least 50 of those trustees (including all the officers of the charity, eg chair, treasurer, etc) should be provided. Where any charity trustee disclosed is a body corporate, the names of the directors of the body corporate on that date.

(e)   the name of any other person who served as a charity trustee or as a trustee for the charity for the financial year in question;

(f)   the name of any Chief Executive Officer or other senior staff member(s) to who day to day management of the charity is delegated by the charity trustees;

(g)   the names and addresses of any other relevant organisations or persons. This should include the names and addresses of those acting as bankers, solicitors, auditors (or independent examiner or reporting accountant) and investment or other principal advisers.'

4.11   For an example of such information, see the extract from the annual report and accounts of Help the Aged on page 53.

Comment

4.12   While it would seem to be a matter of common sense that these details should be given in every annual report, it is surprising how many charities take it for granted that the reader will instinctively know all about them. It is, therefore, helpful to have this checklist when starting to prepare the annual report.

4.13   Apart from the details listed in para 41 of SORP, it is also helpful to give a prominent indication of the main objects of the charity so that the reader is immediately aware of the field in which it operates. It is astonishing how often this is omitted, probably because the writers assume that the readers already know. The objects of the charity, if not obvious from its title, should be clearly stated at the very outset, preferably on the front cover.

3   Narrative information

4.14   The trustees' narrative report is perhaps the most important part of the annual report as it links the financial facts shown by the accounts to the objects of the charity and the policies being pursued to achieve those objects. It enables the trustees to explain both successes and disappointments; it also enables them to explain any unusual items in the accounts which they fear may give a misleading impression to their supporters, for example, a sudden influx of cash at the year end.

4.15   As explained above the narrative information falls within a number of distinct categories with the requirements for each being summarised in paragraphs 44–59 of SORP.

4.16   Regulation 40 of Charities (Accounts and Reports) Regulations 2008 gives further reinforcement to the recommendations of paragraphs 44–59 of SORP. The Regulation is reproduced in its entirety below:

'**40.**—(1) This regulation applies to an annual report prepared in accordance with section 45(1) of the 1993 Act by the charity trustees of a non-parent charity.

(2) The report on the activities of a charity during the year which is required to be contained in the annual report prepared under section 45 of the 1993 Act—

(a)   must specify the financial year to which it relates;

(b)   must—

  (i)   in the case of a charity which is not an auditable charity, be a brief summary setting out—

    (aa)   the main activities undertaken by the charity to further its charitable purposes for the public benefit; and

    (bb)   the main achievements of the charity during the year.

  (ii)   in the case of a charity which is an auditable charity, be a review of the significant activities undertaken by the charity during the relevant financial year to further its charitable purposes for the public benefit or to generate resources to be used to further its purposes including—

    (aa)   details of the aims and objectives which the charity trustees have set for the charity in that year, details of the strategies adopted and of significant activities undertaken, in order to achieve those aims and objectives;

    (bb)   details of the achievements of the charity during the year, measured by reference to the aims and objectives which have been set;

    (cc)   details of any significant contribution of volunteers to these activities;

(dd) details of the principal sources of income of the charity; and

(ee) a statement as to whether the charity trustees have given consideration to the major risks to which the charity is exposed and satisfied themselves that systems or procedures are established in order to manage those risks;

(c) must—

   (i) where—

      (aa) any fund of the charity was in deficit at the beginning of the relevant financial year; and

      (bb) the charity is one in respect of which a statement of accounts has been prepared under section 42(1) of the 1993 Act for that financial year,

   contain particulars of the steps taken by the charity trustees to eliminate that deficit;

   (ii) contain a statement by the charity trustees as to whether they have complied with the duty in section 4 of the 2006 Act to have due regard to guidance published by the Commission; and

   (iii) be dated and be signed by one or more of the charity trustees, each of whom has been authorised to do so.

(3) Subject to paragraphs (4) to (7), the other information relating to a charity and to its trustees and officers which is required to be contained in the annual report is—

(a) the name of the charity as it appears in the register of charities and any other name by which it makes itself known;

(b) the number assigned to it in the register and, in the case of a charitable company, the number with which it is registered as a company;

(c) the principal address of the charity and, in the case of a charitable company, the address of its registered office;

(d) the name of any person who is a charity trustee of the charity on the date when the authority referred to in paragraph (2)(c)(iii) above is given, and, where any charity trustee on that date is a body corporate, the name of any person who is a director of the body corporate on that date;

(e) the name of any other person who has, at any time during the relevant financial year been a charity trustee of the charity;

(f) the name of any person who is a trustee for the charity on the date referred to in sub-paragraph (d);

(g) the name of any other person who has, at any time during the relevant financial year been a trustee for the charity;

(h)   particulars, including the date if known, of any deed or other document containing provisions which regulate the purposes and administration of the charity;

(i)   the name of any person or body of persons entitled by the trusts of the charity to appoint one or more new charity trustees and a description of the method provided by those trusts for such appointment;

(j)   a description of the policies and procedures (if any) which have been adopted by the charity trustees for the induction and training of charity trustees and where no such policies have been adopted a statement to that effect;

(k)   a description of the organisational structure of the charity;

(l)   a summary description of the purposes of the charity;

(m)   a description of the policies (if any) which have been adopted by the charity trustees for the selection of individuals and institutions who are to receive grants or other forms of financial support out of the assets of the charity;

(n)   a statement regarding the performance during the financial year of the investments belonging to the charity (if any);

(o)   where material investments are owned by a charity, a description of the policies (if any) which have been adopted by the charity trustees for the selection, retention and realisation of investments for the charity including the extent (if any) to which social, environmental or ethical considerations are taken into account;

(p)   a description of the policies (if any) which have been adopted by the charity trustees for the purpose of determining the level of reserves which it is appropriate for the charity to maintain in order to meet effectively the needs designated by its trusts, together with details of the amount and purpose of any material commitments and planned expenditure not provided for in the balance sheet which have been deducted from the assets in the unrestricted fund of the charity in calculating the amount of reserves, and where no such policies have been adopted, a statement to that effect;

(q)   a description of the aims and objectives which the charity trustees have set for the charity in the future and of the activities contemplated in furtherance of those aims and objectives;

(r)   a description of any assets held by the charity or by any charity trustee of, or trustee for, the charity, on behalf of another charity, and particulars of any special arrangements made with respect to the safe custody of such assets and their segregation from assets of the charity not so held and a description of the objects of the charity on whose behalf the assets are held.'

Public benefit

4.17   In addition to the requirements of SORP and reg 40, trustees are required to include a statement within their annual trustees' report as to whether they have complied with the duty in s 4 of the Charities Act 2006 to have due regard to public benefit guidance published by the Charity Commission. The type of statement envisaged is as follows:

THE ALLTOWN SCHOOL FOUNDATION CHARITY: CHARITY COMMISSION EXAMPLE REPORT

In setting our objectives and planning our activities our Governors have given careful consideration to the Charity Commission's general guidance on public benefit and in particular to its supplementary public benefit guidance on advancing education and on fee-charging.

Structure, governance and management

4.18   Paragraphs 44–46 of SORP require trustees to ensure that the report gives the reader an understanding of how the charity is constituted, its organisational structure and how its trustees are appointed and trained. The report should also assist the reader to understand better how the charity's decision-making process operates. Essentially this section requires:

(a)   details of the nature of the charity's governing document;

(b)   the method of recruiting and appointing new trustees;

(c)   the policies and procedures adopted for the induction and training of trustees;

(d)   the organisational structure of the charity and how decisions are made – eg which decisions are taken by trustees and which by senior management;

(e)   where the charity is part of a wider network – details of the relationship;

(f)   details of relationships with other charities and organisations; and

(g)   a statement confirming that the charity has considered the risks to which the charity is exposed and that the trustees have reviewed the systems and controls established to manage those risks.

4.19   The following extracts from the trustees' annual reports of Social Care Institute for Excellence (SCIE) and Wandsworth Women's Aid illustrate how charities approach certain of these aspects.

SOCIAL CARE INSTITUTE FOR EXCELLENCE : 31 MARCH 2006

SCIE's board of trustees

New trustees are elected by existing trustees (the Secretary of State for Health being entitled to nominate three trustees, the Welsh Assembly Government one trustee and the Department of Health, Social Services and Public Safety in Northern Ireland one trustee) and serve for a term of three years before retiring from office. Retiring trustees can be nominated to serve a second consecutive term provided that no trustee serves more than two consecutive terms of office, except with the unanimous support of all the other trustees. Constant regard is paid to the skills mix of the trustees to ensure that they have all the necessary skills required to contribute fully to the charity's development.

On agreeing to become a trustee of the charity, the trustees are thoroughly briefed by their co-trustees on the history of the charity, the day-to-day management, the responsibilities of the trustees, the current objectives and future plans. The trustees are also encouraged to attend any courses which they feel are relevant to the development of their role, and to keep up-to-date on any changes in legislation.

WANDSWORTH WOMEN'S AID: 31 MARCH 2006

Trustee Induction and Training

As part of its review of trustee recruitment and induction, the board revised its programme of trustee induction and training in 2005/06. Upon appointment to the board, trustees receive a Wandsworth Women's Aid trustee induction pack that contains the following documentation:

- The charity's Memorandum and Articles of Association
- Rules of Wandsworth Women's Aid
- Wandsworth Women's Aid Trustee Code of Practice and Trustee Agreement
- Job descriptions of Wandsworth Women's Aid Chair, Secretary and Treasurer
- Charity Commission booklet: 'The Essential Trustee'
- Minutes from the last three Wandsworth Women's Aid board meetings
- Contacts list for Wandsworth Women's Aid

In addition to the Trustee Induction pack, we also offer new trustees a one to one meeting with the Director to discuss the operations and issues affecting Wandsworth Women's Aid, a tour of one of the refuges, training on domestic violence issues with one of the staff members and training on Trustee issues. Going forward, we hope to offer training on trustee issues to all members of the board on an annual 'refresher' basis.

Objectives and activities

4.20   This section of the report needs to give the reader an understanding of the aims set by the charity, the strategies and activities to achieve them and how its activities further the charitable purposes of the charity for the public benefit. In particular, this section of the report needs to provide:

(a)   a summary of the objects of the charity as set out in its governing document;

(b)   an explanation of the charity's aims and a clear demonstration that those aims are for the public benefit. This will mean that the trustees will need to demonstrate how their charity has addressed the two principles of public benefit, ie there must be an identifiable benefit or benefits and the benefit must be to the public or a section of the public;

(c)   an explanation of its main objectives for the year in question;

(d)   an explanation of the charity's strategies for achieving its stated objectives; and

(e)   details of significant events, projects, services, etc that have enabled it to achieve its objectives and provide public benefit.

4.21   Where a significant part of the charity's activities comprise grant making, this section of the report needs also to refer to the grant-making policies applied. Similarly, reference needs to be made in this section to programme related investments and the policies applied in making such investments.

4.22   Finally in this section, those charities which make significant use of volunteers should provide sufficient information to enable the reader to appreciate the role and contribution of volunteers by explaining the activities volunteers help provide, quantifying their contribution in terms of hours volunteered and, if possible, giving an indicative value of this contribution.

4.23   The following extracts from the trustees' annual reports of Cats Protection and The Trust of St Benedict's Abbey Ealing illustrate how charities approach certain of these aspects.

CATS PROTECTION ANNUAL REPORT AND ACCOUNTS 2008

Trustee's Report

Cats Protection is the UK's leading cat welfare charity. Founded in 1927, we are dedicated to cat welfare; we find homes for cats in need, promote the benefits of neutering and provide education, information, advice and resources on cat care and welfare. In 2008 we directly helped over 193,000 cats (2007:157,000) and indirectly we help many more.

Our vision is...

"A world where every cat is treated with kindness and an understanding of its needs"

It's an ambitious vision. However, we truly believe that it can be achieved because of our passion and professional approach.

Cats Protection will continue to help cats by *developing and growing* in all three of our objectives:

Homing – finding good homes for cats in need

Neutering – supporting and encouraging the neutering of cats

Information – improving people's understanding of cats and their care through education and advice

Our values,
which underpin everything...

They shine through our work and provide the cornerstones of our charity, enabling us to grow and, as a result, to help more cats and kittens every year. Our values are simple:

- We care about cats
- We value and respect our volunteers, supporters and staff
- We are committed to providing a service of the highest quality
- We are open and honest

THE TRUST OF ST BENEDICT'S ABBEY EALING: 31 AUGUST 2007

Principal aims, objects and activities

The charity exists to promote the charitable works carried out by, or supported by, the monks and which are conducive to the advancement or maintenance of the Roman Catholic religion. These fall into three main areas: *[continued on next page]*

The Trust of St Benedict's Abbey Ealing, continued

Education

School

The monastery operates a Senior and Junior School, providing education for over 830 boys (and girls in the 6th form and nursery) between the ages of 3 and 18. The Junior School admits children who have been baptised Roman Catholic, but it also has a limited number of places for other baptised Christians. The Senior School admits baptised Roman Catholics as well as boys of other Christian denominations and other faiths. Although the direction of the school remains in the hands of the Abbot and Community, there is a lay Advisory Governing Body and a teaching staff of over 70 members, plus ancillary and part-time staff, working for the academic, religious and social growth of the pupils.

Adult Education

The Trust provides adult education through parish lectures and the Benedictine Study & Arts Centre (BSAC) which is on-site. Students and volunteers share in aspects of monastic life by both partaking in courses of study and by learning to understand the monastic tradition of hospitality, fidelity and a life centred on community, reflection and prayer.

Parish work

The abbey church serves also as parish church and 3 of the monks are occupied in ministering directly to the needs of some 6,000 parishioners. In addition to spiritual support, there are many initiatives to promote the material and social well-being of all age groups. Again, there are a number of lay employees and many volunteers involved in these areas.

Counselling

Ealing Abbey Counselling Service (EACS) is currently the largest counselling and psychotherapy provider in London and the South East. It has in the region of 85 practitioners, runs 23 supervision groups a month and provides over 250 client hours a week.

Other works

Individual members of the monastic community are also involved in scholarly writing for publication, retreat work, giving spiritual advice and lecturing. The monks take part in local ecumenical and social initiatives. The Community includes a number of retired members and 2 who are in training.

Achievements and performance

4.24 Information about a charity's achievements and performance is a key element of its accountability to stakeholders. The disclosures in this section of the report will be vital to readers being able to understand the public benefit the charity gives and the very significant contribution it makes to society. This section of the report is likely to contain both qualitative and quantitative information and may be used to highlight any indicators, milestones or benchmarks against which the achievement by the charity of its objectives may be assessed. Paragraph 53 of SORP requires that this section should contain:

(a) A review of charitable activities undertaken that explains the performance achieved against the objectives set. Where qualitative or quantitative information is used to assess the outcome of activities, a summary of the measures or indicators used to assess achievement should be included.

(b) Where significant fundraising activities are undertaken, details of the performance achieved against fundraising objectives set, commenting on any material expenditure which might enhance future income generation, and explaining the effect on the current period's fundraising return and anticipated income generation in future periods.

(c) Where material investments are held, details of the investment performance achieved against the investment objectives set.

(d) Comment on those factors within and outside the charity's control which are relevant to the achievement of its objectives; these might include relationships with employees, users, beneficiaries, funders and the charity's position in the wider community.

Financial review

4.25 The aim of this part of the report is to explain to readers what the figures mean given that many stakeholders will not be experienced in interpreting accounts. It needs to contain an explanation of both the charity's incoming resources and resources expended as analysed in the statement of financial activities and explaining the year on year changes is good practice. The section should explain also the resources the charity has had at its disposal and how they have been utilised. In addition to explaining the resource movements in the year, the report needs to address the financial position of the charity at the end of the year. In particular, continuing emphasis is being placed on the inclusion of a detailed reserves policy stating the level of reserves held and why they are held. In addition, where a particular fund is in deficit, the circumstances giving rise to the deficit and details of the steps being taken to eliminate the deficit need to be given. Finally, when material investment holdings exist, this section of the report should comment on the charity's investment policy and objectives including the extent (if any) to which social, environmental or ethical considerations are taken into account.

4.26 This section need not be purely narrative and some charities find it useful to supplement the text with charts and diagrams.

Plans for future periods

4.27   Paragraph 57 of SORP requires trustees to explain the charity's future plans including the aims and key objectives it has set for future periods together with details of any activities planned to achieve them.

Funds held as custodian trustee on behalf of others

4.28   Where a charity is, or its trustees are, acting as custodian trustees, paragraph 59 of SORP requires that the following matters should be disclosed in the report:

(a)   a description of the assets held in this capacity;

(b)   the name and objects of the charity on whose behalf the assets are held and how this activity falls within their own charity's objectives; and

(c)   details of the arrangements for safe custody and segregation of such assets from the charity's own assets.

Comment

4.29   At first sight, reg 40 and paragraphs 44–59 of SORP look dauntingly bureaucratic and repetitive. Some trustees may think that their report will simply consist of a list of disclosure points for compliance purposes. This, however, is not doing either the regulations or the SORP justice. Broken down to their essentials, they are asking trustees the following:

(a)   To give details about the charity's structure, governance and management. This needs to include narrative demonstrating an awareness of the main risks faced by the charity and the need to implement systems to mitigate them.

(b)   To explain its objects and activities carried out to further its charitable purposes for the public benefit.

(c)   To review its achievements and performance.

(d)   To review its financial results for the year and its financial position at the year end including the fund balances at the year end in the context of the objects of each. Are they adequate? Are they excessive? What are they proposing to do to bring the reserves to the right level?

(e)   To outline the charity's plans for the future.

4.30   The report may be a lengthy document or simply a few paragraphs. The main point is that it should help to explain and interpret the figures shown in the accounts, to make the 'Report and Accounts' a cohesive integral document. The sub-headings of paragraphs 44–59 of SORP are intended to act as a prompt to help trustees to identify relevant matters for inclusion.

4.31   Although succinctly worded, paragraphs 44–50 of SORP demand considerable thought on the part of the trustees, who may find it necessary to lengthen their report significantly to cover fully the subjects on which they are asked to comment. We welcome this as a further move in the direction of greater accountability, but the burden should not be underestimated. The 2005 SORP, building on its predecessors which required trustees to consider the optimum level of reserves and make a statement confirming that they have considered the risks to which the charity is exposed, emphasises the need for trustees to comment on the performance of the charity against its targets and the impact that its activities have had.

4.32   A well-prepared trustee's report will have identified its target audience and communicated the main messages concerning the charity's progress by linking these messages to the salient features in the accounts. The report will also go further and demonstrate the actions taken to maintain good governance and improve the impact that the work of the charity has. Thus supporters of the charity will, by reading the report, be able to judge whether their support has been worth while and whether they feel inclined to continue to support it in the future.

4.33   In reporting on achievements and performance, charities are encouraged to make use of ratios and statistical information as well as narrative information looking at each area of the charity's work. It should be remembered that the report need not contain narrative only but can make use of charts, diagrams, photographs and quotes.

4.34   The following example from the trustees' report of the Olivetan Benedictine Sisters, Turvey Abbey Charitable Trust shows how such messages can be conveyed using a mixture of narrative and photographs.

OLIVETAN BENEDICTINE SISTERS, TURVEY ABBEY CHARITABLE TRUST: 31 MARCH 2009

Achievements and performance (continued)

Review of activities (continued)

- **Liturgy**

  Retreatants, visitors and people living in the locality – of all denominations, faiths and none, continue to attend the religious services held in the chapel and often express their appreciation, as the following comments indicate:

[continued on next page]

> *Olivetan Benedictine Sisters, Turvey Abbey Charitable Trust, continued*
>
> > *"I especially appreciated the time of shared worship…I was sincerely blessed to share this time with you appreciating your simplicity and devotion to the Lord."*
> >
> > *"Grateful thanks for the silence and the liturgy…"*
>
> From a group who brought their own speakers:
>
> > *"The theme for the day was 'Old Age', but the main event was the [community] midday Mass in which we all took part. It was a simple, dignified, Mass and it seemed to encapsulate all that we could wish for."*

4.35   In order to ensure that clear and accurate messages come through, trustees should consider the structure of their report and the structure of their accounts. For example, the main expenditure headings in the 'Statement of Financial Activities' should represent the main charitable activities of the charity on which the trustees are reporting. If they do not, then the structure of the report or the accounts or both should be revised. Similarly, if significant resources are earmarked for one particular purpose, it will make the trustees' report clearer if the balance sheet can show these as a designated fund, separate from the other unrestricted funds. This aspect is considered further in Chapter 5.

4.36   While the trustees' report may sometimes be drafted by the charity accountant or even the auditors, it must be made abundantly clear to the trustees that it is their report and that they must take responsibility for it. This is now dealt with in a 'statement of responsibilities', which may form part of the trustees' report or be shown as a separate statement accompanying the accounts. The auditors have a duty under International Statement of Auditing Standards No 600 (ISAS600) to distinguish their responsibilities from those of the trustees. This is discussed further in Chapter 16.

4.37   Apart from the overall financial picture, the trustees are reminded of the need to consider the finances on a fund-by-fund basis to ensure that each is being used for its own purposes and is capable of meeting its commitments. If one becomes over-extended, the trustees should say what they are doing to rectify the situation.

4.38   Although the trustees' report is fundamentally a narrative explanation, it can be illustrated with pictures, graphs, pie charts, etc, to help emphasise particular points. Indeed, such diagrammatic portrayal of figures extracted from the accompanying accounts helps the ordinary reader to understand the main features of the accounts themselves.

Chapter 5

Accounting policies and accounts structure

1 Guidelines

5.1 Paragraph 356 of SORP emphasises the need to explain the basis of the preparation of the accounts of a charity.

'Charity accounts should include notes on the accounting policies chosen. These should be the most appropriate in the particular circumstances of each charity for the purpose of giving a true and fair view...'

5.2 In paragraphs 60–64, the SORP goes on to say the following.

'Accounts intending to show a true and fair view must be prepared on the going concern assumption and the accruals concept and provide information that is relevant, reliable, comparable and understandable...'

and that they must also comply with recognised accounting standards. These include Statements of Standard Accounting Practice (SSAPs), Financial Reporting Standards (FRSs) and Urgent Issues Task Force (UITF) abstracts, all of which fall within the authority of the Accounting Standards Board. The SORP gives helpful guidance on the application of these standards in an appendix.

5.3 The first thing upon which the trustees need to decide in relation to their accounts is the scope of their accountability. What needs to be included: volunteers' activities; branches; overseas activities; connected charities; subsidiary or associated companies? For many charities such as churches, missionary societies and international relief agencies, these are the most difficult questions to resolve as quite often there is a lacuna between the strict legal responsibility and the practical ability to exercise control. To a large extent, the trustees may have to rely upon the reports and returns made to them by those working for the charity in the field.

5.4 Nevertheless, the first imperative as regards the accounts is to decide and define their scope (see Chapter 2). On occasions, this may result in the accounts being limited, for example, to specific geographical areas or by excluding certain activities deemed not to be under the control of the trustees.

5.5   In the accounts of the Congregation of the Daughters of the Cross of Liege for the year ended 31 March 2008, the trustees make it clear that the accounts exclude the results of a voluntary-aided school which is a separate legal entity over which the charity exercises no control.

---

31 MARCH 2008

Principal accounting policies (extract)

Non-aggregated activities – St Philomena's School, Carshalton and Holy Cross College, Bury

The charity owns the property at St Philomena's, Carshalton, which is a Voluntary Aided School funded by the Local Education Authority and the property at Holy Cross College, Bury, Lancashire, which is a Catholic Sixth Form College funded by the Learning and Skills Council. The School and College are exempt charities and therefore separate legal entities. The charity does not exercise control over the activities nor the management of either organisation and derives no financial benefit from them. The income, expenditure, assets and liabilities are not therefore incorporated into these financial statements.

As the School and College are carrying out activities which further one of the objects of the charity, the properties are let to them at a peppercorn rent and this arrangement will, subject only to major changes in funding, governance or educational needs in those areas, continue indefinitely. The School and College land and buildings cannot be disposed of in the open market nor put to alternative use whilst such occupation continues. The freehold property is therefore considered to have no value for the purpose of these financial statements.

5.6   Having established the boundaries of the accounts, the next step is to decide upon the accounts structure that is needed to control and communicate the financial transactions of the charity. The main considerations are as follows.

(a)   Funds structure: are the trusts upon which funds are given to the trustees clearly known? Do they restrict the trustees further than the general trusts under which they receive other monies for the charity? If they do, then they must be kept separate from the general unrestricted funds.

(b)   Branches: are the branches an integral part of the charity, or have they such autonomy and independence as to make them totally separate from the charity?

(c)   Connected charities: are there parallel charities working in concert with the charity? Are they under common control or administration? Should their activities be aggregated with those of the charity? If not, what if anything needs to be said about them?

(d)   Consolidation: have all subsidiary undertakings, corporate or otherwise, been consolidated with the parent charity's accounts? Does this distort the overall picture of the charity's activities?

(e)   Associated undertakings: does the charity have a material interest, say 20%, in a company owned by a consortium?

5.7   The answers to all these questions will have a significant bearing upon the accounts structure of the charity. It is worth spending considerable time examining each of these aspects which are dealt with later in this chapter.

2   Accounting policies

5.8   Once the trustees have agreed the scope of their accountability and have broadly established the accounts structure that is needed to comply with this, their next step is to define the accounting policies which form the basis for their accounts.

5.9   These are covered in paragraphs 356–370 of SORP. The following is a summary of the matters to be considered:

- accounts are prepared in accordance with the SORP and accounting standards;

- compliance with the Charities Act or Companies Act or other legislative requirement;

- based on historic cost, except for investments (and possibly fixed assets if revalued);

- any material departure from the SORP or accounting standards with explanation and justification;

- details of any branches or other entities not included and why;

- specific policies regarding material incoming resources, eg legacies, gifts, intangible income, grants receivable, deferred income, subscriptions, endowment income, resources received net of expenditure;

- specific policies for the recognition of liabilities including constructive obligations;

- policy for including items within categories of resources expended;

- methods and principles for the allocation and apportionment of costs between different categories of expenditure;

- bases of capitalisation of fixed assets for the charity's use;

- bases of valuation of investments;

- basis of inclusion of unrealised and realised gains and losses on investments;

- basis for inclusion of stocks and work-in-progress;

- description of the different types of fund held by the charity and the policy for transfer between funds and allocations to and from designated funds; and

- other relevant policies eg pension contributions, foreign exchange gains and losses, exceptional items, finance and operating leases, treatment of irrecoverable VAT.

Comment

5.10　The detailed requirement for the disclosure of accounting policies is given in Chapter 13 (**13.4** ff). Suffice it to say at this stage that, in line with the exhortation given in Chapter 2 regarding the trustees' responsibilities in relation to the accounts, it is their responsibility to select 'suitable policies'. These policies are judged against the objectives of relevance, reliability, comparability and understandability. The objectives of the SORP with regard to accounting policies are identical to those of Financial Reporting Standard 18 'Accounting Policies' (FRS 18). FRS 18 aims to ensure that a charity adopts the accounting policies most appropriate to its particular circumstances, that they are reviewed regularly to ensure they remain appropriate and are changed if necessary, and that sufficient information is disclosed in the accounts to enable users to understand the accounting policies adopted and how they have been implemented. Accounting policies, therefore, should reflect the main accounting aspects affecting the charity: its sources of income, its application of those resources and the way in which it accounts for its major assets, including land, buildings and other fixed assets. They will also introduce the main funds structure of the accounts which will indicate the purposes for which the balances on the funds are held (see the example taken from the accounts of Coram Family, below).

CORAM FAMILY: 31 MARCH 2008

Principal accounting policies

Basis of accounting

The accounts have been prepared under the historical cost convention, as modified by the inclusion of certain functional freehold properties at a valuation and the inclusion of investments at market value, and in accordance with the requirements of the Charities Act 1993. Applicable United Kingdom accounting standards (United Kingdom Generally Accepted Accounting Practice) and the Statement of Recommended Practice 'Accounting and Reporting by Charities' (SORP 2005), issued by the Charity Commission in March 2005, have been followed in these accounts.

[*continued on next page*]

Coram Family, continued

Incoming resources

Incoming resources are recognised in the period in which the charity is entitled to receipt and the amount can be measured with reasonable certainty. Income is deferred only when the charity has to fulfil conditions before becoming entitled to it or where the donor or funder has specified that the income is to be expended in a future accounting period.

Grants from government and other agencies have been included as income from activities in furtherance of the charity's objectives where these amount to a contract for services, but as donations where the money is given in response to an appeal or with greater freedom of use, for example monies for core funding.

Legacies are included in the statement of financial activities when the charity is advised by the personal representative of an estate that payment will be made or property transferred and the amount involved can be quantified.

Resources expended and the basis of apportioning costs

Expenditure is included in the statement of financial activities when incurred and includes any attributable VAT which cannot be recovered.

Resources expended comprise the following:

(a)   The costs of generating funds comprises the costs associated with generating voluntary income and the fees paid to investment managers in connection with the management of the charity's listed investments. It includes costs that can be allocated directly to such activities and those indirect costs necessary to support them (see (d) below).

(b)   The charitable activities comprise expenditure on the charity's primary charitable purposes as described in the Trustees' Report i.e. promoting the care and welfare of children.

It includes both costs that can be allocated directly to such activities and those indirect costs necessary to support them (see (d) below).

(c)   Governance costs comprise the costs incurred with the governance arrangements of the charity. These costs include audit, legal advice, costs associated with meeting constitutional and statutory requirements and the costs associated with the strategic management of the charity.

(d)   Support costs are those costs which enable the generation of funds and which enable charitable activities to be carried out. These costs include finance, human resources, property management and information technology. Where expenditure incurred relates to more than one activity it is apportioned using the most appropriate basis.

[*continued on next page*]

Coram Family, continued

Gifts in kind

Assets and gifts in kind donated to the charity for its own use are included in incoming resources and in resources expended at their worth to the charity as at the time of the gift.

Tangible fixed assets

All assets costing more than £750 and with an expected useful life exceeding one year are capitalised.

- Freehold land and buildings

  Freehold land and buildings are included in these accounts at a valuation determined by the trustees, with professional assistance, as at 31 March 2001, based on existing use.

  Freehold buildings are depreciated at an annual rate of 2% per annum.

  No depreciation is charged on freehold land.

- Furniture and equipment

  Expenditure on the purchase and replacement of furniture and equipment is capitalised and depreciated over a four year period on a straight line basis.

- Paintings and other works of art

  Paintings and other works of art are not capitalised for reasons explained in note 10 to the accounts.

Fixed asset investments

Fixed asset investments are included in the accounts at their market value as at the balance sheet date. Realised and unrealised gains (or losses) are credited (or debited) to the statement of financial activities in the year in which they arise.

Fund accounting

The fixed asset permanent endowment fund represents the proceeds from the disposal of the Hospital at Bloomsbury and the Foundling Hospital School at Berkhamsted. These proceeds have been applied to purchase, build and equip Coram's present premises.

Expendable endowment funds comprise monies which are held as capital but which may be spent in certain circumstances as explained in note 14. Income generated by the general endowment fund is credited to general funds and applied for general purposes whereas income generated by those investments underlying the building, repair and maintenance fund and the pension deficit reduction fund is added to that fund.

[*continued on next page*]

Coram Family, continued

Restricted funds comprise monies raised for, or their use restricted to, a specific purpose, or contributions subject to donor imposed conditions.

The furniture and equipment fund represents the net book value of the charity's fixtures and fittings.

Designated funds comprise monies set aside out of unrestricted general funds for specific future purposes or projects.

General funds represent those monies which are freely available for application towards achieving any charitable purpose that falls within the charity's charitable objects.

Leased assets

Rentals applicable to operating leases, where substantially all the benefits and risks of ownership remain with the lessor, are charged to the statement of financial activities as incurred.

Pension costs

The charity contributes to a defined benefit pension scheme which was closed to new members in 2004 and provides benefits based on final pensionable salary. The assets of the scheme are held and managed separately from those of the charity.

Pension scheme assets are measured at fair value at each balance sheet date. Liabilities are measured on an actuarial basis using the projected unit method. The net of these two figures is recognised as an asset or liability on the balance sheet.

Any change in the asset or liability between balance sheet dates is reflected in the statement of financial activities in recognised gains and losses for the period.

Contributions in respect of personal pension schemes and defined contribution schemes are recognised in the statement of financial activities in the year in which they are payable to the relevant scheme.

Liquid resources

Liquid resources represent monies held on short term deposit with United Kingdom banking organisations.

---

3   Accounting for separate funds

5.11   Whilst the main purpose of the accounts is to give an overall view of the incoming and outgoing resources and the resultant financial position at the year end, there are additional requirements for charities that have to account for more than one fund under their control.

'The accounts should provide a summary of the main funds, differentiating in particular between the unrestricted income funds, restricted income funds and endowment funds...'
(para 65)

5.12   This can present complications, particularly where the charity earmarks projects and enters into funding agreements with various trusts or government authorities. The accounts must be capable of producing the overall picture, while at the same time providing an account of the movement on each of the main funds.

5.13   To ensure that both aims are achieved, it is necessary to classify the funds of the charity. Appendix 3 of SORP explains the legal position regarding the funds of a charity. The major distinction is between 'unrestricted funds', ie those that are expendable at the discretion of the trustees in furtherance of the objects of the charity, and 'restricted funds' which are subject to specific trusts declared by the donor within the objects of the charity.

5.14   Further distinctions must be made within the categories of restricted and unrestricted funds. Restricted funds may be restricted income funds or they may be restricted as to the use of capital which must be retained while the income may be used for unrestricted purposes. Such capital funds, if restricted in perpetuity, are called 'permanent endowments'; if the trustees have power to convert them into income funds, they are called 'expendable endowments' until such time as the trustees exercise the power.

5.15   To complicate matters further, the trustees may place their own restrictions on the use of part of the unrestricted funds. They may do this by designating amounts to be set aside, for instance for 'replacement of buildings'. Such designated funds have many of the characteristics of restricted funds but, except where donors give specifically to these funds, they remain unrestricted and the trustees can use their discretion to change their earlier decision if they so wish. Once, however, new money is raised specifically for the designated fund, its character then changes from unrestricted to restricted.

The following chart on 'The Funds of a Charity' may help readers to classify their receipts among their funds.

The Funds of a Charity

Nature of Fund	Restricted	Unrestricted
1. Capital funds		
Property or cash given to the charity to be held in perpetuity as capital, the income from or use of the asset being for either restricted or unrestricted purposes.	Permanent endowment	
Property or cash given to the charity to be held as capital but giving the trustees power to use the capital for income purposes. The end uses may be either restricted or unrestricted, but until the power is exercised, the capital will remain restricted.	Expendable endowment	
2. Fixed asset funds		
Reserves set aside by trustees to represent investment out of income in fixed assets either for the use of the charity or as income-producing investments.		Designated fixed asset fund
(Technically this is an income fund but as it has been applied to achieve the long-term purposes of the charity, it may be helpful to show this designated fund separately from the other income (or designated) funds.)		
3. Income funds		
Property or cash which has been given to fund a particular project, or to be used for a particular purpose, or in a particular region or manner.	Restricted income fund	

Nature of Fund	Restricted	Unrestricted
Property or cash which has been set aside by the trustees for a particular purpose, eg cyclical maintenance, roof replacement, research or staff pensions.		Designated income fund

5.16   In order to cope with the separate accounting that is necessary to distinguish individual funds, a suitable coding structure is essential in order to allocate all incoming and outgoing resources correctly.

5.17   Guidance is given in SORP in paragraphs 65 to 76 and also in SORP Appendix 3.

Funds structure

5.18   Figure 1 of SORP, reproduced below, shows the main classifications of separate funds and requires accounts to provide a summary of the main funds differentiating in particular between the unrestricted income funds, restricted income funds and endowment funds.

'The notes to the accounts should provide information on the structure of the charity's funds so as to disclose the fund balances and the reasons for them...'
(para 75)

In particular, the assets and liabilities representing each type of fund should be summarised and analysed (eg investments, fixed assets and net current assets) between the funds and any which appear in deficit should be explained in the trustees' report.

Figure 1 – The types of funds of charities

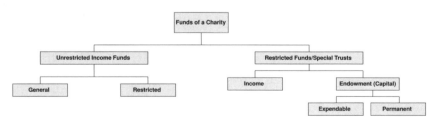

The accounts of the Sisters of Charity of St Vincent de Paul Charitable Trust describe the composition of the charity's funds in the accounting policies.

SISTERS OF CHARITY OF ST VINCENT DE PAUL CHARITABLE TRUST: 31 DECEMBER 2007

Accounting policies (extract)

Fund accounting

The general fund comprises those monies which may be used towards meeting the charitable objectives of the charity and which may be applied at the discretion of the trustees.

The designated funds are monies set aside out of general funds and designated for specific purposes by the trustees.

The restricted funds are monies raised for, and their use restricted to, a specific purpose, or donations subject to donor imposed conditions.

The endowment funds comprise monies which must be held indefinitely as capital. The income therefrom is credited directly to unrestricted or restricted funds in accordance with the terms of the relevant endowment.

Reconciliation of funds

5.19 However the funds structure is presented (and liberal use of the notes is recommended for the detail), there must be a reconciliation of the opening and closing balances of each fund. This not only enables the donors to track their restricted fund, but to see how it fits into the general finances of the charity as a whole.

Thus, paragraph 74 of SORP emphasises the following.

'Reconciliation of funds

The Statement of Financial Activities should reflect the principal movements between the opening and closing balances on all the funds of the charity. It should be analysed between unrestricted income funds, restricted income funds and endowment funds (permanent and expendable combined).'

This is illustrated in the accounts of The British Butterfly Conservation Society Limited.

STATEMENT OF FINANCIAL ACTIVITIES: YEAR TO 31 MARCH 2008

	Notes	Unrestricted funds £	Restricted funds £	Endowment funds £	**2008 Total £**	2007 Total £
Incoming resources						
Incoming resources from generated funds						
Voluntary income	1	654,196	135,701	—	**789,897**	453,851
Activities for generating funds	1	27,946	—	—	**27,946**	34,627
Investment income and interest receivable	1	149,846	29,181	—	**179,027**	156,439
Incoming resources from charitable activities						
Conservation activities – grants receivable	2	40,145	1,425,566	—	**1,465,711**	1,426,410
Contracts and royalties		173,158	56,164	—	**229,322**	211,216
Other primary purpose trading		42,558	2,218	—	**44,776**	65,030
Membership subscriptions		329,861	—	—	**329,861**	305,107
Other incoming resources		661	—	—	**661**	3,613
Total incoming resources		1,418,371	1,648,830	—	**3,067,201**	2,656,293
Resources expended	3					
Cost of generating funds						
Costs of generating voluntary income		33,602	9,866	—	**43,468**	46,165
Fundraising trading: cost of goods sold and other costs		4,839	1,742	—	**6,581**	5,936
Investment management costs		916	251	—	**1,167**	1,179
Charitable activities						
Conservation		413,093	1,657,484	—	**2,070,577**	1,709,695
Membership services		153,767	45,112	—	**198,879**	199,465
Governance		54,321	21,663	—	**75,984**	71,099
Total resources expended		660,538	1,736,118	—	**2,396,656**	2,033,539
Net incoming (outgoing) resources before transfers	4	757,833	(87,288)	—	**670,545**	622,754

[continued on next page]

77

Statement of financial activities: Year to 31 March 2008, continued

	Notes	Unrestricted funds £	Restricted funds £	Endowment funds £	**2008 Total £**	2007 Total £
Transfers between funds	13	(230,600)	230,600	—	**—**	—
Net incoming resources before net investment (losses) gains		527,233	143,312	—	**670,545**	622,754
Net investment (losses) gains		(6,709)	—	(141,309)	**(148,018)**	49,677
Net movement in funds		520,524	143,312	(141,309)	**522,527**	672,431
Balances brought forward at 1 April 2007		1,740,702	1,129,896	1,781,850	**4,652,448**	3,980,017
Balances carried forward at 31 March 2008		2,261,226	1,273,208	1,640,541	**5,174,975**	4,652,448

Chapter 6, which deals with the Statement of Financial Activities, gives further guidance on the separation of funds.

Comment

5.20   The separation of funds is one of the more difficult aspects of charity accounting. It demands first definition and then consistency of treatment. Definition can be achieved by a written memorandum setting out the purposes of each fund, its sources of income and the allocation of expenditure to it.

5.21   Consistency refers to the basis of allocation. For example, a charity may agree to apportion the cost of salaries of a department over the projects administered by that department according to the time spent on each project by each member of staff. Another charity may find such a basis of apportionment of cost too complicated and adopt instead a fixed percentage of the total cost to be allocated to each project. Either method may be acceptable, but what is not acceptable is to chop and change from one to the other.

5.22   If it is thought necessary to change the basis of allocation, then, depending upon its materiality, it may be necessary to explain it in the accounting policies, showing the effect of the change on the respective funds.

4 Branches

5.23 Appendix 1 of SORP is a glossary of terms and defines branches as:

'entities or administrative bodies set up, for example, to conduct a particular aspect of the activities of the reporting charity, or to conduct the activities of the reporting charity in a particular geographical area. They may or may not be legal entities which are separate from the reporting charity.' (GL4.1)

The definition recognises its own limitation by going on to explain different types of branch, including charities which may have nothing to do with the activities of the reporting charity, but which are under the control of the reporting charity (see **5.27**). It helpfully lists some of the characteristics, any one or more of which may indicate that the entity is a branch:

'(a) it uses the name of the reporting charity within its title;

(b) it exclusively raises funds for the reporting charity and/or for its own local activities;

(c) it uses the reporting charity's registration number to receive tax relief on its activities;

(d) it is perceived by the public to be the reporting charity's local representative or its representative for a specific purpose;

(e) it receives support from the reporting charity through advice, publicity materials, etc.' (GL4.4)

5.24 Paragraph 79 of SORP says that 'all branch transactions should be accounted for gross in the reporting charity's own accounts…'. This is normally done in one of two ways, either by aggregating the activities of all branches under generic headings or by identifying the contributions made by each branch.

5.25 If the branch and the reporting charity are both incorporated as companies then the method of accounting for the branch within the accounts of the main charity is by means of consolidation (see **5.31** ff).

5.26 Paragraph 78 of SORP draws attention to the distinction between a branch and a connected charity.

'Separate legal entities which may be known as branches but do not fall within the definition of a branch in the Glossary should prepare their own Annual Report and Accounts and, if they are connected charities, the relationship should be explained in the Trustees' Annual Report…' (see **5.26**)

An example of such a situation is a local charity which raises funds for more than one national charity. It may be regarded as the local branch of each national charity but clearly is not exclusively under the control of any of them.

5.27   *Accounting policies and accounts structure*

Comment

5.27   The biggest practical problems concerning branches are first to identify them, secondly to decide whether they are under the control of the reporting charity or not, and thirdly to set in place a uniform and controllable system
of reporting by branches to the main charity. Control is the key word. If the
trustees are legally responsible for the activities of the branch, they must ensure
that they can account for them and, to do so, they will have to have in place
effective accounting controls and procedures. Having said that, regard should
also be given to the circumstances. Some branches operate in remote parts
of the world with limited resources. A pragmatic view needs to be taken on
the level and quality of reporting expected; but, nevertheless, if material, the
activities of the branch should still be included in the accounts with appropriate
notes if necessary to explain the basis on which they are included.

---

*WESTMINSTER ROMAN CATHOLIC DIOCESAN TRUST: 31
DECEMBER 2007*

Scope of the consolidated accounts

The consolidated accounts include the assets, liabilities and transactions
of the following:

Curial funds

The Curial funds are used to support the Archbishop and Bishops in providing Diocese-wide services and pastoral care and to meet the cost of
central administration. The Curial funds are administered by staff within
the Curial (or Central) Offices in the Westminster Cathedral complex.

Parochial funds

The Parochial funds are administered, with guidance from the Central
Finance Office, by the parish priests and are used to carry out the work of
the Church within local areas and to help fund the Curia.

Fund accounting

The Curial Funds

The Curial Funds can be used across the whole of the Diocese and are
subdivided between:

●   The general fund comprising those monies which may be used
     towards meeting the charitable objectives of the Charity and used
     across the whole of the Diocese at the discretion of the Directors of
     the Corporate Trustee.

[continued on next page]

> *Westminster Roman Catholic Diocesan Trust, continued*
>
> - The designated funds being monies set aside out of general funds and designated for specific purposes by the Directors of the Corporate Trustee.
>
> - The restricted funds being monies received for, and their use restricted to, a specific purpose, or donations subject to donor imposed conditions.
>
> *The Parochial Funds*
>
> These comprise legacies, donations, trust income and interest and relate to specific parishes. As the monies must be utilised by individual parishes and cannot be used across the whole of the Diocese, the funds are all regarded as restricted for the purpose of these accounts.

5   Connected charities

5.28   Connected charities are defined in Appendix 1 of the SORP as 'those which have common, parallel or related objects and activities and either common control or unity of administration. Within this category may be charities which come together under one umbrella organisation'. Often, they are separate charities run by the same people. All that is normally required in the accounts of each is a note to indicate the relationship between each charity and details of any transactions between them.

5.29   Charities which are members of an 'umbrella organisation' should give an indication of how many members there are, their areas of activity and how the reader can contact them. If there have been material transactions between the connected charities and the reporting charity, these should be disclosed.

5.30   Sometimes, however, the relationship amounts to one being integral to or subordinate to the other and, in this case, the controlling charity should account for the activities of the other as though it were a trust established for special purposes of the controlling charity. It will be treated as a branch and be included, probably as a restricted fund, in the accounts of the controlling charity. This situation is referred to in paragraphs 77–81 of SORP (see **5.21**).

WESTMINSTER ROMAN CATHOLIC DIOCESAN TRUST: 31 DECEMBER 2007

Scope of the consolidated accounts

Other registered charities

Other registered charities, which are integral to the Charity and which therefore have been included in these accounts are:

- The Moorfields Charity (Charity Registration No 247198) – a charity providing assistance to the Roman Catholic parishes of Moorfields and Bunhill Row and to Westminster Cathedral.

- Westminster Cathedral Trust (formerly Westminster Cathedral 1995 Centenary Trust) (Charity Registration No 270637) – a charity with the principal objectives of supporting Westminster Cathedral and preserving its fabric and music.

Connected charities

The main charities connected with the Charity are listed below.

All the charities listed are the responsibility of WRCDT but are outside the scope of these accounts as they are separate registered charities and are not controlled by the Charity. In many cases they are administered by the Central Finance Office of the Charity and many have similar or related charitable objectives.

- Westminster Ecclesiastical Education Fund (WEEF) (Charity Registration No 312528)

    WEEF is a charity for the training of students to the priesthood and is the recipient of the Diocesan collection.

- Diocese of Westminster Sick and Retired Priests Fund (Charity Registration No 278136)

    This charity's principal activity is the provision of assistance to sick and elderly and retired clergy.

- Norfolk Fund Charity (Charity Registration No 241675)

    The Norfolk Fund Charity is a charity with the principal objective of fulfilling the social and pastoral works of the Diocese.

Others – a full list of all connected charities is given in note 20 to the attached accounts.

Comment

5.31   One might ask why there is a need to disclose dealings with connected charities. Are they more important than dealings with unconnected charities?

Clearly it is a regulatory matter to ensure that charities which are effectively run from the same office or by the same people are not using one of the charities to hide the reality of the overall situation. For example, two charities with differing year ends could hide accumulated reserves by making donations to each other just before their year end. This regulatory aspect is reinforced by the fact that connected charities are now included in the SORP under 'related parties'.

5.32   Apart from the regulatory aspect, it is important for trustees to determine precisely the relationship between their charity and any other – is it a branch, is it a 'special trust' (ie subsidiary charity), is it connected or is it independent?

6   Consolidation

5.33   Consolidation of accounts is required where there is a corporate hierarchy of parent and self-accounting subsidiary undertakings. The only exception is the 'special trust' subsidiary of an unincorporated charity, as described in **5.21** and **5.28** above and referred to in paragraph 383(d) of SORP.

5.34   In all other cases, the parent charity and its charitable and non-charitable subsidiary undertakings will form a group. Whereas previously consolidation of non-company charities was a SORP and not a statutory requirement, the Charities Act 1993, as amended by the Charities Act 2006 and the Charities and Trustee Investment (Scotland) Act 2005 require consolidation for charity groups which exceed the statutory audit threshold. Charities which are companies and are not small companies are required to prepare group accounts, if relevant, under the Companies Act 2006.

5.35   SORP paragraphs 381–406 set out the detailed rules for preparation and filing of group accounts, including guidance on assessing whether subsidiary entities are charitable or non charitable and the respective treatments to be adopted.

5.36   SORP paragraph 396 states that where group accounts are prepared, the strict legal position is that both charity and group accounts should be filed – though these may be filed as a single document. Following general accounting practice, many charities do not file the Statement of Financial Activities of the parent charity alone as part of the statutory accounts. The regulators are prepared to accept omission of the parent charity Statement of Financial Activities only 'as long as the gross income/ turnover and results of the parent charity are clearly disclosed in the notes'.

5.37   Principal disclosure requirements set out in SORP include the inclusion of identifying information and an overview of the finances of each material subsidiary and the separation within the funds statement of any subsidiary charities with objects narrower than the parent charity (as a restricted fund) and any balances retained in non charity subsidiaries.

5.38

'The normal rules will apply regarding the method of consolidation, which should be carried out on a line by line basis as set out in FRS2.' (SORP para 393)

Comment

5.39   Balancing the SORP's requirement to separately identify the income and results of the parent charity with clarity of presentation can be a challenge. It may on occasion be more straightforward to simply produce a full Statement of Financial Activities for the parent charity than to explain how its results can be divined from group figures.

5.40   Whilst most subsidiaries are owned either to further the charity's objects or to generate profits to provide unrestricted income to support the activities, this is not always the case. Where subsidiaries operate on a social enterprise model, for example, it may be the case that the activities of a subsidiary include activity that could be undertaken by the charity and is to some degree subsidised by it (or by profits from other activity in the subsidiary) and some which are profitable and non charitable.

5.41   Where subsidiaries have such mixed objectives, it is a matter of judgement how these should be presented in the group accounts. Regardless of accounting presentation, clarity over the objectives of the subsidiary is important to ensure trustees can demonstrate that charity funds are not being 'wasted' on loss making commercial ventures and also to ensure that the tax liabilities of the subsidiary (which will generally be relieved by paying over profits to the parent charity) are properly calculated.

5.42   Practical guidance is summarised in paragraph 395 of SORP which recommends charities to:

'choose appropriate line headings within the permissible format of the Statement of Financial Activities and suitable amalgamations of activities. The headings used should reflect the underlying activities of the group'.

5.43   Additional segmental information may sometimes be needed in the notes in order to distinguish the key results of the charity from those of its subsidiary undertakings.

'Examples of those items which should be separately disclosed include the costs of generating funds, the costs of charitable activities and governance costs.'
(para 405)

7   Associates, joint ventures and joint arrangements

5.44   Paragraphs 407–418 of SORP give guidance on how to identify associates and joint ventures and distinguish them from parents or subsidiaries.

Reference is made to FRS 9, which determines the relationship between the entities involved.

5.45

'Where a charity has a long term participating interest in another under-taking and exercises significant influence over its operating and financial policy then this is likely to be an associate undertaking. Where a charity beneficially holds 20% or more of the voting rights in any undertaking it will be presumed to have a participating interest and significant influence…' (para 409)

5.46   Associates should be included in the accounts based on the net equity method, ie the net interest in the results to be shown in one line after the '*net incoming/(resources expended)*' line in the SOFA and the net interest in associ-ates to be shown in a separate line within fixed asset investments.

5.47   A joint venture arises where there is a separate entity controlled by two or more undertakings. The accounting for a charity's share in a joint ven-ture seems rather clumsy, but it is explained in paragraph 414 of SORP as: '*the gross equity method*'. It involves including gross incoming resources from the joint venture on a line-by-line basis, then deducting the total from the total incoming resources and then adding back the net interest in the results as a separate line in the same way as for associates.

5.48   Where a charity carries out activities in partnership with other bodies but without creating a separate legal entity, it should account for its gross share in the incoming resources from the joint arrangement and for its gross share in the resources expended in the same way as for a branch (see **5.23** ff). In this case, there may be a contingent liability in respect of joint and several liability to be considered.

OXFAM 2006/07

At 30 April 2007, Oxfam had an interest in the following subsidiary undertakings:

Organisation name	Country of registration	Nature of business	Class of share capital held	Portion held by parent company	Minority interest	Consolidation
Oxfam Activities Limited	United Kingdom	Raises funds through trading activities	Ordinary	100%	0%	Yes
On the Line Trust Limited	United Kingdom	Dormant	Ordinary	100%	0%	No (not material)

[*continued on next page*]

85

Oxfam, continued

| Progreso Cafés Ltd | United Kingdom | Fair Trade cafés | Ordinary | 50% | 50% | Yes |
| Coffee Producers Company Ltd | United Kingdom | Dormant | Special share | OGB have control of activities but no right to the assets | 100% | No (not material) |

All the subsidiaries have a 30th April financial year end with the exception of the Coffee Producers Company Ltd which has a 30th June year end.

The aggregate total amount invested in all Oxfam's subsidiaries is £1.7m (2005/06: £1.7m).

Their financial results for the year were:

	Oxfam Activities Ltd		Progreso Cafes Ltd	
	2007	2006	2007	2006
	£ m	£ m	£ m	£ m
Income	17.1	16.8	0.6	0.6
Expenditure	(15.3)	(14.7)	(0.6)	(0.6)
Trading profit	1.8	2.1	–	–
Loan interest paid to Oxfam	(0.2)	(0.2)	–	–
Profit gift aided to Oxfam	(1.6)	(1.9)	–	–
Profit for the year	–	–	–	–
Net Assets at 30 April 2007	0.1	0.1	(0.1)	(0.1)

On the Line Trust Limited and Coffee Producers Company Limited were dormant for both 2006 and 2007 and have no net assets.

The Minority Interest of Progreso Cafés Limited for the Statement of Financial Activities was £3,978 (2005/06: £14,980) and for the balance sheet was £40,490 (2005/06: £44,468).

In order to operate in some countries Oxfam is required by local legislation to establish 100 per cent controlled, locally registered organisations. These are listed below. The accounts of these organisations are included within the accounts of Oxfam.

Organisation name	Country of registration	Nature of business
Oxfam UKI Inc	Barbados	As per Oxfam
Associacao Recife – Oxford para a Cooperacao ao Desenvolvimento	Brazil	As per Oxfam
Sociedad De Desarrollo Oxfam Limitada	Chile	As per Oxfam
Oxfam (India) Trust	India	As per Oxfam
Oxfam Great Britain	South Africa	As per Oxfam

Chapter 6

Statement of Financial Activities

1 Purpose

6.1   The Statement of Financial Activities is a single accounting statement which analyses all capital and income resources and resources expended by a charity in the year across all of the charity's funds. The Statement of Financial Activities also contains a reconciliation of those funds, from the funds held by the charity at the start of the financial year to those held at the end of the year.

6.2   Paragraph 82 of SORP summarises the overall objectives of the statement:

'The Statement of Financial Activities is a single accounting statement with the objective of showing all incoming resources and resources expended by the charity in the year on all its funds.

It is designed to show how the charity has used its resources in furtherance of its objects for the provision of benefit to its beneficiaries. It shows whether there has been a net inflow or outflow of resources, including capital gains and losses on assets, and provides a reconciliation of all movements in the charity's funds.' (para 82)

Comment

6.3   The Statement of Financial Activities has a number of benefits over purely reporting the income and expenditure of an organisation. For example:

- there is less focus on the 'bottom line' or the surplus or deficit for the year;

- the Statement of Financial Activities aims to portray the charity's underlying activities and the fact that the primary concern of a charity is to provide benefits to its beneficiaries rather than a corporate pursuit of gain for the benefit of shareholders;

- it concentrates attention on the resources available to the charity and how the trustees have applied them;

- it enables the identification of specific types of fund, particularly restricted funds; and

6.4 *Statement of Financial Activities*

● the Statement of Financial Activities provides the essential link with the second primary statement, the balance sheet, via the reconciliation of funds.

6.4 The Statement of Financial Activities is a columnar statement analysed in appropriate detail to show all incoming resources, both capital and revenue, in the financial year, and how and to what extent the charity's funds have been spent. The following examples taken from the Women's Therapy Centre and the Terrence Higgins Trust show the basic construction of a Statement of Financial Activities.

WOMEN'S THERAPY CENTRE:

Statement of financial activities Year to 31 March 2008

	Notes	Unrestricted funds £	Restricted funds £	**2008** Total funds £	2007 Total funds £
Income and expenditure					
Incoming resources					
Incoming resources from generated funds:					
● Voluntary income	1	1,791	750	**2,541**	9,427
● Activities for generating funds	2	1,580	—	**1,580**	2,313
● Interest receivable		1,860	—	**1,860**	1,369
Incoming resources from charitable activities					
● Provision of psychoanalytical psychotherapy	3	47,372	424,947	**472,319**	429,462
Total incoming resources		52,603	425,697	**478,300**	442,571
Resources expended					
Cost of generating funds:					
● Cost of generating fundraising income	4	19,652	—	**19,652**	14,866
Charitable activities					
● Provision of psychoanalytical psychotherapy	5	24,729	384,027	**408,756**	452,068
Governance costs	6	3,536	—	**3,536**	4,192
Total resources expended		47,917	384,027	**431,944**	471,126
Net movement in funds i.e. net income (expenditure)	7	4,686	41,670	**46,356**	(28,555)
Balances brought forward at 1 April 2007		21,370	9,225	**30,595**	59,150
Balances carried forward at 31 March 2008		26,056	50,895	**76,951**	30,595

There is no difference between the net movement in funds stated above, and the historical cost equivalent.

[continued on next page]

Women's Therapy Centre, continued

All of the charity's activities derived from continuing operations during the above two financial years.

The charity has no recognised gains and losses other than those shown above and therefore no separate statement of total recognised gains and losses has been presented.

TERENCE HIGGINS TRUST

Consolidated statement of financial activities (incorporating an income and expenditure account)

For the year ended 31 March 2008

	Note	Unrestricted £'000	Restricted £'000	2008 Total £000	2007 Total £'000
Incoming resources					
Incoming resources from generated funds					
Voluntary income	2	3,569	1,830	5,399	4,155
Activities for generating funds	3	1,025	2	1,027	862
Investment income	4	76	—	76	51
Incoming resources from charitable activities					
Statutory income					
– Health promotion	5	4,435	341	4,776	4,192
– Care and advice	5	3,580	617	4,197	3,839
Other incoming resources	6	316	—	316	353
		13,001	2,790	15,791	13,452
Net assets transferred on merger	21	25	—	25	166
Total incoming resources		13,026	2,790	15,816	13,618
Resources expended					
Cost of generating funds					
Cost of generating voluntary income	7	1,638	—	1,638	1,465
Fundraising trading	7	361	—	361	273
		1,999	—	1,999	1,738
Net incoming resources available for charitable application		11,027	2,790	13,817	11,880
Charitable activities					
Health promotion	8	6,196	1,500	7,696	5,680
Care and advice	8	4,206	1,460	5,666	5,616
Campaigning, lobbying and advocacy	8	430	45	475	397
Governance costs	10	39	—	39	32
Total resources expended		10,871	3,005	13,876	11,725

[*continued on next page*]

Terence Higgins Trust, continued

	Note	Unrestricted £'000	Restricted £'000	2008 Total £000	2007 Total £'000
Net incoming/(outgoing) resources before other recognised gains and losses and net income/ (expenditure) for the year	11	156	(215)	(59)	155
Investment assets (losses)/gains	15	—	(15)	(15)	9
Actuarial gains / (losses) on defined benefit pension scheme	13	468	—	468	(421)
Net movement in funds		624	(230)	394	(257)
Funds brought forward		4,343	3,145	7,488	7,745
Funds carried forward		4,967	2,915	7,882	7,488

All of the above results are derived from continuing activities. There were no other recognised gains or losses other than those stated above. Movements in funds are disclosed in Note 19 to the financial statements.

The notes on pages 27 to 41 form part of these accounts.

2   The basic construction

6.5   The basic concept behind the Statement of Financial Activities is to analyse all of the charity's incoming resources and resources expended such that the reader of the charity's accounts can gain an immediate understanding of where its resources came from and what it has spent its resources on during the year. As a minimum, it should also distinguish between unrestricted income funds, restricted income funds and the endowment funds of the charity. All the charity's incoming resources and resources expended should be categorised between these funds, although, of course, a charity may not have all three types of fund.

6.6   Where a charity does have more than one type of fund then the Statement of Financial Activities should show, in columns, the movements on each type of fund as well as the total movement on all funds. Comparative figures are required but normally these will be for the total movements only rather than for each type of fund.

6.7   The following table, Table 3 of SORP, provides the structure, format and activity categories of the Statement of Financial Activities.

Reference		Unrestricted Funds	Restricted Funds	Endowment Funds	Total Funds	Prior Year Total Funds
A	**Incoming resources**					
A1	Incoming resources from generated funds					
A1a	Voluntary income					
A1b	Activities for generating funds					
A1c	Investment income					
A2	Incoming resources from charitable activities					
A3	Other incoming resources					
	Total incoming resources					
B	**Resources expended**					
B1	Cost of generating funds					
B1a	Costs of generating voluntary income					
B1b	Fundraising trading: cost of goods sold and other costs					
B1c	Investment management costs					
B2	Charitable activities					
B3	Governance costs					
B4	Other resources expended					
	Total resources expended					

[continued on next page]

91

Reference		Unrestricted Funds	Restricted Funds	Endowment Funds	Total Funds	Prior Year Total Funds
	Net incoming/outgoing resources before transfers					
C	Gross transfers between funds					
	Net incoming resources before other recognised gains and losses					
D	**Other recognised gains/losses**					
D1	Gains/losses on revaluation of fixed assets for charity's own use					
D2	Gains/losses on investment assets					
D3	Actuarial gains/losses on defined benefit pension scheme					
	Net movement in funds					
E	**Reconciliation of funds**					
	Total funds brought forward					
	Total funds carried forward					

Comment

6.8   The above table sets out the standard format for the Statement of Financial Activities. If deemed appropriate, there is nothing to prevent a charity disclosing additional information. For example, in some instances, it may be preferable to split out the unrestricted funds column into two columns – one for the general fund and one for designated funds. This will be particularly relevant where significant amounts of money have been designated for a particular purpose and the charity wishes to emphasise that these are not regarded as 'free' or general reserves. A good example of this is the Catholic Marriage Care accounts for the year ended 31 March 2008.

CATHOLIC MARRIAGE CARE LIMITED

Statement of financial activities Year to 31 March 2008

		Unrestricted funds		Restricted funds	**Total 2008 funds**	Total 2007 funds
		General fund	Tangible fixed assets fund & designated funds			
	Notes	£	£	£	£	£
Income and expenditure						
Incoming resources						
Incoming resources from generated funds						
• Voluntary income	1	135,802	—	423,540	**559,342**	625,348
• Investment income and interest receivable	2	29,709	—	—	**29,709**	27,745
Incoming resources from charitable activities						
• Counselling and training		106,285	—	—	**106,285**	131,496
• Marriage preparation		142,980	—	—	**142,980**	87,433
• Annual conference		16,784	—	—	**16,784**	17,185
Other incoming resources		—	—	—	**—**	22,328
Total incoming resources		431,560	—	423,540	**855,100**	911,535
Resources expended						
Cost of generating funds	3	527	—	13,920	**14,447**	18,610
Charitable activities	4					
• Counselling and training		273,477	—	322,395	**595,872**	553,778

Catholic Marriage Care Limited, continued

	Notes	General fund	Tangible fixed assets fund & designated funds	Restricted funds	Total 2008 funds	Total 2007 funds
		Unrestricted funds				
		£	£	£	£	£
● Marriage preparation		88,442	—	92,107	**180,549**	173,510
● Relationship education		2,109	—	12,002	**14,111**	43,039
● Telephone helpline		6,284	—	19,310	**25,594**	25,542
● Projects		—	—	43,061	**43,061**	72,110
● Annual conference		53,935	—	—	**53,935**	50,192
Governance costs	6	24,715	—	—	**24,715**	26,959
Total resources expended		449,489	—	502,795	**952,284**	963,740
Net outgoing resources before transfers	7	(17,929)	—	(79,255)	**(97,184)**	(52,205)
Transfers between funds	15,16	426,992	(426,992)	—	**—**	—
Net incoming (outgoing) resources		409,063	(426,992)	(79,255)	**(97,184)**	(52,205)
Net realised investment losses		—	—	—	**—**	(1,853)
Statement of total recognised gains and losses						
Net income (expenditure)		409,063	(426,992)	(79,255)	**(97,184)**	(54,058)
Net unrealised investment (losses) gains		(17,239)	—	—	**(17,239)**	4,512
Net movement in funds		391,824	(426,992)	(79,255)	**(114,423)**	(49,546)
Balances brought forward at 1 April 2007		36,650	936,813	117,318	**1,090,781**	1,140,327
Balances carried forward at 31 March 2008		428,474	509,821	38,063	**976,358**	1,090,781

6.9   The current SORP introduced a more obvious link between the incoming resources and resources expended arising from the various activities undertaken by a charity. Paragraph 89 of the SORP states that 'Charities should expand the structure ... in order to ... convey a proper understanding of the nature of all their activities. Charities should, where possible, have a clear link between the incoming and outgoing resources and, in particular, activity analysis'. This can be achieved by inserting additional sub-headings within the income and expenditure categories set out in Table 3 of SORP. In the Catholic Marriage Care accounts above, this guidance has been followed for the counselling and training; marriage preparation and annual conference activities: identical headings have been used in both the incoming resources and resources expended sections of the Statement of Financial Activities.

6.10 A charity may decide to revise the order of the headings within the incoming resources and resources expended headings of the Statement of Financial Activities. This can assist with the presentation of the accounts if certain categories of income or expenditure are more material than others.

Table reference A – Incoming resources

6.11 The first section of the Statement of Financial Activities lists out the various categories of incoming resources by fund. It is important to emphasise that transfers between funds, which are internal to the charity, are not regarded as an incoming resource, and nor are the gains and losses on revaluations of fixed assets or the gains/losses on the disposal of investment assets which are shown separately further down the Statement of Financial Activities (see **6.22** below). Gains on the disposal of tangible fixed assets used by the charity (functional fixed assets), are, however, regarded as incoming resources.

6.12 The details regarding the treatment and analysis of incoming resources are detailed in Chapter 7.

Table reference B – Resources expended

6.13 In the next section of the Statement of Financial Activities, resources expended should be summarised between the cost of generating funds, charitable activities and governance costs, and then totalled, distinguishing between fund types. The detailed requirements regarding the classification and analysis of resources expended are set out in Chapter 8.

6.14 One of the main developments within SORP 2005 from the previous SORP has been the change to the categorisation and disclosure of resources expended within the accounts. For example, the SORP now refers to 'governance costs' rather than 'management and administration costs'; and support costs of the charity are no longer shown in the Statement of Financial Activities, but instead are apportioned between cost categories with the detail provided in the notes to the accounts.

Comment

6.15 The SORP recognises the fact that in practice individual charities may need to expand on the structure set out in the table given at 6.7 above in order for the accounts to show a true and fair view and convey a proper understanding of the nature of the charity's activities. In all cases, however, it is important that there is consistency between the incoming and outgoing resources and, in particular, the functional split of activities.

6.16 The link referred to by the SORP is of fundamental importance to the reader of the accounts. For example, a charity which runs a residential and nursing care home may include within its incoming resources section 'Residential and care fees'. It would therefore be sensible for the charitable expenditure section of the statement of financial activities to include a heading such as 'Residential and care costs'.

Table reference C – Gross transfers between funds

6.17   The next section of the Statement of Financial Activities should record, gross, all transfers between the various categories of funds. Detailed explanations of the movements should be given in the notes to the accounts.

6.18   Paragraph 214 of SORP sets out the purposes for which the transfer row in the Statement of Financial Activities will be used, as follows:

(a)   when capital funds are released to an income fund from expendable endowment;

(b)   for charities following a total return approach to investment when releasing the funds to income from the unapplied total return fund held within the permanent endowment fund;

(c)   if restricted funds have been released and reallocated to unrestricted income funds;

(d)   a transfer of assets from the unrestricted funds to the restricted funds to finance a deficit on the restricted funds; and

(e)   to transfer the value of fixed assets from restricted funds to unrestricted funds: this occurs when restricted funding has been received for the purchase of a fixed asset, but once purchased, the asset can be used for a general, not restricted, purpose.

Comment

6.19   The above guidance considers transfers between unrestricted, restricted and endowment funds. In addition, transfers will take place within the unrestricted funds, for example, to reflect a designation from the general funds.

Generally transfers will be in respect of designations made during the year, where general and designated funds are shown separately; augmentation of restricted funds out of general funds, either to meet expenditure not covered by restricted income or to boost an appeal, for example; or the transfer of restricted funds to general or other funds provided the restriction has been removed by the donor or the Charity Commission.

6.20   The total of transfers between funds should always be zero as the transfers should cancel one another out.

6.21   Immediately following the transfers section should be a sub-total giving the net incoming or outgoing resources for the year before other recognised gains and losses, such as gains/losses arising from the revaluation of tangible fixed assets or from the sale of investment assets.

Table reference D – Other recognised gains and losses

6.22   The next section of the Statement of Financial Activities comprises the gains or losses on revaluations of fixed assets which are held for the charity's use and, as a separate line, the net gains or losses on the revaluation and disposal of investment assets (including property investments).

6.23   The following gains and losses should not be reflected in this section of the Statement of Financial Activities:

- impairment losses on assets held for the charity's own use (ie functional assets rather than investments) should be treated as additional depreciation and included in resources expended;

- gains on the disposal of assets held for the charity's own use should be included in 'Other incoming resources';

- losses on the disposal of assets held for the charity's own use should be included in resources expended.

6.24   The full implementation of accounting standard FRS 17, 'Accounting for Retirement Benefits', and the inclusion of pension surpluses or deficits within the accounts resulted in new sub-headings being included within the Statement of Financial Activities and the Balance Sheet. Within the Statement of Financial Activities, any actuarial gains or losses on a defined benefit pension scheme to which the charity contributes should also be included under the 'Other recognised gains and losses' heading. Further details regarding the treatment of pension schemes are included within Chapter 13.

Comment

6.25   There is no requirement to show realised and unrealised gains on investment assets separately and, in practice, many charities choose not to do so. However, incorporated charities bound by the requirements of Financial Reporting Standard 3 may need to split realised and unrealised gains (or losses) and this is discussed further in Chapters 7 and 10.

Net movement of funds

6.26   By adding the net gains to, or deducting the net losses from, the net incoming resources, we arrive at the figure for the net movement in the charity's funds for the year.

6.27   Paragraph 90 of the SORP addresses the issue of discontinued activities or the acquisition of new ones.

'In order to comply with Financial Reporting Standard 3 (FRS 3) where a charity has discontinued any of its operations or acquired new ones, the accounts should distinguish between continuing, discontinued and acquired operations. This will normally apply to the whole of a distinctive type of activity of a charity but not to the development or cessation of new projects within that activity.'

This would apply to the key figures within the Statement of Financial Activities and would be most appropriately reported via the inclusion of a separate table underneath the Statement of Activities. However, in practice this is unlikely to impact on many charities. An example of disclosure for discontinued activities is included at **6.46**.

3   Reconciliation of funds

6.28   Paragraph 74 of SORP states the following.

'The Statement of Financial Activities should reflect the principal movements between the opening and closing balances on all the funds of the charity. It should be analysed between unrestricted income funds, restricted income funds and endowment funds (permanent and expendable combined).'

Comment

6.29   The reconciliation of funds statement is an integral part of the Statement of Financial Activities and provides the link between the Statement of Financial Activities and the balance sheet, ie the final total of each column of the Statement of Financial Activities should be the balance on each of the fund categories shown in the bottom half of the balance sheet.

6.30   The following is an example of a Statement of Financial Activities for an unincorporated charity which illustrates each of the above points.

ROYAL COLLEGE OF NURSING

Consolidated statement of financial activities for the year ended 31 March 2009

| | Notes | Unrestricted funds | | Restricted funds | Endowment funds | Total 2009 | Total 2008 |
		Representation activities	Other activities				
		£'000	£'000	£'000	£'000	£'000	£'000
INCOMING RESOURCES							
Incoming resources from charitable activities:							
Subscriptions income		29,567	33,688	—	—	63,255	61,192
Education & training	4.1	—	2,496	1,411	—	3,907	3,074
Advancing of the profession	4.1	—	264	65	—	329	353

[continued on next page]

Royal College of Nursing, continued

	Notes	Unrestricted funds Representation activities	Other activities	Restricted funds	Endowment funds	Total 2009	Total 2008
		£'000	£'000	£'000	£'000	£'000	£'000
Promotion of nursing	**4.1**	—	205	—	—	205	257
Assisting nurses	**4.1**	—	155	—	—	155	659
Representation	**4.1**	606	—	104	—	710	1,575
Incoming resources from generated funds:							
Donations		—	43	110	—	153	498
Legacies		—	364	—	—	364	52
Investment income	5	—	1,499	239	—	1,738	1,857
Trading income	**4.1**	—	14,710	—	—	14,710	13,070
Other incoming resources:							
Gain on disposal of fixed asset	**4.2**	—	387	—	—	387	—
Exceptional Items	**4.2**	—	2,486	—	—	2,486	—
TOTAL INCOMING RESOURCES		**30,173**	**56,297**	**1,929**	—	**88,399**	**82,587**
RESOURCES EXPENDED							
COST OF GENERATING FUNDS							
Fundraising and sponsorship costs	**8.1**	—	482	—	—	482	500
Investment management fee	**8.1**	—	43	—	—	43	73
Other trading costs	**8.1**	—	13,322	—	—	13,322	11,333
CHARITABLE ACTIVITIES							
Education & Training	**8.1**	—	13,914	1,508	—	15,422	17,956
Advancing of the Profession	**8.1**	—	6,279	79	—	6,358	5,715
Promotion of Nursing	**8.1**	—	2,770	28	—	2,798	9,031
Assisting Nurses	**8.1**	—	2,040	415	—	2,455	3,792
Representation	**8.1**	29,683	—	104	—	29,787	24,778
GOVERNANCE COSTS	**8.1**	490	1,173	—	—	1,663	1,663
TOTAL RESOURCES EXPENDED	**8.1**	**30,173**	**40,023**	**2,134**	—	**72,330**	**74,841**

[*continued on next page*]

Royal College of Nursing, continued

	Notes	Unrestricted funds Representation activities	Other activities	Restricted funds	Endowment funds	Total 2009	Total 2008
		£'000	£'000	£'000	£'000	£'000	£'000
NET INCOMING RESOURCES FOR THE YEAR		—	16,274	(205)	—	16,069	7,746
Net investment losses	10	—	(2,149)	(753)	(195)	(3,097)	(428)
Actuarial losses on defined benefit pension scheme	19	—	(9,261)	—	—	(9,261)	(66)
NET MOVEMENT IN FUNDS		—	4,864	(958)	(195)	3,711	7,252
Fund balances b/f at 1 April		—	21,670	7,170	1,109	29,949	22,697
Fund balances c/f at 31 March		—	26,534	6,212	914	33,660	29,949

4   Adaptation of formats

6.31   Paragraphs 86 and 89 of the SORP acknowledge that there may be instances when, in order to give a true and fair view of the charity's activities, the format of the Statement of Financial Activities may need to be amended or expanded. For example, paragraph 88 of the SORP suggests that some charities may wish to insert an additional subtotal after the 'Cost of generating funds' heading to give a figure for *'net incoming resources available for charitable application'*. A further subtotal may also be inserted to show the total for charitable expenditure.

Comment

6.32   It is important that the Statement of Financial Activities portrays very clearly the manner in which the charity has applied its resources. Many charities will find that the adaptation referred to in paragraph 88 of the SORP is very useful. It enables the reader to determine very quickly the amount expended on charitable activities and to compare this with the amount available. It might also emphasise the efficiency (or not) with which the charity has generated funds by enabling a clear comparison to be made between the total incoming resources with the net incoming resources available for charitable application.

6.33   The Statement of Financial Activities is a complex statement and for this reason it is important that where there is nothing to report in either the current or the preceding period, the heading is omitted.

5 Summary income and expenditure account

6.34   In addition to producing a Statement of Financial Activities, a number of charities will need to produce a summary income and expenditure account also. This requirement will affect those charities which are governed by the Companies Act, or similar legislation, or have endowment funds.

6.35   A separate summary income and expenditure account will also be needed if required by the charity's governing instrument.

6.36   This summary statement and all relevant notes will need to be appropriately cross-referenced to the Statement of Financial Activities from which the summary amounts are derived.

The problem

6.37   The Statement of Financial Activities includes, in incoming resources, endowment capital receipts and excludes realised gains and losses on the disposal of investments, which are dealt with 'below the line' along with unrealised gains and losses on investments, revaluations of other fixed assets and actuarial gains and losses on defined benefit pension schemes. As a result, the Statement of Financial Activities cannot always double as an income and expenditure account because FRS3 will not allow the inclusion of capital receipts, nor the exclusion of profits or losses on the realisation of fixed assets.

Solution 1 – adapt the Statement of Financial Activities

6.38   Where the Statement of Financial Activities of a charity constituted under the Companies Act does not include movements on endowment funds during the year, and where it is possible to separate out realised and unrealised gains and losses on investment assets, the charity may be able to adapt its Statement of Financial Activities. The changes required are as follows:

(a)   immediately above the heading 'Incoming resources' insert another heading 'Income and Expenditure';

(b)   add to the heading, 'Net incoming/outgoing resources for the year', the total for realised gains on investments and annotate the resultant subtotal with the heading 'Net income/expenditure for the year';

(c)   immediately above the heading 'Net income/expenditure for the year' place another heading 'Statement of Total Recognised Gains and Losses'; and

(d)   add to, 'Net income/expenditure for the year', unrealised gains or losses on investments, gains or losses on the revaluation of fixed assets for the charity's own use and actuarial gains or losses on defined benefit pension schemes to arrive at the 'Net movement in funds'.

6.39   Thus, the Statement of Financial Activities would comprise two distinct sections – an income and expenditure account and a statement of total recognised gains and losses. The format of the latter statement will be:

6.40 *Statement of Financial Activities*

Net income/expenditure for the year

Net unrealised gains (losses) on revaluation

Gains on the revaluation of fixed assets for charity's own use

Actuarial gains (losses) on defined benefit pensions schemes

Net movement in funds

Balances brought forward at start of year

Balances carried forward at end of year

6.40   The following examples taken from the accounts of Age Concern and the Church Housing Trust illustrate the adaptation of the Statement of Financial Activities in order to satisfy the requirements of the Companies Act and FRS3.

AGE CONCERN

Statement of financial activities – Charity ACE only

Year ended 31 March 2008

	Note	Unrestricted funds	Restricted funds	2008 Total funds	2007 Total funds Restated
		£'000	£'000	£'000	£'000
Incoming resources from generated funds					
Voluntary Income					
Legacies	2	6,887	598	7,485	5,914
Grants	3	—	1,493	1,493	1,246
Gifts and donations	4	4,356	2,154	6,510	9,297
Activities for generating funds					
Shop sales		13,671	—	13,671	12,559
Gross income from charitable trading		891	376	1,267	1,356
Investment Income					
Investment and other Income	5	533	26	559	896
Gift aid from trading companies	17	3,745	—	3,745	6,868
Gift aid from joint ventures	18	293	—	293	316

[continued on next page]

Age Concern, continued

	Note	Unrestricted funds	Restricted funds	2008 Total funds	2007 Total funds Restated
		£'000	£'000	£'000	£'000
Incoming resources from charitable activities					
Conferences & events		286	2	288	514
Income from training		7,229	184	7,413	7,351
Total incoming resources		**37,891**	**4,833**	**42,724**	**46,317**
Resources expended					
Costs of generating funds					
Cost of generating voluntary income	6	4,632	24	4,656	6,374
Shop operating costs		11,353	—	11,353	10,714
Cost of managing investments		79	—	79	64
Charitable activities					
Influencing policy and practice	7	4,662	218	4,880	6,578
Enabling older people	7	9,483	2,315	11,798	12,115
Supporting Age Concerns & other organisations	7	12,062	2,055	14,117	14,367
Influencing markets	7	887	—	887	995
Governance costs	10	869	69	938	1,106
Total resources expended		**44,027**	**4,681**	**48,708**	**52,273**
Net (outgoing)/incoming resources for the year	11	**(6,136)**	**152**	**(5,984)**	**(5,956)**
Other recognised gains and losses					
Net (losses)/gains on investment assets	15	(530)	—	(530)	555
Actuarial (losses)/ gains on defined benefit pension scheme	31	4,928	—	4,928	727
Net movement in funds		(1,738)	152	(1,586)	(4,674)
Total funds brought forward (as previously stated)		23,866	2,112	25,978	31,174
Prior year adjustment	32	(10,263)	—	(10,263)	(10,785)
Total funds brought forward (as restated)		13,603	2,112	15,715	20,389
Total funds carried forward		**11,865**	**2,264**	**14,129**	**15,715**

All income and expenditure is from continuing activities.

CHURCH HOUSING TRUST

Statement of financial activities Year to 31 March 2008

	Notes	Unrestricted funds £	Restricted funds £	**Total 2008** £	Total 2007 £
Income and expenditure					
Incoming resources					
Incoming resources from generated funds					
● Voluntary income	1	359,771	288,765	**648,536**	703,780
● Investment income	2	27,839	—	**27,839**	21,768
Total incoming resources		387,610	288,765	**676,375**	725,548
Resources expended					
Cost of generating funds					
● Costs of generating voluntary income	3	80,221	—	**80,221**	78,296
Charitable activities					
● Assisting homeless people and those in housing need	4	325,614	331,338	**656,952**	470,731
Governance costs	6	7,512	—	**7,512**	4,675
Total resources expended		413,347	331,338	**744,685**	553,702
Net (outgoing) incoming resources	7	(25,737)	(42,573)	**(68,310)**	171,846
Statement of total recognised gains and losses					
Net (expenditure) income for the year		(25,737)	(42,573)	**(68,310)**	171,846
Unrealised (losses) gains on investments		(16,616)	—	**(16,616)**	9,982
Net movement in funds		(42,353)	(42,573)	**(84,926)**	181,828
Balances brought forward at 1 April 2007		344,540	209,491	**554,031**	372,203
Balances carried forward at 31 March 2008		302,187	166,918	**469,105**	554,031

Comment

6.41   It is anticipated that, in the course of time, the need to continue to produce a summary income and expenditure account may disappear. This would require the Companies Act accounting regulations to be brought into line with the Charities Act regulations as far as charitable companies are concerned. We continue to hope for a suitably amended FRS3 to accommodate the Statement of Financial Activities.

Solution 2 – a summary income and expenditure account

6.42   The purpose of the summary income and expenditure account is solely to provide a reconciliation between the information given in the Statement of Financial Activities and that required by the Companies Act and FRS3. It is for disclosure purposes only in order to comply with those requirements.

6.43   Paragraph 425 of the SORP sets out the requirements.

'Where a summary income and expenditure account is required, it should be derived from and cross referenced to the corresponding figures in the Statement of Financial Activities. It need not distinguish between unrestricted and restricted income funds but the accounting basis on which items are included must be the same as in the Statement of Financial Activities. It should show separately in respect of continuing operations, acquisitions and discontinued operations:

(a)   gross income from all sources;

(b)   net gains/losses from disposals of all fixed assets belonging to the charity's income funds;

(c)   transfers from endowment funds of amounts previously received as capital resources and now converted into income funds for expending;

(d)   total income (this will be the total of all incoming resources – other than revaluation gains – of all the income funds but not for any endowment funds);

(e)   total expenditure out of the charity's income funds;

(f)   net income or expenditure for the year.

In practice, the format may need to be modified to comply with specific statutory requirements or those of the charity's own governing document.'

6.44   To prepare the summary income and expenditure account, it will be necessary to prepare as a working document a schedule reconciling the net movement in funds as shown in the Statement of Financial Activities to the gross income of continuing operations required by FRS3. Taking the Statement of Financial Activities for the St Albans Diocesan Board of Finance below, we can prepare a reconciliation schedule as indicated.

THE ST ALBANS DIOCESAN BOARD OF FINANCE

Statement of financial activities Year to 31 December 2007

	Notes	Endowment funds £	Restricted funds £	Unrestricted funds Common fund £	Unrestricted funds Other £	Total 2007 £	Total 2006 £
Incoming resources							
Incoming resources from generated funds:							
● Donations, legacies and similar incoming Resources	1	—	120,436	9,805,139	10,913	**9,936,488**	9,733,597
● Investment income and interest receivable	2	—	386,290	1,114,250	435,230	**1,935,770**	1,631,830
Incoming resources from charitable activities	3	—	85,967	763,602	214,243	**1,063,812**	1,047,711
Other incoming resources:							
● Surplus on disposal of tangible fixed assets		1,756,351	—	40	—	**1,756,391**	1,777,939
Total incoming resources		1,756,351	592,693	11,683,031	660,386	**14,692,461**	14,191,077
Resources expended							
Cost of generating funds	4	—	—	94,348	7,483	**101,831**	117,768
Charitable activities							
● Grants payable	5	—	262,752	218,978	116,866	**598,596**	408,858
● Promotion of the work of the Church of England in the Diocese of St Albans	6	—	214,510	11,172,590	411,602	**11,798,702**	11,356,679
Governance	7	—	—	311,370	—	**311,370**	309,342
Total resources expended		—	477,262	11,797,286	535,951	**12,810,499**	12,192,647

[continued on next page]

The St Albans Diocesan Board of Finance, continued

	Notes	Endowment funds £	Restricted funds £	Unrestricted funds		Total 2007 £	Total 2006 £
				Common fund £	Other £		
Net incoming (outgoing) resources before transfers	9	1,756,351	115,431	(114,255)	124,435	**1,881,962**	1,998,430
Gross transfers between funds	18	(1,522,661)	(25,151)	46,147	1,501,665	—	—
Net incoming (outgoing) resources before revaluations and investment asset disposals		233,690	90,280	(68,108)	1,626,100	**1,881,962**	1,998,430
Revaluation of tangible fixed assets	13	2,987,422	—	—	2,036,517	**5,023,939**	3,166,728
Realised gains on disposal of investment property and listed investments		42,825	2,889	—	—	**45,714**	157,005
Unrealised gains (losses) on investment property and listed investments		222,421	(98,803)	—	8,610	**132,228**	2,311,173
Net movement in funds		3,486,358	(5,634)	(68,108)	3,671,227	**7,083,843**	7,633,336
Balances brought forward at 1 January 2007		85,268,769	8,169,997	897,748	8,326,852	**102,663,366**	95,030,030
Balances carried forward at 31 December 2007		88,755,127	8,164,363	829,640	11,998,079	**109,747,209**	102,663,366

[continued on next page]

The charity is unable to prepare a note of historical cost net movement in funds as required by FRS 3. The historic cost of Glebe is unknown because typically such assets have arisen from gifts, tithes, or transfers to the charity over a period of many years. In the opinion of the members of the Board, the omission of such a statement does not detract from the picture of the Board's finances shown by these financial statements.

All of the Board's activities derived from continuing operations during the above two financial periods.

The Board has no recognised gains and losses other than those shown above and therefore no separate statement of total recognised gains and losses has been presented.

The St Albans Diocesan Board of Finance, continued
Reconciliation schedule – workings

The following workings can be derived from the above statement of financial activities.

Total income of continuing operations for the year ended 31 December 2007

		2007	2006
		£	£
Net movement in funds per SoFA		7,083,843	7,633,336
Add:	Total resources expended	12,810,499	12,192,647
	Realised losses on investments	–	–
	Unrealised losses on investments	–	–
	Revaluation losses on tangible fixed assets	–	–
		19,894,342	19,825,983
Less:	Non-charitable trading income	–	–
	Endowment fund receipts	1,756,351	1,513,530
	Realised gains on investments	45,714	157,005
	Unrealised gains on investments	132,228	2,311,173
	Revaluation gains on tangible fixed assets	5,023,939	3,166,728
Total income of continuing operations		**12,936,110**	**12,677,547**

6.45   The example below illustrates the resulting summary income and expenditure account.

THE ST ALBANS DIOCESAN BOARD OF FINANCE

Summary income and expenditure account Year to 31 December 2007

	2007	2008
	£	£
Total income of continuing operations	**12,936,110**	12,677,547
Total expenditure of continuing operations	**(12,810,499)**	(12,192,647)
Net income for the year before transfers and investment asset disposals	**125,611**	484,900
Transfer from endowment fund	**1,522,661**	443,133
Net income before investment asset disposals	**1,648,272**	928,033
Gain on disposal of fixed asset investments	**2,889**	(6,966)
Net income for the year	**1,651,161**	921,067
	[continued on next page]	

108

The St Albans Diocesan Board of Finance, continued

Total income comprises £12,343,417 (2006 – £12,196,997) for unrestricted funds and £592,693 (2006 – £480,550) for restricted funds. A detailed analysis of income by source is provided in the statement of financial activities.

Detailed analyses of expenditure are provided in the statement of financial activities.

Net income before investment asset disposals for the year of £1,648,272 (2006 – £928,033) comprises £1,557,992 net income (2006 – of £884,334) on unrestricted funds and £90,280 net income (2006 – £43,699) on restricted funds, as shown in the statement of financial activities.

The summary income and expenditure account is derived from the statement of financial activities on [page 27] which, together with the notes to the financial statements on [pages 35 to 51], provides full information on the movements during the year on all funds of the charity.

Such a statement is further illustrated by an example from the Butterfly Conservation 2008 accounts.

BUTTERFLY CONSERVATION

Summary income and expenditure account Year to 31 March 2008

	2008 **Total** **funds** **£**	2007 Total funds £
Total income of continuing operations	**3,067,201**	2,656,293
Total expenditure of continuing operations	**(2,396,656)**	(2,033,539)
Net income for the period before investment asset disposals	**670,545**	622,754
Gains on disposal of investment assets	**13,345**	7,420
Net income for the period	**683,890**	630,174

Total income comprises £1,418,371 (2007 – £1,046,149) for unrestricted funds and £1,648,830 (2007 – £1,610,144) for restricted funds. A detailed analysis of income by source is provided in the statement of financial activities.

Detailed analyses of the expenditure are provided in the statement of financial activities and note 3.

The summary income and expenditure account is derived from the statement of financial activities on [page 41] which, together with the notes to the financial statements on [pages 49 to 62], provides full information on the movements during the period on all the funds of the charity.

6 Discontinued and acquired operations

6.46   Very occasionally, a charity will discontinue a particular class of its operations or acquire new ones. When this happens, para 90 of the SORP states that the Statement of Financial Activities should distinguish between continuing, discontinued and acquired operations as required by FRS3.

GIRLS FRIENDLY SOCIETY IN ENGLAND AND WALES: 30 SEPTEMBER 2003

Post balance sheet events – discontinued activities

As referred to in the Trustees' Report, there were two ongoing events at the balance sheet date. These were the sale of the charity's central office, 125–126 Queen's Gate, London SW7, and the charity's disengagement from Supported Housing activities.

Whilst neither of these events requires adjustment to the balance sheet at   , they are significant for an understanding of the charity's accounts.

Contracts for the sale of 125–126 Queen's Gate were exchanged on 17 November 2003 and completion was due to take place on 4 February 2004. Sale proceeds are expected to be £4.4m less selling expenses. The net book value of the property in the accounts at was £462,613. Part of the proceeds relate to the endowment fund and will be invested in accordance with the charity's investment policy. The balance of the proceeds are unrestricted funds.

The charity's disengagement from Supported Housing activities is due to be completed by the end of March 2004. The proceeds from the transfer of housing net assets to other Registered Social Landlords will be invested to generate income for the charity's continuing activities. The extent of Supported Housing activities is shown in note 3. The most significant assets relating to the Supported Housing activities are freehold and leasehold properties as detailed in note 13. The transfer of six housing properties on 10 December 2003, which had a net book value of £667,829 as at 30 September 2003, will generate proceeds of £3m. Negotiations are continuing on the remaining housing properties, which had a net book value of £947,466 as at 30 September 2003 and it is hoped that these will transfer to like-minded registered social landlords by Spring 2004.

In the year ended   , Supported Housing activities gave rise to incoming resources of £1,952,522 (2002 – £1,632,211) and resources expended of £1,788,797 (2002 – £1,475,583).

Chapter 7

Incoming resources

1   Guidelines

7.1   Paragraph 30(a) of SORP states that the accounts should include a Statement of Financial Activities for the year that will show 'all incoming resources and all resources expended by it and [that] reconciles all changes in its funds.'

7.2   In this chapter, therefore, we examine how charities account for the 'incoming resources' received by them.

7.3   Table 3 of SORP requires the following categorisation of incoming resources. The Statement of Financial Activities extracted from the WaterAid accounts illustrates the categorisation of income across these headings.

A1   Incoming resources from generated funds
A1a   Voluntary income (paragraphs 121–136)
A1b   Activities for generating funds (paragraphs 137–139)
A1c   Investment income (paragraphs 140–142)
A2   Incoming resources from charitable activities (paragraphs 143–146)
A3   Other incoming resources (paragraph 147)
Total incoming resources by column

WATERAID

Consolidated statement of financial activities (incorporating an income and expenditure account)

For the year ended 31 March 2008

	Note	Unrestricted £000	Restricted £000	**2008 Total £000**	2007 Total £000
Incoming resources					
Incoming resources from generated funds:					
Voluntary income:					
– Donations	2	21,891	3,196	**25,087**	21,014
– Grants	2	1,912	—	**1,912**	1,459
– Gifts in kind	2	218	—	**218**	177
Activities for generating funds	3	1,695	—	**1,695**	1,028
Investment income		567	62	**629**	484
Incoming resources from charitable activities:	4				
Grant funding for specific activities		25	10,608	**10,633**	6,841
Campaign sales		—	—	**—**	4
Other incoming resources	5	83	—	**83**	—
Total incoming resources		26,391	13,866	**40,257**	31,007
Resources expended					
Costs of generating funds:					
Costs of generating voluntary income	6	7,658	—	**7,658**	6,438
Fundraising trading	6	137	—	**137**	116
		7,795	—	**7,795**	6,554
Charitable activities					
Supporting partners to deliver water, sanitation and hygiene	6	10,442	12,663	**23,105**	19,901
Influencing policy in water, sanitation and hygiene	6	4,247	51	**4,298**	3,143
Governance costs	1f/6	300	—	**300**	385
Total resources expended		22,784	12,714	**35,498**	29,983
Net incoming resources before transfers		3,607	1,152	**4,759**	1,024
Gross transfers between funds	18	—	—	**—**	—
Net income for the year before gains and losses	23	3,607	1,152	**4,759**	1,024
Unrealised (loss)/gain on investment assets		(25)	—	**(25)**	(67)
Net movement of funds in year		3,582	1,152	**4,734**	957

[*continued on next page*]

WaterAid, continued

	Note	Unrestricted £000	Restricted £000	**2008** **Total** **£000**	2007 Total £000
Reconciliation of funds					
Total funds at 1 April		14,666	1,493	**16,159**	15,202
Total funds at 31 March	18/24	**18,248**	**2,645**	**20,893**	**16,159**

The statement of financial activities includes all gains and losses recognised during the year. There were no realised gains during the year on investment assets. All incoming resources and resources expended derive from continuing activities. The notes supporting the financial statements are on [pages 35 to 44].

Comment

7.4   The above example shows how any of the headings set out in Table 3 of SORP may need to be expanded or emphasised as appropriate to describe the main sources of funding to support the activities of the charity.

7.5   This chapter will consider the resources made available to charities under each of the following heads:

- grants and donations receivable;

- contractual arrangements;

- voluntary income;

- legacies;

- gifts in kind;

- donated services and facilities;

- cash collections;

- activities for generating funds;

- investment income;

- incoming resources from charitable activities;

- trading activities;

- gains and losses on fixed assets for charity use;

- gains and losses on investment assets; and

- tax recoverable.

7.6   First, however, we need to examine the general principles which should be followed in recognising incoming resources in the accounts.

2   Recognition – basic principles

7.7   Paragraphs 94 to 97 of the SORP set out the principles to be followed with regard to the recognition and disclosure of incoming resources. In particular, paragraphs 94 and 95 define the basic principles regarding recognition as follows.

'Incoming resources – both for income and endowment funds – should be recognised in the Statement of Financial Activities when the effect of a transaction or other event results in an increase in the charity's assets. This will be dependent on the following three factors being met:

(a)   entitlement – normally arises when there is control over the rights or other access to the resource, enabling the charity to determine its future application;

(b)   certainty – when it is virtually certain that the incoming resource will be received;

(c)   measurement – when the monetary value of the incoming resource can be measured with sufficient reliability.' (para 94)

'All incoming resources should be reported gross when raised by the charity (or by volunteers working at the charity's direction) or its agents. However, where funds are raised or collected for the charity by individuals not employed or contracted by the charity, the gross incoming resources of the charity are the proceeds remitted to the charity by the organisers of the event, after deducting their expenses.' (para 95)

Comment

7.8   Although the above basic principles can be applied to most sources of charity income, there are a vast number of types of activity arising in the charity sector. The SORP seeks to provide further guidance to enable the reader to distinguish between differing transactions but does recognise that judgement will be required in deciding how specific transactions fit into the framework. For example, paragraph 97 of the SORP states that charity trustees must understand the following in order to fully determine how accounting standards apply to funding arrangements:

● the legal arrangements (for example contract or trust law) governing the terms of the arrangements and how any disputes are to be settled;

● whether entitlement to funding requires a specific performance to be achieved (ie under a contract or a performance related grant); and

● whether funds can be used for any purposes of the charity, or whether they can only be used for a specific purpose.

7.9   The current SORP includes an update for the revised Financial Reporting Standard 5 *'Reporting the substance of transactions'*, which became effective for accounting periods ending on or after 23 December 2003. The revised standard states that revenue (income) should be recognised by reference to the '*right to receive consideration*', being the '*sellers*' right to the amount received or receivable in exchange for its performance. This has implications for those charities that receive contractual income and moves away from the previous SORP requirements. One of the impacts of Financial Reporting Standard 5 is the introduction of 'performance related grants' in SORP 2005. This is explored further in paras **7.24** to **7.33** below.

3   Grants and donations receivable – recognition of incoming resources subject to restrictions and conditions

General

7.10   In line with the basic principles for income recognition set out in para 7.7 above, the pre-requisite for recognition of a grant or donation is evidence of entitlement. This will normally occur once the intention to pay the grant or donation to the charity has been expressed in writing. Once entitlement has been demonstrated, the incoming resource will be recognised in the accounts provided that the criteria of certainty and measurement are also met.

7.11   Incoming resources of a restricted fund, which have been recognised in the Statement of Financial Activities and have not been spent by the end of the financial year, will be carried forward in that fund. Paragraph 116 of SORP emphasises the following.

'The fact that a grant or a donation is for a restricted purpose does not affect the basis of its recognition within the Statement of Financial Activities.' (para 116)

Comment

7.12   The following example shows a charity which, having received restricted income during the financial year and not spent it all, has carried forward the balance at the end of the year.

SAMARITANS

Consolidated Statement of Financial Activities

Incorporating an Income & Expenditure Account 12 Months to 31st March 2008

	Note	Unrestricted Funds 2008 £'000	Restricted Funds 2008 £'000	All Funds 2008 £'000	All Funds 2007 £'000
Incoming Resources					
Incoming Resources from Generated Funds:					
Voluntary Income:					
Donations		3,782	10	3,792	3,642
Legacies		1,529	1	1,530	1,343
Donated Advertising Services		331	—	331	1,711
Grants – Public Body	2	—	161	161	179
Grants – Other		457	876	1,333	1,558
Total Voluntary Income		6,099	1,048	7,147	8,433
Activities for Generating Funds					
Merchandising	17	162	—	162	225
Sponsorship & Licensing	17	81	—	81	260
Totals from Activities for Generating Funds		243	—	243	485
Investment Income & Interest	3	316	59	375	338
Total Incoming Resources from Generated Funds		6,658	1,107	7,765	9,256
Incoming Resources from Charitable Activities					
Branch Affiliation Fees/BREF		599	66	665	666
Training & Conferences		483	—	483	369
Total Incoming Resources from Charitable Activities		1,082	66	1,148	1,035
Total Incoming Resources		**7,740**	**1,173**	**8,913**	**10,291**
Resources Expended					
Cost of Generating Funds:					
Fundraising Costs		3,197	—	3,197	2,740
Investment in Information System		—	232	232	—
Merchandising	17	78	—	78	238
		3,275	232	3,507	2,978
Net Incoming Resources Available for Charitable Purposes		4,465	941	5,406	7,313
Charitable Expenditure:					
Branch Support		1,540	291	1,831	1,600
Service Research & Development		492	251	743	1,449
Service Provision & Promotion		613	134	747	531

[*continued on next page*]

	Note	Unrestricted Funds 2008 £'000	Restricted Funds 2008 £'000	All Funds 2008 £'000	All Funds 2007 £'000
Samaritans, continued					
Donated Advertising Services		331	—	331	*1,711*
Training		582	69	651	*570*
Quality Monitoring		211	92	303	*167*
Information & Education		65	—	65	*73*
Total Charitable Expenditure	4	**3,834**	**837**	**4,671**	*6,101*
Governance Costs	5	279	—	279	*224*
Total Resources Expended		**7,388**	**1,069**	**8,457**	*9,303*
Net Income/(Expenditure) for the Year		**352**	**104**	**456**	*988*
Other Recognised Gains and Losses					
Net investment losses	10	(34)	—	(34)	*(87)*
Net Movement in Funds		**318**	**104**	**422**	*901*
Balances brought forward at 1 April 2007		5,577	1,504	7,081	*6,180*
Balances carried forward at 31 March 2008	16	**5,895**	**1,608**	**7,503**	*7,081*

The Restricted Funds column includes a balance of £768,000 of Expendable Endowment, the movement on which can be found in Note 16.

Pre-conditions on use

7.13   Paragraph 116 of SORP goes on, however, to stress the importance of distinguishing between incoming resources that are subject to restrictions on the use to which they can be put and those which will only be received once certain conditions have been fulfilled. The SORP states that incoming resources which are subject to restrictions should be recognised in the Statement of Financial Activities:

'There is an important difference for accounting purposes between restrictions placed on the purposes for which a particular resource may be used and conditions which must be fulfilled prior to entitlement or use by the charity. The existence of a restriction does not prevent the recognition of the incoming resource as the charity has entitlement to (control of) the resource and is simply limited by the restriction as to the purposes to which the resource can be applied.' (para 116)

7.14   Paragraph 105 of the SORP covers the scenario in which conditions are attached to grant or donation income:

'Charities often receive grants or donations with conditions attached that must be fulfilled before the entity has unconditional entitlement (control) of the resources. Meeting such conditions may be either within the recipient charity's control or reliant on external factors outside its control.

Where meeting such conditions is within the charity's control and there is sufficient evidence that the conditions will be met, then the incoming resource can be recognised.

Where uncertainty exists as to whether the recipient charity can meet the conditions within its control, the incoming resource should not be recognised but deferred as a liability until certainty exists that the conditions imposed can be met.' (para 105)

Comment

7.15   A good example of income subject to pre-conditions arises from the current trend for grant-making institutions to award grants subject to the charity obtaining matched funding from elsewhere. Meeting the matched funding conditions is not certain or wholly within the control of the recipient charity, and the charity does not, therefore, have unconditional entitlement to the grant until the funding has actually been secured. Once the conditions have been met, the grant income and the corresponding balance sheet asset will be recognised.

7.16   If the condition for receipt is deemed to be simply an administrative requirement, such as the submission of accounts or certification of expenditure, recognition as income in the Statement of Financial Activities should not be prevented.

7.17   If the existence of a condition prevents the recognition of income, but it is probable that the condition for receipt will be met in the future, the charity should disclose a contingent asset within the notes to the accounts.

Pre-conditions as to timing of use

7.18   Donor imposed conditions as to the timing of related expenditure could also affect the timing of the recognition of the grant or donation income if the restrictions amount to a pre-condition. Paragraph 108 considers this situation:

'Incoming resources may also be subject to donor imposed conditions that specify the time period in which the expenditure of resources can take place. Such a pre-condition for use limits the charity's ability to expend the resource until that time condition is met.

For example, the receipt in advance of a grant for expenditure that must take place in a future accounting period should be accounted for as deferred income and recognised as a liability until the accounting period in which the recipient charity is allowed by the condition to expend the resource.' (para 108)

Comment

7.19   Paragraph 108 is essential to prevent any form of departure from the accruals concept of accounting for donations and grants receivable in charity accounts. Care is needed, however. If taken literally, and to its extreme, the requirement to defer income that will be used for expenditure in a future accounting period could result in grant and donation income being equated exactly to expenditure each year with any excess incoming resources being deferred simply because they have not been spent. Grant and donations income should only be deferred where the person or institution providing it has specifically stated that it is to offset expenditure in a given future period.

7.20   Furthermore, a condition that allows for recovery by the donor of any unexpended part of a grant does not prevent recognition. In this case, a liability for any repayment should be recognised when the repayment becomes probable.

7.21   The following example illustrates the treatment of deferred income in the notes to the Statement of Financial Activities. The notes to the accounts should explain the reason for the deferral of income and also analyse the movement between incoming resources deferred in the current year and amounts released from previous years.

ROYAL COLLEGE OF PSYCHIATRISTS – 2006 ACCOUNTS – NOTE 8

8 Grants receivable

	2006 £000	2005 £000
Member and trainee services		
Department of Health		
• Basic Specialist Training	71	70
• Higher Specialist Training	55	53
• Overseas Doctors Training	78	76
	204	199
Less: Deferred income- grant received in advance (Note 17)	(41)	(40)
	163	159
Research Unit		
• Department of Health (DoH)	381	426
• Department of Health – LD, MH & Young People	—	105
	[continued on next page]	

Royal College of Psychiatrists, continued

	2006 £000	2005 £000
• Gatsby Charitable Foundation	75	360
• Healthcare Commission	207	158
• Health Foundation	246	217
• NICE	1,232	1,173
• Big Lottery Fund – Community of Communities	129	—
• Big Lottery Fund – Community Ethnography Project	19	56
• Finance & Leasing – Community Ethno	8	—
• Eli Lilly	25	55
	2,322	2,550
Other Projects		
• Big Lottery Fund – 6th Form Public Speaking	—	2
• NHS Scotland	4	—
• Young Offenders Project	—	6
	4	8
Total grants receivable	2,489	2,717

7.22   Care should be taken to differentiate the treatment of grants receivable and donations income from accounting for contractual arrangements. Contractual income will often be deferred in a charity's accounts: the accounting treatment for contractual income is set out in paras **7.24** to **7.33** below.

Restricted grants for purchase of a fixed asset

7.23   The treatment of 'capital' grants or grants for the purchase of tangible fixed assets is dealt with in paragraph 111 of SORP.

'Where either incoming resources are given specifically to provide a fixed asset or a fixed asset is donated (a gift in kind), the charity will normally have entitlement to the incoming resources when they are receivable. At this point, all of the incoming resources should be recognised in the Statement of Financial Activities and not deferred over the life of the asset. As explained in paragraph 110, the possibility of having to repay the incoming resources does not affect their recognition in the first instance. Once acquired, the use of the asset will either be restricted or unrestricted (see paragraph 117). If its use is unrestricted, the trustees may consider creating a designated fund reflecting the book value of the asset. The relevant fund will then be reduced over the useful economic life of the asset in line with its depreciation. This treatment accords with the requirements under accounting standards for the recognition of assets and liabilities and provides the most appropriate interpretation of SSAP 4 for charities.'
(para 111)

4   Contractual arrangements

7.24   As noted within para **7.9** above, the current SORP has been updated for the revised Financial Reporting Standard 5, *'Reporting the Substance of Transactions'*, which introduced specific guidance on revenue recognition within Application Note G. The current SORP provides clarification on the treatment of income which is deemed to be contractual in nature, and how this is differentiated from grants and donations receivable.

7.25   Appendix 1, GL 30 of the SORP aims to distinguish between contractual income and grants:

'A payment made to a charity for the purpose of providing goods or services may be by way of grant or contract. The main distinction is that grant payments are voluntary whereas contracts are normally legally binding between the payer and the charity: the payment is not then voluntary and is not a grant. The distinction is important because:

(a)   a contractual payment will normally be unrestricted income of the charity, but a grant for the supply of specific services will normally be restricted income;

(b)   the nature of the payment may be relevant to its VAT treatment.'

(Para GL30.1)

7.26   For those charities that earn contractual income as part of their charitable activities, by providing goods and/or services for a fee, the income should be recognised in the Statement of Financial Activities to the extent that the charity has provided the goods and/or services. If the contract monies are received in advance of the charity providing the goods and/or services, the charity will not have entitlement to the income and the monies should be treated as deferred income on the Balance Sheet, until the charity becomes entitled to the income.

7.27   The SORP goes on further to state that certain grant funding arrangements may contain conditions that closely specify the service to be performed by the charity, for example terms set out in a Service Level Agreement which specify that payment is linked to a particular level of output or service. The SORP gives the example of a grant received to provide a certain number of meals or opening hours of a facility for use by the charity's beneficiaries. Such grants are described as *'performance-related grants'* and, as for contractual income, should be recognised to the extent that the charity has provided the services or goods.

7.28   Appendix 1, GL 45 of the SORP defines a performance-related grant as follows:

'The term performance-related grant is used to describe a grant that has the characteristics of a contract in that:

(a)   the terms of the grant require the performance of a specified service that furthers the objectives of the grant maker; and

(b)   where payment of the grant receivable is conditional on a specified output being provided by the grant recipient.'

(para GL45.1)

7.29   Application Note G to Financial Reporting Standard 5 considers the recognition of income under 'long-term contracts'. This guidance has more recently been updated under Urgent Issues Task Force (UITF) Abstract 40, 'Revenue Recognition and Service Contracts', which applies the requirements of Application Note G to all contractual income for services. Reinforcing this point, paragraph 103 of the current SORP states:

'... A charity should recognise incoming resources in respect of its performance under a long-term contract when, and to the extent that, it obtains entitlement to consideration. This should be derived from an assessment of the
fair value of goods or services provided to its reporting date as a proportion
of the total fair value of the contract.'
(para 103)

7.30   In practice, this means that for contracts which are in progress at the charity's financial year end, the charity should assess the level of completion to determine the proportion of income (ie level of entitlement) which should be recognised in the Statement of Financial Activities. For example, for contracts for which costs incurred to date reflect the extent of work performed, the charity would calculate the proportion of costs incurred to date to total anticipated expenditure. This proportion would then be used to calculate the proportion of total contract income to include in the period's accounts. For service provision, a reasonable estimate of contract performance may be calculated using the proportion of time spent to estimated total time to be spent in fulfilling the contract.

Comment

7.31   It is important that the difference between performance-related grants and restricted grant income is understood. A grant which is restricted for a particular purpose does not mean that it should necessarily be classed as a per-
formance-related grant. For a performance-related grant, entitlement to income should arise only on the performance of a specific output which is a condition for receipt of the grant. In contrast, a restricted grant will limit how a charity can spend the income but will not require a specific and measurable output to be delivered. Such restricted grants should be recognised in line with paras **7.10** to **7.21** above.

7.32   Performance-related grant and contract income is normally treated as unrestricted income within the accounts: the condition for receipt is that a spe-
cific output is performed and, providing that the charity achieves this output, it has a right to retain the income irrespective of the costs incurred in performing the work. The charity is in reality taking the risk of any surplus or loss on the funding arrangement.

7.33   In contrast, grants for restricted purposes are included within the charity's restricted funds as the donor requires the charity to spend all of the income on a specified purpose: any unspent funds will usually be returned to the donor and the charity does not have the ability to generate a surplus on this funding arrangement.

5   Voluntary income

7.34   This section of the Statement of Financial Activities is intended to show incoming resources of a voluntary nature, usually given by the founders, patrons, supporters and the general public, government and non-statutory bodies such as businesses and charitable foundations and trusts. It will include grants which provide core funding or of a general nature but will not include those which are specifically for the performance of a service or production of charitable goods (for example, a service agreement with health authorities for the provision of hospice care in a hospice). In addition, this section of the Statement of Financial Activities may include incoming resources from membership subscriptions, gifts in kind, donated services and facilities and sponsorships where these are regarded as donations rather than payment for goods and services.

7.35   Appendix 1, GL61 of SORP defines voluntary income as follows:

'Voluntary income comprises gifts that will not normally provide any return to the donor other than the knowledge that someone will benefit from the donation. They will thus exclude any gifts that are quasi-contractual (in that a certain service to a certain level must be provided) but they would include gifts that must be spent on some particular area of work (i.e. restricted funds) or given to be held as an endowment. Voluntary income will normally include gifts in kind and donated services ...'
(para GL 61.1)

7.36   If material, the details of the types of activities undertaken to generate voluntary income should be provided on the face of the Statement of Financial Activities or in the notes to the accounts. Following the requirement for an activity based reporting format, the income categorisation should match the analysis of the costs of generating voluntary income.

Legacies

7.37   Paragraphs 123 to 128 of the SORP state the following.

'It is good practice to monitor a legacy from the time when notification is received to its final receipt. A charity should not, however, regard a legacy as receivable simply because it has been told about it. It should only do so when the legacy has been received or if, before receipt, there is sufficient evidence to provide the necessary certainty that the legacy will be received and the value of the incoming resources can be measured with sufficient reliability.'
(para 123)

'There will normally be sufficient certainty of receipt, for example, as soon as a charity receives a letter from the personal representatives of the estate advising that payment of the legacy will be made or that the property bequeathed will be transferred. It is likely that the value of the resource will also be measurable from this time. However, legacies which are not immediately payable should not be treated as receivable until the conditions associated with payment have been fulfilled (eg the death of a life tenant).'
(para 124)

'It is unlikely in practice that the entitlement, certainty of receipt and measurability conditions will be satisfied before the receipt of a letter from the personal representatives advising of an intended payment or transfer. The amount which is available in the estate for distribution to the beneficiaries may not have been finalised and, even if it has, there may still be outstanding matters relating to the precise division of the amount. In these circumstances entitlement may be in doubt or it may not be possible to provide a reasonable estimate of the legacy receivable, in which case it should not be included in the Statement of Financial Activities.'
(para 125)

'Where a charity receives a payment on account of its interest in an estate or a letter advising that such a payment will be made, the payment, or intended payment, on account should be treated as receivable.'
(para 126)

'Similarly, where a payment is received or notified as receivable (by the personal representatives) after the accounting year end, but it is clear that it had been agreed by the personal representatives prior to the year end (hence providing evidence of a condition that existed at the balance sheet date), then it should be accrued in the Statement of Financial Activities and the balance sheet.'
(para 127)

'*Disclosure*

Where the charity has been notified of material legacies which have not been included in the Statement of Financial Activities (because the conditions for recognition have not been met), this fact and an estimate of the amounts receivable should be disclosed in the notes to the accounts. Similarly, an indication should be provided of the nature of any material assets bequeathed to the charity but subject to a life tenancy interest held by a third party. Where material, the accounting policy notes should distinguish between the accounting treatments adopted for pecuniary and residuary legacies and legacies subject to a life interest held by another party.'
(para 128)

Comment

7.38   It is often felt advisable to highlight material outstanding legacies as a separate debtor figure and explain the position with regard to the legacies in the notes to the accounts.

7.39   Trustees will need to assess the likely amount of any legacies which have been notified to them. This may not always be easy, particularly with regard to residuary legacies, and in cases where the amount cannot be estimated or measured, it may be more appropriate to exclude the legacy from the Statement of Financial Activities but to include a note to the accounts disclosing details of the legacy and why it has not been accrued for.

MACMILLAN CANCER RELIEF: 31 DECEMBER 2007

Accounting policies (extract)

Legacies are deemed to be receivable from the date of probate. Those receivable at the year end, where they can be valued, are included at 90% of probate value, reflecting the uncertainty inherent in the fact that a substantial proportion of legacy receivables represent property or other investments whose value is subject to market fluctuations until they can be realised.

7.40   It will be virtually impossible for an auditor or independent examiner of a charity's accounts to test the completeness of legacy income. He or she will be reliant on assurances obtained from the trustees that they have informed the auditor of all legacies of which they have been notified. Additional evidence can be obtained from the charity's solicitors, from published death notices, from specialist agencies such as Smee and Ford and from a review of post-year end receipts.

7.41   In view of the huge impact a legacy can have on the accounts of a charity and its unpredictability both as to amount and timing of receipt, many charities may seek to modify the application of paragraphs 123 to 128 of SORP, for example by including only such legacies as they know they will receive within the early months of the following accounting year. In the past, the argument for doing this might be either that the doubt over the timing of the receipt makes the legacy 'incapable of measurement' or that to include such an amount as an incoming resource in the current period would not show a true and fair view of the position because of the uncertainty as to actual receipt and amount.

7.42   The additional clarity provided by the revised SORP means that the credibility of this argument is now almost non-existent. In very basic terms, if a charity now has a letter informing it of an intended payment or transfer, that amount should be accrued for in the Statement of Financial Activities. Details of all material legacies notified to the trustees at the year end, but not included in the accounts because the recognition factors have not been satisfied, should be given in the notes. In certain cases, it might even warrant special mention in the trustees' report.

7.43 The aim of the SORP is to seek recognition in the accounts of all incoming resources as and when they are known to be due to the charity, when it has a legally enforceable entitlement to them and when they can be quantified. In the case of legacies, this must be when the charity is notified that it is legally entitled to the legacy so that there is reasonable certainty of its eventual receipt and when it is told of an impending payment or transfer of monies, ie it can be quantified for accounting purposes.

7.44 We are aware that the practice of treating legacies as an incoming resource in full in the year they are received still causes anguish for a number of charities, simply because the size and the frequency of receipt of such sums is unpredictable and, therefore, uncontrollable. Trustees naturally wish to retain control and like to compare figures to budget estimates and the previous year. The inclusion of legacies often makes such comparison difficult and, some might argue, misleading. However, it shows the truth. It is not, in the authors' views, helpful to try and hide the event; rather it is better to explain it, if significant, in the trustees' annual report.

HELP THE AGED: 30 APRIL 2008

Financial review (extract)

Lower numbers of high value legacies were received this year against an exceptional amount received last year, and legacy costs have increased this year as we continue to invest in the Wills Advice service, which will reap long term legacy benefits. While legacy income for the year was at a lower level than in 2006/07, the average value of new legacies notified during the year increased by almost 20 per cent with the number of new notifications holding steady. We expect this to translate into increased income in 2008/09.

Gifts in kind

7.45 Paragraphs 129 to 132 of SORP describe the basis of recognising gifts in kind and the related disclosures. The paragraphs state the following.

'Incoming resources in the form of gifts in kind should be included in the Statement of Financial Activities in the following ways.

(a) Assets given and held as stock for distribution by the charity should be recognised as incoming resources for the year within "voluntary income" only when distributed with an equivalent amount being included as resources expended under the appropriate category of the Statement of Financial Activities to reflect its distribution.

(b) Assets given for use by the charity (eg property for its own occupation) should be recognised as incoming resources and within the relevant fixed asset category of the balance sheet when receivable (see paragraph 111). [See **7.47** below]

(c)   Where a gift has been made in kind but on trust for conversion into cash and subsequent application by the charity, the incoming resource should normally be recognised in the accounting period when receivable and where material, an adjustment should be made to the original valuation upon subsequent realisation of the gift. However, in certain cases this will not be practicable and the incoming resource should be included in the accounting period in which the gift is sold. The most common example is that of second-hand goods donated for resale, which, whilst regarded as a donation in legal terms, is, in economic terms, similar to trading and should be included within "activities for generating funds".'

(para 129)

'In all cases the amount at which gifts in kind are included in the Statement of Financial Activities should be either a reasonable estimate of their gross value to the charity or the amount actually realised as in the case of second-hand goods donated for resale. Where gifts in kind are included in the Statement of Financial Activities at their estimated gross value, the current value will usually be the price that it estimates it would have to pay in the open market for an equivalent item.'
(para 130)

'Disclosure

The basis of any valuation should be disclosed in the accounting policies.'
(para 131)

'Referring to 129(a) above, where there are undistributed assets at the year end, a general description of the items involved and an estimate of their value should be given by way of a note to the accounts provided such value is material.'
(para 132)

Comment

7.46   The requirements with regard to gifts in kind should not present any significant problems and most charities are adhering to the principles laid down in paragraphs 129 to 132.

7.47   However, care does need to be taken to ensure that the circumstances surrounding the gift are examined, particularly if the gift is of an asset which is of substantial value. For example, was the gift subject to any conditions? If so, did these conditions impel the trustees to treat the gift as either an addition to the permanent endowment or as a new permanent endowment? If so, the gift should be valued and treated as incoming endowment fund resources, with any income therefrom treated as either unrestricted or restricted income according to the conditions of the gift. Similarly, the gift itself may be subject to conditions on its use. If this is the case, the asset should be treated as incoming resources of restricted funds. Where the asset is to be retained for continuing use by the charity itself, the restricted fund will be reduced by amounts equivalent to any depreciation or amortisation charges over the expected useful life of the asset concerned in accordance with paragraphs 111 and 117 of SORP.

OXFAM: 30 APRIL 2007

Accounting policies (extract)

Gifts in Kind – Food aid, for which Oxfam accepts full responsibility for distribution, is included in 'Voluntary income' at its market value when it is distributed, and under 'Charitable expenditure' at the same value and time.

Gifts in Kind – Properties, investments and other fixed assets donated to the charity are included as 'Voluntary income' at market value at the time of receipt.

BOOK AID INTERNATIONAL REPORT AND ACCOUNTS 2007

4   Value of Gifts in Kind

The table below shows the value of the 508,589 donated books which were distributed to partner organisations during 2007 (2006 = 525,564). The valuation of these gifts in kind is based on prices from online suppliers of discounted new and used books. Seventy-four per cent are new or like new from publishers, and the rest of the books that we distributed were second-hand from other sources, but all were in excellent condition and have been valued at 74% of the value of new books.

At the end of the year there were approximately £1,720,000 (2006 = £2,802,000) of undistributed donated books in our warehouse.

Value of donated books distributed in 2006	Value per book 'new'	Value per book 'used'	Number of books	**2007 Total value***	2006 Total value*
	£	£		£	£
Children's & Teenagers'	2.81	2.11	170,681	**444,000**	544,000
Fiction & Literature	4.28	3.21	23,412	**93,000**	143,000
Non-Fiction	9.60	7.20	5,067	**45,000**	96,000
Reference	12.28	9.21	12,618	**143,000**	78,000
Primary Textbooks	4.91	3.68	55,688	**253,000**	237,000
Secondary Textbooks	9.27	6.95	116,125	**996,000**	519,000
Vocational Skills	13.52	10.14	13,776	**172,000**	175,000
Higher Education	21.82	16.37	36,256	**732,000**	823,000
Education & Teacher Training	12.99	9.74	24,331	**292,000**	199,000

[*continued on next page*]

Book Aid International, continued					
Value of donated books distributed in 2006	Value per book 'new'	Value per book 'used'	Number of books	**2007 Total value***	2006 Total value*
	£	£		£	£
English as a Foreign Language	7.40	5.55	15,153	**104,000**	337,000
Health & Medicine	27.48	20.61	30,657	**779,000**	605,000
Law	21.65	16.24	4,825	**97,000**	108,000
			508,859	**4,150,000**	3,864,000

* The calculation for total value is based on 74% (2006 = 70%) of the books being 'new' and the remainder being 'used' but in excellent condition. The figure is then rounded to the nearest thousand.

Donated services and facilities

7.48   Paragraphs 133 to 136 of SORP state the following.

'A charity may receive assistance in the form of donated facilities, beneficial loan arrangements or donated services. Such incoming resources should be included in the Statement of Financial Activities where the benefit to the charity is quantifiable and measurable. The value placed on these resources should be the estimated value to the charity of the service or facility received: this will be the price the charity estimates it would pay in the open market for a service or facility of equivalent utility to the charity.'
(para 133)

'Donated services and facilities recognised in financial statements would include those usually provided by an individual or entity as part of their trade or profession for a fee. In contrast, the contribution of volunteers should be excluded from the Statement of Financial Activities as the value of their contribution to the charity cannot be reasonably quantified in financial terms. Commercial discounts should not be recognised as incoming resources except where they clearly represent a donation.'
(para 134)

'Where donated services or facilities are recognised, an equivalent amount should be included as expenditure under the appropriate heading in the Statement of Financial Activities.'
(para 135)

'*Disclosure*

The notes to the accounts should give an analysis of donated services or facilities included in the Statement of Financial Activities distinguishing appropriately between the different major items, eg seconded staff, loaned assets, etc. The accounting policy notes should also indicate the basis of valuation used. When donated services are received but not included in the Statement of Financial Activities (eg volunteers) this should be disclosed in

the Trustees' Annual Report if this information is necessary for the reader to gain a better understanding of the charity's activities.'
(para 136)

Comment

7.49   The current SORP revised the guidance for the inclusion of donated services and facilities, previously referred to as 'intangible income'. The 2000 SORP required another party to bear the financial cost of the resources as a criteria for inclusion of donated services or facilities in the accounts. Where no financial cost was borne by another party for the provision of the assistance, the income was not included in the Statement of Financial Activities. The current SORP states that income should be included within the accounts providing that it is possible to quantify and measure the benefit and to attribute an open market price, irrespective of the cost incurred by the third party donor.

7.50   Paragraph 134 of the SORP states that the contribution of volunteers' time should not be included within the accounts. This followed considerable debate within the sector, the key aspects of which were summarised in a consultation document issued in November 2003 by the Charity Finance Directors' Group (CFDG). The document put forward the argument that volunteer time should be valued in order to better reflect the importance of volunteers to the charity sector. CFDG suggested that: (i) the value of volunteer time should be shown as an incoming resource, with an equivalent figure shown as resources expended under an appropriate heading or headings; (ii) all figures should be cross-referenced to a note in the accounts explaining volunteer activities in more detail; and (iii) that volunteer time should be valued at a uniform rate such as the National Minimum Wage. The document acknowledged that this was a controversial proposal.

7.51   The proposal was not taken forward into the current SORP due to a number of potential implementation issues. For example, the definition of 'volunteer' would need to be clarified (is a trustee a volunteer? is an employee doing unpaid overtime volunteering?); are all volunteer services of equal value or should some be valued at a figure above the National Minimum Wage?; how are charities to measure and record volunteer time and ensure that it is done in a manner which can be audited subsequently?; and safeguards would need to be introduced to ensure that the information requirements do not drive behaviour and encourage volunteers or charities, for example, to inflate their hours.

7.52   However, it is fully accepted that the contribution made by volunteers is of considerable importance to many charities. It was concluded, therefore, that donated volunteer time should be disclosed in the Trustees' Report to the accounts where it is of significance to the charity.

Cash collections

7.53   Funds collected for a charity, and to which it is legally entitled but which it has not received by the year-end, should normally be included in its

Statement of Financial Activities as incoming resources and in its balance sheet as 'collections in progress' as a current asset.

7.54   Funds in the form of cash collections in the hands of, or otherwise under the control of, persons other than the charity trustees as at the year-end should, where material, be brought into account as incoming resources of the year in accordance with the returns received from the collectors. Where it is not practicable to ascertain the actual amount, it should, if considered material, be estimated (eg by apportioning the amount subsequently ascertained or received between the relevant accounting years) on a reasonable and consistent basis according to the known circumstances and the results of control checks made from time-to-time.

Comment

7.55   A sensible approach should be adopted when accounting for cash collections. Inevitably there is the difficulty of ascertaining the actual amount collected at the end of each financial year, but as the accounts are not published until some months after the accounting date, it should be a relatively straightforward exercise to estimate the amount collected by reference to the total amount subsequently received and apportioning on a time basis.

Activities for generating funds

7.56   The SORP defines activities for generating funds as:

'the trading and fundraising activities carried out by a charity primarily to generate incoming resources which will be used to undertake its charitable activities'

and includes:

(a)   fundraising events such as jumble sales, firework displays and concerts (which are legally considered to be trading activities;

(b)   those sponsorships and social lotteries which cannot be considered as pure donations;

(c)   shop income from selling donated goods and bought in goods;

(d)   providing goods and services other than for the benefit of the charity's beneficiaries;

(e)   letting and licensing arrangements of property held primarily for functional use by the charity but temporarily surplus to operational requirements.'

(para 137)

7.57   The SORP recognises that, although legally considered to be the realisation of a donation in kind, in economic terms selling donated goods is akin to a trading activity and should be included under the activities for generating funds heading.

Comment

7.58   Trading and fundraising activities have potential direct tax and VAT implications and, as a result, are likely to be routed through wholly owned trading subsidiaries. On consolidation of the trading subsidiary's results with those of the charity, it is likely that the majority of the company's income will be consolidated under the activities for generating funds heading in the group accounts.

7.59   This classification causes greater use of ratio analysis in interpreting charity accounts and, inevitably, to assessing performance and comparing charities. Whilst some charities welcome this, such analysis must be carried out with care. Charities which seem to carry out similar activities are often subtly different and these differences can have a marked impact on financial results (for example, one charity may employ a fundraiser whereas another may be fortunate enough to have volunteers to assist with the raising of funds). Additional disclosure in the notes to the accounts and in the trustees' report explaining ratios that, at face value, may appear far from satisfactory is therefore essential.

Investment income

7.60   Investment income includes all income arising from the charity's investment assets, including dividends, interest and rental income. However, this income category excludes unrealised and realised gains (or losses) on investments which appear towards the foot of the Statement of Financial Activities.

7.61   Paragraph 142 of SORP states the following.

'The notes to the accounts should show the gross investment income arising from each class of investment shown in paragraph 303.' (para 142)

Note: Paragraph 303 referred to above requires that investments should be analysed between the following categories:

- investment properties;
- investments listed on a recognised stock exchange or ones valued by reference to such investments, such as common investment funds, open ended investment companies, and unit trusts;
- investments in subsidiary or associated undertakings or in companies which are connected persons;
- other unlisted securities;
- cash and settlements pending, held as part of the investment portfolio; and
- any other investments.

Comment

7.62   In most cases this should not present charities with any problems but it will enable the reader of a charity's accounts to carry out a crude, but nevertheless relatively meaningful, analysis of investment yields.

THE ENGLISH PROVINCE OF THE INSTITUTE OF THE
FRANCISCAN MISSIONARIES OF MARY CHARITABLE TRUST
– NOTE 2

2 Investment income

	Unrestricted funds £	Restricted Funds £	**Total 2007 £**	Total 2006 £
Income from listed investments				
● UK fixed interest common investment funds	136,014	—	**136,014**	116,982
● UK equities based common investment funds	180,433	—	**180,433**	177,911
Cash instruments	59,307	—	**59,307**	44,563
Government bonds	24,979	—	**24,979**	21,657
	400,733	—	**400,733**	361,113
Income from investment property				
● Rental income	11,411	—	**11,411**	13,154
Interest received				
● Bank interest	93,617	—	**93,617**	55,920
● Cash held by investment managers	13,017	—	**13,017**	6,786
	106,634	—	**106,634**	62,706
Total	518,778	—	**518,778**	436,973

Incoming resources from charitable activities

7.63   Incoming resources from charitable activities comprise those funds received which are a payment for goods and services which are for the benefit of the charity's beneficiaries. This includes income generated from 'primary purpose' trading activities (ie those undertaken in furtherance of the charity's objects) and those grants which have conditions which make them similar in economic terms to trading income, for example, service level agreements.

7.64 *Incoming resources*

7.64 Grants for core funding are excluded from this category of income and are instead included in the section for voluntary income.

7.65 Paragraph 145 of SORP states that this category of incoming resources should include:

'(a) the sale of goods or services as part of the directly charitable activities of the charity (known as primary purpose trading);

(b) the sale of goods or services made or provided by the beneficiaries of the charity;

(c) the letting of non-investment property in furtherance of the objects;

(d) contractual payments from government or public authorities where these are received in the normal course of trading under (a) to (c), eg fees for respite care;

(e) grants specifically for the provision of goods and services as part of charitable activities or services to beneficiaries;

(f) ancillary trades connected to a primary purpose in (a) to (e).'

(para 145)

Comment

7.66 Wherever possible, the face of the Statement of Financial Activities should provide a breakdown of the key components of the incoming resources from charitable activities to enable the reader to gain an understanding of the main activities of the charity. Incoming resources should be analysed using the same categories as used for resources expended and as described in the Trustees' Report. Further details can also be provided within the notes to the accounts.

WRVS

Consolidated Statement of Financial Activities (incorporating the Income and Expenditure Account)

For the year ended 31 March 2008

	Note	Unrestricted funds £'000	Restricted funds £'000	Total 2008 £'000	Total 2007 £'000
Incoming resources					
Incoming resources from generated funds:					
Voluntary income	2	2,308	913	**3,221**	3,391
Activities for generating funds		376	—	**376**	295
Investment income	4	2,271	9	**2,280**	2,039
			[continued on next page]		

134

WRVS, continued

	Note	Unrestricted funds £'000	Restricted funds £'000	Total 2008 £'000	Total 2007 £'000
Incoming resources from charitable activities:					
Hospital services		55,185	—	**55,185**	56,198
Food services		14,335	1,975	**16,310**	15,542
Community services		3,507	—	**3,507**	3,427
Emergency services		367	—	**367**	337
Services welfare		—	2,547	**2,547**	2,378
Property		348	—	**348**	303
Other incoming resources:					
Net (loss)/gain on the disposal of tangible fixed assets		(34)	—	**(34)**	1,047
Defined benefit pension scheme income		—	370	**370**	349
Funds changes during the year		(37)	—	**(37)**	176
Total incoming resources		**78,626**	**5,814**	**84,440**	**85,482**
Resources expended					
Cost of generating funds:					
Costs of generating voluntary income		1,288	—	**1,288**	1,292
Fundraising trading: cost of goods sold and other costs		288	—	**288**	134
Investment management costs		81	—	**81**	28
Cost of charitable activities:					
Hospital services		52,422	—	**52,422**	53,852
Food services		15,494	1,969	**17,463**	16,657
Community services		6,999	—	**6,999**	5,934
Emergency services		1,311	—	**1,311**	991
Services welfare		313	2,566	**2,879**	2,646
Governance costs		437	—	**437**	321
Other resources expended – defined benefit pension expenditure		—	10	**10**	693
Total resources expended	5	**78,633**	**4,545**	**83,178**	**82,548**
Net incoming resources		**(7)**	**1,269**	**1,262**	2,934
Other recognised gains and losses					
Net (losses)/gains on investments	10	(490)	(65)	**(555)**	4,819
Other revaluation gains		—	—	**—**	1,595
Actuarial (losses)/gains on defined benefit pension schemes	18	—	(360)	**(360)**	344
Net movement in funds		**(497)**	**844**	**347**	**9,692**
Fund balances at 1 April 2007		54,623	2,987	**57,610**	47,918
Transfers between funds	13	—	—	**—**	—
Fund balances at 31 March 2008		**54,126**	**3,831**	**57,957**	**57,610**

All the above results derive from continuing activities and there were no gains or losses other than those shown above.   [*continued on next page*]

> *WRVS, continued*
>
> For the purposes of the Companies Act 1985 the surplus for the Group for the year was £1,262,000 (2007 – £2,934,000) and for the Charity was a shortfall of £163,000 (2007 – a surplus of £3,930,000).
>
> The accompanying notes on [pages 37 to 51] are an integral part of this consolidated Statement of Financial Activities.

Trading activities

7.67   As described more fully in Chapter 18, trading activities are not charitable activities and should not, therefore, be carried on by charities. There are, however, two major exceptions to this rule:

- if the trade is exercised in the actual carrying on of a primary purpose of the charity, eg independent schools; or

- if the work in connection with the trade is mainly carried on by the beneficiaries of the charity, eg disabled workshops.

7.68   Thus, a charity established to care for the sick can run a hospital, nursing home, day centre, hospice, etc. If fees are charged for the services provided, the activity is broadly defined as trading, but provided any surplus that is earned is applied towards the charitable objectives, it falls within the first exception. Similarly, any sale by the charity of work made by the patients while in the charity's care will fall within the second exception.

7.69   Other permissible operational income will include regular forms of trading income appropriate to the charity which relate directly to its activities. An operatic society will have receipts from sales of theatre tickets, programmes, advertising, recording royalties, etc; a museum will have receipts from entry fees, private functions, book and poster sales, etc.

7.70   The activities described in paras **7.68** and **7.69** above will fall within the category 'incoming resources from charitable activities'.

7.71   Most charities with substantial trading activities will channel these through a trading subsidiary either to minimise risk or avoid *ultra vires* activity. The trading results of the subsidiary undertakings themselves should be accounted for in accordance with the rules for consolidation. These are detailed and discussed in Chapter 5.

Comment

7.72   Most charities have little difficulty in complying with these requirements although there are often concerns about the 'application' of charity funds invested in non-profitable, non-charitable trading companies and the financing of such companies.

7.73   One area of particular difficulty, however, arises in connection with charity shops which sell mainly donated goods – a charitable activity – but which may also sell bought in goods – a trading activity. This problem is dealt with in paragraph 139 of SORP.

'It may be possible to identify the incoming resources and resources expended for each different component of an activity (this may have to be done for tax purposes) but often these will be viewed as contributing to a single economic activity. Charity trustees should consider the balance of the activities being undertaken to determine the most appropriate place to include the incoming resources from such enterprises but having done this the components of incoming resources need not be analysed further. For example, a shop may mainly sell donated and bought in goods, but it may also sell a small amount of goods made by its beneficiaries and incidentally provide information about the charity. It would be acceptable to classify all the incoming resources from the shop as "shop income" under activities for generating funds.'
(para 139)

Funds received as agent

7.74   A charity may receive income which does not belong to it. For example, when the charity receives monies which the trustees, acting as agents, are legally bound to pay over to a third party and have no responsibility for their future application. In this instance, the original payer remains the principal and is deemed to be legally transferring resources to the specified third party. Hence, the intermediary charity should not recognise the resources in the Statement of Financial Activities or the balance sheet.

7.75   If the intermediary charity is able to control the use of the resources prior to their transfer to a third party or the trustees are required to take legal responsibility for the transfer to the third party, the income should be included in the intermediary charity's Statement of Financial Activities.

Gains and losses on fixed assets for charity use

7.76   Two types of gain or loss can arise with regard to fixed assets. The first is where an asset is revalued, either upwards or downwards, thereby resulting in an unrealised revaluation gain or loss. The accounting of such gains or losses is detailed and discussed in Chapter 10.

7.77   The other type of gain or loss in relation to fixed assets for charity use is a realised gain or loss, arising when an asset is sold, scrapped or otherwise disposed of.

7.78   Paragraph 218(b) of SORP states the following.

'Gains on the disposal of fixed assets for the charity's own use should be included under the heading "other incoming resources". Losses on disposal should be treated as additional depreciation and included appropriately in

the resources expended section of the Statement of Financial Activities.'
(para 218(b))

Gains and losses on investment assets

7.79   Paragraph 219 of SORP states the following.

'Any gains and losses on investment assets (including property investments)
should be included under the gains and losses on the revaluation and disposal of investment assets. Realised and unrealised gains and losses may
be included in a single row on the Statement of Financial Activities. In particular this approach will be necessary where a charity adopts a 'marking
to market' or continuous revaluation approach in relation to its investment
portfolio.'
(para 219)

ROYAL COLLEGE OF PSYCHIATRISTS

Statement of financial activities 31 December 2007

	Notes (pages 25 to 38)	Unrestricted Funds £000	Restricted Funds £000	**Total Funds 2007 £000**	Total Funds 2006 £000
Incoming resources					
Incoming resources from generated funds					
• Voluntary income – donations and gifts		1	—	**1**	1
• Investment income and bank interest	1	383	—	**383**	290
Incoming resources from charitable activities					
• Standard setting and research	2	998	2,351	**3,349**	3,198
• Education and training	3	4,914	1	**4,915**	4,942
• Member services and support	4	3,784	—	**3,784**	3,335
• College campaign and public education	5	44	31	**75**	42
• Central College development		381	—	**381**	330
• Prize funds	19	—	12	**12**	9
Total incoming resources		10,505	2,395	**12,900**	12,147
Resources expended					
Cost of generating funds	1				
• Activities for generating funds		21	—	**21**	20
• Investment management costs		10	—	**10**	9
Charitable activities:					
• Standard setting and research	2	1,959	2,547	**4,506**	4,271

[*continued on next page*]

Royal College of Psychiatrists, continued

	Notes (pages 25 to 38)	Unrestricted Funds £000	Restricted Funds £000	**Total Funds 2007 £000**	Total Funds 2006 £000
● Education and training	3	5,329	1	**5,330**	5,090
● Member services and support	4	1,985	—	**1,985**	1,686
● College campaign and public education	5	747	5	**752**	561
● Prize funds	19	—	9	**9**	25
Governance costs	6	418	—	**418**	351
Total resources expended		10,469	2,562	**13,031**	12,013
Net incoming/(outgoing) resources before transfers	9	36	(167)	**(131)**	134
Transfer between funds		15	(15)	**—**	—
Net incoming resources before other recognised gains and losses		51	(182)	**(131)**	134
Other recognised gains and losses					
● Gains/losses on investment assets		44	—	**44**	72
Net movement in funds		95	(182)	**(87)**	206
Reconciliation of funds					
Total funds brought forward		6,017	661	**6,678**	6,472
Total funds carried forward		6,112	479	**6,591**	6,678

Comment

7.80   The calculation and treatment of gains is discussed in more detail in Chapter 10. In many cases, charities should have little problem complying with SORP, but others may find that their investment managers insist on additional charges for supplying the necessary information.

7.81   Some charities argue that gains on investments should not be included within the Statement of Financial Activities. The 'growth' of an investment is often largely inflationary and merely represents the amount required to maintain the real value of the investment. SORP has recognised this particular point by excluding all investment gains (or losses) from the 'incoming resources' section of the Statement of Financial Activities. However, it is important to show that there has been a movement in the net worth of the charity, be it an increase or a decrease, and this is done by means of the 'gains and losses on investment assets' section.

7.82   The need not to have to show separately realised and unrealised gains and losses is welcome and reflects the fact that the only figures that matter to the charity are the closing values of the investment pool compared to the opening values. It makes no difference whether or not investments were changed in between.

Tax recoverable

7.83   Income received in circumstances where a claim for repayment of tax has been or will be made to HM Revenue & Customs (for example, income received under Gift Aid) should be grossed up for tax recoverable and the gross figure included as income. The tax recoverable should be accounted for as a debtor until the charity recovers the amount involved.

Comment

7.84   The grossing up of income received net of income tax is a good discipline to ensure that tax is reclaimed regularly from HM Revenue and Customs.

MARIE CURIE CANCER CARE: 31 MARCH 2008

Accounting policies (extract)

(f)   Incoming resources

All income is accounted for when receivable and includes associated tax reclaims. Entitlement to legacy income is taken to be the earlier of estate accounts being finalised and cash received. Deferred income includes amounts received in respect of work to be undertaken in the next financial year. Gifts in kind are valued at their realised amount, or the amount equivalent to an alternative commercial supply, and are included in the Statement of Financial Activities as appropriate.

Chapter 8

Resources expended

1 Introduction

8.1   Appendix 1 of SORP defines resources expended as follows.

'Resources expended means all costs incurred in the course of expending or utilising the charity's funds. This includes all claims against the charity upon being recognised as liabilities by the trustees, as well as all accruals and payments made by the trustees of a charity, and all losses on the disposal of fixed assets (other than investments), together with all provisions for impairment of tangible fixed assets or programme related investments.

This is to be distinguished from total expenditure.'
(para GL 52)

Total expenditure is defined as follows.

'Total expenditure is a term used within the Charities Act 1993 to determine the thresholds that govern the requirements (in England and Wales) for accounts scrutiny, submission of reports, accounts and an annual return to the Charity Commission. The Charities Accounts (Scotland) Regulations 1992 define a similar term 'Gross expenditure'. Total expenditure does not include losses on the disposal of fixed assets nor amounts paid for the acquisition of fixed assets nor any amounts paid out of endowment funds.'
(para GL 55)

8.2   Paragraph 177 of the SORP states that resources expended should be split into three main categories, being the costs of generating funds, the costs of charitable activities and governance costs. This is a move away from the previous SORP which included 'management and administration costs' within the categorisation of resources expended. This change came about largely as a result of inconsistencies within the charity sector regarding the allocation of costs to management and administration and the increasing focus upon ratio analysis of key figures in the accounts. Furthermore, the current SORP removed the requirement to show 'support costs' on the face of the statement of financial activities. Instead, support costs should now be allocated to the relevant activity cost category.

8.3   In this chapter we look at how expenditure should be analysed and at each of the recommended headings in some detail. We also consider how to allocate expenditure over each of the expense headings and deal with capital expenditure, aspects of the Companies Acts and accounting for irrecoverable VAT.

2   Analysis of expenditure

8.4   Given the requirement set out in paragraph 177 of SORP that resources expended should be analysed between the costs of generating funds, the costs of charitable activities and governance costs, paragraphs 178 to 213 of the SORP expand on this and identify sub-headings that should be used to categorise expenses. In particular, paragraphs 178 and 179 define what is meant by the costs of generating funds, paragraph 188 defines charitable activities and paragraphs 210 and 211, governance costs.

'Costs of Generating Funds

These are the costs which are associated with generating incoming resources from all sources other than undertaking charitable activities. The main components within this category are:

(a)   Costs of generating voluntary income;

(b)   Costs of fundraising trading, including cost of goods sold and other associated costs;

(c)   Costs of managing investments for both income generation and capital maintenance.'
(para 178)

'Costs of generating funds should not include:

(a)   Costs associated with delivering or supporting the provision of goods and services in the furtherance of the charity's objects; nor

(b)   The costs of any subsequent negotiation, monitoring or reporting relating to the provision of goods or services under the terms of a grant, contract or performance-related grant.'

(para 179)

'Charitable Activities

Resources expended on charitable activities comprise all the resources applied by the charity in undertaking its work to meet its charitable objectives as opposed to the cost of raising funds to finance these activities and governance costs. Charitable activities are all the resources expended by the charity in the delivery of goods and services, including its programme and project work that is directed at the achievement of its charitable aims and objectives. Such costs include the direct costs of the charitable activities together with those support costs incurred that enable these activities to be undertaken.'
(para 188)

'Governance costs

Governance costs include the costs of governance arrangements which relate to the general running of the charity as opposed to the direct management

functions inherent in generating funds, service delivery and programme or project work. These activities provide the governance infrastructure which allows the charity to operate and to generate the information required for public accountability. They include the strategic planning processes that contribute to future development of the charity.'
(para 210)

'Expenditure on the governance of the charity will normally include both direct and related support costs. Direct costs will include such items as internal and external audit, legal advice for trustees and costs associated with constitutional and statutory requirements eg the cost of trustee meetings and preparing statutory accounts. Where material, there should be an apportionment of shared and indirect costs involved in supporting the governance activities (as distinct from supporting its charitable or income generation activities).'
(para 211)

Comment

8.5   As noted within **8.2** above, the current SORP has introduced a revised categorisation of resources expended. The updated guidance resulted from significant inconsistencies which existed within charity accounts prepared under the 2000 SORP. The lack of consistency led the Charity Finance Directors' Group (CFDG) to call for a revision in the headings within the statement of financial activities and their definitions. In the CFDG's document entitled 'Inputs Matter', published in November 2003, CFDG called for clarification on two main issues: the treatment of fundraising costs and costs of generating funds; and the accounting practice for support, management and administration costs. Each of these issues is discussed further in the sections which follow.

8.6   The aim of the current SORP is for a charity to break down its costs by activity which can be matched to the categorisation of income. For example, within income, the charity will have identified the voluntary income received in the accounting period. Within expenditure, the costs of generating that voluntary income should be disclosed separately. By presenting the results in this manner, trustees are disclosing the efficiency of their fundraising activities. Similarly for a service delivery or project based charity, the 'charitable activities' heading under resources expended should be split into the main activity or programme areas. Any primary purpose trading, contract or grant income relating to these activities or programmes will be broken down in the same way under 'Incoming resources from charitable activities'. The Kidney Research UK accounts below show the statement of financial activities prepared in this format.

8.6   *Resources expended*

KIDNEY RESEARCH UK ANNUAL REPORT AND FINANCIAL STATEMENTS 31 MARCH 2008

	Notes	Unrestricted funds £	Restricted funds £	**2008 Total funds £**	2007 Total funds £
Income and expenditure					
Incoming resources					
Incoming resources from generated funds					
• Voluntary income	1	6,740,795	—	**6,740,795**	5,073,431
• Activities for generating funds	2	1,498,792	—	**1,498,792**	1,253,462
• Investment income	3	365,981	—	**365,981**	302,821
Incoming resources from charitable activities	4	176,132	889,870	**1,066,002**	1,260,893
Total incoming resources		8,781,700	889,870	**9,671,570**	7,890,607
Resources expended	5				
Costs of generating funds					
• Costs of generating voluntary income		2,410,170	—	**2,410,170**	2,445,993
• Fundraising trading: cost of goods sold and other costs		1,144,399	—	**1,144,399**	1,272,495
• Investment management costs		61,685	—	**61,685**	33,410
		3,616,254	—	**3,616,254**	3,751,898
Charitable activities					
• Research		1,357,386	889,870	**2,247,256**	2,571,477
• Education and awareness		314,927	—	**314,927**	402,756
• Patient welfare		99,306	—	**99,306**	119,034
Governance costs		84,546	—	**84,546**	108,732
Total resources expended		5,472,419	889,870	**6,362,289**	6,953,897
Net incoming resources for the year		3,309,281	—	**3,309,281**	936,710
Net realised investment (losses) gains	13	(141,061)	—	**(141,061)**	42,077
Statement of total recognised gains and losses					
Net income		3,168,220	—	**3,168,220**	978,787
Net unrealised investment (losses) gains	13	(322,285)	—	**(322,285)**	159,426

[continued on next page]

144

Kidney Research UK Annual Report and Financial Statements,
continued

	Notes	Unrestricted funds £	Restricted funds £	**2008 Total funds £**	2007 Total funds £
Net movement in funds		2,845,935	—	**2,845,935**	1,138,213
Fund balances brought forward at 1 April 2007		4,382,180	—	**4,382,180**	3,243,967
Fund balances carried forward at 31 March 2008		7,228,115	—	**7,228,115**	4,382,180

3   Recognition – basic principles

8.7   Paragraph 148 of the SORP provides the following general rules on the recognition of expenditure:

'Expenditure should be recognised when and to the extent that a liability is incurred or increased without a commensurate increase in recognised assets or a reduction in liabilities. In accounts prepared on the accruals basis, liabilities are recognised as resources expended as soon as there is a legal or constructive obligation committing the charity to the expenditure as described in Financial Reporting Standards 5 and 12. A liability will arise when a charity is under an obligation to make a transfer of value to a third party as a result of past transactions or events.'
(para 148)

Following Financial Reporting Standard 12, Appendix 1 of the SORP defines a constructive obligation as:

'An obligation that derives from an entity's actions where:

(a)   By an established pattern of past practice, published policies or a sufficiently specific current statement, the entity has indicated to other parties that it will accept certain responsibilities; and

(b)   As a result, the entity has created a valid expectation on the part of those other parties that it will discharge those responsibilities.'

(para GL10)

Comment

8.8   In general, expenditure should be recognised in the statement of financial activities if the charity has entered into an obligation during that accounting period to make a payment to a third party. The payment will not necessarily be made during the accounting period and could be made at a future date.

8.9   Constructive obligations most commonly occur in charities which approve grant commitments to third parties in advance of making the payment. Paragraphs **8.59** to **8.66** below consider this in further detail.

4   Costs of generating funds

8.10   As set out in **8.4** above, the costs of generating funds will comprise the following sub-categories:

- costs of generating voluntary income;

- costs of fundraising trading, including cost of goods sold and other associated costs;

- costs of managing investments for both income generation and capital maintenance.

Each of these sub-categories is reviewed in turn below.

Costs of generating voluntary income

8.11   The costs of generating voluntary income are defined in the Glossary of the SORP (GL13) as follows:

'Costs of generating voluntary income comprise the costs actually incurred by a charity, or by an agent, in inducing others to make gifts to it that are voluntary income (see GL 61).

(a)   Such costs will include the costs of producing fundraising advertising, marketing and direct mail materials, as well as any remuneration payable to an agent. It will normally include publicity materials but not those used in an educational manner in furtherance of the charity's objects.

(b)   Such costs will exclude fundraising trading costs (see GL 26).'

8.12   Some charities may also have a wholly owned trading subsidiary which incurs such costs. In the case of consolidated accounts, as costs are consolidated on a line-by-line basis in the statement of financial activities, these costs would also be included under the costs of generating voluntary income heading.

8.13   Paragraph 181 of SORP considers the accounting treatment of certain fundraising costs where they relate to starting up a new source of future income. In general, start-up costs of a new fundraising activity should be treated just as other costs incurred as part of the charity's usual activities. UITF Abstract 24, Accounting for Start-up Costs, does permit the carry forward of start-up costs as prepayments on the balance sheet but only on the basis that the future economic benefits deriving from those costs are sufficiently certain. The SORP takes the view that the carry forward of these costs would not be appropriate as it would be difficult to evidence the future economic benefits. In contrast, the SORP does state that data capture costs of internally developed databases can be capitalised providing that the future benefit can be demonstrated and the database has an ascertainable value.

8.14   Paragraph 183 of SORP requires that where the costs of generating voluntary income are material, the details of the types of activities should be shown in the notes to the accounts. For example, this may include collections, sponsorship, legacy development and direct mail. Following the matching principle of the SORP and to enable a true income/cost comparison to be made, this analysis should follow the analysis of 'voluntary income' within incoming resources.

Comment

8.15   Potential donors to charities will often calculate the cost to the charity of generating £1 of voluntary income. Charities are aware of the importance of the fundraising cost ratio, particularly as donors and potential donors often expect 100% of their donation to be used on charitable activities, and are always looking for more efficient ways of raising money so that the least efficient methods can be dropped. However, this is a difficult problem for trustees since income is money, regardless of whether the fundraising costs associated with obtaining it are 1% or 90%. When cash is needed to carry out the charity's main objects, the trustees face a dilemma when deciding whether to refuse income because its fundraising costs are too high. This is a dilemma facing more and more charities given the continued pressures on charitable giving.

8.16   A charity that undertakes a variety of fundraising activities can use the SORP requirement to provide the voluntary income and cost breakdown to beneficial effect. For example, the cost of generating legacy income can often distort the results for the year. A legacy campaign may only result in funds being received by the charity many years into the future or a very large legacy receipt may have few costs attributed to it. By splitting out the cost of the legacy campaign and legacy income in the notes to the accounts, the reader is able to obtain a clearer picture. Charities may also consider separating out the costs of generating *future* voluntary income, ie those costs which comprise an investment in developing sources of income for future periods, from the cost of generating voluntary income for the current year.

HELP THE AGED ANNUAL REPORT AND ACCOUNTS 2008

Consolidated statement of financial activities

(incorporating a consolidated income and expenditure account) for the year ended 30 April 2008

	Note	Unrestricted funds £'000	Restricted funds £'000	Total 2008 £'000	Restated Total 2007 £'000
Incoming resources					
Incoming resources from generated funds					
Voluntary income:					
Donations and gifts		6,235	11,378	**17,613**	18,341
Legacies		10,616	1,925	**12,541**	17,041
Grants		588	1,140	**1,728**	1,236
Activities for generating funds:					
Merchandising and retail	23	31,385	–	**31,385**	31,684
Other trading income	23	2,525	81	**2,606**	2,425
Events		702	19	**721**	655
Sale of services by joint venture		1,629	–	**1,629**	1,145
Investment income	2	1,121	186	**1,307**	1,177
Incoming resources from charitable activities					
Combating poverty	5	21	291	**312**	271
Reducing isolation	5	113	1928	**2,041**	2,475
Defeating ageism	5	–	–	**–**	–
Challenging neglect	5	280	65	**345**	538
Preventing future deprivation	5	466	282	**748**	928
International	5	170	–	**170**	177
Other incoming resources					
Exceptional item: VAT refund		–	–	**–**	1,743
Gain on disposal of fixed assets		390	-	**390**	897
Total incoming resources including share of joint venture		56,241	17,295	**73,536**	80,733
Less share of joint venture		(1,629)	–	**(1,629)**	(1,145)
Total incoming resources		**54,612**	**17,295**	**71,907**	**79,588**
Resources expended					
Cost of generating funds					
Cost of generating voluntary income:					
Fundraising		4,517	3,588	**8,105**	7,904
Legacies		954	16	**970**	627
Grants		174	17	**191**	218
Activities for generating funds:					
Cost of selling donated and bought-in goods	23	27,016	246	**27,262**	26,765
Merchandising and commission costs		6,440	9	**6,449**	3,073
Events costs		679	–	**679**	819
Investment management costs		113	–	**113**	96
		39,893	3,876	**43,769**	39,502
Net income available for charitable activities		14,719	13,419	**28,138**	40,086
Charitable activities					
Combating poverty		3,155	1,556	**4,711**	4,363
Reducing isolation		5,306	3,625	**8,931**	9,718
Defeating ageism		2,369	590	**2,959**	3,426
Challenging neglect		3,136	613	**3,749**	3,925
Preventing future deprivation		3,259	4,027	**7,286**	5,935
International		3,182	6,501	**9,683**	9,360
Total charitable spend		20,407	16,912	**37,319**	36,728
Governance		329	–	**329**	258
Total resources expended before joint venture and transfers	**6**	**60,629**	**20,788**	**81,417**	**76,488**
Net (outgoing)/incoming resources before joint ventures and transfers		(6,017)	(3,493)	**(9,510)**	3,100

Fundraising trading: Cost of goods sold and other costs

8.17   Paragraph 185 of the SORP defines the 'fundraising trading: costs of goods sold and other costs' as follows:

'... all those costs that are incurred by trading for a fundraising purpose in either donated or bought-in goods or in providing non-charitable services to generate income. This includes:

(a)   the costs of goods sold or services provided;

148

(b) other costs related to the trade, including staff costs, premises costs and other costs incurred in the activity including allocated support costs; and

(c) costs related to the licensing of a charity logo.'

8.18 For charities with a trading subsidiary, this category of expenditure will often include the majority of the trading subsidiary's costs. For example, the costs incurred by a trading subsidiary in running retail shops, when consolidated with the charity's results on a line-by-line basis, will be included under this heading.

8.19 If the fundraising costs are material, the SORP requires disclosure in the notes to the accounts of the cost of separate trading activities. Again, the analysis should match the income breakdown in 'activities for generating funds'.

MARIE CURIE CANCER CARE REPORTS AND ACCOUNTS 2007/08

Consolidated Statement of Financial Activities
for the year ended March 31, 2008 (incorporating consolidated income and expenditure accounts)

	Notes	Unrestricted funds £'000	Restricted funds £'000	TOTAL 2008 £'000	TOTAL 2007 £'000
INCOMING RESOURCES					
Incoming resources from generated funds:					
Voluntary income	2	50,321	21,277	71,598	65,297
Activities for generating funds:					
Retail sales of donated and purchased goods		10,104	4,387	14,491	14,638
Investment and other income	3	4,186	21	4,207	3,205
Incoming resources from charitable activities:					
Statutory and grant funding	4	27,479	1,927	29,406	26,170
Education course fees		166	–	166	337
Other incoming resources:					
Gain on disposal of assets		–	–	–	122
Total incoming resources		**92,256**	**27,612**	**119,868**	**109,769**
RESOURCES EXPENDED					
Cost of generating funds:					
Cost of generating voluntary income:					
Fundraising		19,000	2,981	21,981	19,838
Publicity		2,679	–	2,679	1,761
Fundraising trading: cost of goods sold and other costs		10,357	3,778	14,135	13,901
Investment management costs		110	–	110	236
		32,146	6,759	38,905	35,736
Net incoming resources available for charitable application		**60,110**	**20,853**	**80,963**	**74,033**
Cost of charitable activities:					
Hospices		23,686	13,452	37,138	35,329
Nursing		22,672	4,464	27,136	24,086
Education		1,068	91	1,159	1,392
Palliative care research		4,785	6	4,791	1,335
Supporting and Delivering Choice		1,150	1,361	2,511	1,307
Scientific research		3,820	645	4,465	4,225
		57,181	20,019	77,200	67,674
Governance costs		925	–	925	860
Total resources expended	5	**90,252**	**26,778**	**117,030**	**104,270**
NET INCOME FOR THE YEAR		2,004	834	2,838	5,499
OTHER RECOGNISED GAINS AND LOSSES					
(Loss)/gain on investment assets	8	(4,061)	(8)	(4,069)	2,504
Actuarial gains/(losses) on defined benefit pension scheme	18	130	–	130	(1,100)
NET MOVEMENT IN FUNDS		(1,927)	826	(1,101)	6,903
TRANSFER OF FUNDS		1,724	(1,724)	–	–
RECONCILIATION OF FUNDS					
Total funds at April 1, 2007	15	87,267	6,874	94,141	87,238
Total funds at March 31, 2008		87,064	5,976	93,040	94,141
APPLICATION OF NET INCOME FOR THE YEAR					
Net income for the year		2,004	834	2,838	5,499

Investment management costs

8.20   Investment management costs should be included as a sub-heading of the costs of generating funds for those charities which hold investments, such as a portfolio of listed investments or investment properties.

8.21   The Glossary to the SORP (GL38) includes the following definition of investment management costs:

'Investment management costs include the costs of:

(a)   portfolio management;

(b)   obtaining investment advice;

(c)   administration of the investments;

(d)   rent collection, property repairs and maintenance charges.

Valuations fees incurred for accounting purposes would normally be charged to the governance cost category of the relevant funds that hold the properties being valued.

Costs associated with acquiring and disposing of investments would normally form part of the acquisition cost of the investment or reduce the return on disposals. These costs are therefore not part of investment management costs.'

ROYAL COLLEGE OF NURSING ANNUAL REPORT AND ACCOUNTS 2007/08

Financial statements

Consolidated statement of financial activities for the year ended 31 March 2009

	Notes	Unrestricted funds		Restricted funds	Endowment funds	Total 2009	Total 2008
		Representation activities	Other activities				
		£'000	£'000	£'000	£'000	£'000	£'000
INCOMING RESOURCES							
Incoming resources from charitable activities:							
Subscriptions income		29,567	33,688	-	-	63,255	61,192
Education & training	4.1	-	2,496	1,411	-	3,907	3,074
Advancing of the profession	4.1	-	264	65	-	329	353
Promotion of nursing	4.1	-	205	-	-	205	257
Assisting nurses	4.1	-	155	-	-	155	659
Representation	4.1	606	-	104	-	710	1,575
Incoming resources from generated funds:							
Donations		-	43	110	-	153	498
Legacies		-	364	-	-	364	52
Investment income	5	-	1,499	239	-	1,738	1,857
Trading income	4.1	-	14,710	-	-	14,710	13,070
Other incoming resources:							
Gain on disposal of fixed asset	4.2		387			387	
Exceptional Items	4.2		2,486	-	-	2,486	-
TOTAL INCOMING RESOURCES		**30,173**	**56,297**	**1,929**	**-**	**88,399**	**82,587**
RESOURCES EXPENDED							
COST OF GENERATING FUNDS							
Fundraising and sponsorship costs	8.1	-	482	-	-	482	500
Investment management fee	8.1	-	43	-	-	43	73
Other trading costs	8.1	-	13,322	-	-	13,322	11,333
CHARITABLE ACTIVITIES							
Education & Training	8.1	-	13,914	1,508	-	15,422	17,956
Advancing of the Profession	8.1	-	6,279	79	-	6,358	5,715
Promotion of Nursing	8.1	-	2,770	28	-	2,798	9,031
Assisting Nurses	8.1	-	2,040	415	-	2,455	3,792
Representation	8.1	29,683	-	104	-	29,787	24,778
GOVERNANCE COSTS	8.1	490	1,173	-	-	1,663	1,663
TOTAL RESOURCES EXPENDED	8.1	**30,173**	**40,023**	**2,134**	**-**	**72,330**	**74,841**
NET INCOMING RESOURCES FOR THE YEAR		-	16,274	(205)	-	16,069	7,746
Net investment losses	10	-	(2,149)	(753)	(195)	(3,097)	(428)
Actuarial losses on defined benefit pension scheme	19	-	(9,261)	-	-	(9,261)	(66)
NET MOVEMENT IN FUNDS		-	4,864	(958)	(195)	3,711	7,252
Fund balances b/f at 1 April		-	21,670	7,170	1,109	29,949	22,697
Fund balances c/f at 31 March			26,534	6,212	914	33,660	29,949

All amounts shown relate to continuing activities. There are no material differences between net incoming resources for the year before transfers stated above and their historic cost equivalent. Notes on pages 39 - 55 form part of these accounts.

---

5   Charitable activities

8.22   As stated above, paragraph 188 of the SORP defines the resources expended on charitable activities as follows.

'Resources expended on charitable activities comprise all the resources applied by the charity in undertaking its work to meet its charitable objectives as opposed to the cost of raising funds to finance these activities and governance costs. Charitable activities are all the resources expended by the charity in the delivery of goods and services, including its programme and project work that is directed at the achievement of its charitable aims and objectives. Such costs include the direct costs of the charitable activities together with those support costs incurred that enable these activities to be undertaken.'

8.23 Paragraph 191 of the SORP considers the analysis of resources expended on charitable activities:

'Resources expended on charitable activities should be analysed on the face of the Statement of Financial Activities or in a prominent note to the accounts. The analysis should provide an understanding of the nature of the activities undertaken and the resources expended on their provision. This analysis may, for example, set out the activity cost of the main services provided by the charity, or set out the resources expended on material programmes or projects undertaken by the charity'.

8.24 For those charities providing a combination of direct service provision and grant-making as part of their charitable activities, the total cost of the activity should include the costs incurred directly by the charity together with those costs of providing funding to third parties as part of the grant-making activity. In addition to the costs of activities directly undertaken and the grant funding of activities, each activity, as defined in the Statement of Financial Activities, will include an allocation of support costs. Paragraphs **8.45** to **8.54** below set out the SORP requirements for the treatment of support costs.

8.25 Paragraph 192 of the SORP requires disclosure of the amount of support costs allocated to charitable activities and paragraph 193 the amount of grant-making expenditure by activity type. The SORP suggests that the presentation of these costs in the notes to the accounts could follow the format of the table below:

Activity or Programme	**Activities undertaken directly £**	**Grant funding of activities £**	**Support costs £**	**Total £**
Activity 1				
Activity 2				
Activity 3				
Total				

(Table 5)

The total column on the right hand side should reconcile with the current year's total funds column within the Statement of Financial Activities.

Comment

8.26 For charities which undertake just one core activity, for example a nursing home providing care services, the Statement of Financial Activities may require only one activity heading under charitable activities. The majority

8.27   *Resources expended*

of costs incurred, excluding governance costs and the costs of generating funds, will relate to this one charitable activity.

8.27   In order to provide the reader of the accounts with a clear understanding of the charity's work, it is recommended that the classification of activities within the Statement of Financial Activities is consistent with the discussion of charitable activities within the Trustees' Report. For example, the categorisation may be based on the charitable objectives or the focus of the charity's main programmes and projects.

8.28   Wherever possible, we recommend that the classification of activities is included on the face of the Statement of Financial Activities rather than in the notes to the accounts. This ensures that, simply by reading the primary statements, the reader of the accounts has an understanding of the charity's core activities.

SAVE THE CHILDREN ANNUAL REPORT 2007/08 – STATEMENT OF FINANCIAL ACTIVITIES

Consolidated statement of financial activities

(incorporating an income and expenditure account) for the year ended 31 March 2008

	Notes	Unrestricted funds £000	Restricted funds £000	Total 2008 £000	Total 2007 £000
Incoming resources:					
Incoming resources from generated funds:					
Voluntary income:					
Donations and gifts	2	30,230	27,626	**57,856**	65,302
Legacies	2	15,288	33	**15,321**	13,461
Gifts in kind	5	–	8,602	**8,602**	3,058
Institutional grants	3	6,400	59,042	**65,442**	53,569
Retail income	6	7,639	–	**7,639**	7,101
Investment income	7	2,780	616	**3,396**	3,221
Incoming resources from charitable activities:					
Overseas programme income		535	462	**997**	861
Other income	8	1,421	103	**1,524**	1,858
Total incoming resources		64,293	96,484	**160,777**	148,431
Cost of generating funds:					
Costs of raising voluntary income	9	15,748	355	**16,103**	15,419
Retail costs	6, 9	6,594	–	**6,594**	6,529
Investment management fees	9	148	–	**148**	153
Total cost of generating funds		22,490	355	**22,845**	22,101
Net incoming resources available for charitable applications		41,803	96,129	**137,932**	126,330
Charitable activities					
Promoting children's right to be free from hunger	9	3,311	18,539	**21,850**	11,009
Promoting children's right to protection	9	6,600	14,677	**21,277**	18,801
Promoting children's right to education	9	6,305	23,447	**29,752**	21,485
Promoting children's right to health	9	1,690	13,581	**15,271**	6,570
Tackling HIV and AIDS	9	1,043	2,907	**3,950**	3,962
Safeguarding children in emergencies	9	5,756	20,788	**26,544**	38,728
Tackling child poverty	9	381	1,110	**1,491**	2,473
Promoting children's rights	9	663	491	**1,154**	5,281
Information, campaigning and awareness	9	10,930	365	**11,295**	8,794
Total charitable activities		36,679	95,905	**132,584**	117,103
Governance costs	9	850	–	**850**	691
		37,529	95,905	**133,434**	117,794
Total resources expended		60,019	96,260	**156,279**	139,895
Net incoming resources		4,274	224	**4,498**	8,536
(Losses)/gains on investments	15	(1,067)	148	**(919)**	436
Actuarial losses on defined benefit pension scheme	13	(330)	–	**(330)**	(3,698)
Net movement in funds		2,877	372	**3,249**	5,274
Fund balances brought forward		25,485	31,406	**56,891**	51,617
Fund balances carried forward at 31 March	22	28,362	31,778	**60,140**	56,891

All of the above results are derived from continuing activities. All gains and losses recognised in the year are included above. All restricted funds received and expended relate to income funds.
The surplus for the year for Companies Act purposes, comprising the net incoming resources/(resources expended) for the year plus realised gains on investments, was £4,986,000 (2007: £8,889,000).
The restricted fund balances carried forward include £2,788,000 (2007: £2,640,000), which relate to the endowment funds.
There were no new endowments in this period and the only changes to the funds are investment gains of £148,000 (see note 24).
The accompanying notes are an integral part of this consolidated statement of financial activities.

32

[continued on next page]

154

Save the Children Annual Report, continued

9 Resources expended

	Grants payable £000	Staff costs £000	Other direct costs £000	Depreciation £000	Gifts in kind £000	Allocation of support costs £000	**Total 2008 £000**	Total 2007 £000
Costs of generating funds								
Cost of raising voluntary income	–	4,034	6,350	–	240	5,479	**16,103**	15,419
Retail costs	–	793	4,483	312	–	1,006	**6,594**	6,529
Investment management fees	–	–	128	–	–	20	**148**	153
	–	4,827	10,961	312	240	6,505	**22,845**	22,101
Charitable activities								
Promoting children's right to be free from hunger	1,403	3,489	8,866	1	6,965	1,126	**21,850**	11,009
Promoting children's right to protection	3,393	6,529	10,042	1	217	1,095	**21,277**	18,801
Promoting children's right to education	6,647	7,057	14,440	2	75	1,531	**29,752**	21,485
Promoting children's right to health	1,375	3,731	9,191	1	187	786	**15,271**	6,570
Tackling HIV and AIDS	1,325	914	1,468	–	39	204	**3,950**	3,962
Safeguarding children in emergencies	10,505	5,319	9,078	2	294	1,346	**26,544**	38,729
Tackling child poverty	185	515	590	–	124	77	**1,491**	2,473
Promoting children's rights	40	549	494	–	12	59	**1,154**	5,281
Information, campaigning and awareness	51	4,500	3,799	1	2	2,942	**11,295**	8,794
Support costs	66	7,038	8,342	208	447	(16,101)	**–**	–
	24,990	39,641	66,310	216	8,362	(6,935)	**132,584**	117,103
Governance	–	282	138	–	–	430	**850**	691
Total resources expended	24,990	44,750	77,409	528	8,602	–	**156,279**	139,895
Total resources expended 2007	26,268	42,791	67,083	695	3,058	–	**139,895**	

During the year ended 31 March 2008, Save the Children made grants to partner organisations carrying out work to help children.

A list of grants made is available on the Save the Children website (www.savethechildren.org.uk).

Grants payable to partner organisations are considered to be part of the costs of activities in furtherance of the objects of the charity because much of the charity's programme activity is carried out through grants to local organisations that support long-term, sustainable benefits for a community, which are monitored by the charity. Grants are also made to fund immediate emergency relief provision in times of crisis, catastrophe or natural disaster.

Save the Children's information, campaigning and awareness activities have several key objectives, including:
• informing our supporters and the wider public about the reality of children's lives throughout the world, based on our experience in around 50 countries
• influencing key decision-makers on social and economic policies affecting children, drawing evidence for our advocacy and campaigning work directly from our global programme
• educating children and young people in the UK through initiatives that reflect our programme, which brings global perspectives to the curriculum and youth work by promoting the United Nations Convention on the Rights of the Child.

The Trustees see these initiatives as key activities that further our charitable purposes.

The operational programme is work undertaken overseas by the charity through field offices working through local community groups and other organisations.

40

6 Grant-making

8.29   The Glossary to the SORP (GL29, Appendix 1) defines a grant as follows.

'A grant is any voluntary payment (or other transfer of property) in favour of a person or institution. Grant payments, when made by a charity, are any such voluntary payments made in furtherance of its objects. The payment or transfer may be for the general purposes of the recipient, or for some specific purpose such as the supply of a particular service. It may be unconditional, or be subject to conditions which, if not satisfied by the recipient, may lead to the grant, or property acquired with the aid of the grant, or part of it, being reclaimed.'

It should be noted that any payment which a charity makes in return for the supply of goods or services cannot be a grant.

8.30 *Resources expended*

8.30 Grant-making costs should not just comprise the grants actually made, but also the support costs associated with the activity. The SORP suggests in paragraph 196 that the following support costs will relate to grant-making:

'(a) costs incurred before grants are made (pre-grant costs) as part of the decision making process;

(b) post-grant costs eg monitoring of grants; and

(c) costs of any central or regional office functions such as general management, payroll administration, budgeting and accounting, information technology, human resources, and financing.'

The amount of support costs allocated to grant-making activities should be identified in the notes to the accounts.

8.31 Whether grant-making is the sole activity of the charity or not, an analysis of the grant-making costs, if material, should be provided within the notes to the accounts. The information provided should give the reader a reasonable understanding of the nature of the activities or projects which are being funded and whether the grants are being made to individuals or institutions. For institutional grants, further disclosure should be included regarding the recipient(s) of the funding. The details of the recipients are not required for grants made to individuals.

8.32 An individual grant constitutes a payment to an individual where the individual is the direct beneficiary, such as an educational bursary. All other grants are classed as grants to institutions. The SORP gives the following example:

'... a grant which is made to an individual to carry out a research project should be regarded as a grant to the institution with which the individual is connected rather than as a grant to the individual.'

8.33 Regardless of whether grants are given to individuals or to institutions, the SORP requires an analysis of grant-making activities to be given in the accounts which discloses the total number and the total value of the grants given for different charitable purposes, ie by nature or type of project being supported. The actual classifications used will be left to the specific grant-making charity to decide but could, for example, include social welfare, medical research, the performing arts, etc. Where grant-making is significant, a charity might also decide to provide further analysis, for example, showing a geographical analysis of grants payable. Paragraph 203 of the SORP provides the following as a possible way of disclosing grants:

Analysis	Grants to institutions Total amount £	Grants to individuals Total amount £
Activity or Project 1		
Activity or Project 2		
Activity or Project 3		
Total		

(Table 6)

8.34   The Trustees may decide to provide further details in respect of the grant-making activity within the Trustees' Report or by means of a separate publication. Nonetheless, the Trustees should ensure that the notes to the accounts continue to provide the necessary detail to provide a true and fair view.

Comment

8.35   This definition of what constitutes an institutional grant should encourage greater consistency in disclosure between grant-making charities. However, total consistency is impossible – for example, it is interesting to note the different ways in which grants (or bursaries) towards education costs are classified by different grant-making charities. There are clear arguments for defining such payments as both individual grants and as institutional grants. It is necessary to look into the specific circumstances in which such grants are made before making a final decision on classification.

Grants to institutions

8.36   Paragraphs 206 and 207 of SORP require the following to be disclosed with regard to grants made by a charity to institutions.

'If a charity has made grants to particular institutions that are material in the context of grantmaking, the charity should disclose details, as specified in paragraph 207, of a sufficient number of institutional grants to provide a reasonable understanding of the range of institutions it has supported. This information may be provided either in the notes to the accounts, or as part of the Trustees' Annual Report or by means of a separate publication. Where the analysis is contained in a separate publication, it should be made available by the charity to the public on request. The notes to the accounts should identify the publication and state how copies of it can be obtained.' (para 206)

'The disclosure of institutional grants should give the name of the institution and the total value of grants made to that institution in the accounting year. Where grants have been made to a particular institution to undertake different activities or projects, the total value of the grants made for each activity or purpose should be disclosed. For example, a charity may have made

157

grants to different officers of a particular university for different projects. Such grants should be treated as having been made to the institution.' (para 207)

8.37   The SORP includes provision for non-disclosure of grants to institutions but in very limited circumstances. If grants are material but it is possible that disclosure of the details of one or more of those grants could seriously prejudice the furtherance of the purposes of the recipient or the charity itself, the charity is exempted from disclosing the details of the recipient of the grant. However, the charity is required to undertake the following steps:

- disclose the total number, value and general purpose of those grants for which further disclosure has not been provided;

- write to the charity's regulatory body (eg the Charity Commission) to set out the full details of any grants not disclosed and the reasons for not disclosing them; and

- state in the notes to the accounts whether or not the details have been provided to the charity's regulatory body.

Grants to individuals

8.38   The disclosure requirements with regard to grants made to individuals are less onerous with only the aggregate value and the number of grants needing to be disclosed.

8.39   Further review of the specific disclosure requirements relating to grants payable is contained within Chapter 13 which deals with the notes to the accounts.

Current practice

BBC CHILDREN IN NEED

NOTES TO THE FINANCIAL STATEMENTS
FOR THE YEAR ENDED 30 SEPTEMBER 2007

4 GRANT EXPENDITURE

The grants given to charities and organisations in 2006/2007 fall into the bands detailed below

	No 2007	Amount 2007 £'000	No 2006	Amount 2006 £'000
£1-£1,000	41	32	67	54
£1,001-£5,000	343	1,041	430	1,332
£5,001-£10,000	263	1,991	308	2,273
£10,001-£25,000	309	5,295	320	5,311
£25,001-£100,000	356	18,275	390	20,060
Over £100,000	38	6,338	27	4,063
Total Grant Expenditure	**1,350**	**32,972**	**1,542**	**33,093**

5 SUPPORT, EVALUATION AND TRAINING

A small number of applicant organisations are provided with external consultancy for management support, evaluation or training – this may be as a condition of or instead of grant aid

6 ADJUSTMENTS TO GRANTS GIVEN

An amount of £1,514,577 (2006 £565,360) has been written back to the Statement of Financial Activities This represents adjustments to grants and the full and partial return of grants that have been awarded in the current and the prior year This amount is added back to the total available for distribution

7 OTHER EXPENDITURE

	Governance £'000	Grant Giv- ing Costs £'000	Cost of Generating Income £'000	Investment Manage- ment Fees £'000	2007 Total £'000	2006 Total £'000
Staff Costs	175	1,146	621	-	1,942	1,539
Credit Card and Gift Aid Administration	-	-	62	-	62	77
Computer Systems	-	34	-	-	34	28
Fees and Expenses of External Assessors	-	261	-	-	261	224
Committee and Trustees Expenditure	27	46	-	-	73	56
Fundraising Printing & Publicity	-	10	512	-	522	344
Warehouse and Despatch Costs	-	-	103	-	103	92
Office Costs	38	277	134	-	449	362
Professional Fees	33	-	-	66	99	88
Bank and Credit Card Charges	-	-	16	-	16	13
Children in Need Limited	-	-	139	-	139	203
Total Other Expenditure	**273**	**1,774**	**1,587**	**66**	**3,700**	**3,026**

These Include	Group 2007 £'000	Group 2006 £'000	Charity 2007 £'000	Charity 2006 £'000
Depreciation	32	40	32	40
Operating Leases	23	27	23	27
Reimbursement of Trustees' expenses	14	9	14	9
Auditors remuneration				
Audit of these financial statements	11	9	11	9
Audit of the charity's subsidiaries pursuant to the legislation	3	3	-	-
Legal Fees	22	15	22	15

40

[continued on next page]

159

BBC Children in Need, continued

A selection of Our grants in 06/07

Organisation	Town/City	£
10 LARGEST GRANTS		
Frank Buttle Trust	London	1,750,000
Renfield Centre Children's Fund	Glasgow	344,570
Carers' Association in South Tyneside	South Shields	180,369
African Youth League	Romford	160,633
Asylum Aid	London	145,298
Carers' Federation Ltd	Boston	144,935
Mencap Eden	Penrith	139,223
InterAct	Chelmsford	138,107
Adoption UK	Banbury	137,030
The Nia Project	London	134,109
10 MEDIAN GRANTS		
Shape	London	11,380
Cornerstone Community Care	Glasgow	11,360
Hollybush Centre Ltd	Stoke on Trent	11,300
St Joan of Arc School	Glasgow	11,250
Lambeth Play Association	London	11,233
Mencap & Gateway Sheffield	Sheffield	11,209
Womens Aid Aberconwy	Llandudno	11,209
Manor Street Cliftonville Community Group	Belfast	11,200
West Alness Residents Association	Alness	11,180
Criw Niwbwrch Cyf	Newborough	11,026
10 SMALLEST GRANTS		
Woodside Parish Church Starter Pack Group	Aberdeen	600
Glencolin Residents Assn	Belfast	500
Fauldhouse Pre School Playgroup	Bathgate	475
Girl Guides Rainbows 119th Joanmount Methodist	Belfast	450
Football Club Loughside	Belfast	400
Football Club Upper Ardoyne Juniors	Belfast	400
Extreme Youth	Carrickfergus	386
Boys Brigade 93rd Belfast Company	Belfast	350
Stepping Stones (North Edinburgh)	Edinburgh	350
South Holland User Group (shug)	Spalding	200

A full list of our grants is printed in this year's Grant Report, which
is available to download from our website bbc.co.uk/pudsey

48

8.40   The requirements with regard to grant disclosure continue to cause
some disquiet in the charity world. However, the detailed disclosure does provide a means of controlling the situation where donations from the public are
passed from one grant-making body to another, gradually being eroded before
being passed over to the ultimate beneficiary.

7   Governance costs

8.41   The Glossary to the SORP (GL28, Appendix 1) includes the following definition of governance costs:

'These are the costs associated with the governance arrangements of the charity which relate to the general running of the charity as opposed to those costs associated with fundraising or charitable activity. The costs will normally include internal and external audit, legal advice for trustees and costs associated with constitutional and statutory requirements eg the cost of trustee meetings and preparing statutory accounts. Included within this category are any costs associated with the strategic as opposed to day to day management of the charity's activities.'

8.42   As noted within **8.4** above, paragraphs 210 and 211 of the SORP provide further expansion on this definition.

8.43   The notes to the accounts should provide an analysis of the main items of expenditure included within governance costs and the accounting policies should explain the nature of the costs allocated to governance.

Comment

8.44   The Charity Finance Directors' Group's (CFDG) consultation exercise concluded that the analysis of management and administration costs by different charities was extremely inconsistent. This resulted in the move from 'management and administration costs' in the previous SORP to 'governance costs' in SORP 2005. The governance costs definition is much more specific than that for management and administration costs. To date, this appears to have resulted in a greater degree of consistency between charities: the proportion of governance costs to total costs does not tend to fluctuate significantly if the SORP guidance is adhered to.

MACMILLAN CANCER RELIEF ANNUAL REPORT AND ACCOUNTS 2007

Analysis of governance costs	2007 £'000	2006 £'000
Staff costs	352	321
External audit fees	56	49
Board and Council meeting expenses	14	13
AGM costs	9	77
Legal and other costs	176	203
	607	663

---

8   Support costs

8.45   Paragraphs 164 and 165 of the SORP reflect that, whilst support costs enable a charity to deliver its objectives, they do not constitute a specific activity and should be, therefore, allocated to the activity headings. Support costs comprise those core costs and overheads which cannot be directly attributed to specific headings within the Statement of Financial Activities.

161

'In undertaking any activity there may be support costs incurred that, whilst necessary to deliver an activity, do not themselves produce or constitute the output of the charitable activity. Similarly, costs will be incurred in supporting income generation activities such as fundraising, and in supporting the governance of the charity. Support costs include the central or regional office functions such as general management, payroll administration, budgeting and accounting, information technology, human resources, and financing.'
(para 164)

'Support costs do not, in themselves, constitute an activity, instead they enable output-creating activities to be undertaken. Support costs are therefore allocated to the relevant activity cost category they support on the bases set out in paragraphs 168 to 174. This enables the total cost of an activity category to be disclosed in the Statement of Financial Activities and for the cost of the constituent sub-activities to be presented at a service, programme or project level within the notes to the accounts. There is nevertheless legitimate user interest in both the level of support costs incurred and the policies adopted for their allocation to the relevant activity cost categories that should be addressed through relevant note disclosures.'
(para 165)

8.46   The SORP requires the disclosure of the total support costs incurred by the charity together with a breakdown of the material items or categories of expenditure included within support costs. Furthermore, if support costs are material, the notes to the accounts should provide an explanation of how the costs have been allocated to each of the activity cost categories in the Statement of Financial Activities. The explanation may show percentages or the absolute value of amounts allocated, details of the methods of apportionment or a table setting out this information. Paragraph 167 of the SORP provides an example table for such disclosure:

Support cost (examples)	Fund-raising	Activity 1	Activity 2	Activity 3	Activity 4	Activity 5	Basis of allocation
Management	£X	£X	£X	£X	£X	£X	Text describing method
Finance	£X	£X	£X	£X	£X	£X	Text describing method
Information technology	£X	£X	£X	£X	£X	£X	Text describing method
Human resources	£X	£X	£X	£X	£X	£X	Text describing method
Total	£X	£X	£X	£X	£X	£X	

(Table 4)

MACMILLAN CANCER RELIEF

Notes to the financial statements
For the year ended 31 December 2007

6 Expenditure	Grants £'000	Direct staff costs £'000	Other direct costs £'000	Apportioned support costs £'000	2007 £'000	2006 £'000
Source of support (Note 7)	51,888	6,276	3,096	3,028	**64,288**	55,457
Force for change (Note 7)	3,464	1,497	8,020	1,582	**14,563**	10,268
Governance (Note 7)	–	353	119	135	**607**	663
Total charitable expenditure	55,352	8,126	11,235	4,745	**79,458**	66,388
Cost of generating voluntary and legacy income	–	9,288	13,347	7,882	**30,517**	29,709
Merchandising costs	–	–	687	–	**687**	754
Investment management fees	–	–	222	–	**222**	215
Total expenditure	55,352	17,414	25,491	12,627	**110,884**	97,066

Other direct costs associated with generating voluntary income include direct event costs, travel and accommodation for fundraisers, rent and rates and office costs for regional fundraising offices.

Analysis of apportioned support costs	Human Resources & Facilities £'000	IT £'000	Finance, Legal & Secretarial £'000	Policy & Communications £'000	2007 £'000	2006 £'000
Source of support	1,386	549	461	632	**3,028**	3,826
Force for change	724	287	241	330	**1,582**	1,130
Governance	62	24	21	28	**135**	155
Cost of generating voluntary and legacy income	3,608	1,429	1,200	1,645	**7,882**	7,239
	5,780	2,289	1,923	2,635	**12,627**	12,350

Support costs, including staff costs, were apportioned to activities on the basis of headcount in each of the departments supporting the various activities.

Allocation of costs

8.47   In apportioning costs to activity headings in the Statement of Financial Activities, the SORP requires the following steps to be followed:

(i)   Allocate any direct costs to the relevant activity cost category, including the generating funds and governance activities;

(ii)   For those items of expenditure which contribute directly to more than one cost category, such as a staff member who works on both fundraising and a charitable project, allocate the costs to the relevant headings. The basis of doing so should be reasonable, justifiable and consistent. For example, for staffing resources, the completion of staff timesheets will enable a relatively straightforward allocation of salary costs.

(iii)   Allocate depreciation, amortisation, impairment or losses on the disposal of fixed assets on the basis set out above.

(iv)   The remaining support costs will not be attributable to a single activity and should be apportioned to the activity cost categories on a basis that is reasonable, justifiable and consistent.

8.48   The basis of apportionment of support costs under (iv) above can be performed using a number of different bases. The basis used for a specific cost category should be appropriate to the cost concerned and to the charity's particular circumstances. For example, the human resources department is likely to spend more time on those activities/projects which employ a greater number of staff members. An appropriate basis for apportionment of the human resources department costs would, therefore, be the number of staff members employed by each activity.

8.49   The SORP gives the following examples for bases for cost apportionment:

- Usage – for example, the same basis as expenditure incurred directly in undertaking an activity.

- Per capita – the number of people employed within an activity.

- On the basis of floor area occupied by an activity. For example, this basis of apportionment is likely to be appropriate for premises costs – the greater the amount of office space a specific activity occupies, the higher proportion of premises costs would be charged to that activity.

- On the basis of time, for example where staff duties are multi-activity.

8.50   When allocating costs to specific activity headings in the Statement of Financial Activities, a problem often arises when differentiating between the costs of generating funds and charitable activities for fundraising promotions. For example, information about the aims, objectives and projects of a charity is regularly provided by charities in the context of mail shots, websites, collections and telephone fundraising. The question needs to be asked whether this constitutes a multi-purpose activity and therefore there is a need to apportion costs. The SORP draws the following distinction:

(i)   Publicity or information costs incurred in raising the profile of a charity which is associated with fundraising should be classed as costs of generating funds;

(ii) Publicity or information that is provided in an educational manner in furtherance of the charity's objectives will be classed as expenditure on charitable activities.

8.51   In order for the information supplied to meet the educational criteria, (ii) above, the following must apply:

- the information is targeted at beneficiaries or others who can use the information to further the charity's objectives; and

- the recipient can act upon the information in an informed manner to further the charity's objectives; and

- the information is related to other educational activities or objectives undertaken by the charity.

If the information supplied does not meet the above criteria, the fundraising activity should be treated as targeting potential donors and is wholly related to the cost of generating funds.

8.52　An example of a charity providing joint fundraising and charitable activities would be as follows: A health education charity that supplies documentation to high-risk beneficiary groups and the medical profession which incorporates information on health risks, symptom recognition and advising on steps that can be taken. The information would meet the criteria in **8.51** above as it is targeted at beneficiaries, advises in steps to be taken and is likely to link to the charity's activities or objectives in health education. Hence, if such information is provided during a fundraising promotion, the costs should be apportioned between the cost of generating funds and charitable activities.

Comment

8.53　The method of support cost allocation which has been introduced in the current SORP results in greater transparency of activity based costs and links in with the charity sector's efforts to establish full cost recovery when negotiating contract and grant funding.

8.54　The approach used for cost allocation should be reliable, justifiable and consistent year on year. However, charities should ensure that the methodology used to allocate costs is not overly cumbersome and time consuming. The benefits of achieving a greater degree of accuracy may only be possible at a high incremental cost to the charity.

INTERNATIONAL RESCUE COMMITTEE UK ANNUAL REPORT AND FINANCIAL STATEMENTS 30 SEPTEMBER 2007

4a　Support costs

Support Costs include the costs of general administration and management (both staff and other costs) and have been allocated variously to the Cost of Generating Funds, Charitable Activities and Governance Costs on the basis of the proportion of dedicated staff time attributable to those categories. The support costs charged to the category of Charitable Activities have been allocated to activities within that category on the basis of staff time where appropriate and otherwise on the basis of the proportional value of direct expenditure incurred on those activities during the year.

Total support costs arising including the Cost of Generating Funds (Note 3) and Governance Costs (Note 5) are as follows:

	Total 2007 £'000	Total 2006 £'000
Cost of generating funds	30	36
Charitable Activities	509	382
Governance costs	19	21
Total Support Costs	**558**	439

The increase in support costs reflect in the main the increase in Technical Unit staff numbers during the year (see note 7).

165

9   Accounting for contractual arrangements and grants payable

8.55   In **8.7** to **8.9** we considered the basic principles for the recognition of expenditure. The SORP includes further guidance in paragraphs 150 to 160 on the differences between expenditure under contractual arrangements and grants payable.

Contractual arrangements

8.56   Many activities entered into by a charity will constitute a contract for the supply of goods or services, for example the provision of the electricity supply to the charity's offices or the employment of a staff member under a contract. The expenditure relating to that contract will be recognised in the charity's accounts at the point at which the supplier of the goods or services has performed their part of the contract. For example, when the electricity has been supplied to the charity, a charge should be made in the accounts (say, at the end of each month) to reflect the consumption of electricity even if an invoice has not yet been received or the payment has not yet been made. Similarly, staff costs should be recognised in line with the work undertaken and time spent on the charity's activities.

8.57   Within chapter 7 the notion of performance related grants was introduced for charities which receive grants that are similar in nature to contracts, for example, the income received by the charity under the terms of the grant is based upon specific outputs or milestones being achieved. Paragraph 151 of the SORP considers performance related grants from the point of view of the grant-maker. This would mean that the terms of the grant may be set out in a service level agreement which includes conditions for payment linked to performance by the recipient. The SORP states that expenditure on performance related grants should be recognised as resources expended to the extent that the recipient has provided the specified outputs or services.

8.58   In reality, this may be extremely difficult to measure if the charity provides performance related grants to a number of organisations. Reporting from the recipient to the grant-making charity at the specific year end would require a considerable level of detail in order to ascertain the extent of the service delivery to date.

Grants payable and constructive obligations

8.59   Grants payable exclude all performance related grants and contractual arrangements. Unlike for performance related grants and contractual arrangements, an exchange for consideration does not arise with a grant payment. The expenditure is incurred to further the charity's objects but does not create a contractual relationship with the recipient of the grant or the charity's beneficiaries. However, despite there being no legal contract, the charity still may need to reflect an obligation (liability) within its accounting records.

8.60   A liability will arise in relation to grants payable when a constructive obligation exists. A constructive obligation occurs when events have created a valid expectation in other parties that the charity will discharge its obligations. For example, communication of a grant commitment to the recipient would be evidence that a valid expectation has been created.

8.61   An internal grant approval by the trustees of a charity does not give rise to a constructive obligation as this does not involve a commitment to a third party. Only if the decision to provide grant funding has been communicated to the recipient prior to the balance sheet date, will a valid expectation have been created and a liability for the grant commitment should be included in the accounts. Furthermore, general or policy statements regarding future charitable giving or plans do not create a constructive obligation as discretion is retained by the charity as to their implementation.

8.62   In summary, paragraph 157 of the SORP concludes that a constructive obligation is likely to arise when:

'(a) a specific commitment, or promise to provide goods, services or grant funding is given, and (b) this is communicated directly to a beneficiary or grant recipient.'

8.63   Consideration also needs to be given to conditions which are attached to the grant. If a charity enters into grant commitments that are dependent upon specific conditions being met, for example, that the recipient charity has to obtain planning permission for a particular building project prior to the grant being paid, the liability, and the related grant expenditure, should only be recognised when the conditions fall outside the control of the giving charity. In the example of planning permission being obtained by the recipient charity, this falls outside the control of the grant-making charity and thus, should be recognised as a liability and expenditure in the accounts. In contrast, if the grant-making charity retains the discretion to avoid the future grant expenditure, ie the conditions set remain within the control of the giving charity, the liability should not be recognised.

8.64   This guidance can be applied to multi-year grant commitments. For example, a charity makes a commitment to grant fund a project for three years. There are two possible scenarios:

(i)   The grant is conditional on an annual review of progress that determines whether future funding is provided and discretion is retained by the giving charity to terminate the grant. Providing the discretion retained by the charity has substance (for example, evidence is available from past review practice), this amounts to a condition which is within the giving charity's control and the liability arises only for the first year of the funding commitment.

(ii)   If there is no condition attached to the grant that enables the giving charity to realistically avoid the commitment, the liability for the full three years of the funding should be recognised.

167

8.65   In scenario (i) above, if the annual review process is determined not to have substance, ie it is not in practice used to determine whether future funding is provided in subsequent years, the review stipulation is not classed as a condition and the liability for the full three years should be recognised.

8.66   Charities should be wary of multi-year grant commitments if they are reliant upon the later grant commitments being funded by future income. If the conditions for payment of the grant are outside the charity's control, the total liability required in the accounts may be greater than the reserves level at the point at which the commitment is made. This could potentially lead to solvency issues for the charity.

10   VAT

Current practice

8.67   The majority of charities follow the principle of including irrecoverable VAT with the expenditure to which it relates. This has not necessarily arisen as a positive decision on an accounting policy, but probably because it simplifies the bookkeeping entries.

THE TRUST OF ST BENEDICT'S ABBEY, EALING – 31 AUGUST 2007 – EXTRACT FROM ACCOUNTING POLICIES

'Expenditure is included in the statement of financial activities when incurred and includes any attributable VAT which cannot be recovered.'

8.68   Some charities, however, particularly those in the anomalous position of having to pay VAT while similar state-run operations are able to reclaim it, extract VAT, show the expenditure net and group all the VAT borne as a separate charge disclosed separately under both 'the costs of generating funds' and 'charitable activities' as appropriate.

8.69   Other charities calculate the total sum of irrecoverable VAT paid by them and show this as a separate note in their accounts.

Comment

8.70   The trustees of a charity have a responsibility to the public to inform them of wasteful government burdens such as VAT suffered by their charity and we applaud those who disclose this amount in their accounts.

8.71   There are two preferred methods of disclosing the amounts involved:

(i)   to calculate the total VAT that is irrecoverable and to disclose this in a separate note to the accounts; and

(ii)   to calculate the total VAT irrecoverable on each of the classifications of expenditure to disclose these amounts in the appropriate notes to the accounts supporting each class of expenditure.

Chapter 9

Balance sheet presentation

1 Guidelines

9.1 Paragraphs 244–251 of the SORP, together with the illustrative Table 7, set out the basic requirements relating to the balance sheet of a charity. The 'balance' that is demonstrated by a charity is significantly different from that set out by a commercial business. Whereas the latter is seeking to show how the assets and liabilities of the business represent balances due to its owners (as capital and accumulated profit) or other financiers, a charity has no 'external' interests and so all of its possessions, net of its debts, are held for the benefit of its charitable purposes.

9.2 The purpose of the balance sheet of a charity, para 245 tells us, is to provide information about the 'resources available to the charity' and the degree to which these are legally restricted or free for general use. The balance sheet 'may also show which resources the trustees have designated for specific future use'.

9.3 The format of the balance sheet of a charity is both familiar and conventional, albeit the concept of equity interests does not apply to the funds held. Table 7 sets out the expected format of the balance sheet and usefully cross refers the headings used to the paragraphs in the text which give guidance on each in turn. Whilst the categorisation of assets and liabilities is fixed, the order in which fund categories are presented may be varied 'to accommodate an individual charity's presentational preference' (para 247).

TABLE 7. BALANCE SHEET

		Total Funds £	Prior Years Funds £	Reference
A	**Fixed Assets:**			
A1	Intangible assets			
A2	Tangible assets			252
A3	Heritage assets			253 to 278

[continued on next page]

Table 7. Balance Sheet, continued

		Total Funds £	Prior Years Funds £	Reference
A4	Investments:			
A4a	Investments			295 to 307
A4b	Programme related investments			308 to 312
	Total fixed assets			
B	**Current assets:**			
B1	Stocks and work-in-progress			313 to 316
B2	Debtors			314
B3	Investments			316
B4	Cash at bank and in hand			
	Total current assets			
C	**Liabilities:**			
C1	Creditors: Amounts falling due within one year			317 to 320
	Net current assets or liabilities			
	Total assets less current liabilities			
C2	Creditors: Amounts falling due after more than one year			317 to 320
C3	Provisions for liabilities and charges			321 to 329
	Net asset or liabilities excluding pension asset or liability			
D	Defined benefit pension scheme asset or liability			330 to 332
	Net assets or liabilities including pension asset or liability			
E	The funds of the charity:			
E1	Endowment funds			
E2	Restricted income funds			
E3	Unrestricted income funds			
E3a	Share capital			333
E3b	Unrestricted income funds			
E3c	Revaluation reserve			334
	Unrestricted income funds excluding pension asset/liability			
E3d	Pension reserve			335
	Total unrestricted funds			
	Total charity funds			

9.4   The main functions of the balance sheet in summarising information as a primary statement for a user of the accounts are to:

- group together the funds of the charity according to their kind, ie restricted – further analysed between income funds and endowments – and unrestricted – separately identifying any designated funds;

- analyse the assets between fixed and current categorising fixed assets between intangible fixed assets, tangible fixed assets and investments; and

- analyse the liabilities between current and long-term liabilities.

9.5   As emphasised in previous chapters, a charity's finances cannot generally be interpreted in isolation. A proper understanding of the purposes for which assets are held and liabilities incurred, and of why surplus resources may be generated and held over, or consciously run down, over periods of time can only be obtained through an appreciation of the aims, activities and ongoing strategies of the charity. In particular, para 245 concludes:

> 'It will normally be necessary to read the reserves policy and plans for the future in the Trustees' Annual Report (see paragraphs 55(a) and 57) to gain a fuller understanding of the availability and planned use of the charity's funds.'

9.6   Paragraph 249 requires that further details be given in the balance sheet or the notes to the accounts that enable the reader to gain a proper appreciation of the spread and character of the assets and liabilities. The specific example cited is the requirement to make disclosures regarding debtors recoverable after more than one year; however, the general principle is that all balance sheet items should be analysed over component parts where this is useful. Charities which are companies should follow the standard analyses of debtors, creditors etc set out in company law; those which are not may use a categorisation which fits their own circumstances.

9.7   An important additional requirement is the need to provide a statement showing the division of the assets and liabilities between the main funds of the charity. This can be done either through use of the columnar format, as a separate financial statement, or as a note.

9.8   Here we have presented one example of each presentation. The columnar presentation has not been widely adopted, but readers can see that while the two approaches are effectively equivalent, it is significantly more difficult to ensure an accurate analysis at each line of the balance sheet and the separate note presentation allows a more summarised assessment to be made.

BRITISH RED CROSS

Consolidated balance sheet for the year ended 31 December 2007

	Notes	Unrestricted £000	Restricted £000	2007 Total £000	2006 Total £000
Fixed assets					
Tangible assets	10	53,470	7,025	**60,495**	54,052
Investments	11	47,667	17,729	**65,396**	61,105
		101,137	24,754	**125,891**	115,157
Current Assets					
Stocks		1,350	730	**2,080**	4,822
Debtors	12	11,966	5,281	**17,247**	22,657
Investments	11	6,090	28,757	**34,847**	33,803
Cash at bank and in hand		5,233	5,149	**10,382**	7,048
		24,639	39,917	**64,556**	68,330
Creditors: Amounts falling due within one year	13	(13,471)	(6,153)	**(19,624)**	(12,413)
Net Current Assets		11,168	33,764	**44,932**	55,917
Total assets less current liabilities		112,305	58,518	**170,823**	171,074
Creditors:					
Amounts falling due in more than one year	14		(275)	**(275)**	(275)
Provision for Liabilities and Charges	15	(2,067)	(17,457)	**(19,524)**	(29,161)
Net assets before pension scheme deficit		110,238	40,786	**151,024**	141,638
Defined benefit pension scheme deficit	17	(742)	—	**(742)**	(484)
Net assets	9	109,496	40,786	**150,282**	141,154
Represented by:					
Funds excluding pension scheme deficit		110,238	40,786	**151,024**	141,638
Pension scheme deficit		(742)	—	**(742)**	(484)
Accumulated Funds		109,496	40,786	**150,282**	141,154

The British Red Cross has not prepared a separate balance sheet for the charity as this is not considered to be materially different to the consolidated balance sheet.

MARIE CURIE CANCER CARE

Extract from note 15 to the accounts for the year ended 31 March 2009

The analysis of consolidated net assets between funds was as follows:

	Consolidated Unrestricted funds £'000	Consolidated Restricted funds £'000	Consolidated Total 2009 £'000	Consolidated Total 2008 £'000
Tangible fixed assets	23,491	10,655	34,146	26,452
Investments	71,234	–	71,234	65,560
Stocks	605	–	605	412
Debtors	7,241	–	7,241	6,120
Creditors and cash	(17,106)	167	(16,939)	(5,634)
Defined benefit pension scheme asset/(liability)	(4,200)	–	(4,200)	130
	81,265	10,822	92,087	93,040

	Charity Unrestricted funds £'000	Charity Restricted funds £'000	Charity Total 2009 £'000	Charity Total 2008 £'000
Tangible fixed assets	24,569	10,655	35,224	27,132
Fixed asset investments	71,961	–	71,961	66,287
Stocks	117	–	117	84
Debtors	7,087	–	7,087	7,133
Creditors and cash	(17,119)	167	(16,952)	(6,997)
Defined benefit pension scheme liability	(4,200)	–	(4,200)	130
	82,415	10,822	93,237	93,769

Comment

9.9   What the description of the balance sheet's purpose in para 245 does not bring to a reader's attention is that the assets and liabilities may be recorded using a variety of measurement principles, including historic cost (which may be a very dated indication of their value), market valuation or some approximation of current cost or 'fair values' – which may or may not be discounted to reflect the 'time value of money' – and that some items will be reduced by depreciation or impairment charges or may even be omitted entirely from the balance sheet (though the preceding paragraph does deal with this final point).

9.10   This potential for 'comparing apples and pears' should be borne in mind before setting out to use the balance sheet as a source of information about value – though the key information that many users will be seeking will relate to current assets and liabilities and these will (usually) be reflected at values realisable or to be settled as money.

2   Grouping of funds

9.11   Paragraph 247 of SORP recommends that the balance sheet should:

'distinguish, as a minimum, between, the total funds held as unrestricted income funds, restricted income funds and as endowment funds. Distinctions between funds held as permanent and expendable endowment and held as designated funds can also be made.'

9.12 The principles of fund accounting are dealt with in paras 65 to 76. Paragraphs 74 to 76 deal with the requirements to provide information that reconciles the opening and closing balances on each fund or category of funds (the degree of aggregation will depend upon the number and homogeneity of the funds held) using information that can be traced in total to both the balance sheet and the statement of financial activities.

9.13 Summarising paragraph 75, the key requirements are:

'the notes to the accounts should provide information on the structure of the charity's funds so as to disclose the fund balances and the reasons for them, … in particular:

(a) the assets and liabilities representing each type of fund of the charity should be clearly summarised and analysed …;

(b) disclosure of how each of the funds has arisen (including designated funds), the restrictions imposed and the purpose of each fund …;

(c) any funds in deficit should always be separately disclosed …;

(d) material transfers between different funds and allocations to designated funds should be separately disclosed …;

(e) where, in relation to permanent endowment, a total return approach to investments has been adopted, the notes to the accounts should give particulars …'

Comment

9.14 Although the fund structure of the charity may be complex, the balance sheet should be simple, showing only the year end balances of the main funds or groups of funds. These should be set out in a logical sequence, for example beginning with the restricted funds, then the designated funds, and finally the balance on the unallocated unrestricted funds (often referred to as the 'general' fund). Alternatively, it may be more appropriate to begin with 'Long-term Funds', both restricted and unrestricted to show the amount tied up in property and endowment and move down to 'Revenue Funds' set aside for short-term and general purposes. Care needs to be taken when using 'capital' as a description of a fund or group of funds as the Charities Act uses 'capital' to mean endowment. It would usually be preferable to use a more specific term to avoid potential confusion.

9.15 There is a specific requirement to disclose funds in deficit and explain the nature of the deficit. Generally speaking, a deficit balance on any fund is a serious matter which the trustees must be able to demonstrate an intention to reverse. Paragraph 251 of SORP requires that where deficit balances are material these should be separately disclosed on the face of the balance sheet.

9.16 In relation to the three main categories of income fund the following considerations apply.

- Deficits cannot generally arise on restricted funds as the creation of the restriction relates to specific receipts. Where spending on a project or contract funded by a restricted source exceeds the funding received, the excess should be charged against unrestricted funds. Exceptions will arise, for example in situations where funding is received in arrears and the trustees consider that the expenditure of funds is not wholly sufficient grounds for recognising the income, or where spending is undertaken in anticipation of specific appeal receipts.

- It is not logical to show a deficit balance on a designated fund as these are by definition general funds set aside by the trustees and can not be created where there are no funds to designate – para 75(c) of SORP states clearly 'Designated funds should never be in deficit'. Equally, it is not usually sensible to make designations of funds where this will leave general funds in deficit although there may be compelling reasons to make exceptions, for example commitments to future expenditure which would be difficult but not impossible to reverse – demonstrating a need to generate surpluses on general activities in future periods if plans are to be realised.

- Where the general funds of the charity are in deficit, careful consideration of the application of the going concern principle is required and further disclosures may be necessary regarding this.

9.17   The most common form of fund in deficit is a restricted fund where expenditure is reimbursed in arrears or is paid out in anticipation of specific fundraising receipts. This is anticipated in SORP paragraph 251 and paragraph 4(b) of Appendix 3 to the SORP, which states the following.

> 'Expenditure may be charged to a restricted fund which is not at the time in credit, or not in sufficient credit, where there is a genuine anticipation of receipts which can properly be credited to the fund in order to meet the expenditure (eg where a decision has been taken to invite donations for that fund).'

The example given below from the Annual Report and Accounts of Oxfam for the year ended 30 April 2008 illustrates how this may be disclosed.

OXFAM – ACCOUNTS FOR THE YEAR ENDED 30 APRIL 2008

18 Restricted funds

Oxfam and Oxfam Group

	At 1 May 2007 £m	Income £m	Expenditure £m	At 30 April 2008 £m
REGIONAL FUNDS				
CAMEXCA	1.2	7.7	(6.5)	2.4
HECA	2.2	27.8	(27.2)	2.8

[*continued on next page*]

OXFAM, continued

Oxfam and Oxfam Group

	At 1 May 2007 £m	Income £m	Expenditure £m	At 30 April 2008 £m
West Africa	(0.1)	8.4	(6.9)	1.4
Humanitarian	0.3	1.4	(1.3)	0.4
MEEECIS	1.1	5.3	(3.7)	2.7
Southern Africa	1.8	8.8	(8.4)	2.2
South Asia	2.4	16.7	(15.0)	4.1
UKPP	—	0.4	(0.3)	0.1
South America	1.1	3.3	(4.0)	0.4
East Asia	(0.6)	16.6	(15.5)	0.5
Goods in Kind	—	8.6	(8.6)	—
Oxfam Unwrapped	7.5	8.9	(11.7)	4.7
Other Funds	0.5	1.4	(1.5)	0.4
DFID – Partnership Programme Agreement	0.1	10.4	(10.1)	0.4
APPEALS				
Asian Tsunami	1.9	0.2	(0.6)	1.5
Darfur/Chad	1.2	1.5	(1.8)	0.9
South Asia Earthquake	1.8	—	(0.9)	0.9
South Asia Floods	—	1.4	(1.4)	—
Bangladesh Cyclone	—	1.5	(1.0)	0.5
Other Appeal Funds	2.1	0.5	(1.5)	1.1
	24.5	130.8	(127.9)	27.4

The income and expenditure on the appeals below can be found within both the Appeals and Regional Funds sections as shown above.

9.18   The analysis of funds in the balance sheet can be used to highlight the free reserves of the charity. It is now common practice for charities to separately identify unrestricted funds representing fixed assets which could not be liquidated easily without detriment to charitable activity. These are identified as not available for general purposes, together with designated and restricted funds. The remaining fund balances, broadly speaking the net current assets and treasury investment assets of unrestricted funds, are the free reserves over which the trustees are obliged to exercise a policy and make a statement in their Annual Report.

9.19   With the help of the notes explaining the purpose of each fund within each group and the movement of each since the previous year end, the reader is in a position to appreciate the overall deployment of the assets and liabilities of the charity.

9.20   The following extracts from the accounts of Norwood for the year ended 31 March 2008 illustrate a number of points arising from fund accounting. The relationship between the parent charity and group figures receives additional explanation. The treatment of designated funds in the reserves policy reflects the opinion of Norwood's trustees that whilst they believe designation of the funds is necessary, it is recognised that additional general funds will need to be generated to enable the planned expenditure to occur.

9.21   Although the disclosures are potentially convoluted it is possible to summarise the funds of a charity (see the Oxfam and Marie Curie Cancer Care examples above) succinctly. In Norwood's case, as with many other charities, there are sensitivities that the trustees must balance – ensuring that acknowledgement and thanks are given in the accounts may take precedence over brevity.

NORWOOD RAVENSWOOD 2008

Reserves Policy

Approximately two thirds of our operating income comes from the government, mostly through Local Authority contracts for care services. In the event that those contracts ceased and the income stopped, we would also stop providing the care services thereby reducing costs. Because of this, Norwood does not need to hold financial reserves against the risk that those contracts might cease. Norwood only recovers approximately 85% of the cost of providing those care services.

The remaining one third of Norwood's income comes from voluntary donations and a reduction in this income would directly affect our ability to provide our services. The trustees consider that financial reserves need to be held to allow sufficient time to reduce expenditure and identify alternative funding. The trustees have therefore set a reserves policy which recognises this risk and they seek to hold reserves which would cover a 25% reduction in voluntary income for one year. Based on the year ended 31 March 2008 this would amount to £2.2m.

In considering the risk adjusted reduction in voluntary income, the trustees consider each major source and the likelihood that this might rise, fall or remain stable.

In considering the financial reserves available, the trustees recognise that most of the unrestricted funds are used to finance tangible fixed assets which Norwood uses to provide its services. Although these assets could be sold to release cash, this would take time and the trustees have therefore excluded the tangible fixed assets from the calculations of available financial reserves. The trustees have therefore used unrestricted and designated balance sheet net current assets as the basis for considering the financial reserves available.

[continued on next page]

Norwood Ravenswood, continued

At 31 March 2008 the Group had unrestricted balance sheet net current liabilities of £1.4m and designated balance sheet net current assets of £4.8m. In the event that the reserves were required, the designated funds could be undesignated. The net unrestricted and designated balance sheet net current assets of £3.4m were in excess of the £2.2m target.

The expected timescale for the utilisation of the designated funds is shown in note 12.

12 Funds (Group)

	1 April 2007 £'000	Incoming Resources £'000	Outgoing Resources £'000	Transfers between funds £'000	Investment gains and losses £'000	31 March 2008 £'000
(a) Unrestricted Funds						
Designated funds						
Bike Ride	55	—	—	—	—	55
Dilapidations	150	—	—	—	—	150
Home From Home	1,446	—	—	—	—	1,446
Louise Appeal	104	—	—	—	—	104
New School	—	—	—	1,220	—	1,220
Pamela Barnett Centre	1,000	—	—	—	—	1,000
Properties Improvement	300	—	—	—	—	300
Tager Autistic Centre	546	—	—	—	—	546
Total designated funds	3,601	—	—	1,220	—	4,821
General funds	12,904	35,335	(34,599)	2,744	(12)	16,372
Total unrestricted funds	16,505	35,335	(34,599)	3,964	(12)	21,193
(b) Endowment Funds						
Endowment fund for Jewish Children	205	—	—	—	(13)	192
Ernst and Dola Fischer fund	320	—	—	5	(15)	310
Somers Fund	953	—	—	(11)	18	960
	1,478	—	—	(6)	(10)	1,462
(c) Other restricted funds						
Adult learning disability services	—	1,225	—	—	—	1,225

[continued on next page]

179

Norwood Ravenswood, continued

	1 April 2007 £'000	Incoming Resources £'000	Outgoing Resources £'000	Transfers between funds £'000	Investment gains and losses £'000	31 March 2008 £'000
Bearsted/Surestart project	45	—	(5)	—	—	40
Binoh	102	125	(80)	—	—	147
Harper Collins	124	—	—	—	—	124
Horinsky Overseas Holiday	94	—	—	—	—	94
JAPH	61	—	(5)	—	—	56
Kennedy Leigh Nursery	—	102	—	(86)	—	16
Lira Abeleva	106	24	(24)	—	—	106
New School	6,415	368	(33)	—	—	6,750
Norwood Home for Jewish Children	8,253	138	(138)	—	(280)	7,973
Pamela Barnett Centre	501	851	—	(1,177)	—	175
Peripatetic Outreach	59	—	(19)	—	—	40
Ravenswood Building	235	—	—	(235)	—	—
Redbridge Autistic	35	—	—	—	—	35
Tager Autistic Centre	1,561	706	—	(1,175)	—	1,092
Young People's Focus Group	—	47	(13)	—	—	34
Other funds valued under £50,000	437	177	(99)	(65)	—	450
Total other restricted funds	18,028	3,763	(416)	(2,738)	(280)	18,357
(d) Restricted property fund	2,479	—	—	(1,220)	—	1,259
(e) Total restricted funds	20,507	3,763	(416)	(3,958)	(280)	19,616
Total Funds	38,490	39,098	(35,015)	—	(302)	42,271

12 Funds (Group and parent charity)

Transfer between funds

The transfers from other restricted funds to unrestricted general funds relate to fulfilment of restrictions by capital expenditure during the year from those restricted funds. The transfer from the restricted property fund to the unrestricted designated funds relates to fulfilment of restrictions by the disposal of property assets no longer required for future capital projects.

[*continued on next page*]

Norwood Ravenswood, continued

Designated Funds

The trustees have designated funds to be used for specific purposes. A substantial amount of these funds will be used during the year ending 31 March 2009. The New School fund will be used by September 2010. Where the trustees conclude that these funds are no longer required, they will be undesignated and returned to unrestricted general funds.

Bike Ride

Designated for supporting bike riders during events and recreational activities for learning disabled residents.

Home from Home

Designated for the refurbishment of old homes, and the provision of new homes in London.

Louise Appeal

Designated for supplying a home at Ravenswood.

Pamela Barnett and Tager Autistic Centres

Designated for two new homes under construction at Ravenswood for people with profound multiple learning disabilities and autism.

Properties Improvement and Dilapidations Fund

Designated for major expenditure on buildings and infrastructure.

Endowment Funds

Endowment Fund for Jewish Children

The fund is the permanent endowment for Norwood Homes for Jewish Children and represents the original endowment made on its inception. Income arising from the fund is restricted and can only be used for the provision of services for children.

Ernst and Dola Fischer Fund

This is an endowment, originally of £350,000, where the income is used to fund the charity's home at 94 Station Road, Harrow, Middlesex.

Somers Fund

This is an endowment, originally of £1 million, where the income is used to fund the charity's family centre at Hackney.

[*continued on next page*]

Norwood Ravenswood, continued

Restricted Funds

Restricted funds are funds, the uses of which, are subject to specific restrictions imposed by the donors or by the nature of the appeal. They include both restricted income funds, where the income has to be applied for a specific purpose and restricted endowed funds where the capital is invested and only the income can be applied. The nature of the restrictions on the key funds are explained below.

Adult learning disability services

Incoming resources arising on the merger with the Parry Charitable Foundation to be used for adult learning disability services.

Bearsted/Surestart project

This grant is for the provision of 'wellbeing' services to the Jewish community in Hackney.

Binoh

Funds to be spent on this special educational needs service.

Harper Collins

Copyright money received on sale of "Halliwell Film Guide." Provisionally classed as restricted fund, pending further discussion with the Halliwell family.

Horinsky Overseas Holiday

Providing holidays for Jewish children and their families.

Jewish Association for the Physically Handicapped (JAPH)

The fund is being spent on supporting physically handicapped users.

Lira Abeleva

This fund is set up to provide an educational and respite care facility for disabled children in Minsk, Belarus.

New School Fund

This fund is for the provision of an educational centre in North London for special needs children.

[*continued on next page*]

Norwood Ravenswood, continued

Norwood Home for Jewish Children

This is a trust fund, originally for Norwood Child Care, now for Norwood Ravenswood, which is to be used in aid of Jewish Children's activities.

Pamela Barnett and Tager Autistic Centre

These are funds for two residential homes under construction at Ravenswood Village.

Peripatetic Outreach

Provision of funds, for the peripatetic outreach service to provide information, advice and support service to children and families in their homes. Also, by identifying families with similar needs, establish networking and parent-to-parent support.

Ravenswood Building

Provision of funds for improvement to the property at the Ravenswood, contributed towards the construction of the Tager and Pamela Barnett Centres.

Redbridge Autistic

The fund was originally set up by parents of autistic children. It is being held by Norwood Ravenswood to be used at the discretion of parents who set up the fund. Upon the death of founders of the fund, the remaining balance will be transferred to unrestricted general funds.

Young Peoples' Focus Group

Funded by a grant from the Big Lottery Fund, the Young People's Focus Group will ensure that children and young people using Norwood's disability services will have their voices heard, regardless of their disability.

12 Funds (Parent Charity)

	1 April 2007 £'000	Incoming Resources £'000	Outgoing Resources £'000	Transfers between funds £'000	Investment gains and losses £'000	31 March 2008 £'000
(a) Unrestricted funds						
Designated funds						
Bike Ride	60	—	—	—	—	60
Home from Home	1,446	—	—	—	—	1,446
					[continued on next page]	

183

Norwood Ravenswood, continued

	1 April 2007 £'000	Incoming Resources £'000	Outgoing Resources £'000	Transfers between funds £'000	Investment gains and losses £'000	31 March 2008 £'000
Louise Appeal	104	—	—	—	—	104
New School	—	—	—	1,220	—	1,220
Total designated funds	1,610	—	—	1,220	—	2,830
General Funds	5,586	11,982	(7,660)	6	(12)	9,902
Total unrestricted funds	7,196	11,982	(7,660)	1,226	(12)	12,732
(b) Endowment funds						
Ernst and Dola Fischer Fund	320	—	—	5	(15)	310
Fund for Jewish Children	205	—	—	—	(13)	192
Somers Fund	953	—	—	(11)	18	960
	1,478	—	—	(6)	(10)	1,462
(c) Other restricted funds						
Harper Collins	124	—	—	—	—	124
Horinsky Overseas Holiday	94	—	—	—	—	94
Lira Abeleva	106	23	(24)	—	—	105
New School	580	—	(580)	—	—	—
Norwood Home for Jewish Children	8,253	138	(138)	—	(280)	7,973
Pamela Barnett Centre	52	—	(52)	—	—	—
Peripatetic Outreach	59	—	(59)	—	—	—
Redbridge Autistic	35	—	(35)	—	—	—
Tager Autistic Centre	69	—	(69)	—	—	—
Ravenswood Building	235	—	(235)	—	—	—
Other Funds valued under £50,000	324	48	(63)	—	—	309
Total other restricted funds	9,931	209	(1,255)	—	(280)	8,605
(d) Restricted property fund	1,220	—	—	(1,220)	—	—
(e) Total restricted funds	11,151	209	(1,255)	(1,220)	(280)	8,605
Total funds	19,825	12,191	(8,915)	—	(302)	22,799

[*continued on next page*]

Norwood Ravenswood, continued

16 Analysis of Net Assets between Funds

Group

	Unrestricted funds £'000	Designated funds £'000	Endowment funds £'000	Restricted funds £'000	Total funds £'000
2008					
Tangible fixed assets	24,316	—	—	2,479	26,795
Investments	183	—	1,462	6,806	8,451
Net current assets/ (liabilities)	(1,447)	4,821	—	10,331	13,705
Liability due after one year	(6,680)	—	—	—	(6,680)
	16,372	4,821	1,462	19,616	42,271
2007					
Tangible fixed assets	15,044	—	—	2,479	17,523
Investments	202	—	1,478	6,950	8,630
Net current assets/ (liabilities)	(2,342)	3,601	—	11,078	12,337
	12,904	3,601	1,478	20,507	38,490

Parent Charity

	Unrestricted funds £'000	Designated funds £'000	Endowment funds £'000	Restricted funds £'000	Total funds £'000
2008					
Tangible fixed assets	1,994	—	—	—	1,994
Investments	183	—	1,462	6,806	8,451
Net current assets/ (liabilities)	7,725	2,830	—	1,799	12,354
	9,902	2,830	1,462	8,605	22,799
2007					
Tangible fixed assets	2,004	—	—	1,220	3,224
Investments	202	—	1,478	6,950	8,630
Net current assets	3,380	1,610	—	2,981	7,971
	5,586	1,610	1,478	11,151	19,825

3   Fixed assets

9.22   The principles for the inclusion of intangible and tangible fixed assets are set out in paras 252 to 312 of SORP. The fact that over 60 paragraphs are devoted to the subject explains why an entire chapter is set aside in this book.

9.23   Fixed assets will include:

● intangible assets held for the charity's use, such as intellectual property;

● tangible assets held for the charity's use, such as freehold land and buildings, leaseholds, plant machinery and motor vehicles, fixtures, fittings and equipment and payments on account of assets in course of construction;

- tangible assets classified as heritage assets, for example historic buildings and museum collections;

- investments held for a financial return, including investment properties; and

- investments made wholly or partly to further the charity's objectives – that is programme related investments.

9.24   The values at which fixed assets should be included in the balance sheet are discussed in Chapter 10.

9.25   It will be seen that a separation must be made between fixed assets held for the charity's use and those held for investment purposes. Where part of a building occupied by the charity is sub-let to provide rental income, an apportionment may be made, if material. Otherwise, the primary use of the asset should be the deciding factor – see para 257 of SORP.

4   Current assets

9.26   Current assets will include:

- stock and work in progress;

- debtors, analysed in the notes between trade debtors, amounts due from subsidiary or associated undertakings, other debtors, prepayments and accrued income;

- investments which are to be realised without reinvestment of the sale proceeds (see para 295 of SORP); and

- cash at bank and in hand.

Comment

9.27   Paragraph 249 of SORP draws attention to the need to analyse assets and liabilities in a way that enables 'the reader to gain a proper appreciation of their spread and character'. It may therefore be appropriate to show separately on the face of the balance sheet a significant debtor, for example, which might otherwise be hidden in the notes distorting comparison with the previous year.

9.28   Similarly, where debts or amounts due from subsidiary or associated undertakings remain outstanding for more than 12 months, consideration should be given as to whether they are current assets at all. Perhaps they should be reclassified as loans and included in investments. If so, the terms of interest, repayment and security may also require consideration. Indeed, this may raise the question whether the loan is either a qualifying investment for tax purposes or a justifiable use of charity funds from the point of view of the Charity Commission.

5   Liabilities

9.29   Liabilities should be analysed between their current and long-term elements. Having reminded users that the headings given may be added to or varied if the circumstances warrant, para 318 of SORP recommends that:

'the totals for both short-term and long-term creditors should each be separately analysed in the notes giving amounts for the following:

- loans and overdrafts

- trade creditors

- amounts due to subsidiary and associated undertakings

- other creditors

- accruals and deferred income'

Comment

9.30   The presentation of liabilities in the manner recommended is simple enough to follow. The main area of difficulty is in deciding what is a liability. For example, when does a contingent liability warrant inclusion as a provision; or when does a decision by the trustees amount to a legal commitment? These aspects are considered in Chapter 11.

Chapter 10

Fixed assets, valuations and depreciation

1   Overview of fixed assets

10.1   The SORP sets out the basic principles for recognition and measurement of all assets and liabilities in the balance sheet. With the exception of the compulsory use of valuation rather than cost in the case of investment assets (other than programme related investments), the principles are generally familiar to preparers of accounts in other sectors. This chapter deals with the recognition, initial measurement and subsequent depreciation, revaluation or writing down of fixed assets. The next chapter deals with other assets and liabilities.

10.2   There is extensive guidance in the SORP regarding fixed assets. This is necessary for a number of reasons, principally arising either because the specific reasons for holding assets are different from those common in other sectors or because the accounting principles followed in accounting standards designed to present a true and fair view of commercial activity are not readily applicable by charities.

10.3   'Fixed assets' is a broad heading which encompasses assets acquired or held for operational use, investment purposes or directly in the course of achieving the charity's objects. The common feature is that the assets are held for a period which spans more than one accounting period and are not part of the working capital of the charity. For each class of fixed assets it is possible that where disposal is intended and imminent the asset may be reclassified as a current asset, though this will not apply to investments where proceeds will be reinvested or to other assets unless they are held only with a view to resale.

10.4   Fixed assets fall into three main classes within which there are subdivisions:

*   intangible fixed assets should be included in accordance with Financial Reporting Standard 10 (FRS 10) 'Goodwill and Intangible Assets';

*   tangible fixed assets, which are analysed between those held for charity use, accounted for following the usual accounting rules, and heritage assets, to which special rules apply; and

*   fixed assets held as investments, most commonly held for financial return and held in the accounts at market value or alternatively made for

programme related purposes, in which case specially adapted accounting rules apply.

2 Relevant accounting standards

Intangible assets

10.5 The incidence of intangible assets which require inclusion in the accounts of a charity is uncommon. Only where such assets are purchased as a means to generate future benefits would items such as trademarks, goodwill, etc, be recognised in financial statements.

10.6 In the rare circumstances in which charities acquire such assets – examples would include acquisition of a trading business to generate funds or of intellectual property – intangible assets are recognised at cost and amortised over the period during which the expected economic benefits will arise. FRS 10 sets out the relevant accounting treatments and the reader is referred to that standard for detailed guidance.

Tangible assets

10.7 Generally accepted accounting practice (GAAP) in relation to tangible fixed assets is enshrined in FRS 15. FRS 15 offers two methods of accounting for tangible fixed assets, the most common is to carry the asset in the balance sheet at cost less depreciation, the alternative – most commonly applied to property assets – is to carry assets at revalued amounts, again subject to depreciation.

10.8 The guiding principle is to write off the cost or valuation of an asset, less any anticipated residual value on disposal, over its estimated useful life. If the asset has no recorded cost because it was a gift or because it was written off in the past, an estimate of its present value and its life expectancy should be made and the asset should be capitalised at that value with an appropriate charge for depreciation in future years to reduce the value to nil, or its expected residual value, at the end of its useful life.

10.9 The requirements for initial recognition and subsequent changes in the carrying value of heritage assets included in the balance sheet are no different from those for other tangible assets. However, there is a limited dispensation from the general rules of FRS 15 for certain heritage assets and enhanced disclosure requirements for all heritage assets, whether included in or excluded from the accounts. At the time of writing, FRS 30 'Heritage Assets' had yet to come into force. Mandatory for periods beginning on or after 1 April 2010, the standard further codifies the treatment of heritage assets in all entities' financial statements. Other than increased disclosure requirements, this will not noticeably affect the presentation currently required by SORP and discussed later in this chapter.

Impairment

10.10   In accounting for tangible and intangible fixed assets, regard should also be had to Financial Reporting Standard 11 (FRS 11) 'Impairment of Fixed Assets', regarding the impairment of assets. This standard requires charities to make a provision in the accounts when the carrying value of an asset exceeds its 'recoverable amount'. This is explained in paras 267–272 of the SORP and discussed later in this chapter.

Investments

10.11   There is currently no specific accounting standard comprehensively dealing with investments, although specific Financial Reporting Standards relating to 'Accounting for Subsidiary Undertakings' (FRS 2) and 'Joint Ventures and Associates' (FRS 9) cover some aspects. Statement of Standard Accounting Practice 19 'Investment Properties' (SSAP 19) codifies the appropriate treatment of properties owned as investment assets.

10.12   Recent accounting standards issued as part of the convergence of UK GAAP with International Financial Reporting Standards (IFRS) have introduced new and potentially complex accounting rules for investment assets which are set out in FRS 25 and FRS 26. These standards will usually not apply to charities unless they are companies and have elected to use the fair value accounting option permitted by the Companies Act 2006. As adoption of these rules is generally linked to the adoption of IFRS, what is written here assumes that charities will be following UK GAAP. The SORP appendix which deals with the application of accounting standards signposts preparers to the appropriate treatments in the unlikely event that this is not the case.

10.13   The SORP requires charities to carry investment assets held to generate a financial return, whether income capital or both, at valuation. Investments made wholly or partly to further the charity's objects – programme related investments – are carried at cost less a provision for any impairment in the assets' recoverable amount.

Comment

10.14   The Accounting Standards Board allows very little latitude for variance from the principles set out in Financial Reporting Standards. This is understandable as otherwise the standards would be steadily eroded. One fundamental principle is that expenditure on an asset should be matched against the period over which the asset is used. This can create presentational difficulties, for example in circumstances where an asset's purchase is externally funded and SORP's income recognition rules require the funding to be brought into the SOFA in the year it is receivable but the related cost to be recognised in the SOFA over a period of several years.

10.15   By capitalising such expenditure and depreciating it over the life of the asset, not only does the balance sheet reflect the continuing utility of the assets, but the Statement of Financial Activities will show an annual cost of using the asset. The resulting net book value shown in the balance sheet represents the resource available for use in future years, though this does not necessarily represent the replacement cost or saleable value of the assets held.

3   Recognition and initial valuation of fixed assets for the charity's own use

10.16   The value at which a fixed asset, used by the charity, should be included in the balance sheet is set out in paras 190–196 of SORP. Normally this will be its original cost less depreciation. Recommendations concerning the depreciation of such assets are contained in paras 198–202 of SORP and are considered in the next section.

10.17   Subsequent expenditure relating to an asset should be separated between the costs of maintaining, decorating and replacing component parts of the asset and any expenditure on replacing whole assets, or which substantially improves the assets' functionality or quality. The former, which may include (for example) replacing windows with very similar units, should be written off as expenditure as incurred. The latter, which could include (for example) replacing single-glazed windows with high specification double-glazed units, would be capitalised as a new addition to fixed assets.

10.18   Fixed assets which have been donated should be included at the value at which the gift was included in incoming resources, which should be its estimated market value at the time of the gift. For those assets which have not been capitalised for some years, it may be difficult to ascertain the original cost or even the value at the date of gift. It should, however, be possible to make 'a reasonable estimate of the asset's cost or current value to the charity'. Such a valuation will be regarded as the asset's initial carrying amount and will not be regarded as a 'revaluation' – (para 195).

10.19   Assets which meet the stringent definition of heritage assets set out below are accounted for using the specific rules embodied in the SORP. Other assets which may be of historic interest or held on trusts which bind them to the charity's objects but which do not meet the criteria required of heritage assets should be accounted for as investment assets or assets held for charity use.

Comment

10.20   A particularly substantial asset, for example a new building, may consist of discrete parts, which can clearly be seen to have different expected useful lives. For example, the shell of a building may be expected to stand for more than 50 years whereas other parts, such as the roof or internal partitioning, may be replaced periodically and more frequently. In these circumstances, SORP para 261 encourages separate recording of the components and depreciation over the specific lives of each part. Clearly such a separation should only be considered in cases where it will have a significant impact on the amounts subsequently reported; para 261 refers to 'major components with substantially different useful lives'.

4   Heritage assets

10.21   FRS 15 and SORP both recognise that the requirements to bring all assets into the balance sheet, including assets that have previously been written off on acquisition and assets which were received as a gift, are in practice difficult to apply universally. Whilst functional and investment assets can be valued with reference to likely replacement costs or achievable sale prices, assets of cultural, scientific, artistic or historical significance frequently have intrinsic value which is difficult to express in monetary amounts.

10.22   FRS 15 and SORP make exceptions from the general rules which, in tightly circumscribed circumstances, permit heritage assets to be excluded from the balance sheet. The ability to take advantage of these exemptions is subject to additional disclosure requirements.

10.23   The SORP recognises that the cost of seeking to account for certain heritage assets where reliable or meaningful valuations or costs data are unavailable will often outweigh any benefit that would be derived from the exercise. Paragraphs 279 to 294 of SORP define heritage assets, specify which charities should account for such assets specifically and set out detailed requirements which must be met if assets are to be excluded from the accounts.

10.24   To meet the definition of a heritage asset under SORP the assets must be held 'in pursuit of preservation or conservation objects' (SORP para 281). Although this requirement is broad and extends to assets held as part of broader educational objectives, para 289 of SORP makes it clear that assets which themselves have heritage value may not be classified as heritage assets if not held in pursuit of relevant objects.

10.25   A significant concession in SORP is made in the case of buildings and artefacts used for religious purposes or as part of 'ancient centres of learning'. SORP para 293 acknowledges that while the preservation of the assets may not be part of the objects of the charities which have stewardship of them, their unique historic qualities instil value in them which it would be impossible to capture in any assessment of replacement cost based on functional utility alone. The effect of this is to extend the exemptions discussed below to many historic religious and educational buildings.

10.26   SORP reemphasises that the general requirement to capitalise fixed assets applies equally to heritage assets (para 279). It further explains that for recently purchased assets, assets donated by a benefactor who has themselves recently purchased the asset, or gifts from estates which have been subject to probate or other tax driven valuations there will be an initial cost or value available and so recognition is mandatory.

10.27 Provided the above definitions are met, there are two circumstances in which heritage assets may be exempted from capitalisation. Assets which had not previously been capitalised at the time that SORP 2005 was introduced and donated assets received subsequently may both be excluded, subject to a cost benefit analysis.

10.28 For an asset to be excluded from the accounts, both of the following must apply:

(a) reliable cost information is not available and conventional accounting approaches lack sufficient reliability;

(b) significant costs are involved in the reconstruction or analysis of past accounting records or in valuation which are onerous compared with the additional benefit derived by users of the accounts in assessing the trustees' stewardship of the assets. (SORP para 284)

10.29 SORP requires that the cost benefit analysis is carried out on each class and sub class of heritage assets held. It provides examples of assets more and less likely to be susceptible to valuation and suggestions for sources of information that may be used to provide a valuation.

10.30 Heritage assets which are included in the accounts are included in the balance sheet as a separate row from other tangible fixed assets. The usual requirements for depreciation apply, though it is anticipated that many heritage assets will by their very nature be considered to have indefinite useful lives.

10.31 SORP para 294 sets out disclosure requirements for all heritage assets, both capitalised and excluded. Charities are required to provide narrative details of the nature and scale of the assets held, details of acquisitions and disposals and to set out clearly the accounting policy for heritage assets.

LEEDS CASTLE FOUNDATION REPORT AND FINANCIAL STATEMENTS FOR THE YEAR ENDED 31 MARCH 2008

Accounting policies

1.11 Tangible fixed assets and depreciation

(a) Heritage assets

Heritage assets are the tangible assets of the Charity that are of historical importance and are held to advance the preservation, conservation and educational objectives of the Charity and through public access contribute to the nation's culture and education.

The castle, grounds and contents bequeathed by the late Olive, Lady Baillie, and subsequent development expenditure in these assets, are considered to be heritage assets and are integral to the Leeds Castle Estate.

[*continued on next page*]

Leeds Castle Foundation, continued

Due to the historic and unique nature of the assets concerned conventional valuation approaches lack sufficient reliability. As a consequence the value of heritage assets has not been included in the financial statements.

Notes to the Financial Statements

15. Heritage assets (Group and Foundation)

In accordance with the Foundation's accounting policy, heritage assets are not included within the financial statements as due to the historic and unique nature of the assets concerned, conventional valuation approaches lack sufficient reliability.

The Castle Island buildings are insured for £47.4m and other estate buildings for £9.6m. Castle contents have been valued by Sotheby's at £28.6m, which includes loaned items valued at £14.9m.

Comment

10.32   The rules surrounding heritage assets superseded earlier SORPs' concessions for 'historic or inalienable assets'. By more rigorously restricting the ability of charities to exclude assets from the accounts, the revised rules have ensured that more assets are now recognised in balance sheets. However, as noted earlier in this chapter, accounting standards setters are reluctant to allow inconsistencies in treatment to persist and there have been a number of developments in the accounting for these assets since the introduction of SORP 2005.

10.33   The requirement to include all newly acquired assets whilst continuing to exclude those previously acquired introduces a level of inconsistency which has been uncomfortable for accountants to accept. There has been significant debate on the subject of 'Heritage assets – Can accounting do better?' to which the answer at present appears to be 'no'.

10.34   FRS 30 'Heritage Assets' which was issued in June 2009 and which will be mandatory for accounting periods beginning on or after 1 April 2010 reaffirms the SORP position, whilst adding additional narrative disclosure requirements. Readers with an interest in the development of the accounting rules for heritage assets should refer to FRS 30, which contains a history of the development of the standard.

5   Revaluations of fixed assets, other than investments

10.35   Paragraphs 262 to 266 of SORP deal with the procedures for revaluing fixed assets, other than investments. Apart from investments, revaluation of fixed assets is optional. If a policy of revaluation is applied to one asset it must also be applied to other assets of the same class (SORP para 262). The fact that they have been revalued, together with the date and basis of valuation, should be disclosed in the notes. Once assets have been revalued in the accounts, there is a requirement to periodically update the valuations and adjust accordingly.

10.36 Paragraph 263 of SORP clarifies that where assets are capitalised as a result of a change in accounting policy, or were donated and recognised initially at a valuation, this value will not be subject to periodic revaluation. Similarly, paragraph 264 explains that where assets were held at a revalued amount on the initial adoption of FRS 15, this value is not regarded as a revaluation. In both cases, the value initially recognised is treated for accounting purposes as if it were the cost of the asset and the historic cost rules described above apply.

10.37 For land and buildings – other than investment properties – valuations should be carried out by a qualified person using appropriate recognised valuation methods. This will generally be existing use value (EUV) for non specialised properties or depreciated replacement cost (DRC) for specialised properties. Definitions and an outline of when each method is appropriate can be found in FRS 15. Where there is no recognised market to which to refer, the name and qualification of the person making the valuation should be disclosed. For charities, the requirement for valuations to be carried out by an independent external valuer is relaxed (SORP para 265). If the person undertaking a valuation is also a trustee or employee of the charity, that fact should also be disclosed.

10.38 Trustees are advised by SORP to:

'use any reasonable approach to valuation at least every five years subject only to obtaining advice as to the possibility of any material movements between individual valuations.'
(para 265)

If trustees carry out a revaluation of fixed assets, they should substitute the revalued amount for the book value immediately prior to the valuation in the balance sheet and show the resulting gain or loss in the Statement of Financial Activities (SORP para 218).

10.39 The following example shows how a complete valuation can be explained straightforwardly in a note.

JOHN GROOMS 31 MARCH 2007

12. Tangible fixed assets

John Grooms
NOTES TO THE FINANCIAL STATEMENTS
For the year ended 31 March 2007

12 TANGIBLE FIXED ASSETS

	Freehold Land and buildings	Mobile homes and chalets	Furniture, plant and equipment	Motor Vehicles	Total
GROUP & CHARITY	£'000	£'000	£'000	£'000	£'000
Cost or valuation					
1 April 2006	23,038	143	3,716	592	27,489
Additions	3,351	-	377	65	3,793
Disposals	(30)	(17)	(296)	(31)	(374)
Revaluation	(1,839)	-	-	-	(1,839)
31 March 2007	24,520	126	3,797	626	29,069
Depreciation					
1 April 2006	3,240	76	2,606	421	6,343
Charged in the year	332	7	241	41	621
Disposals	(19)	(7)	(195)	(22)	(243)
Written back on revaluation	(3,553)	-	-	-	(3,553)
31 March 2007	-	76	2,652	440	3,168
Net book value					
31 March 2007	24,520	50	1,145	186	25,901
31 March 2006	19,798	67	1,110	171	21,146

The net book value at 31 March 2007 represents fixed assets used for

	Land and buildings	Mobile homes and chalets	Furniture, plant and equipment	Motor Vehicles	Total
	£'000	£'000	£'000	£'000	£'000
Direct charitable purposes					
Nursing and Care Services	16,264	-	570	115	16,949
Holidays	6,635	50	375	19	7,079
Projects	121	-	39	2	162
	23,020	50	984	136	24,190
Other purposes					
Head office services	1,500	-	161	50	1,711
	24,520	50	1,145	186	25,901

During May 2007 the Charity's freehold property assets were revalued as at 31 March 2007 by an external valuer, Pinder's Professional and Consultancy Service, in accordance with the regulations prescribed by The Royal Institution of Chartered Surveyors The overall impact, an unrealized gain of £1,714,000, has been reflected in these financial statements

Page 15

196

10.40   In the case of fixed assets used by the charity, if the trustees do not have a policy of revaluation, they should have regard to para 207 of SORP, which requires them to disclose significant differences between the carrying value and the market value of interests in land and buildings not held as investments.

Comment

10.41   It is worth emphasising that, although trustees are required by FRS 15 to ascertain an initial cost or valuation for fixed assets used by the charity, they are under no obligation to revalue them thereafter. They must, however, consider their value from year to year in order to decide whether or not there is any significant difference between the book value and the market value which should be disclosed.

10.42   If trustees decide to revalue fixed assets used by the charity, they must be prepared to continue to do so every five years or on a rolling basis. This need not be an expensive process. Trustees can adopt any reasonable approach according to the circumstances.

6   Depreciation of fixed assets (other than investments)

Guidelines

10.43   Paragraph 258 of SORP reminds us that:

'most tangible fixed assets depreciate; that is they wear out, are consumed or otherwise suffer a reduction in their useful life through use, the passing of time or obsolescence. Their value is thus gradually expended over their useful economic life. This expenditure should be recognised by means of an annual depreciation charge in the Statement of Financial Activities and shown in the balance sheet as accumulated depreciation deducted from the value of the relevant fixed assets.'

Comment

10.44   The first point to consider is the first phrase, 'most tangible fixed assets depreciate'. Which ones do not? Obviously one hopes that investments do not, but these are considered at **10.60** ff. Here we are concerned only with assets used by the charity. Many charities would argue that their land and buildings had appreciated in value over the years. But in reality it is only the land value that would have risen. The buildings themselves are likely to have depreciated physically and become expensive to maintain. Where there is a significant annual expense on repairs and maintenance, in order to maintain a property to the highest standards, it may be that its life is prolonged virtually indefinitely and that the residual value of the buildings themselves is not reducing. Perhaps, also, some of the contents or fixtures are of antique and artistic interest. These may well have increased in value rather than depreciated.

10.45   It is allowable in UK GAAP to exclude a fixed asset from depreciation where the difference between its book value and likely residual value is so small, or its expected useful life so long as to be effectively indefinite, such that any depreciation charge would be immaterial. In these cases an annual impairment review, as required by FRS 11, is mandatory (see **10.52–10.57** below).

10.46   It is important at the outset to analyse the fixed assets into categories such as land, buildings, fixtures and fittings, furniture and equipment etc. The cost or book value should be apportioned over each heading and consideration should be given to the length of life of the asset. If it is finite, a depreciation policy is needed; if not, it is not.

10.47   In the specific case of buildings and other very significant assets, it may be desirable to split the asset further into its recognisable components, for example the roof, the superstructure, internal partitioning, etc, which have different useful lives and depreciate these elements at different annual rates.

10.48   This degree of analysis will only be necessary where the fixed assets consist of many items. In such cases it is recommended that a fixed asset register is maintained.

Comment

10.49   The determination of expected useful lives and residual values, if any, is the key judgement in accounting for tangible fixed assets. The estimates should be made with due care as the application of inappropriate rates of depreciation could lead to large gains or losses on disposals of assets or to assets being fully depreciated long before their use ceases.

10.50   For many charities, there is a temptation to write all expenditure off as quickly as possible, to avoid an appearance of excessive wealth and to match the treatment of funds received from donors, who will usually regard the funds as spent on acquisition of the asset.

10.51   This is particularly the case with charities working overseas which often face a greater risk of assets ceasing to be operational in a short timescale. There is also a greater expectation that assets will no longer be of use or of resale value after the end of the project for which they are acquired. It is not acceptable to treat the cost of assets, which will be used for a period of years, as expenditure immediately. It may, however, be prudent to use a shorter expected useful life than might normally apply for assets – in exceptional cases, it may even be appropriate to use an estimated useful life of only one or two years for project assets.

7   Calculation of depreciation charge and impairment of fixed assets

10.52   Having established the estimated life of a fixed asset, the annual rate of depreciation can be determined. This will be established for groups of fixed assets and be disclosed in the accounting policies – para 199 of SORP.

10.53

'Exceptions to charging depreciation may only arise if any of the following conditions apply:

(a)   the asset is freehold land…

(b)   both the depreciation charge and accumulated depreciation are not material because

(i)   the asset has a very long useful life; or

(ii)   the residual value (based on prices at the time of acquisition or subsequent revaluation) of the asset is not materially different from the carrying amount of the asset;

If depreciation is not charged because of immateriality, FRS15 requires that the asset is subject to an annual impairment review (except for charities under the threshold for following the FRSSE);

(c)   the assets are heritage assets and have not been included in the balance sheet …'

(para 259)

Comment

10.54   It is important to note that where a charity has determined that the exception in (b) applies – ie there is no reduction in carrying value – that judgement is subject to mandatory re-evaluation in each subsequent year by way of impairment review. An annual impairment review is also required in cases where the trustees have assessed the expected useful life of an asset as exceeding 50 years, as this will inevitably result in a relatively modest depreciation charge.

10.55   Impairment of fixed assets for use by a charity is considered in paras 224–229 of SORP. Impairment occurs if a functional fixed asset's net book value is higher than its recoverable amount.

'Recoverable amount is the higher of the net realisable value and the value in use. Value in use is normally the present value of the future cash flows obtainable as a result of an asset's continued use …'
(para 225)

Thus, a piece of medical equipment may, as a result of technological change, have a negligible realisable value, but still be capable of generating significant income giving it a higher value in use. In such a case there may be no impairment of value.

10.56   For charities, the concept of value in use requires modification. As we have already seen in the consideration of adopting values for donated and previously uncapitalised assets (in **10.16** ff above), the value of an asset to a charity may not be comparable to its value if held for commercial uses, for investment or for resale. Whereas FRS 11 defines value in use solely in terms of an asset's ability to generate cash flow for a business, charities should assess whether an asset is contributing to the achievement of its charitable objectives. Thus, if the medical equipment referred to above is enabling a medical charity to continue its work and could not be replaced for a lower cost than its book value, then no impairment should be recognised whether or not the charity generates income directly from the use of the equipment. Paragraph 268 recognises that there is no hard and fast rule for establishing value in use to a charity and allows that: 'Each charity can determine its own measure of service delivery but this must be reasonable, justifiable and consistently operated.'

10.57 Where the recoverable amount as defined above, is less than the net book value of the asset, 'the loss should be treated as additional depreciation' (SORP para 272). As a provision for impairment will only be made where the impact is material, it should be shown as a separate line in the disclosure of movements in fixed assets rather than simply aggregated into the heading of depreciation charges for the year.

Comment

10.58 It should be clear that the overriding concept is the consideration of whether it is still appropriate to carry a proportion of the cost of an asset into future periods to spread the expense associated with its use over time. For assets still in use by the charity to fulfil central objects, it is unlikely that this will be in doubt. The process of impairment review should not be used to prematurely write assets off to reduce the apparent 'wealth' of a charity.

10.59 Whilst one wishes to avoid tinkering with depreciation rates, once they have been established, it is useful to consider whether the resulting net book value of the asset is materially different from its value in use. This will only apply to significant fixed assets used by the charity and the application of the impairment review procedure is likely to be rare for most charities.

8   Fixed assets – investments

Guidelines

10.60 Paragraph 296 of SORP requires that investments, including investment properties and cash held for investment purposes, be classified as a separate category within fixed assets. The only exception is where the investment is only being held temporarily and there is an intention to realise it without reinvestment of the proceeds. In such a case, it should be reclassified as a current asset.

10.61 Within the category of investments, programme related investments (see below) should be separately identified and reported.

Valuation

10.62   Paragraph 232 of SORP recommends that:

'All investment assets other than programme related investments … should be shown in the balance sheet at market value or at the trustees' best estimate of market value as described below. Market value best represents a true and fair view of the value of these assets to the charity, given the duty of the trustees to administer the portfolio of investment assets so as to obtain the best investment performance without undue risk. Investment assets should not be depreciated. All changes in value in the year, whether or not realised, should be reported in the "gains and losses on investment assets" section of the Statement of Financial Activities.'

10.63   The majority of assets in which charities invest are likely to have a market value ascertainable from quoted prices – whether by the investment's issuer or on a recognised exchange. The SORP requires the trustees of charities holding assets for which 'no readily identifiable market price' to 'adopt a reasonable approach' to their valuation (SORP para 297). Where such a valuation is given by the trustees, the basis adopted must be disclosed.

10.64   For investments other than shares and securities – most commonly investment properties – the trustees may use 'any reasonable approach' to valuation. As for tangible fixed assets held at revalued amounts, the values should be formally updated at least every five years and advice should be sought in the intervening years to establish whether material changes in value may have occurred.

Analysis of investment assets

10.65   Paragraphs 299 to 312 of SORP explain the degree of analysis of investments which should be given in the notes to the accounts.

10.66   First, there should be an analysis showing the general spread of investments. Typically this would normally include:

● investment properties;

● listed investments and assets based on them such as unit trust and common investment funds;

● investments in subsidiary or associated undertakings;

● other unlisted investments;

● uninvested cash held as part of the portfolio; and

● any other investments.

10.67   Secondly, the investments should be analysed between those in the UK and those outside the UK. For this purpose, a company which is listed in the UK is regarded as being a UK investment.

10.68   *Fixed assets, valuations and depreciation*

10.68   Further disclosure is required of any individual investment considered material to the overall portfolio and any restrictions which might apply on the realisation of any investments, for example holdings that may be difficult to dispose of.

10.69   Thirdly,

> 'the notes to the accounts should indicate the value of investments held in each type of fund. This may be included in the overall analysis of assets held in the different type of funds'
> (para 307).

THE ROYAL COLLEGE OF NURSING CHARITABLE TRUST – NOTES TO THE ACCOUNTS – 31 MARCH 2008

6. Investments – charitable trust

	2008 £'000	2007 £'000
Market value at 31 March	22,699	19,763
Additions at cost	5,097	12,880
Disposals at market value	(12,332)	(10,681)
Realised gain/(loss)	13	(236)
Unrealised (loss)/gain on revaluation	(441)	973
Investments at market value at 31 March	**15,036**	**22,699**
Unlisted securities	9	9
Cash held for reinvestment	456	540
Market value at 31 March	**15,501**	**23,248**
Cost at 31 March	**14,416**	**19,890**

Investments at market value comprise:	2008 £'000	2007 £'000
Listed Investments		
UK equities	6,204	10,601
Overseas equities	3,726	5,675
UK fixed interest	4,096	5,120
Overseas hedged funds	1,009	1,303
	15,035	22,699
UK unlisted securities	9	9
Cash held for reinvestment	457	540
Total	**15,501**	**23,248**

Holdings over 5%

The following investments represented holdings in excess of 5% of the investment portfolio at 31 March 2008.   *[continued on next page]*

202

The Royal College of Nursing Charitable Trust, continued

	2008 £'000	2007 £'000
Sarasin Sterling Class A income bonds	26.4%	23.0%
Sarasin CI Equisar Sterling Global Thematic Fund units	7.0%	2.0%

At 31 March 2008, investments held belonging to other group entities were RCN restricted funds £3,894,000 and RCNMS £4,056,000.

Short term deposits of £8,663,000 were all held in the UK.

Programme related investments

10.70 Programme related investments are defined in the SORP's glossary, GL47, as being 'made directly in pursuit of the organisation's charitable purposes'. Many programme related investments will generate a financial return but this is not their primary purpose. Examples include microfinance schemes, seed funding for social businesses or loans to other charities.

10.71 The accounting and disclosure requirements for programme related investments reflect their difference from investments held primarily for financial return. The requirements are:

- the investments are separately identified on the balance sheet;

- they are carried at cost, subject to review for impairment;

- any provisions for impairment are treated as charitable expenditure charged against the activity which the investment supports;

- any gains on disposal of such assets are recorded as gains on disposal of fixed assets within 'other incoming resources'.

10.72 Where programme related investments are material, analysis of changes in the value of the investments from one balance sheet to the next, the types of investments made and the projects and activities supported should be given.

Chapter 11

Current assets, liabilities and reserves

1 Current assets

11.1

'Current assets other than current asset investments (see paragraph 296) should normally be recognised at the lower of cost and net realisable value' (para 313).

11.2 An asset is current if it is available to be spent in the near future. If it is likely to take longer than 12 months to be converted into cash, it is strictly not available and ought not to be included as a current asset. However, see **11.4** ff for the method of inclusion of long-term debtors.

11.3

'Where investments are held as current assets, the same disclosure is required as for fixed asset investments' (para 296).

2 Debtors and accrued income

11.4

'Debtors should be analysed in the notes to the accounts between short-term and long-term (after more than one year), giving amounts for the following:

(a)   trade debtors;

(b)   amounts due from subsidiary and associated undertakings;

(c)   other debtors;

(d)   prepayments and accrued income.'

(para 314)

In addition to this requirement, it is a requirement of UITF Abstract 4: 'Presentation of long-term debtors in current assets' that where the amount of debtors receivable after one year is sufficiently material, it should be separately shown on the face of the balance sheet.

11.5 In the case of grants, it is necessary to look at the terms of the grant. Paragraphs 104 to 111 of the SORP demonstrate the complexity of grants which may be paid in advance or in arrears or subject to conditions which make them repayable in certain circumstances. For all grants, including those which are performance related, the main factor to be considered is entitlement.

11.6   Generally speaking, for grants which are not performance related, income should be recognised at the earliest of the point of receipt, the due date for receipt if specified in funding terms or the date of recognition of expenditure that can be recovered under an agreed grant arrangement. Where amounts due in line with a schedule of payments but not yet received or amounts expended which are contractually reimbursable exceed receipts to date, a debtor or accrued income balance will be included in the balance sheet.

11.7   There is some divergence of practice in this area. The recognition of a debtor for income relies upon the criteria for recognising income set out in SORP para 94 and charities' interpretation of this paragraph is not uniform. Whilst some charities take the view that the incurring of expenditure recoverable in arrears is an event which creates a reasonably certain and measurable entitlement to income, others argue that further action may be required to establish entitlement.

11.8   Application Note G to Financial Reporting Standard 5 'Reporting the Substance of Transactions', issued in 2003, clarified general practice in accounting for revenue. SORP 2005, most explicitly at para 103, provides guidance on how charities should interpret entitlement to income in the light of this Application Note.

11.9   The argument can be made that a requirement to make a formal claim for the funding or to submit a report on the project is a further condition which must be met, in addition to the incurring of expenditure, before the charity is entitled to the income from the funder. Thus some charities will only recognise funding receivable in arrears as a debtor balance where the expenditure has been incurred and any required claims and reports submitted prior to the accounting date. SORP para 107 clearly discourages this view; however some charities dispute its assertion that:

> 'Conditions such as the submission of accounts or the certification of expenditure can be seen as simply an administrative requirement as opposed to a condition that might prevent the recognition of incoming resources'

11.10   The more prudent treatment (of delaying recognition until all conditions, including technicalities, are met or funds actually received) has implications for fund accounting where the income stream is restricted. In these cases, the expenditure from the fund at the balance sheet date may be greater than the income recognised to date. This would lead to the fund showing a deficit balance at the year end and all of the resulting disclosure implications.

11.11   Legacies should be brought into account when they are known to be receivable. If a legacy is known to be due to the charity at the balance sheet date and the amount is reasonably quantifiable, and there is reasonable certainty of that amount being received in due course, then it should be included as a debtor. (See para 94 of SORP re entitlement, certainty and measurement.)

NORWOOD: NOTES TO THE FINANCIAL STATEMENTS FOR THE YEAR ENDED 31 MARCH 2009 (EXTRACT)

9 Debtors

	Group	Group	Parent charity	Parent charity
	2009	2008	2009	2008
	£'000	£'000	£'000	£'000
Accrued legacies (see note 15)	684	850	684	850
Amounts due from subsidiary undertakings	-	-	1	2,653
Local Authorities and trade debtors	644	1,163	-	-
Other debtors	62	76	30	60
Prepayments and accrued income	521	593	203	389
	1,911	2,682	918	3,952

---

3   Liabilities

11.12

'The totals for both short-term and long-term creditors should each be separately analysed in the notes giving amounts of the following:

(i)   loans and overdrafts;

(ii)   trade creditors;

(iii)   amounts due to subsidiary and associated undertakings;

(iv)   other creditors;

(v)   accruals and deferred income.'

(para 318)

11.13   A liability is current if it is due for payment within 12 months of the balance sheet date. If all or part of a liability is not due for payment until after 12 months, that part of the liability is not current and should be shown with the long-term liabilities. Care needs to be taken over the way in which liabilities are shown which are partly current and partly long-term, such as amounts due on a bank loan repayable over five years.

11.14   The value at which liabilities, whatever their nature, should be shown in the balance sheet is their settlement value.

NORWOOD RAVENSWOOD: NOTES TO THE FINANCIAL STATEMENTS FOR THE YEAR ENDED 31 MARCH 2008 (EXTRACT)

9 Creditors: Amounts falling due within one year

	Group 2008 £'000	Group 2007 £'000	Parent charity 2008 £'000	Parent charity 2007 £'000
Bank overdraft	-	232	-	-
Other taxes and social security costs	673	687	22	18
Trade creditors	800	728	54	29
Accruals and deferred income	1,558	1,116	535	218
Other creditors	28	22	-	-
Amounts due to subsidiary undertakings	-	-	4,908	5,521
	3,059	2,785	5,519	5,786

10 Creditors: Amounts falling due after more than one year

	Group 2008 £'000	Group 2007 £'000	Parent charity 2008 £'000	Parent charity 2007 £'000
Bank loan repayable within four to five years (5 instalments)	65	-	-	-
Bank loan repayable after five years (235 instalments)	6,615	-	-	-
	6,680	-	-	-

The long term bank loan is secured by a charge over Broadway House, Stanmore, bears interest at 1% over base rate and is repayable in 240 monthly instalments, the first payment due in November 2012. To protect the Group against fluctuations in interest rates, a base rate collar has been purchased at a cost of £21,000. The collar ensures that the maximum effective base rate which the Group will pay is 6.5% and the minimum is 5.25%.

Interest paid on the loan during the year amounted to £180,000.

---

4 Commitments

11.15 A particular problem for charities is to decide whether commitments made before the balance sheet date should be included as liabilities or whether they should be shown as designated funds. The question is: are the trustees obliged to pay the money over, or have they simply decided to do so and are setting it aside in anticipation?

11.16 Paragraphs 154 to 163 of SORP deal with charitable commitments where trusts have promised financial support to a recipient as a constructive obligation. A typical example would be a promise to fund the costs of a researcher for three years without conditions such as performance targets to be met. In this case the charity, having created a valid expectation in the mind of the recipient, should include two-thirds of the cost in long-term creditors and one-third in short-term creditors.

11.17 The SORP distinguishes between commitments which have become constructive or legal obligations – those where any conditionality attaching to future payments relates wholly or mainly to acts outside the charity's control – and those which have not. Conditions which remain in the charity's control will generally only relate to terms which provide discretion for future payments to become payable only after successful progress reviews of work undertaken to date.

11.18   The balance sheet treatment of those different grades of obligation is set out in paras 317–329 of SORP. Broadly speaking, legal or constructive obligations should be included in full and split between liabilities due within one year and those falling due after one year. Commitments which do not amount to obligations should not be included as liabilities, but particulars of any material commitments should be disclosed in the notes to the accounts.

'The notes should distinguish between those commitments included on the balance sheet as liabilities and those that are intentions to spend and are not included but in both cases should detail:

(a)   the reason for the commitments ...;

(b)   the total amount of the commitments ...;

(c)   the amount of commitments outstanding at the start of the year;

(d)   any amounts charged in the Statement of Financial Activities for the year;

(e)   any amounts released during the year ...;

(f)   the amount of commitments outstanding at the end of the year ...'

(para 328)

11.19   Where commitments do not amount to obligations and are therefore not included as liabilities, it is recommended, if they are material, that they are shown separately within unrestricted funds as designated funds. This 'earmarks' part of these unrestricted funds to meet these commitments and thereby shows what is left available for future commitments.

11.20   The establishment of a designated fund for committed expenditure could also include situations where the trustees have budgeted deficits in future years either for the organisation as a whole or for specific projects. An example might be the costs of a project for which grants have been awarded where matching funding is required. The trustees have effectively committed to use charity reserves to fund the matched funding element to the extent that future fundraising does not secure the amounts.

THE BARROW CADBURY TRUST 31 MARCH 2008 (EXTRACT)

1 Accounting policies

(c)   **Resources expended and the basis of apportioning costs**

   ...

   (ii)   Grants payable are included in the statement of financial activities when approved and when the intended recipient has

[continued on next page]

The Barrow Cadbury Trust, continued

either received the funds or been informed of the decision to make the grant and has satisfied all related conditions. Grants where the beneficiary has not been informed or has to meet certain conditions before the grant is released are not accrued for but are noted as financial commitments in the notes to the accounts.

13 Creditors: amounts falling due within one year

	Group		Charity	
	31/3/08 **£'000**	31/3/07 £'000	**31/3/08** **£'000**	31/3/07 £'000
Trade creditors	**164**	73	**131**	62
Grants payable	**1,395**	830	**948**	602
Social security and other taxes	**21**	13	**17**	9
Accruals	**69**	15	**62**	11
Other creditors	**14**	5	**13**	5
	1,663	936	**1,171**	689

15 Grant commitments

At 31 March 2008 the Charity had commitments in respect of grants approved for projects and which have not been accrued in these accounts as follows:

	31/3/08 **£'000**	31/3/07 £'000
Payable within one year	**164**	231
Payable between two and five years	**509**	264
	673	495

In addition to the above, at 31 March 2008 the subsidiary company had financial commitments in respect of grants approved and which have not been accrued in its accounts as follows:

	31/3/08 **£'000**	31/3/07 £'000
Payable within one year	**70**	30
Payable between two and five years	**153**	10
	223	40

E5 – Contingent assets and liabilities

11.21

> 'A charity should not recognise incoming or outgoing resources or gains and losses arriving respectively from contingent assets or contingent liabilities in the Statement of Financial Activities or the balance sheet' (para 341).

Only when it is virtually certain that a contingent asset will be received or probable that a contingent liability will be incurred should they be included in the accounts. At that point they cease to be contingent.

> 'The probability of a contingent asset or liability resulting in a future transfer of resources (to or from the charity) should be continually assessed and the recognition of the asset or liability should be reviewed as appropriate' (para 341)

11.22   Material contingent assets and liabilities should be disclosed in the notes to the accounts. These will show the nature of each contingency and uncertainties that are expected to affect the outcome. A prudent estimate of the financial effect, if not included in the accounts, should be given or an explanation as to why it is not practicable to do so (paras 345 to 348 of SORP).

5   Loan liabilities/guarantees

11.23   Paragraphs 349 and 350 of SORP give details of the disclosure requirements where a charity has pledged assets as security for a loan or other liability. They also require similar disclosure in respect of inter-fund loans and loans to subsidiary companies. Apart from details of the assets charged and the amount of the loan and its proportion to the value of the assets charged, the repayment details and interest should also be given.

Comment

11.24   Inevitably, there are many borderline cases when one cannot be sure whether or not to include an item in the accounts, but by giving detailed disclosure in the notes and, if sufficiently material, referring to the matter in the trustees' report, the treatment adopted will be well flagged and explained.

Chapter 12

Cash flow statements

1   The requirement for a cash flow statement

12.1   The preparation of a cash flow statement is a requirement of Financial Reporting Standard 1 (Revised 1996) 'Cash Flow Statements' (FRS 1) for most charities exceeding certain thresholds. This chapter explains the requirements of FRS 1.

12.2   FRS 1 makes a cash flow statement, with comparative figures, a requirement in the accounts of all entities which do not qualify for exemption. The exemptions from preparing a cash flow statement are, however, extensive and cover all charities which are considered 'small' entities with reference to thresholds established for general company reporting as well as most subsidiary charities.

12.3   It should be noted that the thresholds for determining a small entity in this circumstance are in fact rather greater than those used in other circumstances, such as establishing whether an audit is required or whether receipts and payments accounting is permissible. A small entity is one which falls below two or more thresholds. Where a charity exceeds the thresholds in one year but not the next, or vice versa, there are transition rules to avoid the requirement to prepare a cash flow statement being applied to truly exceptional periods.

12.4   The thresholds for small companies are based on European Directives and are frequently updated but as an indication, those in force at 31 August 2009 are:

'(a)   gross income in the year in excess of £6.5million;

(b)   a Balance Sheet total in excess of £3.26 million;

(c)   more than 50 employees.'

12.5   The FRS exempts from the obligation to produce a cash flow statement, 'Subsidiary undertakings where 90% or more of the voting rights are controlled within the group, provided consolidated financial statements in which those subsidiary undertakings are included are publicly available'. This may be applicable where a parent/subsidiary undertaking relationship is considered to exist within a charitable group.

12.6 *Cash flow statements*

12.6   As a 'primary statement', the cash flow statement should be given the same prominence in the accounts as the Statement of Financial Activities and the balance sheet.

12.7   It is not intended to repeat in this chapter all of the requirements and definitions given by FRS 1 with which the SORP states the charity's cash flow statement must comply.

Comment

Definition of 'gross income'

12.8   The limits stated above refer not to 'turnover' as in FRS 1, but to 'gross income'. 'Gross income' is defined in the Charity Commission's guidance notes for the completion of the Annual Return, a copy of which is reproduced in Appendix 3. In summary, it should represent the total incoming resources of all income funds plus gains or profits on the disposal of fixed assets or investments belonging to those funds. Any amounts receivable which are endowments should be excluded. For these purposes, the gain or profit on disposal of fixed assets or investments represents the amount by which the sale proceeds exceed the original cost, not the carrying value. In the case of accounts consolidating the results of a charity and its trading subsidiary, the 'gross income' should be the total of the charity's gross income as defined above (adjusted to remove the profit gifted by the subsidiary) plus the turnover of the trading subsidiary. For the purposes of determining whether a cash flow statement is required, 'gross income' is not therefore the same as the total incoming resources shown on the Statement of Financial Activities. This, in the authors' view, is needlessly confusing.

Definition of 'balance sheet total'

12.9   The 'balance sheet total' limit is not the total net assets of the charity shown as the total of its balance sheet, but is the total of all of its assets, without offsetting any liabilities.

2   The object and nature of the cash flow statement and the disclosure requirements

12.10   The object of the cash flow statement is to show all of the inflows and outflows of cash of the entity which have occurred in the accounting period in such a way as facilitates comparison of the cash flow performance of different entities and provides information that assists in the assessment of their liquidity, solvency and financial adaptability.

12.11   FRS 1 requires all cash inflows and outflows to be analysed under one of the following eight standard headings:

(a)   operating activities;

(b)   returns on investments and servicing of finance;

(c)   taxation;

(d)   capital expenditure and financial investment;

(e)   acquisitions and disposals;

(f)   equity dividends paid;

(g)   management of liquid resources; and

(h)   financing.

12.12   Where applicable, three supporting reconciliations are required by the FRS.

12.13   The FRS requires a reconciliation between the 'operating profit' reported in the 'profit and loss account' and the net cash flow from operating activities. This reconciliation should show the effect of the increase or decrease in stocks, debtors and creditors on cash movements resulting from operating activities. Clearly the FRS was written with commercial entities in mind. How charities can deal with this requirement is discussed below.

12.14   A reconciliation of the movements in 'net debt' is also required in respect of the amounts shown in the financing section of the cash flow statement reconciling from their balance sheet value at the start of the year to their balance sheet value at the end of the year. This reconciliation should disclose separately movements between the two years resulting from cash flow movements (which will appear on the cash flow statement) and other movements with no cash flow effect (e.g. exchange differences) which should be reported in the notes to the cash flow statement only.

12.15   Finally, a reconciliation is also required between the amounts on the balance sheet at the start and the end of the year of those items treated as 'cash'. Movements of a non-cash nature should be shown separately and the net cash inflow or outflow from this reconciliation must agree with the total cash movements given by the cash flow statement.

12.16   Material transactions not resulting in cash movements must be disclosed in the notes to the cash flow statement if the disclosure is necessary for an understanding of the underlying transactions. The commonest disclosure as a result of this is that of material acquisitions of fixed assets which have not resulted in cash movements as they have been given to the charity or have been financed using hire purchase or similar arrangements.

Comment

Categories of inflows and outflows of cash

12.17   The statement should, if applicable, show a net amount for each of the eight categories listed above. Any sub-division of these categories can either be shown on the face of the statement or should be disclosed in the notes. The FRS allows the cash flows relating to the management of liquid resources and financing to be combined under a single heading, provided the cash flows relating to each are shown separately and separate sub-totals are given.

12.18   Clearly, for charities, the categories for taxation and equity dividends paid are unlikely to apply.

The reconciliation between 'operating profit' and cash flows from operating activities

12.19   The FRS requires a reconciliation of the operating results shown on the profit and loss account with the cash flows arrived at from the operating activities shown as the opening category on the cash flow statement.

12.20   In the absence of an 'operating profit' for charities complying with SORP, it is considered that this reconciliation should be from the 'net incoming/outgoing resources' before other recognised gains and losses of the charity, shown on its Statement of Financial Activities, to the 'cash inflow (or outflow) from operating activities'. The treatment of investment income in this reconciliation is dealt with below.

3   Definition of cash

12.21   FRS 1 gives a detailed and restrictive definition of what should be considered to be 'cash' for the purposes of the cash flow statement.

'… Cash in hand and deposits repayable on demand with any qualifying financial institution, less overdrafts from any qualifying institution repayable on demand. Deposits are repayable on demand if they can be withdrawn at any time without notice and without penalty or if a maturity or period of notice of not more than 24 hours or one working day has been agreed. Cash includes cash in hand and deposits denominated in foreign currencies.' (para 2)

A 'qualifying financial institution' is defined as follows.

'An entity that as part of its business receives deposits and other repayable funds and grants credits for its own account.'

12.22   FRS 1 requires the total of the inflows and outflows to agree to the total of the increase or decrease in the charity's 'cash' (as defined above) between the start and end of the reporting period.

4   Problem areas specific to charities

Investment income

12.23   Cash movements resulting from the purchase and sale of investments are required by FRS 1 to be disclosed as cash outflows or inflows from 'capital expenditure and financial investment' activities and any cash inflows coming from investment income are treated as part of the cash flows resulting from 'returns on investments and servicing of finance'.

12.24 FRS 1 assumes that the opening movement in the cash flow is the 'net cash inflow or outflow from operating activities', which, as the FRS has been written mainly with commercial companies in mind, excludes any cash inflows from investing activities. (Most trading companies would exclude investment income from their operating profit or loss.) However, SORP includes investment income as an incoming resource, and investment income is, therefore, included in the Statement of Financial Activities' equivalent of operating profit ('net incoming/outgoing resources before revaluations and investment asset disposals') with which a charity's equivalent reconciliation should begin.

12.25 In order that charities can comply with the FRS 1 requirement to show cash inflows from investment income as part of their cash flows from 'returns on investments and servicing of finance', the reconciliation referred to above from 'net incoming resources' to net cash inflow or outflow from operating activities must treat the amount shown on the Statement of Financial Activities as investment income receivable as a deduction. The net cash inflow or outflow from operating activities will therefore exclude any cash inflow from investment income.

Treatment of cash held as part of investment portfolio

12.26 Paragraph 295 of SORP provides for the inclusion of cash as a fixed asset investment if it is held as part of the investment portfolio.

12.27 This may include uninvested monies held by investment managers or investments in financial instruments made as part of the charity's investment strategy. To the extent that they meet the definition of cash given above, movements in these amounts must be included in the cash flow statement.

12.28 Below is an example of a charity's cash flow statement.

OXFAM 30 APRIL 2008

Consolidated Cash Flow Statement

	2008		2007	
	£m	£m	£m	£m
Net cash (outflow)/inflow from operating activities		(9.1)		2.4
Returns on investments and servicing of finance				
Deposit interest received	3.4		3.5	
		3.4		3.5

[*continued on next page*]

Oxfam, continued

	2008		2007	
	£m	£m	£m	£m
Capital expenditure and financial investment				
Payments to acquire tangible fixed assets – additions	(3.7)		(4.2)	
Receipts from sales of tangible fixed assets	0.6		0.4	
		(3.1)		(3.8)
Net cash (outflow)/inflow before management of liquid resources and financing		(8.8)		2.1
Management of liquid resources				
Cash withdrawn from short term deposit	73.5		83.0	
Cash invested on short term deposit	(65.0)		(81.0)	
(Decrease)/increase in cash in the year		(0.3)		4.1

Notes

a   Reconciliation of net incoming/(outgoing) resources to net cash (outflow)/inflow from operating activities

	2008	2007
	£m	**£m**
Net incoming/(outgoing) resources before revaluations and investment asset disposals	1.3	(6.5)
Deposit interest and investment income receivable	(3.6)	(3.3)
Depreciation charge	4.7	4.6
Profit on disposal of fixed assets	(0.1)	(0.3)
(Increase)/decrease in stocks	(1.2)	0.4
(Increase)/decrease in debtors	(6.2)	5.1
(Decrease)/Increase in creditors and provisions	(1.7)	3.6
FRS17 difference between pension contributions and current service costs	(2.3)	(1.2)
Net cash (outflow)/inflow from operating activities	(9.1)	2.4

[*continued on next page*]

Oxfam, continued

b Analysis of net funds

	At 1 May 2007 £m	Cashflow movement £m	At 30 April 2008 £m
Cash at bank and in hand	29.7	1.1	30.8
Cash on short term deposit	46.0	(8.5)	37.5
Debt due within one year	—	(0.5)	(0.5)
Debt due after one year	(0.1)	(1.0)	(1.1)
Net funds	75.6	(8.9)	66.7

c Reconciliation of net cash flow to movement in net funds

	2008 £m
Decrease in cash	(0.3)
Cash inflow from decrease in liquid resources *	(8.5)
Non-cash movement	(0.1)
Net funds at 1 May 2007	75.6
Net funds at 30 April 2008	66.7

* Liquid resources comprise monies held on short term Money Market accounts.

Endowment fund movements

12.29 Endowment fund movements are very specific to charities and consequently FRS 1 does not address how they should be dealt with within a cash flow statement.

12.30 SORP paragraph 354 instructs us that:

'Movements in endowments should not be included in cash flows from "operating activities" but should be treated as increases or decreases in the financing section.'

12.31 These somewhat complex disclosures are best illustrated in the following extract of the 'gross cash flows' note to a cash flow statement.

Extract from an example charity cash flow statement illustrating endowment fund movements

Gross cash flows

	£	£
Returns on investments and servicing the finance:		
– Interest received		10,000
– Investment income received		7,000
– Interest paid		(2,000)
		15,000
Capital expenditure:		
– Payments to acquire tangible fixed assets		(45,000)
– Receipts from the disposal of tangible fixed assets		14,000
– Payments to acquire endowment investments	(63,000)	
– Receipts from the disposal of endowment assets	71,000	
– Net movement in cash flows attributable to endowment investments		8,000
– Payments to acquire other investments		(30,000)
– Receipts from the disposal of other investments		26,000
		(27,000)
Management of liquid resources:		
– Purchase of treasury bills		(20,000)
– Disposal of treasury bills		16,000
		(4,000)
Financing:		
– Repayment of bank loan		(6,000)
– Net movement in cash flows attributable to endowment investments		(8,000)
		(14,000)

Chapter 13

Notes and disclosures

1 Introduction

13.1 The main thrust of SORP is to concentrate the report and accounts into three principal statements:

- the trustees' annual report;
- the Statement of Financial Activities (SOFA); and
- the balance sheet.

13.2 If these three statements are to be readily understood, they must be succinct and uncluttered. SORP, in relation to the classification of incoming resources and expenditure, suggests that these should be summarised in a manner appropriate to the charity. The accounts should not be excessively detailed. Supporting analyses should be provided in the notes to the accounts.

13.3 This chapter is therefore concerned with those matters which will be dealt with in the notes to the accounts and can be used as a checklist to ensure that all relevant matters have been considered. It covers the following:

accounting policies	transactions with trustees and related parties
funds structure and movements	indemnity insurance
connected charities	emoluments of employees
subsidiary undertakings	auditors' and independent examiner's remuneration
netting off	ex gratia payments
income from charity shops	tangible fixed assets
detail of income and expenditure	investments
grants payable	guarantees
concessionary loans	contingent assets and liabilities
support costs	secured loans

2 Accounting policies

13.4

'Charity accounts should include notes on the accounting policies chosen. These should be the most appropriate in the particular circumstances of each charity for the purpose of giving a true and fair view. The policies should be

consistent with this SORP, Accounting Standards and relevant legislation. FRS 18 explains how accounting policies should be determined.'
(para 356)

13.5   Paragraph 358 of SORP goes on to say that the accounting policies note should state that the accounts have been prepared in accordance with the SORP and accounting standards (or with the FRSSE if applicable), that they comply with the Charities Act or the Companies Act or other relevant statute, and that they are based on historic cost except for investments (and perhaps certain fixed assets) which have been included at revalued amounts.

13.6   If any part of the accounts does not accord with the SORP, the accounting policies note must give the reasons why the trustees judge that the treatment adopted is more appropriate in the circumstances, describe how it departs from the SORP and give an estimate of the financial effect on the accounts (paragraph 359).

13.7   Para 361 of SORP encourages trustees to give brief explanations of specific accounting policies which they have adopted to deal with material items. Examples of such items are contained in paragraphs 362–370 of SORP and cover policy notes on the following.

- Incoming resources: legacies, grants receivable, gifts-in-kind etc.
- Resources expended: recognition of liabilities, grants payable, allocation of costs.
- Assets: capitalisation, valuation, depreciation, heritage assets, investments, stocks and work-in-progress.
- Funds structure: types of fund and policy for transfers and allocations.
- Other items: pension fund, foreign exchange, finance and operating leases, irrecoverable VAT.

Comment

13.8   The first point to make is that the SORP is a guide; it is not to be slavishly followed. It is a question of identifying the material items contained in the accounts and then explaining the accounting policy adopted for each.

13.9   Successive SORPs from 1995 to date have been written with a view to enhancing comparability of charity accounts and clarifying and reducing the scope for differing interpretations of accounting requirements. SORP includes guidance on the recognition, measurement and presentation of almost all items likely to be material to charities' accounts. This has been further reinforced by the current SORP 2005. So why do we still have to disclose accounting policies?

13.10   There are three answers to this question.

- Not all readers of charity accounts are necessarily well-versed in SORP and they have a right to know the main accounting policies on which the accounts are based.

- UK accounting is principles-based rather than imposing rigid rules and so there are still areas in which judgement is applied in applying a general method and which may have a material impact on the results and financial position portrayed in the accounts. These will need to be explained to enable a reader to assess their impact and facilitate comparison with charities that have made different judgements in similar circumstances. Examples include the timing of income recognition, basis of allocation or apportionment of costs between the various headings, non-depreciation of certain assets etc.

- In certain cases, trustees may feel justified in adopting an accounting policy which is at variance to that contained in SORP. If so, and if it is material, this must be both explained and justified on the grounds of showing a true and fair view.

13.11   Many charities may, on practical grounds, find it difficult to comply with every aspect of SORP and will have to compromise. For example, they may not be able to account for all their branch activities and find it necessary to exclude some from the accounts. While this is not to be encouraged and may invite an audit qualification, it will considerably alleviate the situation if the matter is disclosed in the accounting polices, together with an indication as to what steps are being taken to correct the omission in future.

13.12   The accounts of Imperial Cancer Research for 2007/08 contain a very full and clear explanation of their accounting policies.

CANCER RESEARCH UK ANNUAL REPORT AND ACCOUNTS 2007/08

Notes to the Accounts

1. Accounting policies

Accounting convention

These accounts have been prepared under the historical cost convention as modified by the revaluation of investment properties and listed investments. They comply with the Statement of Recommended Practice 'Accounting and Reporting by Charities' as revised in 2005 ('the SORP'), together with the reporting requirements of the Companies Act 1985 – subject to a true and fair override in respect of investment properties – and applicable accounting standards. The significant accounting polices adopted are described below and are consistent with previous years.

Basis of consolidation

The consolidated accounts incorporate the results of Cancer Research UK ('the Charity'), its subsidiary undertakings and its share of the results of

[*continued on next page*]

Cancer Research UK, continued

its associate. The consolidated entity is referred to as 'the Group'. No separate company Statement of Financial Activities (SOFA) has been prepared for the Charity as permitted by section 230 of the Companies Act 1985 and paragraph 397 of the SORP.

Associated undertakings

The Group's share of its associated undertaking is included in the Group SOFA under the equity method of accounting. The Group balance sheet shows the investment in its associate at cost, less amounts written off.

Incoming resources

Incoming resources are included in the SOFA when the Group is entitled to the income and it can be quantified with reasonable certainty. Donations in kind, other than items donated for sale, are recognised at their value to the Group when they are received. No amounts are included for services donated by volunteers. Incoming resources comprise:

Voluntary income

Legacies	Pecuniary legacies are recognised as they are received. Residuary legacies are recognised at the earlier of receipt or agreement of the estate accounts. Reversionary interests involving a life tenant are not recognised due to the intrinsic uncertainties in valuing them.
Donor marketing	Donations are accounted for as received.
National events	Income from major events, including related sponsorship but excluding events registration and merchandise, is recognised in the period in which the event takes place.
Community fundraising	Income from groups of friends and local committees is accounted for when funds are received.
Gift Aid	Gift Aid is included based on amounts recoverable at the accounting date.

Activities for generating funds

Shop income	All retail income – from both donated and bought-in goods – is accounted for when the sale takes place.
Events registration	Registration fees are recognised when the event takes place. Sales of merchandise are accounted for when the transaction occurs.
Investment income	Investment income is accounted for on an accruals basis.

Incoming resources from charitable activities

Grant income	Grant income is recognised when the Group is entitled to receipt.

[continued on next page]

Cancer Research UK, continued

Technology development	Licence fees, royalties, assignment and option fees are recognised gross, before revenue share payments to third parties, on the basis that risk and rewards remain with the Group. Phased contractual receipts are recognised when they are due and on completion of the Group's contractual obligations for the period.

Resources expended

Expenditure is accounted for on an accruals basis. Allocations of support costs are based on the appropriate combination of staff time, department headcount, direct expenditure and activity levels. Irrecoverable VAT is included with the expense items to which it relates. Resources expended comprise:

Costs of generating voluntary income	These include salaries and directly attributable overheads, plus a proportion of central support costs.
Costs of fundraising trading	Shop costs include the cost of goods sold and the direct costs of operating the shops, plus a proportion of central support costs. No value is ascribed to goods donated for sale.
Costs of managing investments	These include salaries and other direct costs of managing the investment portfolio.
Costs of charitable activities	The presentation of charitable activities flows from the Charity's vision and purpose.
Research	This is the work that we carry out to fulfil our first and second purpose statements: 'We carry out world-class research to improve our understanding of cancer and find out how to prevent, diagnose and treat different types of cancer' and 'We ensure that our findings are used to improve the lives of cancer patients'. It includes basic, translational and clinical research.
Cancer information and advocacy	This involves the work to address our third purpose statement: 'We help people to understand cancer, the progress we are making and the choices each person can make.' It includes advocacy and activities to influence public policy.
Governance costs	These are the central running costs of the Charity, including strategic planning and public accountability.

The Group funds research by employees ('direct costs') and grant-funded researchers ('grant costs')

Direct costs	These include an allocation of technical support costs.

[continued on next page]

Cancer Research UK, continued

Grant costs	A research grant liability is recognised when the Group formally notifies the recipient of the award. The liability is measured as the total of expected payments for the period to the next scientific review. Provision is made for the expected total payments on life chairs/fellowships when the appointment is first made. Grant liabilities for awards where more than five years of expected payments are provided at the outset are discounted to current value using the weighted average cost of capital.
Support costs	Overhead costs which are integral to the Group's charitable activities are allocated accordingly as shown in Note 8.

Net investment gains and losses

The SOFA includes realised gains and losses from the sale of investments and unrealised gains and losses arising from the revaluation of investments.

Fixed assets and depreciation

Fixed assets are included at cost where that is greater than £2,500 for the Charity and its charitable subsidiaries and £500 for its trading subsidiaries, except that batches of items individually below those thresholds are capitalised if they form part of one project and together cost more than £50,000. Software is only capitalised where its cost exceeds £50,000. The costs of laboratory refurbishments are written off as they are incurred. Depreciation is provided so as to write off the cost of fixed assets on a straight-line basis over their expected useful economic lives, as follows:

Freehold land	Not depreciated
Freehold buildings	25 years
Leasehold buildings and research facilities	25 years, or lease period if shorter
Plant and equipment	4–5 years
Shop fixtures and fittings	5 years
Computer equipment and software	3 years

Impairment of fixed assets

Fixed assets are subject to review for impairment when there is an indication of a reduction in their carrying value. Any impairment is recognised in the SOFA in the year in which it occurs.

Investments

Listed investments are stated at market value. They are revalued immediately prior to disposal: as a result, no gain or loss arises on sale. Unlisted

[*continued on next page*]

Cancer Research UK, continued

investments are included at cost as an approximation to market value, unless there is specific evidence to the contrary. Subsidiary companies are valued at cost. Cash deposits intended to be held for the long term are shown under investments. All other cash balances are included as current assets. The SOFA includes unrealised gains and losses arising from the revaluation of the investment portfolio in the year.

Investment properties

Investment properties are included in the balance sheet at their estimated market value. Investment properties are formally revalued at least every five years by professional valuers and are reviewed annually to ensure that the most recent formal valuation is still reasonable. No depreciation is provided on investment properties, which represents a departure from the Companies Act 1985 requirements. These properties are held for investment and the Trustees consider that this policy is necessary to give a true and fair view in accordance with accounting standards.

Goodwill

Goodwill is calculated as the difference between the cost of a consolidated entity and the aggregate of the fair values of that entity's assets and liabilities. Negative goodwill arises when the aggregate fair values of the consolidated entity's assets and liabilities exceed any acquisition cost. Negative goodwill is recognised in the SOFA in the periods in which the assets are recovered. Negative goodwill arising from the acquisition of the Beatson Institute for Cancer Research is amortised on a straight line basis over 10 years.

Stock

Stock purchased for sale and research consumables are valued at the lower of cost and net realisable value. Stock does not include the value of goods donated for sale in the Group's charity shops.

Short term deposits

Short term deposits are current asset investments that are readily convertible into cash at or close to their carrying amount.

Fund accounting

Restricted funds can only be used for particular purposes within the objectives of the Charity and its charitable subsidiaries. Restrictions arise when specified by the donor or when funds are raised for particular purposes.

[*continued on next page*]

Cancer Research UK, continued

Permanent endowment funds are funds where the capital is held until the objectives of the Charity, or of the Trust deeds of each fund, are satisfied.

Designated funds are funds set aside by the Trustees out of unrestricted free reserves.

Free reserves are funds that can be used for any purpose within the Charity's objectives.

Pension deficit is reflected separately in reserves in accordance with the SORP.

Pension costs

The current service cost of the two defined benefit schemes which operated during the year is charged to employee costs over the anticipated period of employment. Net pension finance income or costs are included immediately in employee costs. Actuarial gains and losses are recognised immediately on the face of the SOFA. A provision for the combined scheme deficits is shown on the face of the balance sheet. The amounts charged to the SOFA for defined contribution schemes represent the contributions payable in the period.

Property dilapidation provision

The Group recognises dilapidation costs as they crystallise, or when plans to terminate the lease are confirmed.

Foreign currency

Transactions in foreign currency are recorded at the rate of exchange prevailing at the time of the transaction. Foreign currency balances are translated into sterling at the exchange rates prevailing at the balance sheet date. Any gains or losses on exchange are included in the SOFA.

The Group hedges net currency exposures (balances or future income and expenditure) of its trading subsidiaries by means of forward exchange contracts of up to 12 months. Gains and losses on forward exchange contracts are recognised in the SOFA at the same time as the hedged exposure.

Profits and losses of foreign subsidiaries are translated to sterling at average rates of exchange. The opening net assets and profit and loss accounts of those subsidiaries are retranslated to year end rates; exchange differences arising on the retranslation are taken to reserves.

Leases

Rentals payable under operating leases are charged to the SOFA evenly over the period of the lease.

[*continued on next page*]

Cancer Research UK, continued

Taxation

The activities of the Charity and its charitable subsidiaries are exempt from corporation taxation under section 505 of the Income and Corporation Taxes Act 1988 to the extent that they are applied to the organisation's charitable objectives. The trading subsidiaries do not pay UK corporation tax because their policy is to pay taxable profits as Gift Aid to the Charity. Foreign tax incurred by overseas subsidiaries is charged as it is incurred.

3 Funds' structure and movements

13.13   The accounting for separate funds within a charity is dealt with in paragraphs 65 and 66 of SORP and is covered in Chapter 5. This chapter concentrates on the notes to the accounts which help to amplify and explain the separate funds and their movements.

Paragraph 65 of SORP explains that whereas the accounts will *'provide a summary of the main funds, differentiating in particular between the unrestricted income funds, restricted income funds and endowment funds'*, the notes should give the details of material restricted funds, grouping them under suitable headings.

13.14   Paragraph 75 of SORP goes on to say that 'the notes to the accounts should provide information on the structure of the charity's funds so as to disclose the fund balances and the reasons for them...'.

13.15   Such notes will include a summary showing the following.

- The assets and liabilities representing each fund, analysed between investments, fixed assets and net current assets.

- An explanation of how each fund has arisen and its purpose, with details of restrictions imposed. An indication should be given as to whether or not suitable resources are held in each fund to meet any restrictions, eg if the funds have been given to be spent immediately, are they in liquid assets?

- Details of any funds in deficit. The Trustees' Report should contain an explanation of any such fund and what action they propose to remedy the position.

- Disclosure and explanations of material transfers between different funds, details of allocations to designated funds, and an explanation of the nature of transfers or allocations and reasons for them. In each case, transfers or allocations should be shown gross, ie without any netting off.

- Details relating to the unapplied total return if a total return approach to investments has been followed.

13.16 *Notes and disclosures*

Comment

13.16   As the reconciliation of funds will have to include the transfers between funds, it is likely that most charities having more than one fund will need only one note, or possibly two, to explain their funds structure and their movements.

13.17   Examples of the notes on fund accounting are given in Chapter 9.

4   Connected charities

13.18   Paragraph 44(f) of SORP says that the Trustees' annual report should provide information on the relationships between the charity and related parties, including its subsidiaries, and with any other charities and organisations with which it co-operates in the pursuit of its charitable objectives.

13.19   The Glossary of SORP defines connected charities as those:

'which have common, parallel or related objects and activities; and either

(a)   common control; or

(b)   unity of administration (eg shared management).

Within this category may be charities which come together under one umbrella organisation or are part of a federal structure.'
(para GL9)

Comment

13.20   The first point to note regarding the disclosure of information on connected charities is that SORP asks for this to be given in the annual report – not in the notes. This is reinforced by paragraph 44(d) to (f) of SORP which, in connection with the annual report, says that the narrative information should include a description of:

'(d)   The organisational structure of the charity and how decisions are made. For example, which types of decisions are taken by the charity trustees and which are delegated to staff..

(e)   Where the charity is part of a wider network (for example, charities affiliated within an umbrella group) then the relationship involved should also be explained where this impacts on the operating policies adopted by the charity.

(f)   The relationships between the charity and related parties, including its subsidiaries, and with any other charities and organisations with which it co-operates in pursuit of its charitable objectives.'

(para 44)

13.21 Clearly, therefore, reference must be made to connected charities in the trustees' annual report, but the detail concerning the names and addresses and material transactions should be given in the notes to the accounts, to which reference should be made in the annual report (see also **13.65** ff regarding related party transactions generally).

5   Subsidiary undertakings

13.22 Paragraph 383 of SORP requires a parent charity to prepare consolidated accounts including all its subsidiary undertakings. The only exceptions are:

- FRS 2 provides for the exclusion of certain subsidiary entities from the consolidation. Paragraph 384 of SORP states that this is unlikely to apply to chartable groups;

- The gross income of the group, after consolidation adjustments, is below the audit threshold, currently £500,000;

- The subsidiary undertakings' results are not material to the group;

- The accounts have to be aggregated under charity legislation, for example by virtue of being a special trust or a charity subject to a uniting direction.

13.23 Paragraph 381 of SORP says that consolidated accounts should be prepared for the reporting charity and its subsidiaries irrespective of whether the subsidiaries are also companies.

13.24 Disclosure notes relating to consolidation are contained in paragraphs 398 to 404 of SORP. In summary, these are as follows.

- A separate comment in the Trustees' Annual Report concerning the performance of the subsidiaries.

- An accounting policy note of the method of consolidation and which subsidiaries are included and which excluded.

- Figures given in the notes should generally show the position for the group as well as for the parent undertaking.

- The aggregate amount of the total investment by the charity in its subsidiaries and, unless the subsidiary is not material, the following details: its name; the parent charity's shareholding or other means of control; how its activities relate to those of the charity; the aggregate amount of the assets, liabilities and funds of each subsidiary and a summary of the turnover, expenditure and profit or loss of each.

- If any subsidiaries are excluded or if consolidated accounts are not prepared, 'the trustees should explain the reasons in a note to the charity's accounts with reference to each excluded subsidiary undertaking' (para 404).

13.25 *Notes and disclosures*

Comment

13.25 Whilst the rules relating to consolidation are clear, there is a danger that the amalgamation of figures from both charitable and non-charitable subsidiary companies and other undertakings may obscure some of the main messages contained in the accounts of a charity. This point is recognised in paragraph 405 of SORP which recommend that trustees should choose appropriate line headings to reflect the underlying activities of the group and, if that is insufficient, segmented information should be given in the notes so that the results of the parent charity and each subsidiary undertaking are transparent.

'Examples of items that should be separately disclosed include the costs of generating funds, the costs of charitable activities and governance costs.' (para 405)

NATIONAL TRUST ANNUAL REPORT 2007/08

7   Notes to the Financial Statements

Charitable Trading and Commercial Activities Contribution

The National Trust owns 100% of the share capital of The National Trust (Enterprises) Limited, which during the year was responsible for activities including retailing, events, sponsorship income and the national raffle. Arrangements are in place to donate by Gift Aid the whole of the company's surplus income to the Trust each year.

The income, expenditure and contribution of The National Trust (Enterprises) Limited to Trust funds were:

	Income		Expenditure		Contribution	
	2008 **£'000**	2007 £'000	**2008** **£'000**	2007 £'000	**2008** **£'000**	2007 £'000
Commercial operations	**34,984**	32,540	**27,933**	25,953	**7,051**	6,587
Events and functions	**5,889**	6,195	**4,356**	4,670	**1,533**	1,525
Sponsorship and licences	**2,707**	2,125	**1,038**	811	**1,669**	1,314
National raffle	**1,947**	1,640	**360**	127	**1,587**	1,513
Other activities	**5,604**	5,501	**5,455**	5,330	**149**	171
Pension costs	**—**	—	**(15)**	(34)	**15**	34
	51,131	48,001	**39,127**	36,857	**12,004**	11,144

Certain charitable trading activities are undertaken by the National Trust itself. The contribution from these activities was as follows:

[*continued on next page*]

National Trust, continued

	Income		Expenditure		Contribution	
	2008 **£'000**	2007 £'000	**2008** **£'000**	2007 £'000	**2008** **£'000**	2007 £'000
Catering	**30,903**	26,619	**25,062**	21,924	**5,841**	4,695
Holiday cottages	**7,118**	6,455	**4,717**	4,162	**2,401**	2,293
Other	**4,128**	3,568	**3,035**	2,516	**1,093**	1,052
	42,149	36,642	**32,814**	28,602	**9,335**	8,040
Total	**93,280**	84,643	**71,941**	65,459	**21,339**	19,184

Other charitable trading activities include income from car-parks and basecamps.

The reserves of The National Trust (Enterprises) Limited as at 29 February were:

	2008 £	2007 £
Share Capital	100	100
Profit and Loss Account	—	—
Revaluation Reserve	532,920	755,000
	533,020	755,100

6 Netting off

13.26 Paragraph 95 of SORP states:

'All incoming resources should be reported gross when raised by the charity (or by volunteers working at the charity's direction) or its agents. However, where funds are raised or collected for the charity by individuals not employed or contracted by the charity, the gross incoming resources of the charity are the proceeds remitted to the charity by the organisers of the event, after deducting their expenses.'
(para 95)

13.27 The general rule should be that all income is shown gross.

13.28 In the past, charities have occasionally been tempted to net 'capital' grants off the cost of any asset purchased from the grant and capitalise and depreciate the net amount. This would be comparable to the deferral of grants for capital purposes required by Statement of Standard Accounting Practice 4 – Accounting for government grants. That standard provides for matching of income and expenditure where SORP rules require incoming resources to be recognised immediately and expenditure (as depreciation charges) over the whole life of the assets concerned. Paragraph 255 of SORP makes it clear that this approach is not permissible:

'If a functional fixed asset is acquired in full or in part from the proceeds of a grant it should be included at its full acquisition cost (or in the case of a joint arrangement at the gross value of the charity's share in the asset (see paragraph 416)) without netting off the grant proceeds .'
(para 255(b))

Comment

13.29 The rule against netting off is welcome as it not only ensures that the cost/benefit ratio of fundraising activities is disclosed, but also ensures that the scale of trading activities carried on by subsidiary companies is prominently disclosed. The rule forbidding the netting off of a grant against the cost of an asset purchased with the grant ensures that the asset is capitalised at its true costs or worth and that the depreciation charge is based on that cost, thereby ensuring that the full cost of the asset is charged to expenditure over its useful life. It should be noted that for a charitable company, the netting off is also specifically prohibited by the Companies Act accounting rules.

7 Income from charity shops

13.30 One of the main areas where 'netting off' has been a particularly contentious and common area is the treatment of income from charity shops. However, paragraph 95 of SORP (see above) is categoric that all incoming resources, including proceeds from the sale of donated and bought goods, should be accounted for gross.

13.31 Paragraph 137 of SORP requires that the income from charity shops should be included within the Statement of Financial Activities heading 'Activities for generating funds'. Although requiring this categorisation, the SORP acknowledges that income from the sale of donated goods might also be regarded as the realisation of a gift-in-kind. In the past, many charities have taken this view and included the sale proceeds within donations and voluntary income. However, the SORP states that such income is essentially no different from trading income and hence should be classified as income from activities for generating funds.

'Whilst selling donated goods is legally considered to be the realisation of a donation-in-kind (see paragraph 129(c)), in economic terms it is similar to a trading activity and should be included in this section.'
(para 138)

Comment

13.32 This is reasonable and easy to comply with if the charity shops only sell donated and bought-in goods. If this is the case, in most instances the shops will be operated directly by the charity.

13.33 The situation becomes more complex where the shop engages in broader activities such as promoting the charity's campaigning or recruiting volunteers. SORP implies, at first glance, that the different types of activity should be treated differently in the accounts of the charity.

- The sale of goods made by the beneficiaries is a primary purpose trading activity, not an activity for generating funds.

- The sale of donated and bought-in goods is regarded as trading income and should be accounted for as explained above.

Paragraph 139 of SORP addresses this issue and permits all incoming resources from the shop to be classified as 'retail income' under 'activities for generating funds'. This is a common sense approach and is welcomed.

> 'It may be possible to identify the incoming resources and resources expended for each different component of activity (this may have to be done for tax purposes) but often these will be viewed as a single economic activity. Charity trustees should consider the balance of the activities being undertaken to determine the most appropriate place to include the incoming resources from such enterprises but having done this the components of incoming resources need not be analysed further. For example a shop may mainly sell donated and bought in goods, but it may also sell a small amount of goods made by its beneficiaries and incidentally provide information about the charity. It would be acceptable to classify all the incoming resources from the shop as "shop income" under activities for generating funds.'
>
> (para 139)

The issue is further complicated where shops are operated through a trading subsidiary and sell a mixture of donated goods and bought-in goods for resale. The sale of donated goods is not a trading activity and, in theory, could be carried out by the charity itself. It might be argued, therefore, that income from the sale of donated goods should be accounted for gross within activities for generating funds. The sale of bought-in goods is a trading activity and will be carried out by the trading subsidiary and should be accounted for in that entity's accounts in accordance with normal accounting rules. All operating costs (excluding those incurred in the sale of donated goods) should be deducted from the proceeds to arrive at an accounting and a taxable profit, the latter of which will be paid over to the charity as a Gift Aid payment and shown as a receipt from the trading subsidiary in the accounts of the charity.

13.34 There are a number of implications arising from this.

- Income from the sale of donated goods is credited gross directly to the charity's accounts even though the goods have been sold through a charity shop operated by a trading subsidiary of the charity. None of the overheads incurred by the trading subsidiary should be deducted from the sale proceeds. Instead, they should be shown as costs of generating funds.

- All other overhead costs (including apportioned salaries of shop staff) are deducted from the proceeds of the sale of bought in goods prior to calculating the Gift Aid payment to be made to the charity by the trading subsidiary.

- The shops need to maintain detailed records showing the proceeds from the sale of donated goods and the proceeds from the sale of bought-in goods. In addition, to ensure that such records are accurate, the two types of goods will have to be clearly identifiable within the shop.

13.35 Clearly the practical problems caused by this differentiation of the sale of donated and bought-in goods demands the application of a common sense solution. Two such solutions would appear to present themselves.

1 One solution is to split out the income from the sale of donated goods from that of the sale of bought-in goods, but to allocate overheads to each of the two categories. The gross sale proceeds of donated goods would then be shown as income from activities for generating funds in the charity's Statement of Financial Activities with the costs charged separately as costs of generating funds, but both would be cross-referenced to a note showing gross proceeds and the expenses deducted to arrive at the net benefit to the charity. The sale of bought-in goods less the remaining overhead costs would be accounted for within the subsidiary's accounts and then shown on the charity's Statement of Financial Activities as part of 'Income from generating funds'.

2 An alternative solution is to account for all the sales, regardless of whether they arise from donated goods or from bought-in goods, through the trading subsidiary and to show the total income on the face of the charity's Statement of Financial Activities as 'Retail income'. The figure would be cross-referenced to a note to the accounts giving details of the two types of sale with no attempt to allocate expenditure between them.

13.36 Of the two possible solutions, the first is more in keeping with the spirit of SORP and should, in most instances, provide a fair representation of the charity's activities while the second solution may be better at minimising the practical problems.

8 Detail of income and expenditure

13.37 As discussed in Chapter 8, expenditure should be analysed according to its activity based classification on the face of the Statement of Financial Activities. In other words, the analysis of expenditure contained within the Statement of Financial Activities should be sufficient to enable the reader to identify the key charitable activities.

13.38 Paragraph 177 of the SORP states that 'the Statement of Financial Activities or the notes to the accounts should include an analysis of the sub-activities, programmes, projects or other initiatives that contribute to a particular activity category'.

THE THOMAS CORAM FOUNDATION FOR CHILDREN
ANNUAL REPORT AND ACCOUNTS 31 MARCH 2008

Balance sheet

	Notes	2008 £	2008 £	2007 £	2007 £
Fixed assets					
Tangible assets	10		4,211,904		4,256,740
Investments	11		12,641,748		13,909,405
			16,853,652		18,166,145
Current assets					
Debtors	12	1,051,727		908,713	
Short term deposits		2,044,366		859,087	
Cash at bank and in hand		429,782		433,849	
		3,525,875		2,201,649	
Creditors: amounts falling within one year	13	1,096,636		1,233,448	
Net current assets			2,429,239		968,201
Total net assets excluding pension liability			19,282,891		19,134,346
Pension liability	9		(1,185,000)		(1,582,000)
Total net assets including pension liability			18,097,891		17,552,346
Represented by:					
Funds and reserves					
Capital funds:					
● General endowment fund	14		6,036,900		6,165,517
● Pension deficit reduction fund	14		3,117,319		3,000,000
● Building, repair and maintenance fund	14		3,645,289		3,750,000
● Fixed asset permanent endowment fund	15		3,997,356		4,066,888
Income funds					
General funds	16				
● Free reserves		346,418		339,176	
● Pension reserve		(1,185,000)		(1,582,000)	
			(838,582)		(1,242,824)
Designated funds	17		855,965		591,045
Furniture and equipment fund	18		214,547		189,851
Restricted funds	19		1,069,097		1,031,869
			18,097,891		17,552,346

Approved by the trustees
and signed on their behalf by:

Chairman

Treasurer

Approved on

THE CHILDREN'S SOCIETY ANNUAL REPORT AND ACCOUNT 2007/08

9   Resources Expended

Analysis of resources expended

	Direct Costs £000	Support Costs £000	Total Costs 2008 £000	Total Costs 2007 £000
Cost of generating funds				
Cost of fundraising activities				
Events and other activities				
Charity	876	31	**907**	754
Trading Company	441	15	**456**	617
Shops operating costs	3,381	302	**3,683**	3,681
Total cost of fundraising activities	4,698	348	**5,046**	5,052
Cost of generating voluntary income	5,772	491	**6,263**	5,833
Fundraising costs for income in future years	2,640	136	**2,776**	2,958
Investment management costs	–	–	**–**	32
Total cost of generating funds	13,110	975	**14,085**	13,875
Charitable activities				
Childcare and protection				
Unrestricted	17,649	2,871	**20,520**	20,456
Endowment and restricted	1,099	179	**1,278**	845
Total childcare and protection	18,748	3,050	**21,798**	21,301
Campaigning	3,672	406	**4,078**	2,935
Policy and research	1,356	211	**1,567**	1,409
Public education	2,047	–	**2,047**	184
Governance costs	225	18	**243**	276
Total expenditure on charitable activities	26,048	3,685	**29,733**	26,105
Total resources expended	**39,158**	**4,660**	**43,818**	**39,980**

[continued on next page]

The Children's Society, continued

Support costs	£000	Basis of allocation
Financial management	**1,309**	Estimate of time spent on supporting the various activities
People and Organisation Development	**1,020**	Head count
Information Systems	**1,142**	Number of PCs held
Facilities	**631**	Head count
Estates	**558**	Head count
	4,660	

Resources expended also include:

	Note	2008 £000	2007 £000
Operating lease rentals (land and buildings)		**1,477**	1,472
Depreciation charge	*14*	**593**	473
Auditors' remuneration			
Audit of these financial statements [Society £51,650 (2007: £49,200)]		**5**	49
Audit of financial statements of subsidiaries pursuant to legislation		**5**	5

10 Governance costs

	2008 £000	2007 £000
Internal audit	**45**	76
External audit	**57**	54
Trustee board administration costs	**58**	80
Trustees' indemnity insurance	**8**	8
Apportionment of executive directors' costs	**33**	30
Health and safety	**42**	28
	243	276

9   Grants payable

13.39   Since the late 1980s there has been criticism of grant-making charities over their secrecy and apparent unwillingness to disclose to whom they made grants and for what purpose. As a consequence, the requirements for grants payable disclosure contained within the SORP are detailed and extensive.

Definition

13.40   The SORP defines a grant as 'any payment which, in order to further its objects, a charity makes voluntarily to another institution or individual'. The

SORP makes it clear that the definition does not include any payment made in consideration of the supply to the grantmaker of assets or services, ie the grant must be given for nil consideration. If the payment is made in pursuance of a contract, it is not a grant.

The requirements for disclosure

13.41   Whether grantmaking is the sole activity of the charity or not, an analysis of the grantmaking costs, if material, should be provided within the notes to the accounts. The information provided should give the reader a reasonable understanding of the nature of the activities or projects which are being funded and whether the grants are being made to individuals or institutions. For institutional grants, further disclosure should be included regarding the recipient(s) of the funding. The details of the recipients are not required for grants made to individuals.

Comment

13.42   This distinction is extremely sensible and ensures that for those charities where grantmaking is only a small part of their total activities, grant disclosure does not detract from the charity's other work.

Specific disclosure requirements

13.43   SORP itself splits grants payable into two categories:

- those payable to institutions;
- and those payable to individuals.

An individual grant constitutes a payment to an individual where the individual is the direct beneficiary, such as an educational bursary. All other grants are classed as grants to institutions. The SORP gives the following example:

> '... a grant which is made to an individual to carry out a research project should be regarded as a grant to the institution with which the individual is connected rather than as a grant to the individual.

> Regardless of whether grants are given to individuals or to institutions, the SORP requires an analysis of grant-making activities to be given in the accounts which discloses the total number and the total value of the grants given for different charitable purposes, ie by nature or type of project being supported. The actual classifications used will be left to the specific grant-making charity to decide but could, for example, include social welfare, medical research, the performing arts, etc. Where grant-making is significant, a charity might also decide to provide further analysis, for example, showing a geographical analysis of grants payable. value of grants made.'

Grants payable to institutions

13.44   Paragraphs 206 and 207 of SORP require the following details to be disclosed with regard to grants made by a charity to institutions.

'If a charity has made grants to particular institutions that are material in the context of grantmaking, the charity should disclose details, as specified in paragraph 207, of a sufficient number of institutional grants to provide a reasonable understanding of the range of institutions it has supported. This information may be provided either in the notes to the accounts, or as part of the Trustees' Annual Report or by means of a separate publication. Where the analysis is contained in a separate publication, it should be made available by the charity to the public on request. The notes to the accounts should identify the publication and state how copies of it can be obtained.'
(para 206)

'The disclosure of institutional grants should give the name of the institution and the total value of grants made to that institution in the accounting year. Where grants have been made to a particular institution to undertake different activities or projects, the total value of the grants made for each activity or purpose should be disclosed. For example, a charity may have made grants to different officers of a particular university for different projects. Such grants should be treated as having been made to the institution.'
(para 207)

13.45   Whether grant-making is the sole activity of the charity or not, an analysis of the grant-making costs, if material, should be provided within the notes to the accounts. The information provided should give the reader a reasonable understanding of the nature of the activities or projects which are being funded and whether the grants are being made to individuals or institutions. For institutional grants, further disclosure should be included regarding the recipient(s) of the funding. The details of the recipients are not required for grants made to individuals.

13.46   An individual grant constitutes a payment to an individual where the individual is the direct beneficiary, such as an educational bursary. All other grants are classed as grants to institutions. The SORP gives the following example:

'… a grant which is made to an individual to carry out a research project should be regarded as a grant to the institution with which the individual is connected rather than as a grant to the individual.'

Regardless of whether grants are given to individuals or to institutions, the SORP requires an analysis of grant-making activities to be given in the accounts which discloses the total number and the total value of the grants given for different charitable purposes, ie by nature or type of project being supported. The actual classifications used will be left to the specific grant-making charity to decide but could, for example, include social welfare, medical research, the performing arts, etc. Where grant-making is significant, a charity might also decide to provide further analysis, for example, showing a geographical analysis of grants payable.

THE HENRY SMITH CHARITY ANNUAL REPORT AND
FINANCIAL STATEMENTS FOR THE YEAR ENDED 31
DECEMBER 2007

Review of Grant-Making

A Summary of 2007

The Trustees awarded grants of £26.2m, an increase of £0.1m from 2006.
Total awards on our main grants programme increased by £0.7m but we
awarded £0.7m less on Major Grants.

Administration costs were approximately 3% of grants awarded.

Grant expenditure	2007 £m	2006 £m
Main grant programme (grants above £10k)	21.9	21.2
Small grants (up to £10k)	1.6	1.5
Major Grants – East Lancashire and Domestic Violence Advocacy	0.7	1.4
Grants to Poor Kindred	0.5	0.4
Grants to Needy Clergy	0.5	0.6
Grants for the furtherance or promotion of knowledge and religion	0.4	0.4
Estates Fund distributions	0.5	0.5
Holiday grants	0.1	0.1
Total grant awards	**26.2**	**26.1**
Less: grants cancelled or returned	(0.4)	(0.5)
Add: grant administration costs	0.8	0.8
Total grants expenditure	**26.6**	**26.4**

A Review of the Main Grants Programme

	2007 £m	2006 £m
Number of applications	1,449	1,327
Number of grants awarded	314	331
Application success rate	22%	25%
Number of one-off grant awards	47	89
Number of multi-year grant awards	267	239
Average size of one-off grant awards	£65,000	£56,000
Average size of multi-year grant awards	£70,000	£68,000

The number of applications to our main grants programme increased by
9%. Around a quarter of applications were successful, giving a total of
314 grant awards.

The number of one-off grants fell by almost 50%, despite a similar volume
of capital appeals to 2006. Overall expenditure on one-off grants fell from
£5m to £3m. [*continued on next page*]

The Henry Smith Charity, continued

The number and size of multi-year awards was slightly higher than 2006, giving total multi-year grants awarded of £19m. Around 30% of these awards were given as continuation funding, following the completion of previous awards.

Size of Awards

Number of One-Off Grants

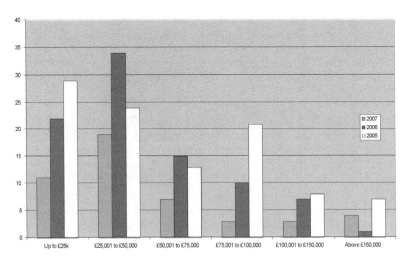

Fewer one-off grants of all sizes were made, with the exception of 4 grants above £150,000 (1 in 2006).

Number of Multi-Year Grants

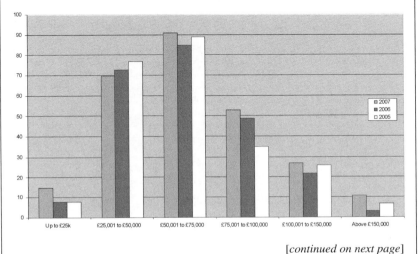

[*continued on next page*]

The Henry Smith Charity, continued

The spread of multi-year grants was very similar to 2006, except for grants above £150,000 where 11 were awarded compared to 3 in 2006.

Total grants awarded by region

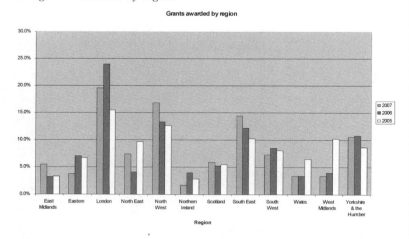

London and North-West regions continued to receive the highest amount of grant awards. There were increases in East Midlands and North-East funding, with falls in Eastern and Northern Ireland regions.

Northern Ireland funding was the lowest at 1.4% of total awards. We will be funding a pilot programme in partnership with the Esmee Fairbairn Foundation in late 2008, which we hope will substantially increase our funding in the region.

Total grants awarded by programme area

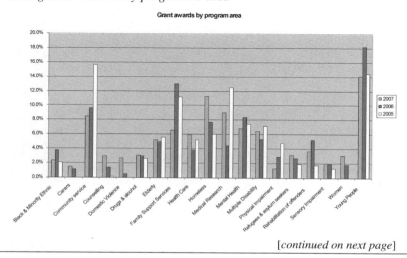

[*continued on next page*]

The Henry Smith Charity, continued

Young People continued to receive the highest funding. Of the major funding areas, Family Support Services saw a large decrease in funding, while our new working relationship with Action Medical Research gave rise to a substantial increase in Medical Research funding.

A review of major grants

We have just completed making awards for programmes focussed on Independent Domestic Violence Advocates and East Lancashire. On our East Lancashire programme we awarded grants totalling £1.5m with a focus on children, youth and intergenerational projects aiming to increase the support and stability of families and the mutual understanding of communities. We awarded grants totalling £0.9m under our Domestic Violence Advocates programmes.

Evaluations have just started for these programmes, and will be carried on throughout the lifetime of the grants, up to 2010.

Looking forward

The Trustees have agreed a total grants budget of just over £27m for 2008. We hope to increase total awards on our main grants programme by 4%.

The Trustees have also agreed a Major Grants budget of £2m to be spent over 2008 to 2010. A pilot programme in Northern Ireland has been agreed with a budget of £0.5m, to be launched in late 2008, jointly with the Esmee Fairbairn Foundation. We have also agreed in principle to invest £0.75m over 3 year in Inspiring Scotland, the venture philanthropy venture launched in 2008.

Notes to the Accounts

4. Grants awarded

	2007 £'000	2006 £'000
Grants to organisations		
Main Grants	21,920	21,153
Small Grants	1,569	1,529
Major Grants	734	1,512
Holiday Grants	64	86
Grants for the promotion of religion and knowledge	349	470
Estates Fund distributions	530	465
	25,166	25,215

[*continued on next page*]

The Henry Smith Charity, continued

	2007 £'000	2006 £'000
Grants to individuals		
Grants to Clergy	532	560
Grants to Poor Kindred	466	439
	998	999
Less: grants returned or cancelled	(346)	(519)
Total Grants Awarded	25,818	25,695

Further analysis of our main grant awards is given in the Trustees' Report and a full grants listing is available on our website.

Grants to individuals

13.47   Charities which give grants to individuals need only disclose the aggregate value of such grants and the total number given.

Comment

13.48   The disclosure of grants payable is a contentious area and a number of concerns have been voiced about the requirements of SORP.

These concerns include the following.

(a)   Why do the grant payments have to be disclosed in detail and not, for example, the payments made under largest projects or any other area of the charity's expenditure? The Charity Commission find grants more difficult to monitor than other charitable expenditure.

(b)   Why distinguish between grants to individuals and grants to institutions?

(c)   Will not such detailed disclosure detract from the overall message of the charity's accounts, particularly when the charity is not only involved in grantmaking? It should not if the detail is contained in a separate publication or the Trustees' Annual Report.

(d)   What is the responsibility of auditors with regard to verifying grant disclosure details, particularly when the details are given in a separate publication? They must ensure that the accounts are not misleading in any material respect and if the accounts rely upon information contained in a separate document then, if material, the auditors will have to satisfy themselves that the content of that other document justifies the accounts' reliance upon it.

13.49   The question of the recognition of liabilities is also very relevant with regard to grants payable. The recognition of liabilities is dealt with in Chapters

8 and 11 and so we only refer to it briefly here. Where a charity's trustees are under an unconditional obligation to make a grant (even if that obligation is only a moral one), and also if that grant is to be paid in a number of instalments over a number of years, it will be necessary to recognise, as expenditure, the full grant in the year in which the commitment is made and treat the amounts payable in future years as liabilities. However, where a grant commitment is made in principle, but the charity has retained the discretion to avoid making the future grant payments, then it may not be appropriate to account for the grant as a liability but simply to disclose the commitment in the notes to the accounts.

10   Concessionary loans

13.50   Many charities, particularly benevolent associations, make interest-free loans (or loans with interest at non-commercial rates) to their beneficiaries, in furtherance of their charitable objectives. Although not explicitly required by SORP, it is generally deemed good practice for the notes to the accounts of such charities to give information regarding such loans and that the charity should regularly consider whether such loans are recoverable or not. More substantial loans, particularly if extended on formal terms over longer periods, would be regarded as programme related investments.

Comment

13.51   Most charities should have little difficulty in meeting these requirements.

11   Support costs

13.52   While it may be obvious to which category of expenditure many over-heads relate, for example the salary of the fundraiser will be attributed to costs of generating funds, the SORP emphasises the need to apportion certain over-heads between the various expenditure heads. Support costs comprise those core costs and overheads which cannot be directly attributed to specific headings within the Statement of Financial Activities.

13.53   The basis of such apportionment may vary according to the type of overhead and the sophistication of the charity's accounting system but it should be reasonable, practicable to apply and be such that the same basis can be used from one year to another unless there is a fundamental change in circumstances. Paragraphs 164 and 165 of the SORP reflect that, whilst support costs enable a charity to deliver its objectives, they do not constitute a specific activity and should be, therefore, allocated to the activity headings.

'In undertaking any activity there may be support costs incurred that, whilst necessary to deliver an activity, do not themselves produce or constitute the output of the charitable activity. Similarly, costs will be incurred in supporting income generation activities such as fundraising, and in supporting the governance of the charity. Support costs include the central or

regional office functions such as general management, payroll administration, budgeting and accounting, information technology, human resources, and financing.'
(para 164)

'Support costs do not, in themselves, constitute an activity, instead they enable output-creating activities to be undertaken. Support costs are therefore allocated to the relevant activity cost category they support on the bases set out in paragraphs 168 to 174. This enables the total cost of an activity category to be disclosed in the Statement of Financial Activities and for the cost of the constituent sub-activities to be presented at a service, programme or project level within the notes to the accounts. There is nevertheless legitimate user interest in both the level of support costs incurred and the policies adopted for their allocation to the relevant activity cost categories that should be addressed through relevant note disclosures.'
(para 165)

13.54   The SORP requires the disclosure of the total support costs incurred by the charity together with a breakdown of the material items or categories of expenditure included within support costs. Furthermore, if support costs are material, the notes to the accounts should provide an explanation of how the costs have been allocated to each of the activity cost categories in the Statement of Financial Activities. The explanation may show percentages or the absolute value of amounts allocated, details of the methods of apportionment or a table setting out this information. Paragraph 167 of the SORP provides an example table for such disclosure:

Support cost (examples)	Fund-raising	Activity 1	Activity 2	Activity 3	Activity 4	Activity 5	Basis of allocation
Management	£X	£X	£X	£X	£X	£X	Text describing method
Finance	£X	£X	£X	£X	£X	£X	Text describing method
Information technology	£X	£X	£X	£X	£X	£X	Text describing method
Human resources	£X	£X	£X	£X	£X	£X	Text describing method
Total	£X	£X	£X	£X	£X	£X	

13.55   The importance of determining the bases for allocation should not be underestimated, nor should the time and thought charities will need to put into deciding on appropriate bases, particularly in the first year in which the revised SORP is applied.

13.56   Typical examples of the ways in which support costs can be apportioned are as follows.

Floor space

13.57   This may be used as a basis for allocating costs such as light, heat, rent, rates, maintenance of properties, property depreciation, etc, between the various headings of costs of generating funds, costs of charitable activities and governance costs.

Time spent

13.58   The chief executive of the charity may spend his or her time involved in all aspects of the charity's activities. In order to allocate his or her salary across the appropriate headings, it may be necessary to take a typical week in his or her working life and record the amount of time spent involved in each of the main expense categories. This information can then be used to determine percentages to be used when allocating the chief executive's annual salary for statutory accounts purposes. A similar exercise may be necessary for other staff members who are involved in several areas of the charity's work.

Actual usage of common services

13.59   By careful logging and recording, it may be possible to allocate certain overhead costs such as printing, postage, stationery, telephone, photocopying, etc, on an actual usage basis. This will probably only be applicable for charities with significant expenditure under any of these headings.

Disclosure of basis used

13.60   Whichever basis is used to allocate overhead costs across the headings shown on the face of the Statement of Financial Activities, Paragraph 154 of SORP requires: 'The basis and principles used for the allocation of all costs should be disclosed clearly in the accounting policies.'

Comment

13.61   Common sense should be the guiding principle. Charities should ensure that the methodology used to allocate costs is not overly cumbersome and time consuming. The benefits of achieving a greater degree of accuracy may only be possible at a high incremental cost to the charity.

GIRLS FRIENDLY SOCIETY IN ENGLAND AND WALES –
EXTRACT FROM THE ACCOUNTS FOR THE YEAR ENDED
30 SEPTEMBER 2007

Resources expended and the basis of apportioning costs (extract)

a.   The costs of charitable activities comprise expenditure on the charity's primary charitable purposes as described in the trustees' report. Such costs include:

- staff costs and associated expenses

[continued on next page]

Girls Friendly Society, continued

- day to day running expenses of schemes and projects

- special projects and equipment

- maintenance and building costs for the schemes and projects.

The majority of costs are directly attributable to specific activities. Certain shared costs are apportioned on the basis of the relative size of the schemes and projects.

b.   Head office costs represent indirect charitable expenditure. In order to carry out the primary purposes of the charity it is necessary to provide support in the form of personnel development, financial procedures, provision of office services and equipment and a suitable working environment. These costs are allocated out to the activities they are supporting on the basis described in note 8.

Note 8 'Head Office cost' (extract)

Head Office costs are allocated across the activities as follows:

	Community projects £	Parish-based branch work £	Other activities £	**Total £**	Basis of apportionment
Staff costs	110,074	3,870	4,129	**118,073**	
Staff and volunteer expenses	3,067	100	107	**3,274**	
Legal and professional fees	—	—	—	**—**	Headcount
Bank charges	2,948	122	130	**3,200**	
Office administration and miscellaneous	36,269	1,185	1,264	**38,718**	
	152,358	5,277	5,630	**163,265**	

CAFOD – ACCOUNTS FOR THE YEAR ENDED 31 MARCH 2007 (EXTRACT)

Accounting policies (extract) – Resources expended:

All expenditure is accounted for on an accruals basis.

Grants payable:

These are charged to the Statement of Financial Activities when they have been approved. Programme grants approved but not disbursed at the balance sheet date, are carried forward as programme creditors in the balance sheet.

Resources expended: Operating and support costs:

Operating costs include the costs of the trading company and the costs of all teams in CAFOD, other than Finance, Facilities, IT and Organisational Development and Personnel, which represent Support Costs.

Operating costs are classified under the expenditure activity headings on the basis of the contribution the teams make to each activity. Support costs are apportioned on the basis of the number of staff included within each activity.

The expenditure activity headings are:

- *Costs of generating funds* which is the costs incurred in attracting voluntary income, and those incurred in trading activities that raise funds;

- *CAFOD's international programme* which is its work with partners on long term development and immediate relief in emergencies situations;

- *CAFOD's education, policy and campaigning programme* which is its work to change the unjust policies and systems that trap people living in poverty; and

- *Governance* which includes costs incurred on the governance of CAFOD's assets and is primarily associated with the constitutional and statutory requirements.

[*continued on next page*]

CAFOD, continued

Note 4 – Operating and Support Costs

	Operating Costs £000	Support costs £000	Total 2007 £000	Total 2006 £000
Staff costs	8,437	1,766	10,203	8,841
Printing postage & stationery	429	160	589	720
Rent, rates, utilities & telephone	325	143	468	376
Repairs & maintenance	257	206	463	396
General office costs	-	40	40	43
Travel costs	905	50	955	864
Advertising & publications	1,420	2	1,422	1,223
Professional fees & consultancies	760	186	946	712
UK audit fee	35	-	35	33
Capacity building with partners	1,113	-	1,113	303
Other fees to UK auditors	-	2	2	3
Depreciation & disposal of assets	(20)	299	279	294
Trading	118	-	118	98
Irrecoverable VAT	-	320	320	295
Operating and support costs	**13,779**	**3,174**	**16,953**	14,201

12   Transactions with trustees and related persons

13.62   The Charities (Accounts and Reports) Regulations require disclosure of any transaction undertaken in the name of the charity (or on its behalf) in which any trustee, or person connected to a trustee, has a material interest. These requirements are linked closely with the need under FRS 8 'Related party Transactions' to disclose material transactions with those deemed to be a related party to the charity. The SORP ensures that charity accounting requirements are consistent with those of FRS 8 by requiring disclosure, in a note to the accounts, of situations where the reporting charity or any institution connected with it (see below) enters into a 'related party transaction'. A related party transaction is one where the charity has a relationship with another party or parties (the related party) which might inhibit it from pursing its own separate interests.

Definitions

13.63   In assessing whether a transaction needs to be disclosed or not the following definitions are important.

Material

13.64   An item is defined as being material if its inclusion (or exclusion) would be likely to influence a reader of the report and accounts either in relation to the report and accounts as a whole or in relation to the context of which the item forms part. It is for the trustees to decide whether an item is material or not. The requirements are complex because they require consideration of whether the transaction is material to the related party, in addition to the charity. Hence, it is possible for a transaction to require disclosure even though it may be immaterial to the charity.

Related parties

13.65   Related parties include all of the following:

● 'Institution Connected with a Charity'

An institution is connected with a charity if it is controlled by (in Scotland managed or controlled by), or if a participating interest in it is beneficially owned by, the charity.

● 'Related to the Charity'

The following should be treated as related to the charity:

(a)   any charity trustee and custodian trustee of the charity;

(b)   any person or body with the power to appoint or remove a significant proportion of the charity trustees of the charity, or whose consent is required to the exercise of any of the discretions of those trustees, or who is entitled to give directions to those trustees as to the exercise of any of those discretions. All or a majority of the trustees should always be treated as a 'significant proportion'. Fewer than 50% of the trustees may be a 'significant proportion' if they collectively have a dominant influence on the operation of the charity, as, for example, is likely to be the case if one body has the power to appoint/remove 7 of a body of 15 trustees, and 8 other different bodies had the right to appoint/remove 1 each.

(c)   any institution connected with the charity, and any director of such an institution;

(d)   any other charity with which it is commonly controlled;

(e)   any pension fund for the benefit of the employees of the charity, and/or of any other person who is a related party of the charity;

(f)   any officer, agent or employee of the charity having authority or responsibility for directing or controlling the major activities or resources of the charity; and

(g)   any person connected to a person who is related to the charity.

● 'Connected with a charity trustee or to a person related to the charity'

The following should be treated as 'connected with a charity trustee' or 'connected to a person who is related to the charity':

13.66   *Notes and disclosures*

(a)   members of the same family or household of the charity trustee or related person who may be expected to influence, or be influenced by, that person in their dealings with the charity;

(b)   the trustees of any trust, not being a charity, the beneficiaries or potential beneficiaries of which include a charity trustee or related person or a person referred to in (a) as being connected with a charity trustee or to a related person, as the case may be;

(c)   any business partner of a charity trustee or related person, or of any person referred to in (a) or (b) as being connected with a charity trustee or to a related person, as the case may be;

(d)   any body corporate, not being a company which is controlled entirely by one or more charitable institutions, in which:

(i)   the charity trustee has, or the charity trustee and any other charity trustee or trustees or person or persons referred to in (a), (b) or (c) above as being connected with a charity trustee, taken together, have a participating interest; or

(ii)   the related person has, or the related person and any other related parties of the charity, taken together, have a participating interest.

(e)   Any person or body who makes available to the charity the services of any person or body as a charity trustee is connected with a charity trustee.

13.66   Common control exists if:

(i)   the same person, or persons have the right to appoint a majority of the charity trustees of both or all the charities; or

(ii)   the same person, or persons, hold a majority of the voting rights in the administration of both or all of the charities.

Persons who are related with each other through family or business relationships should be treated as the same person for the present purposes.

13.67   'Controlled' means that the charity is able to secure that the affairs of the institution are conducted in accordance with its wishes.

13.68   'Participating interest' means that the charity:

'(a)   is interested in shares comprised in the equity share capital of the body of a nominal value of more than one fifth of that share capital; or

(b)   is entitled to exercise or control the exercise of more than one-fifth of the voting power at any general meeting of the body.'

13.69   Thus a charity can be a related party of another charity, for example, if one is the trustee of the other, or if it has the power to appoint or remove a significant proportion of the charity trustees of the other, or if the two charities are subject to common control (ie a majority of the trustees in common). This should not, however, be interpreted as meaning that two charities are related simply because a particular person happens to be a trustee of both.

13.70   The reasoning behind related party disclosure is one of transparency and demonstrating good stewardship. Any decision to enter into a transaction ought to be influenced only by the consideration of the charity's own interests. This requirement is reinforced by legal rules which, in certain circumstances, can invalidate transactions where the charity's trustees have a conflict of interest.

13.71   Transparency is particularly important where the relationship between the charity and the other party or parties might suggest that the transaction could possibly have been influenced by interests other than the charity's.

Related party transactions

13.72   Paragraph 225 of SORP states that related party transactions potentially include:

'(a)   purchases, sales, leases and donations (including donations which are made in furtherance of the charity's objects) of goods, property, money and other assets such as intellectual property rights to or from the related party;

(b)   the supply of services by the related party to the charity, and the supply of services by the charity to the related party. Supplying services includes providing the use of goods, property and other assets and finance arrangements such as making loans and giving guarantees and indemnities;

(c)   any other payments and other benefits which are made to trustees under express provisions of the governing document of a charity or in fulfilment of its charitable objectives.'

(para 225)

Transactions should be disclosed whether or not they are at arm's length.

Disclosure

13.73   The disclosure requirements are summarised in para 163 of SORP:

'The required disclosure is as follows (also see paragraph 303(c) re investments);

(a)   the names(s) of the transacting related party or parties;

(b)   a description of the relationship between the parties (including the interest of the related party or parties in the transaction);

(c)   a description of the transaction;

(d)   the amounts involved;

(e)   outstanding balances with related parties at the balance sheet date and any provisions for doubtful debts from such persons;

(f)   any amounts written off from such balances during the accounting year; and

(g)   any other elements of the transactions which are necessary for the understanding of the financial statements.'

(para 227)

Clearly some transactions are such that they are unlikely to influence the pursuance of the separate independent interests of the charity. Such transactions need not be disclosed unless there is evidence to the contrary. Paragraph 229 of SORP gives the following examples of transactions where no disclosure is usually necessary:

'(a)   donations received by the reporting charity from a related party, so long as the donor has not attached conditions which would, or might, require the charity to alter materially the nature of its existing activities if it were to accept the donation (but any material grant by the reporting charity to a charity which is a related party should be disclosed);

(b)   minor or routine unremunerated services provided to a charity by people related to it;

(c)   contracts of employment between a charity and its employees (except where the employees are the charity trustees or people connected with them):

(d)   contributions by a charity to a pension fund for the benefit of employees; (also see paragraph 235);

(e)   the purchase from a charity by a related party of minor articles which are offered for sale to the general public on the same terms as are offered to the general public;

(f)   the provision of services to a related party (including a charity trustee or person connected with a charity trustee), where the related party receives the services as part of a wider beneficiary class of which he is a member, and on the same terms as other members of the class (for example, the use of a village hall by members of its committee of management, as inhabitants of the area of benefit); and

(g)   the payment or reimbursement of out of pocket expenses to a related party (including a charity trustee or person connected with a charity trustee-but see paragraphs 231 to 233).'

(para 229)

Transactions with trustees

13.74   All transactions, whether directly or indirectly, with a trustee (including persons connected with them), are deemed to be material and therefore require disclosure unless one of the exemptions in paragraph 229 of SORP applies. The fact that remuneration has been paid to a trustee directly or indirectly by the charity or a company which the trustee controls must be disclosed, together with details of the source and the amount, the legal authority under which the payment was made (eg provision in the governing document of the charity, order of the Charity Commission, etc), and the reason for such remuneration. Similar disclosure is required when a person with a family or business connection has received such remuneration (ie when a connected person has received the remuneration). If no such remuneration has been received by trustees this fact must be stated. A company is deemed to be controlled by the trustees if they are able to exercise or direct the exercise of voting power at general meetings of the company.

13.75 Similarly, where any expenses have been reimbursed to a trustee, the aggregate amount of the reimbursed expenses should be disclosed, together with the number of trustees who have been reimbursed during the year. If no expenses have been reimbursed this fact should be stated. Where expenses have been reimbursed, the nature of the expenses (eg travel, subsistence etc) should be disclosed.

13.76 Occasionally trustees act as agents for a charity and make purchases on its behalf and are reimbursed for this expenditure, eg payment for office stationery or equipment. Such expenditure is not related to the services provided by the trustee and need not be disclosed. Similarly there is no need to disclose routine expenditure which is attributable collectively to the services provided by the trustees eg providing refreshments at a trustees meeting or hiring a room for the meeting.

Comment

13.77 SORP provides very prescriptive guidance to the preparers of accounts to determine whether a transaction requires disclosure as being one 'with trustees and related parties'. The decision as to whether a transaction should be disclosed depends on how the criteria set out above apply to the circumstances of the individual case. The ultimate decision on the disclosure or otherwise of a transaction with a trustee or a connected person of the charity rests with the trustees and, in cases of doubt, items should be treated as material and should be disclosed.

13.78 When considering transactions, one should not forget the requirement to disclose details of transactions involving not only those connected to the charity but also those connected to the trustees. Further consideration should be given to not only the materiality of the transaction to the charity but also to the related party. For both trustees and auditors, the identification of these transactions will be difficult. Auditors and trustees may find that the use of an annual certificate completed by each trustee and by senior management in which such persons give details of disclosable transactions may be a useful starting point.

13   Indemnity insurance

13.79   If funds of the charity have been used to purchase indemnity insurance this fact, together with the cost of such insurance, should be disclosed in the notes to the accounts.

13.80   The types of insurance to be disclosed would either protect the charity from loss arising from the neglect or default of its trustees, employees or agents, or indemnify the trustees against the consequences of any neglect or default on their part.

Comment

13.81   Under company law, a company may purchase for any officer or auditor insurance against any liability which by virtue of any rule of law would otherwise attach to him in relation to the company. Where any such insurance has been purchased or maintained in the year, that fact must be stated in the directors' report.

13.82   If the charity indemnified trustees directly for the cost of any neglect or default on their part, this fact would need to be disclosed in the notes to the accounts as a transaction with a trustee (see **13.84**). Care is needed here as there are limitations on the extent to which a charity can indemnify trustees against the effects of their own actions – see Charity Commission Leaflet CC3 and **2.20** ff.

14   Emoluments of employees

13.83   The SORP requires the disclosure in the notes to the accounts of the costs of employing staff who work for the charity whether or not the charity itself has incurred the cost. This includes seconded and agency staff and staff employed by connected or independent companies. For instance, staff working for a charity may have contracts with and be paid by a connected company. Payments may also be made to third parties for the provision of staff (eg agencies), where such arrangements are in place and the costs involved are material in relation to the charity's expenditure, SORP requires that the notes to the accounts should include an outline of the arrangements in place, the reasons for them and the amounts involved.

Comment

13.84   Part of the reasoning behind including so much disclosure in respect of employees, it is to clearly demonstrate the true cost of providing the charity's services. It will also enable the reader of the charity's accounts to gain a better understanding of the charity's efficiency and of the scale of its activities.

Specific disclosure

13.85   Paragraph 235 of SORP sets out the specific disclosures required:

'The total staff costs should be shown in the notes to the accounts giving the split between gross wages and salaries, employer's national insurance costs and pension costs (those pension costs included within resources expended excluding pension finance costs) for the year. The average number of staff during the year should be provided and where material to the disclosure, eg due to the number of part-time staff, an estimate of the average number of full time equivalent employees for the year may be provided in the notes to the accounts providing sub-categories according to the manner in which the charity's activities are organised.'
(para 235)

13.86   The notes should also show the number of employees whose emoluments for the year (including benefits in kind but excluding pension contributions) fell within each band of £10,000 from £60,000 upwards (ie from £60,001 to £70,000, from £70,001 to £80,000 etc). There is no requirement to provide this disclosure for bands into which no employee's emoluments fell in the current or preceding accounting period.

13.87   In addition, the SORP requires details to be given regarding pension details for staff whose emoluments exceed £60,000 per annum. Paragraph 237 of SORP states:

'In addition the following pension details should be disclosed in total for higher paid staff in paragraph 236:

(a)   contributions in the year for the provision of defined contribution schemes (normally money purchase schemes); and

(b)   the number of staff to whom retirement benefits are accruing under defined contribution schemes and defined benefit schemes respectively.'

(para 237)

Comment

Definition of 'total emoluments'

13.88   The SORP defines 'total emoluments' as remuneration and benefits-in-kind, in the same way as defined for taxation purposes. For tax purposes 'emoluments' includes 'all salaries, fees, wages, perquisites and profits whatsoever'. It would normally exclude contributions made by the employer to approved pension schemes which do not form part of the employee's taxable income.

13.89   Redundancy costs would not normally be included in 'total emoluments', although, if material, their separate disclosure should be considered.

Volunteers and part-time employees

13.90   As volunteers are, by definition, excluded from those persons whose remuneration is included in 'total emoluments', they should similarly be excluded from the average number of employees of the charity. The SORP recommends that the extent to which the charity is dependent on the services of unpaid volunteers should be appreciated from the narrative contained in the trustees' annual report or should be reported in the notes to the accounts.

Banding of emoluments

13.91   Surprisingly, the SORP's requirement in respect of the banding of employees' emoluments goes further than the company law requirements which, for years ending on or after 31 March 1997, require the specific disclosure of the emoluments of the highest paid director only. For these Companies Act purposes, 'emoluments' excludes pension contributions made on behalf of the director, but includes benefits-in-kind. Incorporated charities may therefore need to make additional disclosure to meet these requirements.

15   Auditors' and independent examiners' remuneration

13.92   The SORP requires the separate disclosure in the notes to the accounts of the total amounts payable to the charity's auditor or independent examiner in respect of:

(a)   audit or independent examination services, ie the costs of their respective external scrutiny; and

(b)   other services, such as taxation advice, consultancy, financial advice and accountancy.

13.93   The total fees for each of the 'other services' must be analysed by the nature of the service provided (eg taxation advice, consultancy, financial advice and accountancy). Where the accounts are consolidated, the amounts to be disclosed should be the total for the whole group.

13.94   In addition, where a charity has incurred other non-statutory costs of external scrutiny, eg the audit of a branch, the total of these costs should be identified and disclosed separately.

16   Pensions

13.95   Accounting for the provision of pension benefits to an organisation's staff is a complex and often contentious area of accounting. The current accounting standard governing pension contributions, FRS 17 Retirement Benefits has attracted significant comment in the commercial world. As the statement is of general application and affects a minority of charities, we will confine ourselves to an overview of its requirements.

13.96   The primary aim of FRS 17 is to bring the full impact of employers' obligations to their employees through funded pension arrangements into the accounts. The requirements for defined benefit or 'final salary' arrangements are considerably more complex than those for defined contribution or 'money purchase' schemes. The reason for this is that the obligations of the employer are met in full once contributions are paid over to the latter type of scheme. Conversely the obligations of a final salary based pension commitment will fall to the employer to make good if the scheme itself is unable to meet them from its assets and so the employer's obligations remain potentially open until the point at which the promised pension is actually secured.

13.97   It should be noted that the following only apply to 'funded schemes', that is schemes established on behalf of one or more employers, held in a ring-fenced fund administered by trustees. Charities making contributions into employees' personal pension plans – even where these are organised in a group arrangement sponsored by the employer, have no specific disclosure require-ments beyond disclosing the contributions themselves

13.98   FRS 17 seeks to introduce into the accounts for the first time the employer's exposure to the actuarial liabilities (future pension and other obli-gations) of the pension scheme, and the extent to which those liabilities are covered by the assets secured by contributions made to fund the obligation. In recent years, increasing protection to members of employer backed pen-sion schemes has increased the exposure of employers to liability even where defined benefits are not provided. Where employers have potential exposure to statutory penalties and charges for exiting a scheme other than a defined benefit scheme, these will be dealt with under the general accounting rules for liabilities and provisions.

13.99   Accounting for the cost of a defined contribution scheme is straight-forward – paragraph 432 of SORP tells us:

'The cost of a defined contribution scheme recognised in the accounts is equal to the contributions payable to the scheme in the accounting period. These pension costs should be allocated across the relevant resources expended categories of the Statement of Financial Activities ...'

13.100   Under FRS 17 a charity is required to analyse the components of the changes in the assets and liabilities of the pension scheme into those relating to service cost, past and current, investment returns and finance charges arising from discounting, actuarial gains and losses arising from differences between actuarial assumptions and experience or revised assumptions and amounts aris-ing from early termination.

13.101   The net financial position of the scheme, as assessed on the particular bases set out in FRS 17, is presented as a separate fund within unrestricted funds in the charity's balance sheet with a corresponding pension scheme asset or liability also highlighted separately.

13.102   The SORP refers preparers to FRS 17 itself for detailed guidance. It offers clarifications of the rules in the context of the construction of charity accounts. Paragraph 437 explains where in the statement of financial activities the movements in the fund each year should be allocated and paragraphs 438 to 442 highlight the very rare circumstances in which the asset or liability on a scheme would be allocated to a restricted fund.

13.103 Paragraphs 444 to 448 summarise the main disclosure requirements of FRS 17 which include details of the scheme, disclosure of the assumptions underlying the actuarial valuation and more detailed analysis of how the amounts included in the primary statements are arrived at.

13.104 Many charities participate in pension schemes operated for a number of different employers. Historically, these have mainly been public sector schemes such as those for teachers or local authority employees, but also many funds operated in the private sector by specialist pensions administrators who offer pooled arrangements. Recognising that within many such schemes, the actuary will be unable to specifically identify the actuarial liabilities relating to each employer, FRS 17 allows employers participating in such schemes to account for them as if they were defined contribution schemes. SORP paragraph 431 states:

> 'A charity participating in a multi-employer defined benefit scheme, where the contributions are set in relation to the current service period only, or where the charity is unable to identify its share of the underlying assets and liabilities on a consistent or reasonable basis, should account for its contributions to the scheme as if it were a defined contribution scheme. Where a charity is unable to identify its share of the underlying assets and liabilities of the scheme, the disclosures set out in paragraph 446 should be provided.'

Comment

13.105 The disclosures required under FRS 17 are complex and potentially onerous. In practice, however, the detail required is provided to employers by the scheme's actuary. It is important to realise that many of the amounts determined by the actuary are dependent upon assumptions regarding the future performance of the scheme's assets and the cost of servicing future pension obligations – which are directly affected by the longevity of pensioners, inflation and other factors which are uncertain. Although trustees have little scope to consider the output of the actuary's work, they should critically review the assumptions made by the actuary – which are set out in a statement as part of each valuation – to ensure that they are realistic.

13.106 One of the main concerns raised about FRS 17 is that it introduces into the accounts balances and movements in funds that arise from a combination of current valuations of assets and a judgemental valuation of very long term obligations. Not only are the amounts reported potentially volatile as a result of short term market conditions but they also incorporate accounting balances that result from assessments of very long term liabilities which are based on often subjective assumptions. The net asset or liability reported in the balance sheet may significantly alter the overall view of the charity's financial position. In order to ensure that trustees' were not inadvertently driven to make decisions about short term finances based on long term obligations, the Charity Commission issued guidance in 2005 on 'Charity Reserves and Defined benefit Pension Schemes' and this can be viewed on the Charity Commission website. The general thrust of the guidance is that trustees should not regard pension scheme deficits as a reduction in their reserves when assessing financial strategy unless that deficit is such that it makes currently required pension contributions such that the organisation cannot balance its budget.

NATIONAL TRUST ANNUAL REPORT AND ACCOUNTS 2008/09

30   The National Trust Retirement and Death Benefits Scheme

The Trust operates a funded group pension scheme, established under trust, providing defined benefits based on final salary. The Defined Benefit Pension Scheme (the 'Scheme') was closed to new members on 1 June 2003. Schroder Investment Management Limited and Partners Capital LLP act as investment managers to the Trustees of the Scheme.

A new, defined contribution scheme has been offered to regular staff from 1 June 2003. This is a Stakeholder Scheme with Legal & General. In addition to this, the subsidiary, Historic House Hotels Limited, operates a defined contribution scheme. The assets of the schemes are held separately from those of the Trust.

The National Trust Annual Report 2008/09   67

[continued on next page]

National Trust, continued

Notes to the Financial Statements

30   **The National Trust Retirement and Death Benefits Scheme** *(continued)*

The financial assumptions used by the actuary to calculate the scheme liabilities under FRS17 were as follows:

	2009 %	2008 %
Rate of increase in pensionable salaries	4.1	4.4
Rate of increase in pensions in payment pre-March 2007	3.1	3.3
Rate of increase in pensions in payment post-March 2007	2.2	2.4
Discount rate	6.7	6.4
Inflation	3.1	3.4

The mortality assumptions have been updated and are based on standard mortality tables which allow for future mortality improvements. The assumptions are that the average life expectancy of a male is currently 87 and a female 89. By 2029, this is expected to increase to 89 and 90 respectively.

The expected rates of return on the assets of the scheme were:

	2009 %	2008 %	2007 %
Equities	7.9	8.1	8.1
Government Bonds	4.4	4.5	4.6
Other	1.8	4.1	4.1
Average rate of return for all classes of assets	6.2	7.1	7.6

The value of the assets of the scheme were:

	2009 £'000	2008 £'000	2007 £'000
Equities	150,436	257,226	273,970
Options	-	10,594	-
Derivatives*	129,835	-	-
Government Bonds	1,819	54,671	41,632
Other	1,551	9,855	5,204
Total market value of assets	283,641	332,346	320,806

* Includes £93,861,000 of cash and cash-related investments. Derivatives are held in order to ensure a closer match between the assets and the liabilities of the Scheme.

The following table provides the reconciliation of funded status to the balance sheet:

	2009 £'000	2008 £'000
Fair value of Scheme assets	283,641	332,346
Present value of funded Scheme liabilities	(336,256)	(326,006)
Net pension (liability) / surplus	(52,615)	6,340

The National Trust expects to pay £8.5 million of employer contributions to the Scheme in 2009/10.

Changes to the present value of the Scheme liabilities during the year:

	2009 £'000	2008 £'000
Value of Scheme liabilities at 1 March	326,006	366,908
Current service cost	4,957	8,011
Interest cost	20,727	18,798
Contributions by Scheme participants	3,459	3,435
Actuarial gain on Scheme liabilities	(7,972)	(61,028)
Net benefits paid out	(11,234)	(10,142)
Past service cost	313	24
Value of Scheme liabilities at end February	336,256	326,006

[*continued on next page*]

National Trust, continued

30   The National Trust Retirement and Death Benefits Scheme *(continued)*

Changes to the fair value of Scheme assets during the year:	2009 £'000	2008 £'000
Fair value of Scheme assets at 1 March	332,346	320,806
Expected return on Scheme assets	22,569	24,351
Actuarial loss on Scheme assets	(71,734)	(14,311)
Contributions by the employer	8,235	8,207
Contributions by Scheme participants	3,459	3,435
Net benefits paid out	(11,234)	(10,142)
Fair value of Scheme assets at end February	283,641	332,346

The amounts recognised in net incoming resources are as follows:	2009 £'000	2008 £'000
Current service cost	4,957	8,011
Past service cost	313	24
Interest cost	20,727	18,798
Expected return on Scheme assets	(22,569)	(24,351)
Expense recognised in net incoming resources	3,428	2,482

The current and past service costs (2009: £5,270,000 and 2008: £8,035,000) are included in resources expended and the interest cost and expected return on the Scheme assets (2009: £1,842,000 and 2008: £5,553,000) are reported within Other Incoming Resources in the Consolidated Statement of Financial Activities (Income arising on the defined benefit pension scheme).

Actual return on Scheme assets:	2009 £'000	2008 £'000
Expected return on Scheme assets	22,569	24,351
Actuarial loss on Scheme assets	(71,734)	(14,311)
Actual return on Scheme assets	(49,165)	10,040

Analysis of amount recognised in Statement of Financial Activities:	2009 £'000	2008 £'000
Total actuarial (loss) / gain	(63,762)	46,717
Total (loss) / gain in SoFA	(63,762)	46,717
Cumulative amount of gains recognised in SoFA	17,002	80,764

History of asset values, present value of liabilities and surplus/deficit in Scheme:

	2009 £'000	2008 £'000	2007 £'000	2006 £'000	2005 £'000
Fair value of Scheme assets	283,641	332,346	320,806	298,305	242,841
Present value of Scheme liabilities	(336,256)	(326,006)	(366,908)	(348,797)	(327,967)
(Deficit) / surplus in Scheme	(52,615)	6,340	(46,102)	(50,492)	(85,126)

Experience gains and losses:	2009 £'000	2008 £'000	2007 £'000	2006 £'000	2005 £'000
Experience (losses) / gains on Scheme assets	(71,734)	(14,311)	(2,256)	31,992	13,175
Experience (losses) / gains on Scheme liabilities	(19,028)	(1,041)	1,887	2,424	(17,333)

17   Ex gratia payments

13.107   Where ex gratia payments are made not as an application of funds or property for charitable purposes, but in fulfilment of a compelling moral obligation, the total amount should be disclosed in the notes to the accounts. 'Payments' for this purpose include the transfer of non-monetary benefits or other expenditure of any kind or waiver of rights to property to which a charity is entitled.

13.108 The types of payment which may be included under this head would include the surrendering of part of a bequest where disinherited relatives of the deceased press a 'moral' claim to the estate.

13.109 Payments which the trustees reasonably consider to be in the interests of the charity, ie more than a moral obligation, should not be treated as ex gratia even though there is no legal obligation to make them. For example, a redundancy payment over and above the statutory level may be made in order to motivate retained staff and hence benefit the charity.

13.110 The nature and date of the authority for each ex gratia payment should be disclosed in the notes to the accounts where the trustees require the authority of the court, the attorney general or the Charity Commissioners to make such payment.

18   Fixed assets

13.111 Most of the disclosure requirements concerning fixed assets have been covered in Chapter 10. It may be helpful however to recap the main items here. Reference should be made to the examples given in that chapter which illustrate these requirements.

13.112 Paragraphs 273 to 278 of SORP give a detailed explanation as to how the fixed assets held for use by the charity should be analysed:

- Freehold property, leasehold property, plant and machinery including motor vehicles, fixtures and equipment and assets in course of construction are all examples of likely headings.

- Changes in values of each from the beginning of the year to the end distinguishing between the cost or valuation of assets and their depreciation and giving figures of additions, disposals, revaluations, impairments and transfers.

- Separate totals for each class of asset, together with a combined total should be shown and the depreciation charge for the year for each should also be identifiable.

13.113 If any functional fixed assets have been revalued the notes should record:

- the name and qualification of the valuer;
- the basis of valuation;
- the historical cost (if available) and depreciation;
- date of the previous valuation; and
- if the value has not been updated, a statement by the trustees that they are not aware of any material changes.

13.114 In the case of impairment in the value of a functional fixed asset, the notes should show 'the methods used in the impairment review to determine the net realisable value and value in use ...' (para 278). Details of the valuer should also be given as set out in **13.113** above.

13.115 Where heritage assets are held – whether or not these have been capitalised – information should be provided in the notes to enable a reader to assess the age, nature and scale of the assets and their function in achieving the charity's objects. Disclosures are also required of cost or value of additions and disposals in the period or if unavailable, the proceeds and a description of the assets sold.

13.116 For fixed asset investments, there will normally be a quoted market price to which reference may be made in the notes. If not the notes should indicate who is responsible for the valuation giving their qualification and position (eg trustee, employee or external valuer). An indication should also be given as to how the valuation was carried out.

13.117 Paragraph 301 of SORP deals with the situation where the charity holds such a significant proportion of a company's shares that the quoted price may give an exaggerated view of the total value, bearing in mind the effect that a sale of such a large holding might have on the market. The trustees may in such circumstances make adjustments to the valuation but should give an explanation.

13.118 An analysis of investment assets is required by paragraph 238 of SORP, distinguishing between:

- investment properties;
- quoted investments, including unit trusts;
- shares in subsidiary or associated companies;
- unlisted securities;
- cash held as part of the investment portfolio; and
- other investments.

There should be a further analysis between investment assets within the UK and those outside the UK.

13.119 Any holdings that are 'considered material in the context of the investment portfolio' should be separately disclosed (para 306). Whilst the SORP offers no guidance as to what proportion might be considered material, many preparers use a benchmark of 5 per cent of the portfolio, as this follows practice established under previous SORPs, which were more prescriptive on this point.

13.120 Where material, details of programme related investments should be provided. These will set out changes in carrying value – including impairment losses – and categorise the investments by type and by the area of the charity's work supported.

19   Provisions and commitments

13.121

'Particulars of all material provisions for liabilities and charges accrued in the balance sheet as liabilities should be disclosed in the notes. Similar particulars of all material commitments in respect of specific charitable projects should be disclosed if they have not been charged in the accounts' (para 326)

13.122   Where a provision has been made previously the note should show any movement during the year, ie payments made and further provisions required.

Comment

13.123   Paragraph 328 of SORP says that 'the notes should distinguish between those commitments included in the balance sheet as liabilities and those that are intentions to spend and are not included...' and then goes on to list the details of each that should be disclosed. Whilst it seems sensible to give details of commitments which are included as liabilities, it seems to us that it would be more appropriate in the case of material intentions for future expenditure to set up a designated fund and key any explanatory note to that. This is provided for in paragraph 68 of SORP and following.

20   Guarantees

13.124   Paragraph 260 of SORP requires the disclosure of 'all material guarantees given by the charity and the conditions under which liabilities might arise' for the charity as a result of the guarantees.

Comment

13.125   Examples would include the guarantee of a bank overdraft of a trading subsidiary or of a loan obtained by an employee or beneficiary of the charity. In this case it is suggested that the disclosure should include the amount of the guaranteed overdraft or loan at the balance sheet date and the maximum amount of the guarantee.

13.126   Where consolidated accounts are prepared, it is suggested that any guarantees given by the parent charity to its subsidiary charities should be disclosed, even if the results and assets and liabilities of the subsidiary charities concerned are included in the consolidated accounts. This is because, technically, consolidated accounts are additional to the entity accounts of the charity and if the charity is seeking to avoid filing more than the consolidated accounts it must ensure that all disclosures relevant to the entity are made. See Chapter 5 on Consolidation.

21 Contingent assets and liabilities

Definition

13.127 A contingent asset is 'a possible asset that arises from past events and where existence will be confirmed only by the occurrence of one or more uncertain future events not wholly within the entity's control.' (Appendix 1)

A contingent liability is:

'(a) A possible obligation that arises from past events and whose existence will be confirmed only by the occurrence of one or more uncertain future events not wholly within the entity's control; or

(b) A present obligation that arises from past events but is not recognised in the primary statements because:

   (i)   it is not probable that a transfer of economic benefits will be required to settle the obligation; or

   (ii) the amount of the obligation, cannot be measured with sufficient reliability.'

Treatment as accrual or not

13.128 The degree of certainty, timing and measurement of the prospective asset or liability will dictate whether or not it should be brought into the accounts. It is this decision which marks the distinction between an actual asset or liability which should be accrued in the accounts and a contingent asset or liability which should not. If the decision is that the asset or liability is contingent then the only concern is its materiality and how it should be disclosed, if at all.

Disclosure of contingency

13.129 In respect of each contingency which is required to be disclosed, the accounts should show:

(a) the nature of the contingency;

(b) the uncertainties which are expected to affect the ultimate outcome; and

(c) a prudent estimate of the financial effect, where an amount has not been accrued, at the date the accounts are approved. Where it is not practicable to make such an estimate, a statement to this effect should be included – see paragraph 346 of SORP.

13.130 Where a contingent loss may be capable of being reduced by a related counter-claim (eg an insurance claim), the amount accrued or disclosed should take into account the probable result of any such counter-claim. Full details of such counter-claim should be disclosed in the accounts.

22 Loan liabilities

13.131 A note to the accounts is required if any asset of the charity is subject to a mortgage or charge given as security for a loan or other liability.

13.132 Such a note should disclose:

'(a) particulars of the assets which are subject to the mortgage or charge;

(b) the amount of the loan or liability and its proportion to the value of the assets mortgaged or charged.'

(para 349)

13.133 SORP also requires the disclosure in the notes to the accounts of all inter-fund loans existing at the balance sheet date, including details of amounts, interest and repayment terms. This disclosure can be in a summarised form if necessary.

13.134 Separate disclosure is required of amounts loaned to trading subsidiaries, including details of any security provided by the subsidiary.

Comment

Security given on behalf of others

13.135 Although not specifically stated in SORP, disclosure requirements for secured loans will cover not only secured loans of the charity, but also security given in respect of another person's liabilities.

Present value of assets

13.136 It is interesting that SORP requires disclosure of the proportion of the secured loan to the value of the assets on which it is secured. As this is an attempt to disclose how much of a charity's liabilities are covered by the assets on which they are secured, it is assumed that for the purposes of this disclosure, 'value' should be taken to be the market value or realisable value of the charity's secured assets.

ROYAL COLLEGE OF NURSING OF THE UNITED KINGDOM
CONSOLIDATED REPORT AND ACCOUNTS 2008/2009

Notes to the accounts – 31 March 2009

12.2   Amounts falling due after more than 1 year

	RCN 2009 £'000	RCN 2008 £'000	Representation Activities 2009 £'000	Representation Activities 2008 £'000	Group 2009 £'000	Group 2008 £'000
Deferred income	—	—	—	—	—	3,806
	—	—	—	—	—	3,806

The £3.8 million deferred income balance relating to RCNMS was settled in October 2008.

Chapter 14

Summarised accounts

1 Introduction

14.1   In addition to producing an annual trustees' report and full accounts prepared in accordance with applicable legislation such as the Charities Act 1993 or companies legislation many charities also produce, and publish, an annual review.

14.2   An annual review typically contains only summarised accounts or summary financial information rather than the full audited accounts and is normally produced for public consumption.

14.3   Summarised accounts (or financial statements) will comprise an extract (possibly in abbreviated form) from the full accounts of the Statement of Financial Activities, the balance sheet and some of the notes to the accounts.

14.4   Summary financial information, on the other hand, comprises financial data expressed purely by way of statistics, charts, diagrams, narrative, etc.

14.5   The inclusion of summarised accounts or summary financial information in an annual review enables the charity to communicate key financial information to readers who may not be familiar with accounts, so providing them with an overview of the charity's financial activities. It also provides the charity with an opportunity to concentrate on a particular target audience and to emphasise more clearly, often with the aid of charts and diagrams, the salient points within the accounts. For example, a charity may wish to highlight a particular area of its work and use the annual review in order to appeal for more funds for those activities.

14.6   Table 10 of the SORP contrasts the characteristics of summarised financial statements (accounts) and summary financial information:

Characteristics of:

Summarised financial statements	*Summary financial information*
Includes a summary of the Statement of Financial Activities and/or Balance Sheet	Draws information from only parts of the accounts
The summary is derived from statutory accounts	May be based on interim accounts or other financial information as well as statutory accounts
A financial statement that purports to be a Statement of Activities or Balance Sheet or summary thereof	Makes no reference to either if these primary statements
Represents the entire finances of a charity or a charity group	Represents analysis eg of a particular activity or region

14.7   It is essential, however, that the annual review, including the summarised accounts or summary financial information, is consistent with the full audited accounts and does not give a false picture. It is also important to remember that a full annual report and accounts should always be prepared, regardless of the intended circulation of any summarised accounts.

14.8   If summarised accounts are produced, or if summary financial information is provided, they should follow certain general principles which are set out in the SORP. Charitable companies must follow the provisions of s 435 of the Companies Act 2006 concerning non-statutory financial statements but there are no legal provisions for other charities.

2   SORP and legislative requirements

14.9   Paragraphs 377 to 379 of SORP set out the general principles to be applied when preparing summarised accounts and summary financial information:

'**Summarised financial statements**

Summarised financial statements should be accompanied by a statement, signed on behalf of the trustees, indicating:

(a)   that they are not the statutory accounts but a summary of information relating to both the Statement of Financial Activities and the balance sheet;

(b)   whether or not the full financial statements from which the summarised financial statements are derived have as yet been externally scrutinised (whether audit, independent examination, or reporting accountant's report); and

(c)   where they have been externally scrutinised, whether the report contained any concerns such as a qualified opinion, limitation of scope etc;

(d)   where the report contains any concerns, eg is qualified, contains an explanatory paragraph or emphasis of matter, sufficient details should be provided in the summarised financial statements to enable the reader to appreciate the significance of the report;

(e)   where accounts are produced only for a branch of a charity, it must be clearly stated that the summarised financial statements are for the branch only and have been extracted from the full accounts of the reporting charity (giving its name);

(f)   details of how the full annual accounts, the external scrutiny report (as applicable) and the Trustees' Annual Report can be obtained;

(g)   the date on which the annual accounts were approved; and

(h)   for charities registered in England and Wales, say whether or not the Trustees' Annual Report and accounts have been submitted to the Charity Commission.' (para 377)

'If the full accounts have been externally scrutinised, a statement from the external scrutineer, giving an opinion as to whether or not the summarised financial statements are consistent with the full annual accounts, should be attached.' (para 378)

'Summary financial information

Any other summary financial information, in whatever form, should be accompanied by a statement on behalf of the trustees as to:

(a)   the purpose of the information;

(b)   whether or not it is from the full annual accounts;

(c)   whether or not these accounts have been audited, independently examined or subject to a reporting accountant's report;

(d)   details of how the full annual accounts, trustees report and external scrutiny report (as appropriate) can be obtained.' (para 379)

3   How the information is shown

14.10   The wide diversity of charities and the different emphasis each places on its objectives and needs means that, in particular, there is a wide variety as to the manner in which charities design and produce summarised accounts or summary financial information. In the pages that follow it is only possible to give a few examples.

Summarised financial statements

14.11   The Nightingale House summarised financial statements provide an example of the basic information that needs to be produced if a charity wishes to produce summarised financial statements. The example illustrates the inclusion of a statement by the auditors stating that the information is consistent with the full audited accounts and a statement by the trustees that the auditor's report on the full accounts was unqualified. In most cases it would be unsuitable to quote the auditor's report and, in the case of incorporated charities, the Companies Act strictly forbids this.

NIGHTINGALE HOUSE SUMMARISED ACCOUNTS
30 SEPTEMBER 2008

Nightingale House: Summarised financial statements

Consolidated Statement of Financial Activities for
the year ended 30 September 2008

	General funds £'000	Designated funds £'000	Restricted funds £'000	Endowment funds £'000	2008 Total Funds £'000	2007 Total Funds £'000
		Unrestricted funds				
Incoming resources						
Incoming resources from generated funds	5,871	85	429	198	**6,583**	4,789
Incoming resources from charitable activities	7,381	—	—	—	**7,381**	7,383
Other incoming resources	132	—	—	—	**132**	135
Total incoming resources	13,384	85	429	198	**14,096**	12,307
Resources expended						
Cost of generating funds	390	—	—	—	**390**	452
Charitable activities	10,411	693	1,022	—	**12,126**	14,127
Governance costs	63	—	—	—	**63**	60
Total resources expended	10,864	693	1,022	—	**12,579**	14,639
Net (outgoing) incoming resources before transfers	2,520	(608)	(593)	198	**1,517**	(2,332)
Transfers between funds	(251)	107	250	(106)	—	—
Net (outgoing) incoming resources for the year	2,269	(501)	(343)	92	**1,517**	(2,332)
Other gains and losses on investment assets	(2,290)	(39)	—	(92)	**(2,421)**	670
Net movement in funds	(21)	540	(343)	—	**(904)**	(1,662)
Balances brought forward at 1 October 2006	8,390	20,302	4,131	3,511	**36,334**	37,996
Balances carried forward at 30 September 2007	8,369	19,762	3,788	3,511	**35,430**	36,334

Consolidated Balance Sheet as at 30 September 2007

	2008 £'000	2007 £'000
Fixed assets	**28,145**	31,638
Current assets	**8,631**	6,717
Creditors: amounts falling due within one year	**(1,246)**	(1,510)
Net current assets	**7,385**	5,207
Total assets less current liabilities	**35,530**	36,845
Pension scheme liability	**(100)**	(511)
Total net assets	**35,430**	36,334
Represented by:		
Funds and reserves		
Charitable funds		
Income funds		
. Unrestricted funds		
.. General fund	**8,469**	8,901
.. Designated funds	**19,762**	20,302
.. Pension reserve	**(100)**	(511)
. Restricted funds	**3,788**	4,131
Capital funds		
. Permanent endowment funds	**3,511**	3,511
	35,430	36,334

[continued on next page]

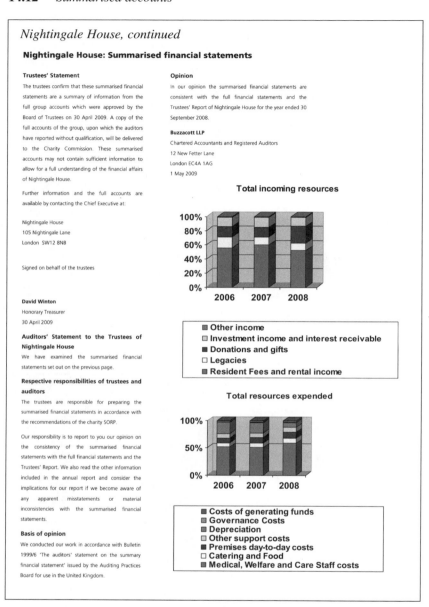

Nightingale House, continued

Nightingale House: Summarised financial statements

Trustees' Statement

The trustees confirm that these summarised financial statements are a summary of information from the full group accounts which were approved by the Board of Trustees on 30 April 2009. A copy of the full accounts of the group, upon which the auditors have reported without qualification, will be delivered to the Charity Commission. These summarised accounts may not contain sufficient information to allow for a full understanding of the financial affairs of Nightingale House.

Further information and the full accounts are available by contacting the Chief Executive at:

Nightingale House
105 Nightingale Lane
London SW12 8NB

Signed on behalf of the trustees

David Winton
Honorary Treasurer
30 April 2009

Auditors' Statement to the Trustees of Nightingale House

We have examined the summarised financial statements set out on the previous page.

Respective responsibilities of trustees and auditors

The trustees are responsible for preparing the summarised financial statements in accordance with the recommendations of the charity SORP.

Our responsibility is to report to you our opinion on the consistency of the summarised financial statements with the full financial statements and the Trustees' Report. We also read the other information included in the annual report and consider the implications for our report if we become aware of any apparent misstatements or material inconsistencies with the summarised financial statements.

Basis of opinion

We conducted our work in accordance with Bulletin 1999/6 'The auditors' statement on the summary financial statement' issued by the Auditing Practices Board for use in the United Kingdom.

Opinion

In our opinion the summarised financial statements are consistent with the full financial statements and the Trustees' Report of Nightingale House for the year ended 30 September 2008.

Buzzacott LLP

Chartered Accountants and Registered Auditors
12 New Fetter Lane
London EC4A 1AG
1 May 2009

Total incoming resources

- Other income
- Investment income and interest receivable
- Donations and gifts
- Legacies
- Resident Fees and rental income

Total resources expended

- Costs of generating funds
- Governance Costs
- Depreciation
- Other support costs
- Premises day-to-day costs
- Catering and Food
- Medical, Welfare and Care Staff costs

14.12   In addition to producing the summarised financial statements some charities also give summary financial information either in the form of a short narrative financial review or in the form of charts and diagrams. Above, the Nightingale House summarised financial statements include two graphs to provide a visual summary of incoming resources and resources expended. Further examples for the Royal College of General Practitioners and the Coram Family Foundation are set out below.

ROYAL COLLEGE OF GENERAL PRACTITIONERS IMPACT REPORT 2008

Summarised Financial Statements

Statement of Financial Activities for the Year Ended 31 March 2008

	Unrestricted Funds £	Restricted Funds £	Endowment Fund £	Total 2008 £	Total 2007 £
INCOMING RESOURCES					
Incoming resources from generated funds:					
Voluntary income	39,120	3,505	-	42,625	219,635
Activities for generating funds	1,201,750	111,303	-	1,313,053	914,030
Investment income and interest receivable	609,370	95,602	-	704,972	548,144
Incoming resources from charitable activities:					
Professional standards	7,028,352	1,668,374	-	8,696,726	6,572,544
Professional development	1,405,996	2,387,207	-	3,793,203	2,845,698
Individual support (includes Membership)	9,931,777	245,547	-	10,177,324	7,777,897
Promotion of the profession	442,228	125,225	-	567,453	389,233
Total incoming resources	20,658,593	4,636,763	-	25,295,356	19,267,181
RESOURCES EXPENDED					
Costs of generating funds:					
Fundraising and publicity	37,702	-	-	37,702	85,024
Investment management fees	9,138	22,416	-	31,554	25,693
Charitable expenditure:					
Professional standards	9,626,492	1,569,215	-	11,195,707	8,564,928
Professional development	3,743,469	1,872,442	-	5,615,911	4,535,304
Individual support (includes Membership)	3,809,419	271,460	-	4,080,879	3,212,091
Promotion of the profession	2,027,619	127,275	-	2,154,894	1,933,509
Governance	390,694	-	-	390,694	308,705
Total resources expended	19,644,533	3,862,808	-	23,507,341	18,665,254
Net incoming resources before transfers	1,014,060	773,955	-	1,788,015	601,927
Transfers between funds	208,490	(208,490)	-	-	-
Net incoming resources					
before (losses)/gains on the revaluation and disposal of investments	1,222,550	565,465	-	1,788,015	601,927
(Losses)/gains on the revaluation and disposal of investments	(72,072)	(177,488)	-	(249,560)	79,204
Actuarial gain on defined benefit pension scheme	2,379,000	-	-	2,379,000	76,000
Net movement in funds	3,529,478	387,977	-	3,917,455	757,131
Fund balances brought forward as at 1 April 2007	(772,689)	5,930,405	1,390,027	6,547,743	5,790,612
Fund balances carried forward at 31 March 2008	2,756,789	6,318,382	1,390,027	10,465,198	6,547,743

Balance Sheet as at 31 March 2008

	2008 £	2007 £
Fixed assets	6,624,168	6,308,894
Current assets	10,553,601	10,246,940
Creditors (amounts falling due within one year)	(4,574,571)	(4,804,091)
Net current assets	5,979,030	5,442,849
Net assets excluding pension liability	12,603,198	11,751,743
Defined benefit pension scheme liability	2,138,000	5,204,000
Net assets including pension liability	10,465,198	6,547,743
Represented by:		
Income funds:		
Unrestricted funds:		
Free reserves	1,902,164	1,643,281
Pension reserves	(2,138,000)	(5,204,000)
	(235,836)	(3,560,719)
Designated funds	2,992,625	2,788,030
	2,756,789	(772,689)
Restricted funds	6,318,382	5,930,405
Capital funds:		
Endowment fund	1,390,027	1,390,027
Funds	10,465,198	6,547,743

48

[*continued on next page*]

Royal College of General Practitioners, continued

Income and Expenditure, 2008

Trustees' statement
The trustees of the RCGP confirm that these summarised financial statements are consistent with the full financial statements that were approved by the Finance Committee on behalf of Council on 24 July 2008, and which comply with the Charities Act 1993 and the Statement of Recommended Practice 'Accounting and Reporting by Charities' 2005. A copy of the full accounts, upon which the auditor has reported without qualification, will be delivered to the Charity Commission. These summarised financial statements may not contain sufficient information to allow for a full understanding of the financial affairs of RCGP.

Further information and the full accounts are available by contacting:

Head of Finance
RCGP, 14 Princes Gate, London SW7 1PU
mbirungi@rcgp.org.uk
Telephone: 020 7581 3232

Signed on behalf of Council
Dr Colin M Hunter OBE FRCPEd FRCGP FIHM
Honorary Treasurer, 24 July 2008

Auditor's statement to the trustees of the Royal College of General Practitioners
We have examined the summarised financial statements set out on page 48.

Responsibilities of the Members of Council and auditor
Members of Council, who constitute trustees for the purpose of charity legislation, are responsible for preparing the summarised financial statements in accordance with the recommendations of the Charities SORP.

Our responsibility is to report to you our opinion on the consistency of the summarised financial statements with the full financial statements and Annual Report.

We also read the other information contained in the Impact Report and consider the implications for our report if we become aware of any apparent misstatements or material inconsistencies with the summarised financial statements.

Basis of opinion
We conducted our work in accordance with Bulletin 1999/6 'The auditors' statement on the summary financial statement', issued by the Auditing Practices Board for use in the United Kingdom.

Opinion
In our opinion the summarised financial statements are consistent with the full financial statements and Annual Report of the Royal College of General Practitioners for the year ended 31 March 2008.

Chantrey Vellacott DFK LLP
Chartered Accountants and Registered Auditor
London, 24 July 2008

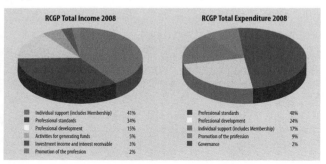

RCGP Total Income 2008	
Individual support (includes Membership)	41%
Professional standards	34%
Professional development	15%
Activities for generating funds	5%
Investment income and interest receivable	3%
Promotion of the profession	2%

RCGP Total Expenditure 2008	
Professional standards	48%
Professional development	24%
Individual support (includes Membership)	17%
Promotion of the profession	9%
Governance	2%

49

CORAM ANNUAL REVIEW 2006/07

Summary financial information for
the year ended 31 March 2007

Income and Expenditure	2007 £000	2006 £000	2007 %	2006 %
Income				
Fees for services provided	2,709	3,204	40.8%	42.3%
Investment & Property Income	609	623	9.2%	8.2%
Donations, Legacies and similar Income	540	794	8.1%	10.5%
Trust & Government Grants	2,778	2,958	41.9%	39.0%
	6,636	**7,579**	**100.0%**	**100.0%**
Expenditure				
Charitable projects and grants made	6,873	7,076	93.4%	93.6%
Cost of generating funds	463	459	6.3%	6.1%
Governance costs	23	19	0.3%	0.3%
	7,359	**7,554**	**100.0%**	**100.0%**
Surplus/deficit for year	**-723**	**25**		
Gains on Investments	522	1,861		
Acturial (losses) gains on defined benefit pension schemes	383	(161)		
Increase in assets	**182**	**1,725**		

Balance Sheet	2007 £000	2006 £000
Capital Funds		
General Endowment fund	6,165	8,736
Pension Deficit Reduction Fund	3,000	0
Tangible fixed assets fund	4,067	4,136
Development Fund	0	4,388
Building, repair and maintenance Fund	3,750	0
Restricted funds	1,032	936
Unrestricted funds	339	577
Pension Reserve	(1,582)	(1,975)
Designated Funds	591	336
Furniture and Equipment Fund	190	236
	17,552	**17,370**
Net Assets		
Fixed assets	4,257	4,372
Investments	13,909	14,061
Net Current Assets	968	912
Pension Liability	(1,582)	(1,975)
	17,552	**17,370**

277

Coram Annual Review 2006/07, *continued*

16_Coram Annual Review 2006/07
Detailed charitable expenditure 2006/07

Detailed charitable expenditure 2006/07

Detailed charitable expenditure	Total 2007	%
A Adoption Service	1,982,878	28.9%
B Housing & Support Service	1,177,288	17.1%
C Child Contact Services	425,697	6.2%
D Parents' Centre	868,243	12.6%
E Coram Children's Campus	303,779	4.4%
F Development	16,702	0.3%
G Family Support & Vulnerable Children Services	2,076,714	30.2%
H Listening to Young Children	23,204	0.3%
I Other Services	(1,871)	0.0%
	6,872,634	100.0%

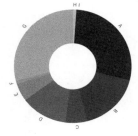

Total incoming resources of Coram's child care services have reached £6,636,517 for the year (down by 12.4% from the previous year), with total resources being expended of £7,359,431 (down 2.6% from the previous year).

Coram's net outgoing resources before other recognised gains and losses for the year was £722,914. Investment income for the year was £608,708.

Reserves
The general endowment is expendable. In the absence of significant unrestricted fundraising income, it provides reserves to protect the charity's working capital to finance day-to-day activities and funds for the development of new and existing child care services.

The net assets of the charity on the balance sheet has increased by £181,980 to £17,552,346 after allowing for pension liabilities under new accounting reporting standards. The Trustees decided to set aside from the expendable endowment the Pension Deficit Reduction Fund with a value of £3,000,000, to enable Coram to meet its future defined benefit pension scheme obligations, which has a current deficit of £1,582,000). Trustees also set aside funds from the expendable endowment to meet our ongoing commitments to the maintenance and upkeep of a substantial and aging campus, with buildings at different stages of repair. The Building, Repair and Maintenance Fund, has a value of £3,750,000. The net value of the expendable endowment, therefore, was £6,165,517 as at 31st March 2007.

Restricted funds of £1,031,869 are earmarked for specific future projects, and have been carried over for expenditure in subsequent financial years. The Fixed Asset Permanent Endowment Fund represents the value of buildings and other tangible fixed assets owned by the charity.

Statement by the Trustees
The financial information given here is an accurate summary of data extracted from the Charity's Report and Accounts which were approved by the Trustees on 31st October 2007, and on which our auditors gave an unqualified opinion. These summarised accounts may not contain sufficient information to give a full understanding of the results and financial affairs of the Charity. Please contact the Secretary for a copy of the full financial statements, which have been submitted to the Charity Commission.

Independent Auditors' statement to the Trustees of Coram Family
We have examined the summarised financial information set out on pages 15 and 16 of the Annual Review.

Respective responsibilities of Trustees and auditors
The Trustees are responsible for preparing the summarised financial information in accordance with recommendations of the Charities SORP. Our responsibility is to report to you our opinion on the consistency of the summarised financial information with the full financial statements and Trustees' Annual Report. We also read the information contained in the summarised annual report and consider the implications for our report if we become aware of any apparent misstatements or inconsistencies with the summarised financial information.

Basis of opinion
We conducted our work in accordance with Bulletin 1999/6 "The auditors' statement on the summary financial statement" issued by the Auditing Practices Board for use in the United Kingdom.
Opinion
In our opinion the summarised financial information on pages 15 and 16 is consistent with the full financial statements and the Trustees' Annual Report of Coram Family for the year ended 31 March 2007.
Buzzacott LLP
12 New Fetter Lane, London EC4A 1AG, 26 October 2007

A financial review

14.13   A short financial review, often presented in the form of a treasurer's report, is an extremely useful tool for highlighting a particular aspect of the accounts or for giving further explanation on the charity's finances. Many readers of the charity's annual review will find narrative easier to understand than figures.

14.14   The report, which can be in the form of a short financial commentary, can be used to enable the reader to appreciate how the charity's funds have been applied, the purposes for which assets are held and the charity's reserve policy. More importantly, in terms of fundraising and marketing, the report can set out the charity's financial position in terms of its future plans and commitments.

14.15   An example of such a financial review published to accompany accounts is that of The Prostate Cancer Charity. In its 2008 Annual Review the charity's treasurer uses such a report to highlight the importance of voluntary income to the charity and the success of recent fundraising efforts.

THE PROSTATE CANCER CHARITY ANNUAL REVIEW 2008

| 2007/08 Financial highlights | annual review 2008 |

Treasurer's message

The Charity's accounts for 2007/08 show exceptional growth in income of £1,599,000, an increase of 36% over the previous year.

For the first time, these figures show separately, the income arising from Prostate Cancer Trading Limited, the Charity's trading subsidiary which was set up in April 2007.

Investment income rose by £46,000, an increase of 39% over the last year, mainly as a result of an increase in interest bearing deposits, arising from the exceptional increase in income.

The main factor contributing to the unprecedented growth in income was 'Movember', a new fundraising project, which raised £1,157,000. With 'Movember' now into a second year here in the UK, we hope to have even greater success for the future.

Excluding 'Movember's' contribution to income, there was an increase of £442,000, up 10% on last year, on a like for like basis.

And finally on income, of the total sums raised, 85% was unrestricted income, an increase of 10% over the previous year.

Expenditure

Total expenditure rose from £4,224,000 in the previous year to £5,390,000, an increase of £1,166,000 (28%). This was largely due to additional spend in both the cost of charitable activities (£2,468,000 to £2,990,000) and generating funds (from £1,553,000 to £2,134,000).

Governance costs rose from £172,000 to £219,000, an increase of £47,000 (or 27%), but still remained at 4% of total overall expenditure for the year.

The Charity spent £719,000 on new research projects in 2007/08. This increases the number of grants funded by the Charity in line with its strategy of spreading and widening research.

Statistics on fundraising income versus cost of generating funds

	£'000 2007/8	£'000 2006/07	% Increase	£'000 Variance
Fundraising income	5859	4320	36%	1539
Cost of generating funds	2134	1553	37%	581
Net contribution	3725	2767	35%	958
ROI	2.75	2.78		

19

[continued on next page]

The Prostate Cancer Charity, continued

annual review 2008 | **2007/08 Financial highlights**

Surplus

The closing surplus at the year end amounted to £663,000 compared to £230,000 at the beginning of the year. But when unrealised losses on investments are included, the surplus was £395,000 at the year end.

Balance sheet

Turning to the Balance Sheet, the significant movements were:

Fixed Assets

There was a reduction of £206,000 resulting from share disposals of £9,000 and unrealised losses on investments of £268,000 as a result of volatility in the financial markets, offset by a net increase of £71,000 in lease improvements on the Charity's premises.

Cash deposits

These increased by £1,065,000, as a result of exceptional growth in funds generated.

Reserves

Free reserves stood at £2,558,000 at the year end which represented four and a half months of unrestricted expenditure against the Charity's stated policy of three months. So the Charity started the new financial year, 2008/09, in a very healthy position.

Income

Direct fundraising	£1,462,000
Community fundraising	£2,347,000
Other incoming resources	£30,000
Investment and interest	£164,000
Trading	£82,000
Donated services	£220,000
In memory	£118,000
General donations	£6,000
Major gifts	£203,000
Legacies	£356,000
Corporate donors	£499,000
Charitable trusts	£502,000
Events	£28,000
Gala dinner	£36,000
TOTAL	**£6,053,000**

20

Charts and diagrams

14.16   Charts and diagrams are also often used by charities to provide read-ers of the annual review with a clear picture of the charity's finances. If charts and diagrams are to succeed in illustrating the facts they should be clear, strik-ing and original in design.

14.17   Charts and diagrams may be used to show a variety of information including where the charity obtains its resources from, how those resources are spent either in total or in specific areas and to provide trend analyses over a past number of years.

14.18   AMREF, for example, provide diagrams showing a breakdown of both income and expenditure. The diagram illustrates clearly the sources of income and the proportion of expenditure devoted to project grants, charitable activities and governance.

AMREF UK ANNUAL REVIEW 2008

Treasurer's Report

This year, 2007–08, has been another excellent one for AMREF UK, as the organisation has continued to grow in profile, size, capacity and influence.

Gross income (including gifts in kind) for the year was £5,069,234 (by comparison — £3,201,769 in 2007) an increase of over 58%. This increase was largely due to the continued increase in the grant funding for projects in Africa from institutional and corporate donors in particular Europe Aid (European Commission), AstraZeneca and Barclays Bank.

For every £1 of gross income, 15p is spent to generate the income and provide technical support to AMREF in Africa, and 1p on governance, office and administrative support. The balance of 84p is available for funding projects in Africa. This is an indication of AMREF UK's commitment to be as cost-effective as possible in all its activities.

We continue to be generously supported by Institutions, Companies, Trusts and Foundations and individuals, to all of whom we are extremely grateful and have been pleased to receive support from new donors during the year.

Gautam Dalal
Treasurer

Income

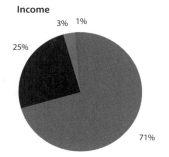

3% 1%
25%
71%

■ Grants for projects £3,572,962
■ Fundraising £1,267,842
■ Gifts in Kind £162,109
■ Bank interest £66,322

Gross income for the year was £5,069,234 – an increase of more than 58% (2007: £3,201,769)

Expenditure

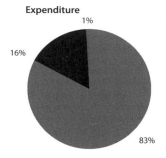

1%
16%
83%

■ Grants for projects £3,658,973
■ Cost of charitable activities & fundraising £717,814
■ Governance costs £39,337

19

14.19   Similar approaches were adopted by the Fairtrade Foundation in its 2007 Annual Review and Kidney Research UK in its 2008 Annual Review. Diagrams were used by both charities to indicate how income was expended and where the income had been derived from.

FAIRTRADE FOUNDATION ANNUAL REVIEW 2007/2008

Our figures: summary of accounts 2007

UK income year ending 31 December 2007

Nearly three quarters of our income comes from licence fees paid by companies selling goods carrying the FAIRTRADE Mark. This is in line with our guiding principle that the Fairtrade system should be sustainable, covering the majority of the costs of its operations.

However, we rely on additional income to invest in developing new products as well as supporting the most disadvantaged producers to enter Fairtrade. This income is supplemented from other sources, principally grant income used to fund, amongst other things, public awareness activities. Grant income, which represents around one quarter of our total income, comes from government sources both UK and European Union, our member agencies such as Oxfam and CAFOD, and other grant funding organisations. Overall, for 2007, our income exceeded our expenditure – partly due to funding for our Africa programme from Comic Relief. This vitally needed income will be invested during 2008 to ensure we achieve the ambitious objectives set out in our strategy Tipping the Balance.

Where our money comes from	£000s
Licence fees	4,644
Other grants	1,061
Government grants	439
Member agency grants	102
Donations	116
Other income	93
Total income	**6,455**

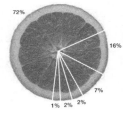

UK income
72% Licence fees
16% Other grants
7%   Government grants
2%   Member agency grants
2%   Donations
1%   Other income

14

[continued on next page]

Fairtrade Foundation, continued

UK expenditure year ending 31 December 2007

About 60% of our expenditure is allocated to our core work of licensing the FAIRTRADE Mark on products, auditing companies and working with both licensees and retailers to develop the Fairtrade market, launch new products and build opportunities for producers. This expenditure includes the monies the Fairtrade Foundation pays to the global umbrella body Fairtrade Labelling Organisations International based in Bonn, Germany, which sets standards, supports producers and inspects and certifies both producers and traders.

A further one third of our costs goes to our public education and awareness programmes that help build and sustain the UK public's support for Fairtrade. It includes the work on Fairtrade Towns, Schools and Universities, Fairtrade Fortnight activities and supporter materials.

Our remaining expenditures include the money we spend on fundraising to secure and report on our grant income and the governance costs we incur in running the Foundation as a charitable organisation.

How we spent it	£000s
Certification, product and market development	2,812
Public education and awareness	1,559
Governance	297
Fundraising	142
Total expenditure	**4,810**

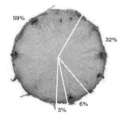

UK expenditure
59% Certification, product and
market development
32% Public education and awareness
6% Governance
3% Fundraising

The figures above were extracted from the full audited unqualified annual accounts. Copies can be obtained from **www.fairtrade.org.uk/accounts**. The annual accounts were approved on 19 May 2008 and have been submitted to the Charity Commission and Companies House.

15

285

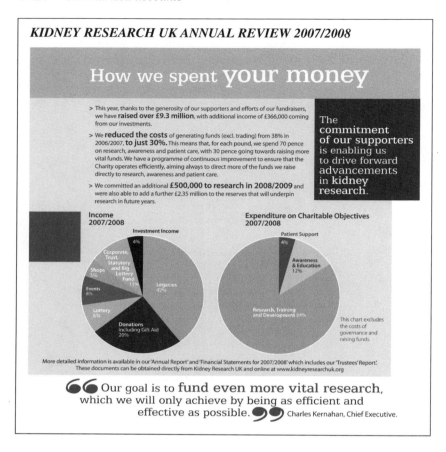

KIDNEY RESEARCH UK ANNUAL REVIEW 2007/2008

How we spent your money

> This year, thanks to the generosity of our supporters and efforts of our fundraisers, we have **raised over £9.3 million**, with additional income of £366,000 coming from our investments.

> We **reduced the costs** of generating funds (excl. trading) from 38% in 2006/2007, **to just 30%.** This means that, for each pound, we spend 70 pence on research, awareness and patient care, with 30 pence going towards raising more vital funds. We have a programme of continuous improvement to ensure that the Charity operates efficiently, aiming always to direct more of the funds we raise directly to research, awareness and patient care.

> We committed an additional **£500,000 to research in 2008/2009** and were also able to add a further £2.35 million to the reserves that will underpin research in future years.

The commitment of our supporters is enabling us to drive forward advancements in kidney research.

Income 2007/2008

Investment Income 4%

Corporate, Trust, Statutory and Big Lottery Fund 13%

Shops 5%

Events 8%

Lottery 8%

Legacies 42%

Donations including Gift Aid 20%

Expenditure on Charitable Objectives 2007/2008

Patient Support 4%

Awareness & Education 12%

Research, Training and Development 84%

This chart excludes the costs of governance and raising funds.

More detailed information is available in our 'Annual Report' and 'Financial Statements for 2007/2008' which includes our 'Trustees' Report'. These documents can be obtained directly from Kidney Research UK and online at www.kidneyresearchuk.org

Our goal is to fund even more vital research, which we will only achieve by being as efficient and effective as possible. Charles Kernahan, Chief Executive.

Faults to be avoided

14.20   Despite the general principles for summarised accounts and summary financial information being set out clearly within SORP, charities continue to make a number of mistakes when producing this information. The most common faults can be summarised as follows.

Omissions

14.21   Several charities produce an extract of their Statement of Financial Activities only, failing to provide a summary of their balance sheet. Others omit to refer to the full audited accounts or fail to provide a warning statement.

Adaptation of accounts

14.22   Some charities adapt the information contained within their full accounts or exclude certain information from the summarised statements altogether, such as the results of trading subsidiaries.

14.23   If summary financial information, such as charts and diagrams, is produced, it is essential that the information is consistent with the information in the full accounts and that creative license is not taken too far.

Proof-reading

14.24   Often typographical errors are not spotted at the proof-reading stage.

14.25   Sadly, all of these faults can detract from the overall message portrayed by the summarised accounts.

Chapter 15

Scottish, Irish and exempt charities

1 Introduction

15.1   Many people, particularly those living in England, think that there is one law governing all charities in the United Kingdom and that they are subject to the supervision of the Charity Commission. This is not so. Some may think that it would be better if it were so but that is unlikely to happen for some time, if at all, given the moves towards ever greater devolution over the past decade.

15.2   The Charity Commissioners in England and Wales were established in the nineteenth century in response to the specific needs of England and Wales at that time. In particular, because of the cost and delay experienced by petitioners in the Court of Chancery, it was thought fit to establish a speedier and cheaper way of helping trustees of charitable foundations to obtain the court's permission to do things in connection with their trust to facilitate its development for the benefit of its beneficiaries.

15.3   It was also recognised that some so-called charitable foundations were run more for the benefit of the kith and kin of the founder than for the beneficiaries.

15.4   The Charity Commissioners therefore were established to represent the interests of all those objects of charity in England and Wales: the poor, the sick, the young and the old, as well as foundations to promote the arts, sciences and other charitable objects.

15.5   Certain charitable activities were regarded by Parliament as having adequate protection and control already and were therefore left outside the control of the Charity Commission as it is known following the Charities Act 2006. These included:

(a)   Scottish charities;

(b)   Irish charities (non-Northern Irish charities); and

(c)   those exempted by the Charities Act, mainly bodies which were already well regulated by other statutes. Typically in the past these have included organisations such as:

    (i)   registered places of public worship;

    (ii)   ancient schools and universities; and

    (iii)   museums, galleries and the British Library.

15.6   The list of exempt charities was brought up-to-date in the early 1990s and was included in the Charities Act 1993 Sch 2 but, under the Charities Act 2006, exempt charities are to be radically reduced and, over time, phased out altogether.

15.7   The purpose of this chapter is to identify those charities which currently are not subject to the Charity Commission in whole or in part and to see to what extent they need not comply with the precepts put forward in the rest of this book.

2 Exempt charities

15.8   All charities which fall within the Charities Act 1993 Sch 2 (as amended by s 11 of the Charities Act 2006) are exempt from the jurisdiction of the Charity Commission. They are, however, required by the Charities Act to keep proper accounting records and to produce accounts and to make these available to the public on request.

15.9   The way in which exempt charities keep their accounting records and prepare accounts is dependent upon the regulations that each has to obey. Thus, Universities will follow their particular SORP and account in accordance with the requirements of the Higher Education Funding Council. Friendly, Industrial and Provident Societies have their own reporting procedures. Churches, museums and exempt scholastic institutions will report under their own specific statutes.

15.10   The charities' SORP will, however, apply to the form and content of all exempt charities' reports and accounts, unless superseded by another SORP as in the cases of universities, common investment funds and registered social landlords.

15.11   It is now unlikely that more SORPs, specific to certain charitable activities will be developed and therefore the Charities SORP is likely to gain in importance and influence. The Accounting Standards Board is reluctant to recognise any more sub-sectors with a need for a specific SORP.

15.12   It has been felt for some time that the existence of exempt and excepted charities (ie those charities excepted from registration by order of the Commission because they have umbrella organisations which have some form of regulatory role – examples would include Scouts, Guides, and some religious organisations) has led to anomalies in the way charities are regulated. The 2006 Act provides for the removal of exempt or excepted status from many charities entirely in the longer term. Accountability is to be tightened up for those that retain exempt status and for those that remain excepted in the short term.

15.13   Every charity must now register with the Charity Commission except those with gross income of less than £5,000 per annum or which remain exempt or excepted.

15.14   The list of exempt charities as set out in Sch 2 to the Charities Act 1993 has been reduced. Those exempt charities which have been removed from the list will be re-designated excepted charities in due course. Charities that will be affected by this include the Church Commissioners, Industrial and Provident Societies, Friendly Societies, Oxford and Cambridge University Colleges and Eton and Winchester Schools.

Comment

15.15   The success of the Charity Commission in getting most of the registered charities, over 90%, to file their annual report and accounts, compared with about 20% fifteen years ago, is driving the charity legislative reform in England and Wales. It is, therefore, not surprising that the accountability of exempt and excepted charities is now being revised.

15.16   As in any time of change, such charities should be wary – for some, the changes will require major adjustments.

3   Scottish charities

15.17   In Scotland the regulation of charities is in the hands of the Office of the Scottish Charity Regulator (OSCR).

15.18   The format and independent scrutiny of Scottish charity accounts is regulated by the Charities and Trustee Investment (Scotland) Act 2005 (the Act), and the Charities Accounts (Scotland) Regulations 2006 (the Regulations).

15.19   Scottish charities must prepare their accounts in accordance with s 44 of the Act and the Regulations for financial years starting on or after 1 April 2006. This will include charities governed by other statutes, for example, charitable companies which are also governed by company law.

15.20   For accounting periods that started before 1 April 2006 charities that are not companies must, for these accounting periods only, continue to maintain accounting records and prepare accounts in accordance with the Law Reform (Miscellaneous Provisions) (Scotland) Act 1990 and the Charity Accounts (Scotland) Regulations 1992. (In brief these require that 'a recognised body' (ie a charity) shall produce annual accounts giving an income and expenditure account and balance sheet; and an auditor shall be appointed by the trustees and his report will be annexed to the balance sheet and income and expenditure accounts.

15.21   Charitable companies with accounting periods starting before 1 April 2006 must prepare accounts that comply with the 1985 Companies Act.

15.22   The Scottish legislation requires that charity accounts must be prepared in one of two ways. Charities with gross annual income of less than £100,000 and which are not incorporated may prepare receipts and payments accounts. As in England and Wales, these are a simple form of accounting that consist of a summary of all monies received and paid via the bank and in cash by the charity during its financial year, along with a statement of balances. Charities with gross annual income of £100,000 or more or which are companies must prepare accounts on an accruals basis. Accounts prepared using the accruals basis must be prepared in accordance with the methods and principles of SORP ie the *Accounting and Reporting by Charities: Statement of Recommended Practice* (the 2005 Charities SORP).

15.23   If the charity's constitution requires accrued accounts to be prepared then these must be prepared even if the charity's gross income would otherwise allow accounts to be produced on the receipts and payments basis.

15.24   The accounts of a charity registered in Scotland must be filed with OSCR within nine months of the charity's year end. This is one month earlier that the filing deadline for charities registered in England and Wales with the Charity Commission and needs to be noted by those charities registered in both jurisdictions – see 'cross border' charities at **15.34** below.

15.25   There are two main types of external scrutiny to which a Scottish charity's accounts may be subject:

- independent examination;

- audit.

A report from an Independent Reporting Accountant may be relevant for some charitable companies.

15.26   As in England and Wales, an independent examination is a form of external scrutiny of the accounts which is less rigorous than an audit and offers an assurance that nothing has been found that needs to be brought to the attention of readers of the accounts rather than the positive expression of a professional opinion based on an audit.

15.27   An audit provides reasonable assurance that the accounts are free from material misstatement, whether caused by fraud or other irregularity or error. In undertaking an audit of a Scottish charity, a registered auditor must comply with the UK Auditing Practices Board's ethical standards for auditors and International Standards on Auditing (UK and Ireland).

15.28   The type of external scrutiny appropriate for a particular charity is determined by:

- any reference to audit in the constitution or governing document of the charity;

- whether the charity is a company;

- the charity's gross income and the value of *assets* held (before deduction of liabilities) for the accounting period. The limits for determining whether an audit or independent examination is required are consistent with those in England and Wales. In other words an audit is required if the charity's annual gross income is equal to or more than

£500,000 or if its assets (before deduction of liabilities) are more than £2.8 million;

- a decision of the charity trustees to carry out an audit.

15.29   Every year, charities registered in Scotland are issued with an Annual Return. This already has details about the charity from its Register entry completed (eg the accounting reference date) but details will need to be confirmed and additional information given. In particular, charities need to state their annual gross income.

15.30   Charities which have declared a gross income of £25,000 or above in respect to the preceding year also receive a supplementary Monitoring Return. This seeks additional information about:

- annual accounts;
- fundraising activities;
- transactions with trustees;
- dealings with connected trading companies.

15.31   The Monitoring Return for charities with an income of £100,000 or above asks for slightly more information.

15.32   Every charity must file its Annual Return, supplementary Monitoring Return (if appropriate) and annual accounts with OSCR within nine months of the charity's financial year end (ten months for accounting periods starting before 1 April 2006). The accounts should be submitted at the same time as the Annual Return. All of these documents must be signed with original signatures (not photocopies) and dated.

Comment

15.33   For several years there were a number of inconsistencies between the accounting and independent scrutiny requirements required under the law of England and Wales and those required by Scottish law. In recent years the laws of the two countries have become far more consistent – this can only be a good thing.

'Cross border' charities

15.34   Following the enactment of the Charities and Trustee Investment (Scotland) Act 2005 the activities of all charities in Scotland are now regulated by OSCR, regardless of whether the charity was first registered in England and Wales and regardless of the charity's size. Exempt and excepted charities will also be caught by the Act. As a result, any organisations registered or recognised as charities outside Scotland, such as those registered by the Charity Commission, may now be required to register with OSCR also.

15.35   The legislation does try to distinguish between charities with large operations in Scotland and those with only an occasional connection. A cross border charity will be required to register if it:

• owns or occupies land or premises in Scotland; or

• carries out activities in any office, shop or similar premises in Scotland.

15.36   In its guidance to cross border charities, OSCR sets out the following examples:

• **Organisations will have to register with OSCR if they**:

– Own or lease premises in Scotland

– Pay rates in Scotland

– Claim relief for non-domestic rates from a local authority in Scotland

– Hold open meetings in Scotland

– Charge for events held in Scotland

• **Organisations are less likely to have to register with OSCR if they simply**:

– Advertise in the Scottish press or other media

– Award grants to recipients in Scotland by correspondence only

– Conduct street collections only

– Hold occasional members' conferences in Scotland

– Use secretarial support provided by volunteers operating from their own home

15.37   In all cases it is the responsibility of the charity to register with OSCR.

15.38   There are several other impacts as a result of this legislation. These include:

(a)   Terminology

English and Welsh charities once registered with OSCR may refer to themselves as a charity, a charitable body, a registered charity or a charity registered in Scotland. However, charities not registered with OSCR must make this clear when referring to themselves in Scotland. For example, they must state that they are 'a charity registered with the Charity Commission'. The terms 'Scottish Charity' or 'Registered Scottish Charity' are only to be used by those charities established in Scotland or managed and controlled wholly or mainly from Scotland.

(b)   Scottish Registration Numbers

Charities registered with OSCR will have a Scottish registration number. Such charities have to quote both this and their English and Welsh registration number on documents in the public domain in Scotland.

(c)   Branches

English and Welsh charities with branches in Scotland which are not autonomous only need to register once in Scotland, ie it is not necessary for each branch to register.

(d)   The Charity Test

All charities operating in Scotland are subjected to a 'charity test'. This is similar to the public benefit test to be used in England and Wales although care is needed because the definitions of charitable purpose and public benefit differ slightly between the two jurisdictions.

(e)   Annual Returns and Monitoring Returns

All charities registered with OSCR are required to submit an Annual Return and those charities with annual income in excess of £25,000 will be required to submit a Monitoring Return as well. There is also a legal requirement to notify OSCR of certain changes such as an alteration to the principal address of the charity or amendments to the charity's constitution.

(f)   Accounts

OSCR has agreed not to insist on separate Scottish accounts. However, OSCR has indicated that it expects a cross border charity to include some narrative within its trustees' report on the charity's activities in Scotland.

(g)   Enquiries and investigations

OSCR has the power to conduct enquiries and investigations into charities and their trading subsidiaries for both general or specific purposes. However, in the case of a charity registered with the Charity Commission, the consensus is that on receipt of a complaint or referral, OSCR Case Officers would contact Charity Commission Case Officers to determine whether enquiries should be delegated or whether, in the circumstances, a joint enquiry would be appropriate.

15.39   These new arrangements for 'cross border' charities became effective from April 2006.

Comment

15.40   The need for certain charities operating in both England and Wales and in Scotland to register with OSCR has been seen by some as overly bureaucratic. The registration process has not been without its teething problems and many charities have been severely frustrated by the process. Many of the problems have arisen because of the differences in the definitions of charitable causes and public benefit in the two jurisdictions. These differences have led to OCSR refusing to register certain charities because of the wording of the objects or dissolution clauses within their governing documents. Section 7(4) of the 2005 Scottish Act states:

'(4) A body … does not meet the charity test if –

(a) its constitution allows it to distribute or otherwise apply any of its property (on being wound up or at any other time) for a purpose which is not a charitable purpose.'

15.41 The difficulty for OSCR arises where instead, or in addition to, specific purposes an objects clause contains a reference to 'other charitable purposes'. Also, or alternatively, a dissolution clause may provide for a body's assets at wind-up to be used for 'some other charitable purpose'. The small differences in the legal definitions mean that it is possible for something to be charitable in England and Wales but not in Scotland!

15.42 In order to address this dilemma, OSCR has agreed with the Charity Commission the wording for standard amendments which meet the requirements of the Scottish charity test and also concerns raised concerning the England and Wales regulatory situation.

15.43 For charities which operate in Scotland and which refer to general charitable purposes in their objects and dissolution clauses the following overriding provision should be added, ensuring that it applies throughout the constitution:

'"Charitable" means charitable in accordance with the law of England and Wales provided that it will not include any purpose which is not charitable in accordance with section 7 of the Charities and Trustee Investment (Scotland) Act 2005.

For the avoidance of doubt, the system of law governing the constitution of the charity is the law of England and Wales.'

15.44 An alternative overriding provision which might be sufficient where the actual objects met the charity test in Scottish legislation although the dissolution clause or other powers did not is:

'Nothing in this constitution shall authorise an application of the property of the charity for purposes which are not charitable in accordance with section 7 Charities and Trustee Investment (Scotland) Act 2005.'

15.45 Charities registered in England and Wales which face this problem should discuss their own individual position with their legal advisers and the Charity Commission.

4 Irish charities

15.46 Charity law in Ireland is undergoing fundamental changes. The new Charities Act 2009 was signed in to law on 28 February 2009 and will be implemented in stages. It is believed it will take two years before all provisions have been implemented. The Act provides for the establishment of a statutory body for the regulation, protection and registration of charities, to be called the Charities Regulatory Authority.

15.47   *Scottish, Irish and exempt charities*

15.47   The accounting bodies in the Republic of Ireland have recognised the charities SORP, hence the reference in para 8 of SORP to the fact that charities in the Republic may choose to comply with its recommendations.

15.48   It can be expected, therefore, that those charities in the Republic of Ireland which present audited accounts showing a true and fair view will follow many of the recommendations of the SORP until such time as specific guidance is drafted for them to follow.

15.49   The Charities Act 2009, in establishing a new statutory framework for charities operating in the Republic of Ireland whether or not the charity is established in that jurisdiction, provides for:

- definitions of 'charitable purposes' and 'purposes for the benefit of the community';

- Charities Regulatory Authority ('this Authority') to secure compliance by charities with their legal obligations and to encourage and facilitate better administration of charities;

- all charities are obliged to register with this Authority;

- charities required to maintain 'proper books of account';

- charities to prepare an annual statement of accounts, to be audited and included in the charities annual report to be submitted to this Authority;

- Revised Statutory Framework for fundraising, including street collection and direct debit and similar non cash methods;

- Charities Appeal Tribunal;

- Consultation Panels to assist this Authority in its work; and

- Dissolution of the Commissioners of Charitable Donations.

15.50   The format and detailed content of the annual statements of account as well as provisions to the audit thereof will be determined by Ministerial Regulations. The relevant Department officials will consult with the accounting profession in the Republic of Ireland on the development of those Regulations.

15.51   Law in Northern Ireland has been updated recently also and in due course, after provisions set out in the Charities Act (NI) 2008 have been implemented, the charity reporting and accounting requirements will be similar to those elsewhere in the UK.

15.52   The Charities Act (NI) 2008 gives an explanation of what a 'charity' is and describes 'charitable purpose'. A new form of charitable body will be created called a charitable incorporated organisation and there will be a compulsory register of all charities operating in Northern Ireland.

15.53   The Act also sets up a new organisation, the Charity Commission for Northern Ireland (CCNI), and a process for anyone to make an appeal against the decision made by the CCNI, the Charity Tribunal for Northern Ireland.

Sections 6 to 11 (and Schedule 1) of the Act list the Charity Commission's objectives, purpose, general duties and powers. The Commission will be a non-Departmental Public Body (NDPB) supported by the Department for Social Development (DSD).

Comment

15.54   It is extremely pleasing that developments in the laws in both the Republic of Ireland and Northern Ireland have progressed as speedily as they have. We are now in touching distance of achieving the goal of ensuring the whole of the UK and the Republic of Ireland has charity laws which contain significant consistency and conformity. This is something that seemed impossible just five years ago.

5   Common Investment Funds

15.55   Common Investment Funds (CIFs) are charities established by schemes made by the Charity Commission. They are administered by trustees who appoint investment managers to manage the funds and a corporate trustee to hold them and oversee the investment manager in a similar manner to a unit trust. Trustees of other charities are then invited to invest in the units issued by the CIF. The essential distinction between these funds and 'pooled' funds is that the trustees of a CIF are entrusted with funds belonging to charities of which they are not necessarily trustees, whereas trustees of 'pooled' funds have to have control of the trusts which pool their funds together.

15.56   Essentially, the accounts of a CIF are drawn up to comply with the requirements of authorised unit trusts. These are designed to show their total returns on investments with comparisons to relevant indices as well as an income and expenditure account and balance sheet.

Comment

15.57   Following discussions between the Charity Commission and the managers of CIFs during 1998 and 1999, amendments have been made to the constitution of CIFs to bring them within the jurisdiction of the Financial Services Authority. With the appointment of a Corporate Trustee, each CIFis now in a similar regulatory framework to that of an authorised unit trust. Indeed the only significant difference is that CIFs have a supervisory board of trustees who have responsibility for appointing the corporate trustee, the investment managers and auditors and for establishing the investment guidelines. The supervisory board of trustees needs to ensure that either the corporate trustee or the managers also report on the reserves policy, the risks analysis and other aspects normally covered in the trustees' report (see Chapter 4) and, if not, include it in their own report.

Chapter 16

Audit and other external scrutiny

1   Introduction

16.1   The accounts of charities are rightly subject to a higher degree of public interest than those of equivalent sized business organisations. As custodians of funds held on trust and often raised from a combination of donations from the general public and support from the public purse, through both direct grant funding and tax concessions, most charities are, by nature, public rather than private entities.

16.2   This is manifested in the extent to which the finances of charities are subjected to independent, external scrutiny. The most common instance of such scrutiny is the statutory obligation for many charities to have their accounts independently audited, or for smaller charities subjected to independent examination.

16.3   Since the mid 1990s, the audit requirement for most smaller private companies has been abolished. Under company law, and based on thresholds prevailing in August 2009, which are subject to change, an audit is not required for the majority of companies. Only those which are part of a listed group, carry out certain financial services business or exceed specified financial thresholds are required to have an audit. The thresholds in the Companies Act are discussed below, but as an indication, the turnover threshold as at August 2009 is £6.5 million.

16.4   This contrasts noticeably with the maintenance of a threshold of £500,000 for all charities, including those which are companies, and with the ongoing requirement for some scrutiny of charities with income as low as £25,000 in England and Wales and with no lower limit in Scotland.

16.5   This chapter sets out the statutory requirements for external scrutiny of the accounts and the respective responsibilities and roles of the charity trustees and the auditor or independent examiner. The chapter is written from the perspective of the charity, in order to understand the role of the audit; it does not purport to be an auditing treatise.

16.6   For ease of reference, this chapter has only attempted to set out and compare the main requirements of the three sources of legislation most likely to apply to a charity in Great Britain. These are the Charities Act 1993 (as amended by the Charities Act 2006), the Charities and Trustee Investment (Scotland) Act 2005 and Regulations issued thereunder, and the Companies Act 2006. Charities which are incorporated as Industrial and Provident Societies or Friendly Societies, and/or are Registered Social Landlords, etc, as well as those in Ireland or Northern Ireland will be subject to audit requirements governed by the legislation under which they prepare their accounts.

16.7   There have been many changes to the legal requirements for audit as a result of the implementation of new company legislation for the UK as a whole and charity legislation in Scotland and England and Wales respectively in recent years. Professional standards for auditors are also under development; in particular ISA 700 which governs the format of an audit report has been significantly revised to reflect the provisions of the Companies Act 2006. At the time of writing, revised guidance for auditors of charities, whether or not they are companies, is being finalised.

16.8   In order to avoid over complication of this chapter – which reflects an already complex interaction of legislation – the legal position applicable to charities, including those which are companies, for years beginning on or after 6 April 2008 is described below. For earlier years the underlying legislation and regulations should be consulted. Additionally, further changes to detailed guidance are very likely to emerge in 2009 and 2010 and what follows may be superseded to some extent by that guidance.

16.9   Some charities are not subject to statutory audit but may, through the requirements of their constitution or through the specific request of major funders, lenders, members or trustees, choose to have their accounts audited. In these cases the scope of the audit, including the required report, will be a matter of agreement between the charity and the auditor, but will generally follow an analogous pattern to that of a statutory audit. The auditor will also be subject to the same Auditing Standards as apply to a statutory audit.

16.10   Alongside the statutory audit or independent examination, there are many other forms of activity referred to as 'audit' and commonly undertaken in the charity sector. Of these this chapter deals briefly only with other reports which may be required of the statutory auditor, or equivalent, by funders. The role of internal auditors and of non-financial audit exercises, such as social, environmental or human resource audits, is outside the scope of this book.

Forms of scrutiny and source of requirements

16.11   Following the enactment of the Charities and Trustee Investment (Scotland) Act 2005 in Scotland, the Charities Act 2006 in England and Wales and the Companies Act 2006 in the whole of the UK, determining the legislation under which a charity may require audit or other external scrutiny has become considerably more complex.

16.12   As we will see below, for charities which operate both in England and Wales and in Scotland, dual regulation now applies in many cases. In England and Wales, for smaller charities which are companies, there is now effectively a choice between audit under company or charity law. Small groups headed by a charity may have obligations to prepare charity only accounts under company law and group accounts under charity law with the former audited under either legislation and the latter under charity legislation only.

16.13   In general, these complexities can be left for the appointed auditor to unravel and advise trustees upon. Provided trustees have identified the need for an auditor and appointed wisely there is little if any practical impact on the audit process as a result of the legal distinctions.

16.14   A charity will determine whether it is subject to scrutiny and, if so, whether its accounts must be audited or subjected to a more limited form of scrutiny by referring to the legislation under which it prepares its accounts. The principles applying under each Act are outlined below, with the detail presented in the Appendices.

What level of scrutiny applies?

England and Wales only

16.15   The following conditions apply to charities registered in and operating only in England and Wales. For charities registered in and operating in Scotland the rules are set out in the following section, together with the position for 'cross border' charities which are simultaneously subject to both regulatory regimes.

16.16   For charities preparing accounts under the Charities Act 1993, all but the smallest charities are required to have some form of independent examination of their accounts. Where neither gross income nor total expenditure of the charity (see definition in Appendix 3) for the year in question exceed £25,000, no such scrutiny is required. An unincorporated charity, with income below £500,000 in the current financial year and gross assets below £2.8 million (or if assets exceed this threshold, income below £100,000), may elect to have an independent examination – this is a form of independent scrutiny that falls short of the full requirement of an audit. These thresholds also apply to company charities which fall below the Companies Act thresholds and have taken advantage of exemption from audit under that Act.

16.17   A charity which is a company must comply with the audit requirements of the Companies Act 2006 unless exempt. Where a company has gross income of less than £6.5 million, has total assets of less than £3.26 million and is a 'small company' as defined from time to time, it is exempt from the requirement for audit – subject to any overriding requirement of the Articles of Association and safeguards for the charity's members, 10% of whom may demand an audit by depositing a request in writing at least one month prior to the relevant year end.

16.18   For years beginning after 6 April 2008 company charities which take advantage of audit exemption under company law are subject to audit or independent examination under the Charities Act. Where this is done, the charity is required to make statements regarding the audit exemption in its balance sheet.

16.19   The detailed conditions for exemption from audit are set out in the Companies Act 2006 s 477. Although not explicitly stated, the conditions have the effect of making exemption from audit elective. Many charities have concluded that as there is little substantive difference between Companies Act and Charities Act audit and the required disclosures are cumbersome and potentially confusing, there is nothing to be gained by taking this exemption. Such charities continue to be audited under the Companies Act. Conversely, where a company charity qualifies for independent examination, exemption from audit may be a significant benefit.

Scotland

16.20   The position in Scotland differs significantly from that in England and Wales. Whereas in the latter jurisdiction generally either one or the other of charity and company law will apply to the audit of charity companies, in Scotland the Charities and Trustee Investment (Scotland) Act 2005 will always apply whether exemption from audit under the Companies Act 2006 has been taken or not.

16.21   In Scotland, the same thresholds for audit exemption apply as in England and Wales, ie assets of less than £3.26 million, gross income below £500,000 and qualification as a small company. Unlike England and Wales, the Scottish regulations require all audit exempt charities to be independently examined – meaning that a 'cross border' charity with income of less than £25,000 would be exempt from external scrutiny in England and Wales but require independent examination in Scotland (though admittedly such a charity is not very likely to exist).

16.22   Non company charities and company charities which have elected for audit exemption under the Charities Act 2006 will be audited or independently examined only under the Charities and Trustee Investment (Scotland) Act 2005. Company charities unable to elect for audit exemption, or which choose not to do so, will be audited under both the Companies Act 2006 and the Charities and Trustee Investment (Scotland) Act 2005.

Cross border charities

16.23   All charities with tangible operations in Scotland, including those registered elsewhere, are required to register with the Office of the Scottish Charity Regulator (OSCR) and in so doing will fall into the accounting and audit regime of the Charities and Trustee Investment (Scotland) Act 2005 and the regulations issued in accordance with that Act. For charities registered in England and Wales, this results in double regulation and such charities are referred to as 'cross border charities'.

16.24   For cross border charities which are companies audited under the Companies Act 2006, the position is equivalent to that of Scottish charities which are companies. For non company charities and those electing to take exemption from Companies Act audit, both the Charities Act 1993 and the Charities and Trustee Investment (Scotland) Act 2005 apply.

Who can be appointed?

Auditor

16.25   Eligibility for the appointment as auditor of a charity is determined by whether a person (or firm) is:

- eligible to act as company auditor under the Companies Act 2006 s 1211 et seq;

- a person eligible for appointment as auditor of the charity under regulations made under the Charities Act 1993 ss 43–44 (England and Wales only); or

- the Auditor General for Scotland (Scotland only).

There are detailed requirements for qualifying as an auditor of statutory financial statements, but these are generally not the concern of the charity making the appointment. A person or firm eligible to be appointed as an auditor will identify themselves as such and a charity can check with the auditor's professional body to verify that status.

16.26   Although a charity is free to appoint any firm of auditors qualified by law to undertake such work, it will of course be in the interests of the charity to appoint a firm which has demonstrable experience in handling the specific accounting and audit requirements of charities. This will add to the confidence of the trustees and other stakeholders that the appointed auditor will address relevant issues in an efficient (and therefore less costly) and effective way.

Independent examiner

16.27   Following the doubling of the audit threshold for charities to £500,000, a two tier regime has been implemented for the appointment of independent examiners. In both Scotland and England and Wales the smallest charities are allowed great flexibility in who may be appointed as an examiner whilst larger charities must appoint a person who is a member of one of a list of prescribed bodies.

16.28   In England and Wales those charities with gross income falling between £25,000 and £250,000 are able to appoint an examiner who does not hold a specified qualification. In Scotland it is only charities using the receipts and payments basis of accounting that are able to take that course. In both regimes, the list of bodies eligible for appointment as examiner to the larger charities is more widely drawn than those bodies that are recognised supervisory bodies for auditors.

16.29 Regulation 11 of the Charities Accounts (Scotland) Regulations 2006 specifies the following:

'Independent examination of statement of account

11.

(1) A charity with a gross income in a financial year of less than £500,000, which is required to prepare a statement of account in accordance with regulation 8 or 9 and which is not required to have its statement of account audited in accordance with regulation 10, must have its statement of account for that year examined by an independent examiner who is reasonably believed by the charity trustees to have the requisite ability and practical experience to carry out a competent examination of the accounts.

(2) If the charity prepares a statement of account in accordance with regulation 8, the independent examiner must also be–

(a) a member of–

(i) the Institute of Chartered Accountants in England and Wales,

(ii) the Institute of Chartered Accountants of Scotland,

(iii) the Institute of Chartered Accountants in Ireland,

(iv) the Association of Chartered Certified Accountants,

(v) the Association of Authorised Public Accountants,

(vi) the Association of Accounting Technicians,

(vii) the Association of International Accountants,

(viii) the Chartered Institute of Management Accountants,

(ix) the Institute of Chartered Secretaries and Administrators,

(x) the Chartered Institute of Public Finance or Accountancy,

(b) a full member of the Association of Charity Independent Examiners, or

(c) the Auditor General for Scotland.'

The equivalent provisions in England and Wales are substantively the same with the omission of the Auditor General for Scotland.

16.30 'Independence' means that the examiner should have no connection with the charity trustees, which might inhibit an impartial conduct of the examination. Such individuals as the charity's trustees themselves, anyone closely involved in the administration of the charity, major donors or beneficiaries of the charity or any close relative, business partner or employee of any of the preceding would be deemed inappropriate.

16.31 As to 'requisite ability', as mentioned above, it is difficult to envisage anyone other than an accountant familiar with accountancy principles and accounting standards being competent to examine complex accounts prepared on an accruals basis. (For receipts and payments accounts and accruals accounts of small uncomplicated charities, a bank manager or local authority treasurer, for example, may be competent.)

16.32 'Practical experience' involves experience of the financial administration of a charity or other institution of similar nature, structure and size, or prior experience as an independent examiner or investigator. An independent examiner should be conversant with the Charity Commission Directions, and the requirements of an independent examiner's report prescribed in accordance with the regulations. Where accruals accounts are concerned, the examiner should also be conversant with the regulations as to form and content of the accounts and the charities' SORP.

16.33 It is the charity trustees' responsibility to ensure that the prospective independent examiner is appropriate for the assignment. The terms of engagement should be recognised in a letter of engagement between the trustees and the independent examiner.

What is an audit?

16.34 The practice of auditing in the UK is governed by International Standards on Auditing (United Kingdom and Ireland), generally referred to as ISAs. The ISAs were developed principally to guide the audit of large commercial concerns. Their application to the specific circumstances of charities is informed by the Auditing Practices Board's Practice Note 11 'The Audit of Charities in the UK'.

16.35 ISA (UK and Ireland) 200 explains that:

'2. The objective of an audit of financial statements is to enable the auditor to express an opinion whether the financial statements are prepared, in all material respects, in accordance with an applicable financial reporting framework. The phrases used to express the auditor's opinion are 'give a true and fair view' or 'present fairly, in all material respects,' which are equivalent terms.

2-1. The 'applicable financial reporting framework' comprises those requirements of accounting standards, law and regulations applicable to the entity that determine the form and content of its financial statements.

3. Although the auditor's opinion enhances the credibility of the financial statements, the user cannot assume that the audit opinion is an assurance as to the future viability of the entity nor the efficiency or effectiveness with which management has conducted the affairs of the entity.'

16.36 For UK charities, the 'applicable accounting framework' is United Kingdom Generally Accepted Accounting Practice (UK GAAP). This comprises principally the relevant legislation, United Kingdom Accounting Standards and by extension of these, the charities SORP. The core reporting obligation set out in ISA 200 is added to by the specific requirements of the legislation. Each Act adds a number of opinions to those the auditor is required to form and express, some of which are stated positively and some negatively (ie by exception).

16.37   The core elements of all audit reports issued under the regimes described above are: positive opinions that the accounts show a true and fair view, have been properly prepared in accordance with UK GAAP and have been prepared in accordance with the relevant legislation; and reporting by exception where the auditor has not received full explanations, proper accounting records have not been maintained or the accounts are not in agreement with the accounting records.

16.38   The Companies Act 2006 includes a requirement for a positive statement that the information given in the directors' report is consistent with the financial statements whereas the Regulations made under the Charities Act 1993 and the Charities and Trustee Investment (Scotland) Act 2005 require a report if the information is not consistent. Company law also requires reporting – if not already made in the financial statements – of details of remuneration of directors, ie the charity trustees.

16.39   The precise requirements of the different charity and company legislation under which a charity's auditors may now be reporting leads to subtle differences in the form of report offered. As noted above, the general layout and content of audit reports is currently undergoing revision and it is expected that by the time this book is published the requirements extant at the time of writing will have been superseded.

16.40   The following paragraphs discuss the general objectives of an audit report, readers interested in the detailed requirements or seeking example reports are referred to guidance issued by the Auditing Practices Board, principally Practice Note 11 and ISA 720 and bulletins and updates issued to supplement these for ongoing developments.

16.41   One of the key common features of all audit reports is clearly distinguishing the respective responsibilities of trustees and auditors – it is the charity's trustees who are responsible for the preparation of accounts, while the auditors are responsible for reporting an independent opinion on those accounts. The responsibilities of the trustees are generally set out in the trustees' report or in a separate statement adjacent to it.

16.42   Company law additionally requires each of the trustees to confirm in the trustees' report that they have provided all relevant information and that they have made such enquiries as they believe are necessary to satisfy themselves that no further relevant information exists.

16.43   The following excerpt from the trustee's report of Skillshare, together with the auditors' report, illustrates how these requirements are met in practice. As is hopefully clear from the above, care is needed to ensure the right statements are made and at the time of writing, the Auditing Practices Board had just issued 'Auditors' reports – Supplementary guidance for auditors of charities with accounting periods commencing on, or after, 6 April 2008' in an attempt to assist auditors in this. The audit report below is taken directly from that guidance.

---

*EXTRACT FROM THE REPORT OF THE TRUSTEES OF
SKILLSHARE INTERNATIONAL FOR THE YEAR ENDED 31
MARCH 2009*

'Statement of trustees' responsibilities

Company law requires the trustees to prepare financial statements which
give a true and fair view of the state of affairs of the charity at the end
of the financial year and of its surplus or deficit for the financial year. In
preparing financial statements giving a true and fair view, the trustees are
required to:

- select suitable accounting policies and then apply them consistently;

- make judgements and estimates that are reasonable and prudent;

- state whether applicable accounting standards have been followed,
  subject to any material departures disclosed and explained in the
  financial statements; and

- prepare the financial statements on the going concern basis unless
  it is inappropriate to presume that the charity will continue in
  operation.

The trustees are responsible for maintaining proper accounting records
which disclose with reasonable accuracy at any time the financial position
of the charity and which enables them to ensure that the financial statements comply with the Companies Act 1985.

The trustees are also responsible for safeguarding the assets of the charity
and hence for taking reasonable steps for the prevention and detection of
fraud and other irregularities.

This report and financial statements are posted on the charity's website.
Every reasonable measure is taken to ensure that the report and financial
statements are unaltered. The trustees are responsible for the maintenance
and integrity of the financial statements presented on the charity website.
Legislation in the United Kingdom governing the preparation and dissem-
ination of financial statements may differ from that of the place in which
these financial statements are viewed.

Each of the trustees confirms that:

- so far as each of the trustees is aware, there is no relevant audit
  information of which the charity's auditors are unaware; and

- the trustee has taken all the steps that he/she ought to have taken as
  a trustee in order to make himself/herself aware of any relevant audit
  information and to establish that the charity's auditors are aware of
  that information.

This confirmation is given and should be interpreted in accordance with
the provisions of s 234ZA of the Companies Act 1985.'

Although the statutory references in the above statement refer to the Companies Act 1985, the forms of words which will be used under the incoming requirements are the same.

AUDITOR'S REPORTS – SUPPLEMENTARY GUIDANCE FOR AUDITORS OF CHARITIES WITH ACCOUNTING PERIODS COMMENCING ON, OR AFTER, 6 APRIL 2008

Example 7: Large charitable company group registered in Scotland, whose consolidated accounts are required to be prepared and audited under the Companies Act 2006 (can also be used for large cross-border charity groups audited under the Companies Act 2006)

Independent Auditor's Report to the Members and Trustees of XYZ Charity (Limited)

We have audited the financial statements of [name of charity] for the year ended [5 April 2009] which comprise [state primary financial statements such as the Consolidated Statement of Financial Activities, the Consolidated Summary Income and Expenditure Account, the Consolidated and Parent Company Balance Sheets, the Consolidated Cash Flow Statement] and the related notes. These financial statements have been prepared under the accounting policies set out therein.

RESPECTIVE RESPONSIBILITIES OF TRUSTEES AND AUDITORS

The trustees' (who are also the directors of the company for the purposes of company law) responsibilities for preparing the Annual Report[1] and the financial statements in accordance with applicable law and United Kingdom Accounting Standards (United Kingdom Generally Accepted Accounting Practice) and for being satisfied that the financial statements give a true and fair view are set out in the Statement of Trustees' Responsibilities.

We have been appointed auditors under section 44(1)(c) of the Charities and Trustee Investment (Scotland) Act 2005 and under the Companies Act 2006 and report to you under those Acts.

Our responsibility is to audit the financial statements in accordance with relevant legal and regulatory requirements and International Standards on Auditing (UK and Ireland).

We report to you our opinion as to whether the financial statements give a true and fair view, have been properly prepared in accordance with United Kingdom Generally Accepted Accounting Practice and have been prepared in accordance with the Companies Act 2006, the Charities and Trustee Investment (Scotland) Act 2005 and regulations 6 and 8 of the Charities Accounts (Scotland) Regulations 2006. We also report to you whether in our opinion the information given in the Trustees' Annual Report is consistent with the financial statements.

[*continued on next page*]

Auditor's Reports, continued

In addition we report to you if, in our opinion, the charity has not kept adequate and proper accounting records, if the charity's statement of account is not in agreement with these accounting records, if we have not received all the information and explanations we require for our audit, or if certain disclosures of trustees' remuneration specified by law are not made.

[We read other information contained in the Annual Report, and consider whether it is consistent with the audited financial statements. The other information comprises only [list all documents published with the financial statements such as the Trustees' Annual Report, the Chairman's Statement]. We consider the implications for our report if we become aware of any apparent misstatements or material inconsistencies with the financial statements. Our responsibilities do not extend to other information[2].]

OR

[We read the Trustees' Annual Report and consider the implications for our report if we become aware of any apparent misstatements within it[3].]

BASIS OF AUDIT OPINION

We conducted our audit in accordance with International Standards on Auditing (UK and Ireland) issued by the Auditing Practices Board. An audit includes examination, on a test basis, of evidence relevant to the amounts and disclosures in the financial statements. It also includes an assessment of the significant estimates and judgments made by the trustees in the preparation of the financial statements, and of whether the accounting policies are appropriate to the group's and charitable company's circumstances, consistently applied and adequately disclosed.

We planned and performed our audit so as to obtain all the information and explanations which we considered necessary in order to provide us with sufficient evidence to give reasonable assurance that the financial statements are free from material misstatement, whether caused by fraud or other irregularity or error. In forming our opinion we also evaluated the overall adequacy of the presentation of information in the financial statements.

OPINION

In our opinion:

- the financial statements give a true and fair view of the state of the group's and the parent company's affairs as at [5 April 2009] and of the group's incoming resources and application of resources, including its income and expenditure, for the year then ended;

- the financial statements have been properly prepared in accordance with United Kingdom Generally Accepted Accounting Practice;

[*continued on next page*]

Auditor's Reports, continued

- the financial statements have been prepared in accordance with the Companies Act 2006, the Charities and Trustee Investment (Scotland) Act 2005 and regulations 6 and 8 of the Charities Accounts (Scotland) Regulations 2006; and

- the information given in the Trustees' Annual Report is consistent with the financial statements.

[Signature]   Address

[Name] Senior Statutory Auditor   Date

for and on behalf of ABC [LLP], Statutory Auditor(s)

ABC LLP is eligible to act as an auditor in terms of section 1212 of the Companies Act 2006

1	Use the title of the document issued by the charity containing the audited financial statements.
2	This paragraph is used where the financial statements are published with surround information in addition to the Trustees' Annual Report.
3	This paragraph is used where the financial statements are not published with surround information other than the Trustees' Annual Report.

Comment

16.44   It is common practice for the firm of accountants appointed as auditors to assist in the preparation of the statutory report and accounts. It is important that trustees are reminded of the separation of functions between assisting them in the fulfilment of their own duties and the independent duty of forming and reporting an audit opinion.

16.45   The benefit of an audit is primarily the assurance that the trustees, and/or the members, receive from an external scrutiny in accordance with statutory requirements and professional standards of the charity's activities over the financial period, and the state of affairs at a given point in time (the balance sheet date).

16.46   There is no formal assurance given – or legal responsibility owed – by the auditor beyond the statutory opinion given to the members or trustees – a fact that auditors generally draw attention to in their audit reports. However, in practice the fact that a charity's accounts have been independently audited adds to the credibility of a charity's accounts with other stakeholders and also, for example, with funders and interested members of the general public or the media.

What is an independent examination?

16.47   As mentioned above, this is a less onerous form of scrutiny than an audit and provides less assurance. An independent examination involves:

- a review of the accounting records kept by the charity – this is something that is not required of a charitable company audit exemption report;

- a comparison of the accounts presented with the accounting records; and

- a review of the accounts and the consideration of any unusual items or disclosures identified.

16.48   The depth of work carried out during an independent examination is less than an audit: for example, verification procedures are only necessary when material concerns or doubts arise during the examination and where satisfactory explanations cannot be obtained from the trustees.

16.49   The Regulations governing independent examination are substantively the same in both Scotland and England and Wales. Both OSCR and the Charity Commission produce detailed guidance for charities and independent examiners on the form and content of independent examiners' reports and the steps to be undertaken by an examiner in preparing a report.

16.50   The report of an independent examiner is required to state whether or not any matter has come to his attention in connection with the examination which gives reasonable cause to believe that in any material respect:

- proper accounting records have not been kept;

- the accounts do not accord with such accounting records; and

- the accounts fail to comply with relevant regulations.

16.51   The independent examiner is also required to state in his report whether or not any matter has been identified, in connection with the examination, to which attention should be drawn to enable a proper understanding of the accounts to be reached.

16.52   Where they have become apparent, additional details that need to be included within the report are:

- any material expenditure or action contrary to the trusts of the charity;

- any failure to provide information or explanations to which the examiner is entitled; and

- evidence that accounts prepared on an accruals basis are materially inconsistent with the trustees' annual report.

16.53   As can be seen from the form of an independent examiner's report, a positive opinion on the accounts does not need to be supported by a body of detailed evidence, nor is an opinion required as to whether the accounts show a 'true and fair view'. As can be seen, however, the benefits of an independent examination are a level of scrutiny commensurate with the relative size and materiality of the charity and the clearly defined items required by the regulations.

2   Auditing standards

16.54   The auditor of a charity is required to carry out his work following relevant auditing standards. In the UK, these are the International Standards on Auditing (United Kingdom and Ireland) – which we will refer to here as 'the ISAs'.

16.55   In 2008 the APB issued a revised version of its Practice Note 11 *The Audit of Charities in the United Kingdom* (PN11). As well as setting the ISAs in a charity context, the Practice Note provides auditors with an overview of the regulatory regime for charities, specific 'commercial' and operating considerations and gives examples of the principal documentation that is generated, such as letters of engagement (the standard document setting out the terms of the relationship between an auditor and client) and example audit reports (though note as set out above, the latter have been recently superseded).

16.56   The revised practice note consolidates guidance issued as a supplement to the Practice Note when the ISA's were first introduced in the UK in place of the former nationally produced Statements of Auditing Standards. The ISAs did not generally introduce new concepts into auditing but have greatly increased the level of documentation auditors are required to keep regarding the assessment of risks that could lead to the accounts being misstated and the development of procedures to detect any misstatement that may have arisen.

16.57   The Practice Note places great emphasis on the need for auditors to have a detailed working knowledge of the charity sector in addition to the general requirement of auditors to obtain a thorough understanding of their client's 'business'. This feeds into the risk assessment as set out principally in ISA's 240, 315 and 320 (see table below.)

16.58   The table set out below details the ISAs governing the work of auditors.

ISAs (UK and Ireland)

200	Objective and General Principles Governing the Audit of Financial Statements
210	Terms of Audit Engagement
220	Quality Control for Audits of Historical Financial Information
240	The Auditor's Responsibility to Consider Fraud in an Audit of Financial Statements
250	Section A – Consideration of Laws and Regulations in an Audit of Financial Statements
	Section B – The Auditors' Right and Duty to Report to Regulators in the Financial Sector
260	Communication of Audit Matters with Those Charged with Governance

300   Planning an Audit of Financial Statements

315   Obtaining an Understanding of the Entity and Its Environment and Assessing the Risks of Material Misstatement

320   Audit Materiality

330   The Auditor's Procedures in response to Assessed Risks

402   Audit Considerations Relating to Entities Using Service Organisations

505   External Confirmations

510   Opening Balances

520   Analytical Procedures

540   Audit of Accounting Estimates

545   Auditing Fair Value Measurements and Disclosures

550   Related Parties

560   Subsequent Events

570   The Going Concern Basis in Financial Statements

580   Management Representations

600   Using the Work of Another Auditor (Revised)

700   The Auditor's Report on Financial Statements

720   Section A – Other Information in Documents Containing Audited Financial Statements

Section B – The Auditor's Statutory Reporting Responsibility in Relation to Directors' Reports

16.59   Of the above, it is ISAs 260, 580, 700 and 720 that most directly influence what a charity will 'receive' as a result of an audit. The audit report – the subject of the last two listed standards – has been discussed in some detail above. ISAs 260 and 580 deal with the other documents generally produced as output during an audit.

16.60   ISA 260 'Communication of audit matters with those charged with governance' sets out requirements for the auditor to engage in two way communication with 'those charged with governance'. Matters considered relevant for this communication include, among other things:

● exchange of ideas regarding risks, particularly any arising from actual incidence of or heightened perceived risk of fraud;

● an overview of the audit strategy;

● significant audit findings such as breaches of or weaknesses in controls;

● an assessment of the overall quality and appropriateness of reporting – particularly policy judgements, estimates etc.; and

● details of misstatements discovered during the audit, both those for which adjustment has been made and those which remain unadjusted.

16.61   The ISA requires at least some of this communication to be in writing – this will usually be in the form of a memorandum or letter issued at the planning stage and a report of findings issued at the end of the audit. Auditors will usually use the communication to manage audit logistics and to include additional information to 'add value' to the audit such as advance notice of impending regulatory change and assessments of the impact of current developments on the charity.

16.62 ISA 580 'Management representations' requires the auditor to obtain written confirmation from management regarding matters which have been disclosed orally but for which no written evidence exists and of general assertions which are implicit in the preparation of financial statements and their submission for audit. The representations are usually obtained by the issuing of a letter to the auditors by the trustees which is drafted by the auditors.

16.63 Such letters of representation are a standard feature of audits in all sectors but in the charity sector can cause concern among the trustees. While some representations such as the confirmation by trustees of acceptance of their responsibility for the financial statements cannot be given by management, many of those generally included may be so given. Trustees are often anxious that the representations requested are outside their immediate knowledge and can only be given on the basis of assurances by management.

16.64 It is common practice for trustees to request that management either co-sign the letter of representations or provide the trustees with a supporting set of representations to demonstrate that they have made all reasonable enquiries and taken due care prior to making representations to the auditors themselves. In large geographically dispersed charities, it is common for central management to seek representations from functional and regional managers regarding the representations made. Charities which are companies are required to include a formal statement in the trustees' report from the trustees, as directors, regarding provision of information to auditors. Similar considerations apply to this statement.

3 'Whistle blowing'

16.65 Under the Regulations issued under both the Charities Act 1993 (s 44 as amended by the Charities Act 2006) and the Charities and Trustee Investment (Scotland) Act 2005 (s 46), an auditor of an unincorporated charity is required to communicate in writing to the Charity Commissioners and/ or OSCR any matters of 'material significance' which come to his attention (in his capacity as auditor) relating to the activities or affairs of the charity (or any institution or body corporate connected with the charity) which the auditor reasonably believes is (or is likely to be) of material significance for the exercise of the regulators' functions under the relevant legislation.

16.66 The Regulations do not require auditors to perform any additional audit work for the purposes of the statutory duty of 'whistle blowing' and nor are they required specifically to seek out any breaches of the requirements applicable to a particular charity. However, auditors should anticipate any requirements and include procedures within their planning to ensure that members of the audit team are able to recognise reportable matters that may be encountered during the audit.

16.67   The types of matter which give rise to a duty to report to the regulator are those which, in the auditors' opinion, are of material significance in determining whether action may be appropriate in order to protect the property of the charity, or ensure that its property is used for proper purposes. This would, of course, exclude minor breaches of trustees' obligations. The statutory duty on the auditors to report to the regulator(s) arises primarily from the identification of any significant loss, or misapplication, of the charity's property or funds, or from the identification of a significant risk to the charity's property or maladministration or misuse of assets.

16.68   The Practice Note provides auditors with guidance on the form of report and e-mail contact details for their submission. It also reminds them of their responsibilities to report promptly once the duty to report is clear and of the possible consequences of failure to report, which can include investigation by their own regulating body.

4   Contractual requirements of the auditor

16.69   In addition to carrying out the statutory audit, the auditor may carry out specific contractual assignments at the request of the trustees or management. For example, the trustees may request the auditor to comment on the nature and adequacy of the internal controls of the organisation, or matters such as management reporting, budgeting or forecasting with a view to enabling the trustees to fulfil their obligations. Matters of particular concern, for example irregularities, suspicion of fraud, weaknesses in the accounting system, could also be the subject of a special investigation by the auditor. All these special assignments are quite separate from the statutory responsibilities of the auditor to express an opinion on the annual accounts of the charity.

16.70   One specific requirement may be to provide an opinion on the application of specific grant funding, as is often required by the providers of funds, especially in the public sector. These reports may vary from a confirmation that the amounts shown in funding claims are properly extracted from the charity's records, to very specific opinion that the funds have been applied for the purposes for which they were provided.

16.71   As a result of concerns in the audit profession relating to the duty of care that such engagements create between the auditor and the funder, the Institute of Chartered Accountants in England and Wales have issued guidance (AUDIT 03/03 Public Sector Special Reporting Engagements – Grant Claims) for auditors. This guidance recommends in many cases that the reports should only be made if a specific contract, governed by a letter of engagement, is entered into which includes the funder as a party. It also sets out the scope such reports might take, including examples of reports which an auditor could not acceptably agree to give.

The relative merits of audit and independent examination

16.72   The respective thresholds for audit and independent examination were discussed at the beginning of this chapter. In circumstances where a charity is not wholly exempt from external scrutiny but may be exempt from audit, the trustees must elect to have an independent examination carried out. If they choose not to do so, an audit is still required. The decision whether to have an audit or independent examination will depend upon several factors, including cost and the level of reassurance required.

16.73   If the trustees require specific advice that is outside the scope of an independent examiner, who may be a private individual for example, they are always entitled to seek that advice from the most appropriate source, including independent professional accountants. The trustees will always need to weigh up the costs and benefits of the type of external scrutiny that they require and ensure that they receive value for money – a particularly pertinent factor where charitable funds are concerned. Certainly for a small charity, if the audit in itself adds no value it may well be best to opt for an independent examination. This will be particularly appropriate, for example, where the charity is closely controlled and subject to direct supervision by the trustees personally.

16.74   In essence, an audit provides a high, positive level of assurance; an independent examination on the other hand, provides only a moderate and negative assurance in the sense of reporting only by exception. The independent examination makes no attempt to provide an opinion on whether the accounts show a true and fair view.

16.75   In considering the accounting records, the review work carried out within an independent examination is made with a view to identifying major failures to maintain accounting records in accordance with the relevant legislation, whereas under the principles of audit, procedures are carried out with a view to forming an opinion of whether accounting records have been maintained in accordance with the statutory requirements. An independent examination does not necessarily involve substantive testing, that is examining source documentation, obtaining independent third party confirmations or physical inspection of assets for example. Unless the analytical review work of an independent examination shows unusual items for which the trustees cannot give satisfactory explanations, no substantive testing is required under independent examination.

16.76   Whenever accruals-based accounts are prepared, it will be seen that the major differences between audit and independent examination are:

- the level of overall independent assurance;

- whether or not an opinion on a true and fair view is required;

- whether accounting records are maintained to a satisfactory level required by statute;

- whether the comfort of detailed substantive testing is required.

16.77   From the above it will seem that in many instances an independent examination will provide a perfectly adequate level of assurance.

16.78   For accounts prepared on the basis of receipts and payments, where the gross income or total expenditure does not exceed £250,000, an independent examination would normally be more appropriate, in the absence of special requirements of funding bodies, or of the membership in the case of an unincorporated association.

16.79   The auditors of an unincorporated charity, which prepares accounts on a receipts and payments basis, are not required to issue an opinion in 'true and fair view' terms, but to report that in their opinion the receipts and payments account, and statement of assets and liabilities 'properly present' the receipts and payments of the charity for the year under review, together with its statement of assets and liabilities as at the year end.

5   Comments and conclusions

16.80   Wherever a charity has a choice between an audit and independent examination, an audit is invariably preferable for those organisations with a high profile, as this represents a high risk for the trustees' reputations. As mentioned above, for a small, closely controlled, low risk organisation, perhaps with few volunteers and no 'members', an independent examination may be preferable.

16.81   As the Charity Commissioners relate in their Direction and Guidance Note, 'The Carrying out of an Independent Examination', the independent examiner must obviously be competent for the task and be familiar with accountancy methods, but does not need to be a practising accountant.

Chapter 17

Tax exemptions and charities

1 General

17.1 There is no overall tax exemption for charities. The lack of a general exemption means that awareness of the tax issues and careful organisation are sometimes necessary if charities are to keep their tax liabilities to the minimum and preserve their funds for charitable works.

Important exemptions exist for income tax, corporation tax and capital gains tax, as do significant reliefs for stamp duty, stamp duty land tax and value added tax.

17.2 Many of these exemptions have been added or amended over the years, and a major criticism of the way charity tax exemptions operated was that there were a number of glaring inconsistencies in the way exemption for direct and indirect taxes often worked. A government review of charity taxation gave rise to a number of changes in the Finance Act 2000 (FA 2000) to attempt to address this issue, and further changes in following Finance Acts have extended charity tax reliefs but also introduced further regulatory and anti-avoidance legislation for charities. VAT regulations, exemptions and reliefs are dealt with in Chapter 20 and partly in Chapter 18.

2 Income tax and corporation tax

17.3 Charities which are constituted as trusts (charitable trusts) are subject to income tax and all other charities (and CASCs) are subject to corporation tax. Although a charity may have 'trust' within its name and make no reference to a limited company it may still be subject to corporation tax. For instance, charities whose inception arose by an Act of Parliament or by Royal Charter are subject to corporation tax.

17.4 Reliefs from income tax are now contained within the Income Tax Act 2007 (ITA 2007) ss 520 to 537, and exemption for corporation tax is still currently contained within s 505 of TA 1988 and apply for income tax purposes for tax years up to 2006/07. The new income tax exemptions applicable from 2007/08 broadly mirror those contained within the Income and Corporation Taxes Act 1988 (TA 1988) which previously applied to both income and corporation tax. We shall discuss some of the minor differences introduced with ITA 2007 later in this book. Needless to say, the current legislation is not a general exemption from taxation, but provides a range of specific exemptions for which claims must be submitted. For income tax, claims must be made within five years of 31 January next following the end of the year of assessment. A charity constituted as a company must claim within six years from the end of the accounting period concerned. These time limits are to reduce by two years from April 2010. See Chapter 19 for time limit changes and Gift Aid.

17.5   Claims for repayment of income tax suffered on investment income and both income and transitional relief are made on Form R68, obtainable from the HM Revenue & Customs (HMRC) on request. Transitional relief claims have a two-year time limit.

17.6   Under the UK taxation system of self-assessment, any charity, whether constituted as a trust or company, must self-assess its income and gains if required by notice to file a tax return. The HMRC 's detailed guidance notes for charities, found on the HMRC website (www.hmrc.gov.uk), state that the majority of charities will not be required to make tax returns every year but that returns will be issued to charities based on a risk assessment or on a random basis. Nevertheless, the reality is that once a charity has been issued with a return it can expect to have to complete returns on a regular basis.

17.7   However, a charity must complete a self-assessment tax return if the charity has income (note not necessarily profit) or gains which either does not fall within one of the taxation exemptions or is income or gains used for non-charitable purposes (*non-charitable expenditure,* see part 4 of this chapter)

17.8   There are special supplementary pages to the standard tax returns which charities must complete if called upon to do so (copy of forms in Appendices). These pages form part of the tax return of the charity and require the disclosure of figures, exempt income and gains, related expenses and details of a charity's general administration expenses and assets. It is important to note that these pages legally constitute the charity's claim to tax exemption. The charity must also declare:

- that all its income and gains are exempt; and

- that all income and gains have been applied for charitable purposes only; or

- that some income or gains may not be exempt or may not have been applied for charitable purposes.

17.9   Whilst most of the information required to file these forms will be readily available from the charity's accounting records, some of the questions demand such a degree of detail that further sub-analysis of the records is usually required. For example, one question asks for the total amount of grants made by the charity, splitting these between those made within the UK and those outside. In addition, the way the SORP requires charities to disclose their income does not always make it easy for the questions on the tax return to be answered from the accounts.

17.10   More importantly, however, the person responsible for the form should carefully consider the implications of the answers to the question. Some of these are carefully chosen to reveal the extent to which the charity may not be applying its income and gains for charitable purposes only, for example, making grants outside the UK without taking the necessary reasonable care to ensure that they are applied for charitable purposes or making loans to a subsidiary company at less than a commercial rate of interest (see **18.17**).

The exemptions

17.11   TA 1988 s 505 exempts from corporation tax:

(a)   profits or gains taxable under Schedule A or D, arising in respect of rents or other receipts from an estate, interest in or right over any land, whether situated in the United Kingdom or elsewhere, to the extent that the profits or gains:

    (i)   arise in respect of rents or receipts from an estate, interest or right vested in any person for charitable purposes; and

    (ii)   are applied to charitable purposes only;

The exemption has been extended to include distributions from Real Estate Investment Trust introduced with the Finance Act 2006.

The provisions in (a) (i) and (ii) above are reflected for income tax purposes in ITA 2007 s 531(2). The exemption for income tax is extended to the unusual circumstances where rent is treated as trading income (s 531(1)) but this will not apply to income from a property business.

(b)

    (i)   income chargeable under Schedule D Case III, for example, interest, annuities and other annual payments, including covenants, and some royalties;

    (ii)   income that would be taxable under Schedule D Case III if UK-sourced, but which is not so sourced, and is therefore taxable under Schedule D Case IV or V;

    (iii)   dividends and other distributions taxable under Schedule F;

    (iv)   dividends and other distributions taxable under Schedule D Case V because they have an overseas source, but which would be taxable under Schedule F if they had a UK source; and

    (v)   non-trading gains on intangible fixed assets charged under Schedule D Case VI;

and applied to charitable purposes only;

(c)   public revenue dividends on securities in the name of trustees, taxable under Schedule D, to the extent that the dividends are applicable and applied only for the repair of any cathedral, college, church or chapel, or other building used only for the purposes of divine worship (also exempt for *income tax* under ITA 2007 s 533);

(d)   profits of trade carried on by a charity, whether in the UK or elsewhere, if the profits are applied solely to the purposes of the charity and either:

   (i)   the primary purpose of the charity; or

   (ii)   work in connection with the trade is mainly carried on by benefici- aries of the charity; and

(e)   profits accruing in respect of a lottery if:

   (i)   exempt in accordance with Schedule 11 part 1 or 4 of the Gambling Act 2005; or

   (ii)   promoted in accordance with a lottery operating licence within Part 5 of the above Act, (or promoted and conducted under Northern Ireland equivalent) AND

   the proceeds are applied solely to the charity's purpose.

The exemption for public revenue dividends applied for the repair of cathe- dral, college, church or chapel, or other building used only for divine worship, was introduced by the Finance Act 1996, and means that local appeals such as 'Friends of the Church Steeple' are now exempted.

Small trades

17.12   A major change introduced by FA 2000 s 46 was the addition of a general exemption for small trades carried on by charities (now charita- ble companies). The profits of any trade will be exempt from corporation tax either where gross trading or other income chargeable under Schedule D Case I or Case VI does not exceed certain limits, or the charity could reason- ably have expected at the beginning of any year that the limits would not be exceeded.

17.13   The turnover limit is the greater of two sums:

(a)   £5,000; and

(b)   the lesser of £50,000 and 25% of a charity's total incoming resources.

An equivalent income tax exemption applies for charitable trusts within ITA 2007 s 526 (referred to as *small-scale trades*) and s 527 for miscellaneous types of income within ITA 2007 s 1016, (essentially income previously taxed under Schedule D Case VI but now falling within Part 5 of the Income Tax (Trading and Other Income) Act 2005 (ITTOIA 2005)). The exemptions now applicable to charitable trusts under ss 526 and 527 have removed the require- ment for trades to be carried on wholly or partly in the UK, applicable under FA 2000 s 46.

17.14   Exemption applies on the condition that the income or profits received by the charity are applied solely for charitable purposes. Where not all income or gains are so applied, restrictions of a charity's tax exemptions may occur (see **17.39**). There is a subtle difference between the wording of the condition attaching to exemption for most types of income, which must be applied for charitable purposes only, and that for trading income (both in TA 1988 s 505 and FA 2000 s 46, where the income has to be applied solely to the purposes of the charity, ie ploughed back into the charitable activity).

17.15 A number of types of income or profits are not exempted by TA 1988 s 505 or Part 10 of ITA for charitable trusts. Schedule E income is not exempt, but this is not relevant since individuals cannot themselves be charities.

17.16 The exemption in respect of Schedule F income ceased to have effect from 6 April 1999, when Advance Corporation Tax (ACT) was abolished, since, as a consequence, the tax credit on UK dividends became notional and not repayable. This change alone was calculated by some observers to cost the charity sector as a whole about £400 million. To soften the blow, a transitional relief was introduced on a sliding scale which ceased in 2003/04.

Trading activities

17.17 Trading profits are not exempted unless as described above, namely carried out by the beneficiaries of the charity or in the course of the carrying out of a primary purpose of the charity, or within the small scale limits, mentioned above.

17.18 The tax issues relating to trading activities carried on by charities, and the ways in which the profits of trading activities carried on for the benefit of charities can flow through in a form which is exempt under TA 1988 s 505 and ITA 2007 s 524 are discussed in detail in Chapter 18.

Interest and annual payments

17.19 Exemption from income and corporation tax applies to all forms of interest, whether annual or short and with a UK or overseas source. It also includes interest payable gross by building societies.

17.20 Annual payments are exempt from tax. The question as to what constitutes an 'annual payment' for tax purposes is dealt with in more detail at **19.3** below in connection with deeds of covenant. Suffice to say that it must be pure profit in the charity's hands, so that a charity receiving an annual payment does not have to do anything to earn it, nor be obliged to offer anything in return.

17.21 Copyright or other royalties may constitute annual payments, especially if given or bequeathed to the charity, but care needs to be taken where a charity takes action to exploit such rights, as such activities can often constitute trading. Royalty payments or other income from intellectual property, certain telecommunication rights and foreign distributions are now specifically exempt for income tax purposes under ITA 2007 s 536, again, providing they do not constitute a receipt from trading (per Chapter 2 of Part 2 ITTOIA 2005) and are applied to charitable purposes only.

Land transactions

17.22   Other one-off receipts may not be exempted from tax unless derived from land (see TA 1988 s 505(1)(a) or ITA 2007 s 531), or for non-trading intangible assets (s 505(1)(c)(iic)).

17.23   Thus, for example, certain types of one-off income, such as share underwriting commission, enjoyed by a charity may be taxable.

17.24   Charities are exempt from capital gains tax (or corporation tax on capital gains) where land or buildings are sold which were either used for charitable purposes or held as investments, (see **17.36** on capital gains tax). However, TA 1988 s 776 imposes on a charitable company a charge to tax under Schedule D Case VI where land is obtained, held or developed with the sole intention of realising a gain on its disposal. HMRC do not accept that TA 1988 s 505(1)(a) exempts a charge under s 776. For charitable trusts, an equivalent charge to income tax arises under ITA 2007 s 755 and there is no exemption within s 531 for gains from land. Charity trustees are under a duty to obtain the best possible result for the charity and when seeking to do this by selling land with development potential may often achieve a sale which includes a share of the developer's profit if certain profit levels are achieved, often referred to as an 'overage' within the sale contract. If such a sale is in prospect, professional advice should be sought as early as possible in the negotiations before proceeding (see *Page v Lowther* [1983] STC 199, where the trustees did exactly that and were caught by s 776). Alternatively, HMRC could seek to remove exemption from such a disposal by assessing the transaction as an adventure in the nature of trade. Either way, professional advice should be obtained before entering into any significant land transaction.

Fundraising events

17.25   Fundraising events that might technically be defined as trading are exempted from income and corporation tax provided they fulfil the requirements for VAT exemption laid out in Chapter 20. This exemption is contained in extra-statutory concession ESC C4 and enacted for trusts within ITA 2007 s 529. Whereas the old pre-2000 concession generally only applied to one-off events, the current concession and legislation can apply to a series of events.

17.26   Following the new alignment of the direct and indirect tax exemptions concerning the raising of money through holding events, the criteria for exemption are laid out in full in Chapter 20. By keeping within those criteria, a charity will be exempt from both income or corporation tax and VAT.

Miscellaneous exemptions

17.27   A number of other minor exemptions from tax can be found elsewhere in the legislation. Charities are exempted from special charges in connection with certificates of deposit by TA 1988 s 56(3)(c) and ITA 2007 s 534. They are also exempted from the accrued income scheme (TA 1988 s 715(1)(d) and ITA 2007 s 645) and from the 40% tax charge on the repayment of pension fund surpluses as the employer (TA 1988 s 601(4)).

Contemplative orders

17.28   ESC B10 grants specific relief to contemplative religious communities and their members, as some communities are not entitled to the exemptions from tax contained in s 505. This is because purely contemplative orders are not seen as carrying on the charitable purpose of the advancement of religion because their activity is inward looking rather than evangelistic. The question as to whom the income of such a community actually belongs is another difficult point to determine.

17.29   ESC B10 assists with these difficulties. It allows an amount being equal to an individual's personal allowance to be regarded as the income of a member of the community, and the aggregate of the members' personal allowances to be offset against the income of the community. Where this aggregate exceeds actual income, the excess can be used against capital gains in that tax year. Carry forward of the excess used to be allowed, but this is no longer possible, with the exception of allowances unused as at 5 April 1995, which can be carried forward until exhausted.

Anti-avoidance

17.30   In addition to the anti-avoidance legislation contained in TA 1988 s 776 relating to capital gains on land (see **17.24**), HMRC has significant other powers to counteract the abuse of charitable status. Although there is no general exemption from tax for charities, favourable exemptions make charitable status an attractive prospect for the avoidance of tax. Although artificial schemes are less common, there are traps in place to catch opportunists but these are also wide enough to catch many innocent transactions.

17.31   One of the most controversial pieces of anti-avoidance legislation is the substantial donors anti-avoidance rules introduced in the Finance Act 2006. These rules were designed to prevent transactions where a donation is effectively returned to a donor. This applies to transactions entered into on or after 22 March 2006.

17.32   Under these rules it is the donor who benefits from tax relief on the donation and from the value extracted by the donor, but it is the charity that is denied relief by treating the value of the transaction as *non-charitable expenditure* (see part 4 of this chapter) restricting the charity tax exemptions mentioned above. The current rules may trap transactions which would appear to be innocent transactions carried out on an arm's length basis, for example remuneration to employees who are also substantial donors may be caught under the current rules. Charities must also monitor transactions with substantial donors for periods which could span over a decade. The government has acknowledged the concerns of the sector and the substantial donors' legislation is currently under consultation.

17.33   There are general anti-avoidance provisions under TA 1988 s 703 which deals with the cancellation of tax advantages accruing from certain transactions in securities. Exempt bodies are not outside this legislation, which was made clear in *Commissioners of the Inland Revenue v Universities Superannuation Scheme Ltd* [1997] STC 1. In this case, a company purchased its own shares from the appellant, a pension scheme otherwise exempt from tax, giving rise to a distribution. The monies received by the appellant consisted of repayment of capital and a dividend. They then claimed a tax credit of over £850,000. The Revenue challenged this as the credit had arisen from a dividend which was of an 'abnormal amount' and they succeeded in raising an assessment under Case VI for the amount of the tax credit. Advance clearance should be sought from HMRC's Technical Division if this section could apply to a transaction.

Claiming relief

17.34   Charities should remember that claims for relief from tax under TA 1988 s 505 and ITA 2007 s 524 onwards can be made as soon and as often as they wish, providing they hold the necessary tax vouchers. It is not necessary to wait until the end of the tax year or to accumulate vouchers to a specific threshold.

17.35   In addition, it is possible to receive interest gross on certain holdings. The Bank of England will pay interest on government securities gross on receipt of an application accompanied by the charity registration slip issued by the Charity Commissioners. Banks and building societies will also pay interest gross as long as they are provided with proof of charitable status. It is important to provide this proof when the relevant account or deposit is opened to avoid tax being deducted automatically.

3   Capital gains tax

17.36   Charities are exempt from CGT provided that the gains are applied for charitable purposes, except in one circumstance. To prevent temporary charities being used to avoid liability to CGT, TCGA 1992 s 256(2) revokes the exemption where assets held on charitable trusts cease to be subject to such trusts. If this occurs, the trustees are treated as if they had disposed of and immediately reacquired the assets at open market value. The gain on the deemed disposal is chargeable to CGT. Assessments must be raised by the HMRC within three years of the end-of-the-year of assessment in which the asset ceases to be held on charitable trusts.

17.37   Unfortunately, as with several anti-avoidance provisions, this withholding of exemption can affect genuine transactions by charities, as well as transactions with the aim of avoiding tax. One example would be where property has been given to a charity for a fixed term, after which it passes to a member of the donor's family. The Charity's trustees would then be liable for CGT on the unrealised gains attaching to the property when passed on. This treatment can carry back to any earlier disposals that were reinvested in other assets which continued to be held at the end of the fixed term. This carry back is not restricted by the six-year limit. The carry back to previous disposals may also be made on those who were trustees at the time of those disposals, rendering them potentially personally liable to CGT. Therefore, trustees in such a situation must ensure that they retain sufficient assets to meet this liability before they transfer the property to the ultimate beneficiary, and obtain an indemnity from them.

17.38   Another situation in which this can be an issue is where a charity has run its course and no longer has charitable objects to which income and gains can be applied. Trustees in this position should apply to the Charity Commissioners for a scheme under Charities Act 1993 s 16 to widen the charitable objects of the charity in order that property can continue to be held with the income and gains being applied for charitable purposes.

4   Application for charitable purposes

17.39   For CGT purposes, a gain is not a chargeable gain if it accrues to a charity and is applied for charitable purposes (TCGA 1992 s 256). However for charitable companies under corporation tax, TA 1988 s 505 requires income or profits to be applied to charitable purposes only. Similarly, for trusts ITA 2007 s 524 requires income or profits to be applied to the purposes of the charitable trust only. Although a charity's administrators may think that this is a simple condition to meet, being a charity and application for charitable purposes is not one and the same thing. Tax relief is restricted where particular expenditure is not incurred for charitable purposes or incurred partly for charitable purposes (for income tax and corporation tax) or specified by legislation as non-charitable expenditure. The rules on non-charitable expenditure were revised from 22 March 2006 and changes how the restriction applies.

17.40   Prior to these and earlier changes, charitable purposes were not defined in statute and reliance was placed on Lord McNaghten's judgment in *Income Tax Special Purposes Comrs v Pemsel* [1891], which summarised charitable purposes as the relief of poverty, the advancement of education, the advancement of religion and other purposes beneficial to the community. As explained in Chapter 1, a new modern definition of charitable purposes is contained in the Charities Act. Provided the charity applied its income and gains within the bounds permitted by its articles or trust deed and within these charitable purposes, there should be no problem. However, there may still be grey areas or differences of emphasis as to what does or does not come within charitable purposes. HMRC current guidance states that they will not necessarily treat expenditure as non-charitable expenditure where it is not specifically authorised within the articles or trust deed if it is clearly of a charitable nature. They will often seek guidance from the Charity Commission in such cases, but they will consider expenditure which is prohibited or restricted in the charity's articles or deed as non-charitable expenditure.

Non-charitable expenditure

17.41   The meaning of non-charitable expenditure is now contained in ITA 2007 s 543 and can be summarised as:

- any expenditure which is not incurred for charitable purposes only;

- losses made in a trade which is not a charitable trade or would not fall within one of the other tax exemptions if a profit had been made;

- payment or restriction as a result of a transaction with a substantial donor;

- investments or loans which are not qualifying investments or loans (ITA 2007 ss 558 and 561 and TA 1988 Sch 20);

- certain payments to an overseas body (ITA 2007 s 547).

For corporation tax the definition is treated as broadly the same, although TA 1988 refers to charitable expenditure instead.

Payments to an overseas body

17.42   Where payments are made to overseas bodies including overseas registered charities TA 1988 s 506(3) (and ITA 2007 s 547) requires the trustees of the donor charity to take reasonable steps to ensure that the money is used by the foreign body for charitable purposes. Any failure to do this, or carelessness by a UK charity in these circumstances, would leave the donor charity in the UK within the rules on non-charitable expenditure and faced with a consequent restriction of its tax exemptions. Please note that HMRC will only accept what is considered 'charitable purposes' under UK law. This legislation is primarily designed to counter artificial tax avoidance schemes. The legislation does not define 'reasonable steps'. HMRC have issued guidance on their interpretation of reasonable steps and where payments are small and one-off they will expect no more than an exchange of correspondence between the two bodies confirming the details of the payment, intended purpose and confirmation that the sum has been applied accordingly. For large payments or ongoing commitments HMRC will expect further evidence such as independent verification that sums have been used for charitable purposes.

Qualifying investments and loans

17.43   Charity law requires that charities making investments avoid speculation or undue risk with a proper spread of investments. A charity must also avoid making investments which contradict its charitable purpose.

17.44   For charitable trusts, the legislation now refers to approved charitable investments and loans but this is used synonymously with qualifying investments and loans still used for corporation tax in TA 1988 Sch 20. Although the list of qualifying investments for trusts is wider, these are generally the same and can be summarised as follows:

- Investments in common investment funds, common deposit funds and similar funds established for the exclusive benefit of charities.

- Any interest in land other than an interest held as security or debt.

- Investments authorised under the Trustee Investment Act 1961 which includes National Savings Certificates/UK Government Treasury Bills including Northern Ireland Treasury Bills, certificates of tax deposit,

- Bank deposits where interest is payable at a commercial rate and is not part of an arrangement where a loan is made to some other person.

- Deposits with a building society, National Savings or other credit institution authorised with mutual principles.

- Shares or securities listed on a recognised stock exchange or (per Schedule 20 and corporation tax) are dealt in on an Unlisted Securities Market (see **17.45** below).

- Investments in unit trust schemes or an open-ended investment company.

- A loan or other investment as to which HMRC are satisfied is made for the 'benefit of the charity' and not for the avoidance of tax by the charity or any other person.

17.45   An interesting point is that the Unlisted Securities Market is no longer in existence, rendering this section of Sch 20 without impact. The effective 'replacements' for the USM, the Alternative Investment Market and PLUS (or previous OFEX market), are not included within the specifically qualifying investments listed in Sch 20. However, HMRC regard stocks quoted on AIM as being listed on a recognised stock exchange for the purposes of the relief for gifts of quoted shares to charity in FA 2000 s 43 – see **19.47** below. It appears that AIM stocks would be regarded as qualifying but PLUS investments should be considered on a case-by-case basis as to whether they are qualifying investments.

17.46   HMRC will accept that a loan or investment is 'for the benefit of the charity' where made on sound commercial terms based on the facts of each case. They will accept a loan which carries a commercial rate of interest, is adequately secured and is made under a formal written agreement with reasonable repayment terms. Although HMRC may give an opinion as to whether a loan or investment is qualifying there are no formal pre-clearance procedures.

17.47   As the shares in a trading subsidiary company, discussed in the next chapter, are not listed shares, this investment falls into the last category listed above and will need to satisfy HMRC that it is for the benefit of the charity. Often the activities of a trading subsidiary will further the charitable purpose of a charity and for commercial or other reasons the charity has chosen to carry out this trade or activity in a separate entity. This would clearly be for the benefit of the charity by furthering its charitable purpose. Where the intention is for the subsidiary to carry on other income generating activities, HMRC will want the charity to have evidence that the charity has made an informed decision demonstrated by say a business plan with cashflow forecasts and illustrating an expected reasonable rate of return. Investments in subsidiaries are discussed further in the next chapter.

Transactions with substantial donors

17.48   As discussed in **17.32** these anti-avoidance rules are currently under government consultation and therefore this is only a brief summary of the main principles contained in TA 1988 ss 506A–506C and ITA 2007 ss 549–557.

17.49   These provisions restrict charity tax exemptions by deeming a charity to incur non-charitable expenditure where certain transactions are entered into with substantial donors from 22 March 2006. A substantial donor is a person, which includes a company, if that person has made 'relievable gifts' to a charity of at least:

- £25,000 in a 12-month period; or

- £100,000 (an increase announced in Budget 2009 from 23 April 2009) in a six-year period

falling within the charity's Chargeable Accounting Period (tax years to 5 April for a trust). The above test applies to donations from connected persons, which has a wide definition within ITA 2007 s 993 and TA 1988 s 839, and will also apply to transactions with connected persons. Connected charities are treated as one charity for this purpose although there is no strict definition of what constitutes a connected charity and is assumed to be those with similar trustees. A person who has become a substantial donor carries this status for the next five chargeable accounting periods.

17.50   A substantial donor will not include another charity, housing association or Registered Social Landlord. A wholly-owned subsidiary of a charity (or more than charity) is excluded in so far as it is donating to one of the charities which own the company.

17.51   'Relievable gifts' is a gift qualifying for tax relief (other than just IHT relief) and includes Gift Aid donations, gifts of shares/securities and real property, payroll giving, gifts of assets with CGT relief, gifts of trading stock, plant and machinery and gifts from settler-interested trusts.

17.52   Types of transaction that fall within these rules are:
- the sale or letting of property;
- the provision of services;
- the provision of financial assistance, whether provided to a charity from a substantial donor or vice versa;
- exchange of property between a charity and a substantial donor apart from certain disposals to charities at an undervalue;
- investment by a charity in the business of a substantial donor unless shares are listed on a recognised stock exchange;

- remuneration by a charity to a substantial donor unless remuneration to a trustee approved by the regulatory body or court.

Exceptions apply to the sale or letting of property, provision of services or financial assistance where from a substantial donor to a charity in the ordinary course of their business on arm's length terms and which is not part of an arrangement to avoid tax.

Accumulating income

17.53   Often there can also be significant delays between the receipt of income or gains and their application, specifically where funds are being built up for a specific but long-term project or charitable purpose. If there appears to be no application of funds, HMRC may seek to withdraw or deny the tax exemptions available to a charity. The question of application was the subject of the Court of Appeal case *IRC v Helen Slater Charitable Trust Ltd* [1981] STC 471. This case was concerned with the payment of income by the trustees of the appellant to the trustees of the Slater Foundation Ltd, another charitable company, with the same trustees as the first. The Inland Revenue claimed that as the money paid over had been accumulated to no specific purpose and had not been spent and, they believed, there had not been any change in the beneficial ownership of the funds, the payment did not constitute application for charitable purposes.

17.54   The court held that, despite the trustees of both charities being the same people, they were separate trusts, with neither trust having power in law to direct the affairs of the other. The appellant trustees had, therefore, applied the funds for charitable purposes by passing them to another charity. The recipient charity had received a capital sum and was, therefore, only liable to account for the application of any income arising therefrom.

17.55   Although the case was not decided on the precise point, the remarks of Lord Justice Oliver in the *Helen Slater* case are of prime importance. In commenting on two conflicting dicta of the judges in the earlier case of *General Nursing Council for Scotland v IRC* [1929] 14 TC 645, he said:

> 'Charitable trustees who simply leave surplus income uninvested cannot, I think, be said to have applied it all, and, indeed, would be in breach of trust. But if the income is reinvested by them and held, as invested, as part of the funds of the charity, I would be disposed to say that it is no less being applied for charitable purposes than if it is paid out in wages to the secretary'.

17.56   As the Revenue in the *Helen Slater* case had conceded that, subject to the trustees not acting ultra vires, accumulation for a specific purpose does represent application for charitable purposes, the only problem appears to lie with accumulation for general purposes. The remarks of Lord Justice Oliver seem to indicate that even general accumulations can constitute application for charitable purposes. This is as long as the very minimum that has been done by the charity in question is consciously to reinvest any surplus income so that it can be said to have been applied. However, the point is still not totally free from doubt, and it may be legislated in the future or tested again by HMRC through the courts in an extreme case. However, the Inland Revenue did mount an attack in the case of *Nightingale Ltd v Price* [1996] STC (SCD) 116 before the Special Commissioners. They had sought to deny charitable exemption under the precursor of TA 1988 s 505 on the grounds that the income received by way of covenant from the property development and trading subsidiaries of the charitable company Nightingale Ltd was not applied for charitable purposes. The income was re-lent at interest to a property holding company controlled by the director of the charity and the charity's subsidiary companies. The Inland Revenue was not successful before the Special Commissioners, who found that the income was applied for charitable purposes only, since the charity's policy was to increase its own resources by lending money to subsidiaries and associated companies at high rates of interest. The Inland Revenue did not pursue this case through the courts, and it remains to be seen whether HMRC will attempt to pursue a similar case in the future.

17.57 HMRC guidance states that accumulations of income will not normally be challenged unless they are kept in cash or a current account or are being accumulated for a project where there appears to be a conflict of interest between the interests of the charity and the interests of the trustee(s) or provider of the funds.

17.58 To counter avoidance by using the *Helen Slater* principle, an amendment to TA 1988 s 505(2) was made in FA 1996. This provides that any payments by one charity to another, being not for full consideration, not otherwise chargeable to tax or otherwise eligible for relief under s 505(1), are taxable under Schedule D Case III as an annual payment. This follows the *Slater* case in that the charity making the payment has applied those funds for charitable purposes, but requires the recipient also to show that they have applied the funds for charitable purposes. The recipient can still claim exemption for tax on these grounds, and the donor does not have to deduct tax before making the payment.

17.59 Where, however, the recipient charity is not resident in the UK, the onus of proving that the money has been applied for charitable purposes falls on the UK-resident donor charity. See **17.42** above.

17.60 Positive misuse of a charity's income in applying it for non-charitable purposes is rare, but inadvertently using income for such purposes can endanger the tax exemptions of any charity, however well-intentioned. There are two ways in which the application of income can slip into dangerous territory: administration costs and non-charitable activity. While HMRC allows that reasonable administrative costs are necessary for the achievement of a charity's objects, and are therefore indirectly applied for charitable purposes, they or the Charity Commission can investigate excessive administration costs. Although this is a subjective question, expenditure by the officers of a charity that is seen as 'extravagant', such as unnecessary foreign trips, is an example of what could be investigated (see Chapter 8 for the accounting requirements concerning administrative expenses).

17.61   A strict legal definition of charitable purposes would exclude activities that are political. An occasional foray into this field, subject to the rules governing non-qualifying expenditure, will generally be tolerated by HMRC, but sustained and significant political or other non-charitable activity will not be. Activity at such a level should be contained within a separate body with separate sources of income if at all possible. The worst case scenario if this is not done is that a charity's tax exemptions may be totally withdrawn, and their very charitable status may be in danger.

5   Non-charitable expenditure – the restriction of tax exemptions

For chargeable accounting periods from 22 March 2006

17.62   The current rules for calculating the amount of any restriction for non-charitable expenditure are contained in ITA 2007 ss 539–542 and the amended TA 1988 s 505 (subsections (3)–(7)). If a charity incurs non-charitable expenditure or is deemed to incur such expenditure within a chargeable accounting period, the equivalent amount of tax relief on income or gains are forfeited, referred to as attributing income, to the non-exempt amount, per ITA 2007 s 540. The legislation is more concise than the complex rules applicable to periods commencing before 22 March 2006. The new rules are to a certain extent less generous as charitable expenditure can no longer be matched with income in a chargeable period before non-charitable expenditure. However, ITA 2007 s 542 does allow the charity to chose which sources of income are to lose exemption. This may affect the level of tax payable if any but the trustees of the charity must specify to HMRC its allocation within 30 days of HMRC notifying the charity of the requirement to restrict relief. HMRC will accept details disclosed in a tax return as notification. A charity must complete a self assessment tax return and account for any tax due for the period it has incurred non-charitable expenditure.

17.63   'Relievable income and gains' is income and gains which would otherwise be eligible for relief or exemption mentioned at **17.11–17.29** and **17.36**. Non-charitable expenditure is allocated firstly to the charity's relievable income and gains of the current chargeable accounting period. Any 'unrelieved' non-charitable expenditure is then allocated to the remainder of total income and gains in the chargeable accounting period. Total income and gains will include the relievable income and gains, income and gains not subject to relief or exemption, and receipts from all other sources such as legacies, other gifts and non-taxable grants. If there is further excess non-charitable expenditure this is carried back to the previous chargeable accounting period and treated as non-charitable expenditure of the previous period. If there still remains a surplus it is then carried back to previous years ending up to six years before the end of the current chargeable period.

17.64   It appears strange that relievable income or attributable income as referred to in legislation for trusts in ITA 2007 s 540(3) includes all income which have exemptions under that part (Part 10). Exemptions under s 521(4) include donations under Gift Aid. It could be argued that there is not a source of income as they are purely gifts.

Example 1

17.65   In Example 1, Charitable company A has the following:

Year ended 31 December 2008	£
Legacies	200,000
UK dividend income	70,000
Bank interest	30,000
Non-charitable expenditure	80,000

Both UK dividend income and bank interest is relievable income. The charity selects to allocate non-charitable expenditure to the £70,000 dividend income first and the remaining £10,000 to bank interest. As a company, the charity will pay no further tax on the dividend income so £10,000 will be payable at the prevailing corporate tax rate.

Example 2

17.66   As in Example 1, with results for the following year:

Year ended 31 December 2009	£
Legacies	40,000
UK dividend income	10,000
Bank interest	5,000
Non-charitable expenditure	100,000

The £100,000 non-charitable expenditure is first offset against relievable income of £15,000, the interest and dividends, with £5,000 chargeable to tax. £40,000 is allocated to the remainder of total income and gains, legacies which are not subject to tax. The remaining surplus of £45,000 is carried back and allocated to the previous year, first to the relievable income of £20,000 bank interest (giving rise to a tax charge) and then £25,000 to the legacies.

17.67   The six year carry back period may include periods under the old rules, commencing prior to 22 March 2006. Carry back is permitted to the extent that a restriction for non-charitable expenditure would have arisen under the previous regime.

For chargeable accounting periods starting before 22 March 2006

17.68   The basic rules for calculating the amount of any restriction of tax exemption for non-qualifying expenditure were contained in the previous version of TA 1988 s 505(3) for periods commencing before 22 March 2006. This laid down that if in any chargeable period a charity had:

(a)   relevant income and gains not less than £10,000; and

(b)   relevant income and gains exceeding qualifying expenditure; and

(c)   the charity incurs or is deemed to have incurred non-qualifying expenditure;

then tax relief will be restricted.

17.69   The amount of income and gains to which the restriction applied is found by comparing the excess of relevant income and gains over qualifying expenditure with the amount of non-qualifying expenditure. Tax exemption is withdrawn for so much of the excess of relevant income and gains over qualifying expenditure as does not exceed the amount of non-qualifying expenditure.

17.70   Similarly to the new rules, for the purposes of this test, relevant income and gains do not necessarily include all the income and gains a charity receives. Relevant income and gains are only those income and gains which would be taxable if they were not exempted by TA 1988 s 505(1) or TCGA 1992 s 256(1).

17.71   Qualifying expenditure includes all expenditure in the period laid out solely for charitable purposes and any commitments made for such expenditure to be entered into in the period. It will obviously include any investments, loans or expenditure connected with them and permitted by Sch 20. It also includes reasonable fundraising and administration expenditure. Where, however, the charity makes payments to bodies outside the UK, it will only be regarded as making qualifying expenditure provided the charity concerned has taken reasonable steps to ensure that their payment will be applied for charitable purposes. Non-qualifying expenditure, in addition to investments or loans outside Sch 20, will include all non-chargeable expenses, for example, trading expenses, political activities, excessive administration costs, etc.

17.72   Thus, the purpose of the legislation is to penalise any charity which misapplies its income and gains by denying tax relief on the appropriate proportion of its income and gains up to the limit of the expenditure misapplied. The de minimis limit should not be forgotten in that, for the rules on non-qualifying expenditure to apply, the charity must have relevant income and gains of £10,000 or more in any one year. In addition, relevant income and gains do not include any income or gains which are exempt under separate provisions from TA 1988 s 505(1) or TCGA 1992 s 256. Contrast the following examples.

Example 3

17.73   In Example 3, Charity X has the following income:

	£
Grants from other UK charities	250,000
UK dividend income	50,000
Gift Aided donations	40,000

Its expenditure comprises:

	£
Grants to UK charities	30,000
Administration costs (of which 60% is deemed excessive by the Inland Revenue)	100,000
Grants to overseas bodies (£80,000 of which was handed over without prior research on the part of Charity X to a little known tax haven charity which promptly misappropriated it)	180,000

Charity X will have its tax exemptions and reliefs restricted as follows:

	Income	Relevant Income
	£	£
Grants from other UK charities	250,000	250,000
UK dividend income	50,000	50,000
Gift Aided donations	40,000	40,000
	340,000	340,000

	Total expenditure	Qualifying expenditure
	£	£
Grants to UK charities	30,000	30,000
Administrative expenses	100,000	40,000
Grants to overseas bodies	180,000	100,000
	310,000	170,000

17.74 Thus, non-qualifying expenditure is £140,000. The excess of relevant income and gains over qualifying expenditure is £170,000. Charity X will therefore have its tax reliefs and exemptions restricted by the lesser of these two amounts, and will therefore pay tax on £140,000 of relevant income and gains.

Example 4

17.75 In Example 4 (in the same year), Charity Y, with exactly the same qualifying and non-qualifying expenditure as Charity X in example 3, has the following income:

	£
Grants from UK charities	150,000
UK dividend income	50,000
Donations from the public (including £40,000 donations under Gift Aid)	140,000

17.76   The computation for Charity Y is:

	Income	Relevant Income
	£	£
Grants from UK charities	150,000	150,000
UK dividend income	50,000	50,000
Donations	140,000	40,000
	340,000	240,000

17.77   Whereas non-qualifying expenditure, as for Charity X, is £140,000, the excess relevant income and gains over qualifying expenditure is only £70,000 (£240,000 less £170,000). Charity Y will therefore suffer restriction of its tax reliefs and exemptions only on £70,000 of relevant income – the lesser of the two amounts. In other words, part of the non-qualifying expenditure is effectively deemed to have been met from income which is not relevant income.

6   Value Added Tax

17.78   There is no general relief from VAT available to charities. Once the registration threshold of taxable supplies has been exceeded, a charity must register and account for VAT as any other trader. This is a complex area discussed in Chapter 20.

7   Inheritance tax

17.79   The aspects of inheritance tax relating to giving to charity are considered in Chapter 19. Charities themselves benefit from the relief in the Inheritance Tax Act 1984 s 58(1)(a), which applies to charities constituted in the form of a trust. Charities constituted as trusts are almost invariably drawn up as discretionary trusts.

17.80   The relief applies to the charges made under the system by which a periodic ten-year charge is imposed on discretionary trusts. This system involves tax being due, albeit at a reduced rate, on the value of the assets held by a discretionary trust on every tenth anniversary of its foundation. Property held for charitable purposes only by permanent charitable trusts is exempted from this periodic charge.

17.81   If the property ceases to be held for charitable purposes, however, the charge can be triggered unless it is given to another charity or applied for such purposes. It will also arise if the trustees make a disposition reducing the value of the settled property otherwise than for charitable purposes.

8   Business rates and council tax

Business rates

17.82   Local taxation is divided into business rates (which apply to businesses) and council tax (which applies to individuals).

Charities receive a mandatory reduction of 80% on uniform business rates. Further relief, up to the total amount otherwise due, can be given to charities at the discretion of local authorities. Following the case *Oxfam v City of Birmingham District Council* [1976] AC 126, the Rating (Charity Shops) Act 1976 was introduced, which entitles charity shops to qualify for the relief, provided that they wholly or mainly sell donated goods and the profits are applied for charitable purposes.

Council tax

17.83   Council tax is chargeable on private dwellings, and is determined by the value of the property, graded in eight valuation bands (A to H). Certain properties can be exempt from the tax and occupants may qualify for reductions or discounts. Charities also receive both specific and partial exemptions. Subject to these properties, where charities will be liable to council tax, are:

- residential care homes, hostels, nursing or mental homes;

- staff flats or accommodation in residential property;

- houses in multiple accommodation; and

- convents, monasteries and church houses.

17.84   Properties exempt from council tax include those occupied only by students or as armed forces' barracks and married quarters. Also included are properties that are vacant for certain reasons, including those waiting to be occupied by a minister of religion, or vacated by someone who has gone into care or gone to care for another person. Residential properties owned by charities that are vacant for up to six months are partly exempt.

17.85   Claims must be made for other reductions. The disabled reduction scheme applies where at least one resident is substantially and permanently disabled, and the property contains either space for a wheelchair to be used inside, or a room other than a kitchen, bathroom or toilet, mainly used by that person and essential to their needs. Under the scheme, valuation can be on the band below the one that would otherwise apply, apart from Band A.

17.86   Where all adult residents of a property fall into the following categories, council tax is reduced by 50%. If one resident is outside the categories, the reduction is 25%, but if two or more are outside, there is no reduction. The categories are:

- patients in homes receiving treatment or care in a residential care home, nursing home, mental home or hostel;

- some care workers, where the person being cared for receives specified benefits and the carer is resident and works at least 35 hours per week (the spouse or child of the recipient is excluded); and

- care workers employed by the Crown, a charity or a local authority, or introduced by such to a third party, where they reside in premises provided by their employer, work at least 24 hours per week, and do not earn more than a certain limit.

17.87   If a claim for relief under the above schemes is rejected, an appeal can be made to a Valuation Tribunal.

9   Benefits-in-kind, stamp duty, betting duty

17.88   Where charities act as employers, they are subject to the normal PAYE (pay as you earn) and NIC (National Insurance Contributions) regimes. Where a director of a charity has total emoluments of less than £8,500, expenses reimbursed to that director are not subject to the benefits in kind legislation. Volunteer drivers who are paid a mileage allowance may be seen as receiving a taxable profit element if the allowance paid exceeds amounts necessary to merely reimburse the cost of fuel and running costs. HMRC can tax this profit element, and so it would be more sensible to limit mileage allowances to agreed rates published by HMRC.

17.89   The introduction of the national minimum wage may affect charities that make nominal payments to volunteers. Where such payments are being considered, a charity should carefully structure the method by which they are made.

17.90   Charities are not liable for stamp duty on conveyances, transfers or sales or leases (FA 1982 s 129), but where stamp duty does apply, it will apply to the full amount of the consideration for sale, including VAT, where that tax is applicable. VAT does not apply to the amount paid to HMRC as stamp duty as this does not form part of the consideration for the supply for VAT purposes (SP 11/91).

17.91   Small lotteries or raffles incidental to exempt entertainments, or private lotteries or societies lotteries defined by Sch 11 to the Gambling Act 2005, may be organised by a charity and exempt from pool betting duty. Additional regulations govern lotteries run by charities and information about them can be obtained from the Gaming Board.

10   Landfill tax

17.92   Landfill tax is a tax per tonne of waste disposed of at licensed landfill sites. It is accounted for by landfill site operators. Bodies registered for landfill tax that make 'qualifying contributions' to approved bodies can get credit for landfill tax paid or payable in respect of 90% of the amount of each qualifying contribution in any accounting period. This credit can only be claimed, however, up to 20% of the annual landfill tax liability of the contributing body.

17.93   An approved body for the purposes of landfill tax is one that is concerned with the environment, including the fields of waste management, reclamation, pollution control, and that is precluded from distributing any profit it may make. Any charities active in areas as described above may wish to seek advice in order to attract as many qualifying contributions as possible by maximising the extent of the credit available for contributors.

11 Community amateur sports clubs

17.94   The Finance Act 2002 s 58 and Sch 18 apply some of the charity exemptions described above to Community Amateur Sports Clubs (CASCs) which are not charities. From 1 April 2004, such bodies became exempt from corporation tax on trading income where turnover is less than £30,000 per annum and property income is less than £20,000 per annum. Between 1 April 2002 and 31 March 2004, these limits were £15,000 and £10,000 respectively.

17.95   Individuals are entitled to Gift Aid relief and CASCs can claim basic rate tax (and transitional relief from 6 April 2008 to 5 April 2011) from donations but not subscriptions. Gifts to CASCs are exempt from Capital Gains Tax and Inheritance Tax and, from 1 April 2004, the 80% mandatory relief from business rates also applies to CASCs in England and Wales.

17.96   To become a CASC, a club's constitution must comply with certain conditions and register with HMRC. The club must be open to all members of the community without discrimination for the purpose of facilitating and encouraging participation in a wide range of sports which are listed together with the registration form on the HMRC website, www.hmrc.gov.uk/charities/casc/register.htm#1. The constitution of the club must prevent the distribution of surpluses to members and for any proceeds on dissolution to be applied for charitable purposes or given to charity. Once registered as a CASC, there is no provision allowing deregistration.

Chapter 18

Tax and trading activities of charities

1   General principles

18.1   The requirement to find continual sources of income with which to pursue the objects of a charity results in competition both between charities, and between charitable and commercial concerns. Where this competition involves adventures in the nature of trade, direct and indirect taxation must be taken into account. Continual trading activities such as the operation of charity shops are one example of charities entering the world of business, while occasional activities, such as the sale of Christmas cards, are another. Charities should ask themselves if they can trade and the Charity Commission has produced guidance on 'How charities may lawfully trade', Booklet CC35.

18.2   'Trade' for direct tax purposes is not the same as 'business' for VAT purposes. The latter is discussed in Chapter 20. However, it should always be kept in mind that if a charity is doing anything that could be construed as making supplies in return for a consideration, VAT will be an issue. If a charity is trading for the purposes of the Income and Corporation Taxes Act 1988 (TA 1988) and the Income Tax Act 2007 (ITA 2007), the making of supplies for VAT purposes is a near certainty.

18.3   Unless a specific exemption is available, trading profits are taxable, no matter what the motive for the activity or the use made of the profits. This is because if the charity was in competition with commercial traders, a blanket exemption would unfairly disadvantage non-charitable traders and would distort competition. This rationale applies to both direct tax and, under the Principal VAT Directive, to VAT. One specific exemption available is that the sale of donated goods is not treated as trading for the purposes of TA 1988 and ITA 2007, being seen as the conversion of a donation into cash, and is zero-rated for VAT. This is one area in which both taxes treat the same subject in the same way. However, see Chapter 19 in relation to where goods are instead sold by charities as agents for 'supporters' and the proceeds are then gifted to the charity under Gift Aid.

2   The trading exemption

18.4   The exemption for trading income is far stricter than that for other income under TA 1988 and ITA 2007. The main conditions to be met in this case are that:

- the trade is exercised in the course of carrying out a primary purpose of the charity; or

- the work in connection with the trade is mainly carried out by the beneficiaries of the charity.

Thus, where a museum, zoo or art gallery charges for admission, they are achieving their charitable goals, carrying out their primary purpose of advancing education and art. The same applies for orchestras, etc, charging for tickets to a performance.

18.5   A typical example of beneficiaries of a charity carrying out work in connection with trade is where a charity established to help disabled people sets up a workshop to employ them and sells the items manufactured.

18.6   Where a charity is trading, whether all year round or on an occasional basis, its profits will only escape tax if the trade is within these specific exemptions. If a charity carries on trading activities on a regular basis which are not within either of the two exemptions, problems will result. At best, the profits of the trade will be liable to tax, but the rest of the charity's tax exemptions will be unaffected. At worst, where the trading activity becomes so significant that it has effectively become the raison d'être of the organisation, the charity may be held not to be pursuing exclusively charitable objects, and its charitable status may be vitiated so that all tax exemptions are lost.

18.7   A further point needs to be made on the working of the exemption. For charitable companies, instead of stipulating that the profits must be applied for charitable purposes only, the exemption makes it a condition that the profits must be applied solely to the purposes of the charity. Similarly for trusts, the profits must be applied to the purposes of the charitable trust. Thus, in an extreme case, if a charity established for strictly educational purposes only and trading as such were to make a large donation for famine relief out of profits, it would be liable to tax on those profits. Even though the trade was exercised in the course of carrying out the primary purpose of the charity, and even though the payment was applied for charitable purposes in a general sense, the exemption would not apply because profits were not applied solely for the purposes of the charity itself. Thus, the wording of the legislation encourages a charity with an exempt trade to plough back all profits into the same activity. It is hoped that in practice this point would not be taken by HM Revenue and Customs (HMRC). The exemptions for other income, such as investment income provide more broadly that the income is applied to charitable purposes only.

18.8   It is important to note that HMRC accept that certain trading activities *ancillary* to the carrying out of a primary purpose trade are also covered by this exemption. For example, the exemption is regarded as covering the sale of food and drink in a cafeteria or bar to visitors to an art gallery or the audience in a theatre, and the sale of textbooks or past exam papers by a college or school.

18.9   Sometimes, however, these ancillary activities go beyond what HMRC are prepared to accept as being within primary purpose trading. There are some trades which are considered partly primary and partly non-primary purpose. These trades are often referred to as *mixed trades*. For example, the facilities provided in a theatre bar may be made available to the general public as well as the audience. For chargeable accounting periods beginning after 21 March 2006, as introduced by the Finance Act 2006 s 56, the sales to audience members (primary purpose) and the sales to the general public (non-primary purpose) must be treated as two separate trades. This causes practical issues for the charity as the separation of the two trades is not easily achieved. If primary purpose and non-primary purpose goods are sold, the separation of the trades may be achieved through detailed sales records. For example, the sale of historical books (primary purpose) in a history museum shop can be separated from sales of promotional mugs (non-primary purpose). Using the Theatre Bar example it would be difficult to separate trades unless we can demonstrate or HMRC allow us to assume that the sales between and around theatre performances relate to audience members.

18.10   For periods beginning on or after 21 March 2006, HMRC operated their own rule-of-thumb concession to allow exemption in situations where the part of the trade which is not either primary purpose or ancillary is not large in itself and is less than 10% of total trading turnover. If these guidelines were breached, HMRC sought to deny the primary purpose exemption to the whole trade.

3   Small traders

18.11   The Finance Act 2000 s 46 introduced a measure to allow charities to carry on small trading operations, such as the sale of Christmas cards or commemorative items, without the complications of setting up a trading subsidiary or the danger of becoming subject to tax.

18.12   Providing that the governing instrument of a charity allows it, non-qualifying trading is now, within certain limits, exempt from tax. The maximum trading income allowed (and charities should note that this is income, not profit) is £5,000 per annum or, if over this amount, up to the lesser of 25% of total incoming resources or £50,000. Profits must be applied solely for the use of the charity. There is also room in the Finance Act 2000 for these amounts to be accidentally exceeded, as exemption applies where the charity had reasonable expectation at the start of the accounting period that they would be within the relevant limit. This applies for both the expectation of the level of income from trading and the expectation of the level of total incoming resources. HMRC may require evidence such as minutes, cash flow forecasts and business plans to demonstrate a reasonable expectation. Levels of income shown in the previous financial statements will also be considered. The exemption has been extended for charitable trusts to miscellaneous income within ITA 2007 s 527.

18.13   There is a separate tax exemption in TA 1988 s 510 in respect of profits from shows or exhibitions held by agricultural societies with corporation tax status but who do not have charitable status. The requirement is that any profits are used solely for the purposes of the society.

4 Trading subsidiary

18.14   Where more substantial trading activities are carried on, standard pro-cedure is to set up a trading subsidiary company to carry on the trade while the parent charity concentrates on qualifying charitable activities. A deed of covenant was previously the most popular means of changing profit, liable to corporation tax in the hands of the subsidiary, into an annual payment exempt from tax in the hands of the charity itself. The Finance Act 2000 s 41 effec-tively abolished the tax effect of deeds of covenant and treated all payments to be made under existing deeds as Gift Aid payments. Transfer of profit is now achieved using the Gift Aid provisions, whereby the gross amount is paid over to the charity, who need make no claim for the tax, and the company is able to get tax relief on the amount paid over. For full details of the current Gift Aid rules, see Chapter 19.

18.15   Providing the necessary capital to set up a subsidiary is a contentious area. As subscription for the share capital of an unquoted company is not a qualifying investment within TA 1988 Sch 20 (ITA 2007 s 558 for charitable trusts), it can only be qualifying expenditure if HMRC can be satisfied that it is for the benefit of the charity and not for the avoidance of tax. As a trading subsidiary is commonly set up to avoid taxing a charity on its trading profits, it can be argued that funding the subsidiary is non-qualifying expenditure.

18.16   The continuing funding of a subsidiary suffers from many of the same problems. The financial situation of most charities means that they would be loath to tie up large sums of money in share capital which would not be easily accessible and that the working capital of the company is therefore likely to be substantially funded by borrowing. To borrow from a bank or other outside source may be difficult, given the payment of profits up to the parent charity. The subsidiary may find it difficult to achieve sufficient liquidity to repay the borrowing.

18.17   Therefore, funding is often achieved by a loan from the parent char-ity. Formal loan agreements should be made with set repayment terms and provision for recovery of the loan in due course. The investment decision should be minuted and for any significant investment decision, business plans and projections should be considered. Given that the trustees have to apply funds for charitable purposes, a loan must be at a commercial rate of interest, and the Charity Commission also requires that the loan be secured, wherever possible. This is also not specifically covered by TA 1988 Sch 20 Part II, so can also only be regarded as qualifying expenditure where HMRC is satisfied that the loan is made for the benefit of the charity and not for the avoidance of tax.

18.18   However, accepted practice is that the use and loan funding of trading subsidiaries by parent charities, unless being blatantly used to misappropriate funds or otherwise misuse charitable status, has the tacit approval of HMRC. In fact, HMRC actually endorses the use of a trading subsidiary by a charity in their guidance notes. In support of the practice is also that most charities will have strong reasons for trading through a subsidiary that are unconnected with tax avoidance– for example, preservation of charitable status– and compliance with their governing instrument.

18.19   Trading involves risk and this may not sit well with the responsibility of managing a charity. A charity's governing document may also prevent the carrying on of trade, either at all or at 'significant' levels. Prior to the Finance Act 2000, the Charity Commission advised and required charities to use a sub-sidiary company for trading, with the benefits of limited liability. This practice is still adopted as there are a number of areas where charity responsibility should be separated from trading risk.

18.20   Both the Charity Commission and HMRC provide a wealth of advice in information leaflets (such as CC35 mentioned above) and on their websites. The information provided includes advice concerning the establishment and maintenance of a trading subsidiary, with reminders about the requirements to stay within the powers laid out in a charity's governing document and within the terms of charity law with regard to avoiding undue risk or speculation. In order to be seen as being for the benefit of the charity, the trading company should be run on efficient lines and aim to make a profit. All decisions concerning such a company, in the course of setting it up and in the course of its operation, should be recorded. HMRC have published detailed guidance notes on this topic and others for charities. These notes can be accessed on their website at www.hmrc.gov.uk/charities.

5   Profit-shedding

18.21   The standard method of passing trading income up to the parent charity used to be for the subsidiary to covenant all or part of its profits to the charity in each successive accounting period. Such covenants have now been replaced by the extension of the Gift Aid scheme to cover payments by companies to their parent charities.

18.22   Whether a charity subsidiary trading company has a covenant in place or not, the profits are now transferred tax-efficiently to the charity by a Gift Aid payment. This converts trading income, which would otherwise be taxable if the trade were carried on by the charity, to donations and not subject to tax. By donating all its taxable profits, the subsidiary receives a deduction by way of a charge on income and reduces the taxable profits to nil. Prior to 1 April 1997, the payment, whether covenant or Gift Aid, had to be made within the period to which it related in order to qualify as a charge on income for the purposes of corporation tax. After that date, new rules were specifically introduced governing subsidiary companies wholly owned by charities, allowing the payment to qualify as a charge if paid within nine months of the end of the relevant period. This allows time for proper determination of the amount to be paid.

18.23   Some charities may prefer to maintain a profit-shedding covenant from their subsidiary for greater security. Although the Deed of Covenant per se has no tax effect, the payments made under it are still tax-effective under the Gift Aid scheme as a normal Gift Aid payment. More importantly, the covenant is still a legally binding document requiring the company to pay its profits to the charity. Conversely, there may be instances where it is desirable to maintain profits in the subsidiary so it may be preferable to make a Gift Aid payment but not a payment under a Deed of Covenant.

18.24   Mention has been made above of the need to operate a charity's trading subsidiary in a sensible and prudent manner. HMRC guidance comments that such a company needs to be provided with enough capital to enable it to operate consistently despite shedding the whole of its profit every year. They warn of the need to avoid a charity having to make frequent injections of cash into the subsidiary.

18.25   The subsidiary may not be able to shed all of its profits for other reasons. In order to shed tax in the subsidiary, it is the taxable profits which are donated which often differs to the accounting profits. This is due to profit adjustments required such as non tax deductible expenditure and more commonly differences between accounting depreciation and capital allowances claimed for taxation purposes. This mismatch between profits for accounting and taxation purposes can often result in having insufficient accounting reserves to make a Gift Aid donation. Although it is often not practical to do so, it is advisable to avoid asset purchases or bring claims made for capital allowances in line with the depreciation policy adopted in the accounts.

6   Payments by a company to a charity under Gift Aid

18.26   The Gift Aid scheme can be used by individuals or companies to make donations to a charity in a tax-efficient manner. For companies, including trading subsidiaries of charities, the procedure is simple.

Since 1 April 2000, the company simply pays over the gross amount and claims tax relief on that, with no claim required or allowed by the charity.

18.27   The Gift Aid scheme was extended by the Finance Act 2000 ss 40 and 41 to cover payments that would previously have been made under a deed of covenant. Existing covenants simply move within the new scheme, with the covenant documentation serving as that necessary for the Gift Aid rules to apply. The Finance Act 2000 s 40(7) allows trading subsidiaries of charities to make the Gift Aid payment up to nine months after the end of the accounting period. The Finance Act 2006 s 57 clarified that the nine month extension would apply to companies which are wholly owned by more than one charity. The Gift Aid scheme in general is described in more detail in Chapter 19, as it can also be used by individuals to make payments to charities.

18.28   The most recognised and reliable method of passing trading profits up to a charity was, prior to changes in the Finance Act 2000, a deed of covenant.

Since then, the Gift Aid legislation has made transfer of profits to a charity by a subsidiary company very much simpler. The ability to make a payment up to nine months after the end of the accounting period for companies wholly owned by charities should enable accurately calculated Gift Aid payments to be made in nearly every case. An accounting period for tax purposes is restricted to 12 months, and care must be taken if the company accounts are prepared for a longer period. There will be separate periods for tax and Gift Aid must be paid within the time limit of each accounting period.

18.29   There may be cases where charities enter into joint ventures with others. Profits may still be shed by the joint venture company with a Gift Aid donation but this must be paid within its accounting period. However, care must be taken that payments are not a distribution to the charity in respect of its shareholding. This was discussed in detail in the case of *Noved Investment Co v HMRC Comrs* [2006] STC (SCD) 120 which found that a donation may also be a distribution, as a transfer of assets to a shareholder by virtue of TA 1988 s 209(2)(b). The Finance Act 2006 introduced provisions to exclude payments being deemed distributions where companies are wholly owned by one or more charities, but extended the rules to cover payments by all other companies. Where a company is not wholly charity owned, HMRC will review evidence such as minutes to determine whether payment has been made by virtue of its shareholding and deny Gift Aid treatment. A distribution or dividend is not deductible from the taxable profits of the company.

7   VAT implications

18.30   Chapter 20 deals with the VAT aspects of charities trading, but it should be mentioned now that a profit motive is not necessary to make an activity subject to VAT. Any supply of goods or services for a consideration is a supply for the purposes of VAT. Although the VAT legislation does not define 'business' exactly, it does state that it includes every trade, profession or vocation.

18.31   If a charity chooses to establish a trading subsidiary, this can mean that the company, rather than the parent charity, is liable to register for VAT. Although this can be a desirable outcome from the point of view of the parent, a close eye must be kept on its relationship with its subsidiary; supplies between the two may result in a VAT cost to the parent, or in a need for it to register.

18.32   As VAT applies to turnover rather than to profits, if a charity is making trading profits that embroil them in direct tax consideration, VAT will almost certainly be an issue. However, it is possible for both direct and indirect taxes to generate problems quite independently of each other, and it should not be assumed that safety from one point of view will prevent unfortunate repercussions from the other.

8   Sponsorship

18.33   Sponsorship has such a wide meaning in charities and charity fundraising activities that it is imperative that clear thought is given to the direct and indirect tax implications of the transactions or activities to be carried out. At its most innocent, for example, a sponsored bicycle ride by an individual in support of his favourite charity, this form of sponsorship will be totally outside the scope of tax. At its most commercial, for example, a charity's endorsement in commercial advertising of a commercial product, significant direct and indirect tax liabilities may be at stake. At their most complex, sponsorship deals, such as affinity credit card schemes and the like, may be a mixture of these two extremes.

18.34   The penalties for ignoring the underlying commerciality of sponsorship deals can be very serious for charities, and significant tax liabilities to income or corporation tax and VAT can be incurred if correct structures are not set up.

18.35   When considering the structure of a sponsorship deal from a tax point of view, it is essential to analyse the component parts of the arrangements thoroughly. In this type of activity, both the VAT (Customs) and Revenue sections of HMRC will look closely at the substance of the transactions. Customs will regard the commercial element of any sponsorship deal as a taxable supply, but it may be possible to persuade them that only part should be regarded as subject to VAT, with part being regarded as a philanthropic donation. The Revenue side is likely to take a far stricter approach and tax the whole payment as relating to the sale of advertising services.

18.36   This is particularly true where a charity, in some sort of joint venture, allows its name or logo to be used by a commercial organisation. The marketing by a charity of its name or logo directly to a commercial organisation which then advertises its support for the charity can be regarded either as promotional trading, or as the sale of copyright or trademark by the charity. Either activity is likely to be subject to VAT and direct tax.

18.37   HMRC provides detailed guidance for charities on the issue of sponsorship. For direct tax, if the charity does not provide goods or services in return for a payment, they will normally accept that the payment is a donation and not trading income. If by making a payment to a charity, the 'sponsor' merely receives the benefit of good publicity or exploits the affinity with a charity this will not in itself constitute trading, unless the charity publicises the affinity. Simple acknowledgements by the charity of donations or support are accepted by Customs and usually the Revenue side depending on the context of the acknowledgment.

18.38   Where a charity merely acknowledges the support of a corporate benefactor, trading will not be in point. Where something beyond mere acknowledgement is involved, the Revenue will seek to tax sponsorship money as trading income. The Revenue will regard reference to a sponsor as trading in the form of advertising if this entails a description of the sponsor's goods or services, or a large and prominent display of the sponsor's logo or corporate colours. Where a charity lends its own good name alongside that of a corporate sponsor, allows its logo to endorse a sponsor's products (see **18.36**) and if the charity goes further and sells its mailing list, the charity promotes the products, links its website to the sponsor's sales website or gives exclusive rights to sell products or services on the charity's premises, the receipts will be treated as trading income. Trading income may still be exempt if it is primary purpose trading, for example, sponsorship of an exhibit for a charity museum or gallery where the benefits received are fairly modest.

18.39   If payments are made solely for use of the charity's logo there are now different rules for charitable companies under where the logo came into existence from 1 April 2002 as introduced by the intangibles fixed asset rules in the Finance Act 2002 Sch 29. Where there is non-trading gain on the logo, this is exempt provided the gain is applied for charitable purposes. Where a charitable trust or the logo was in existence before 1 April 2002, there is no exemption for a one off payment other than potentially the small trader's exemption mentioned above. If payments recur each year under a legal obligation and are accepted as a donation in the hands of the charity (not trading), they are exempt as annual payments.

18.40   This whole area has been complicated even more by the requirements in the Charities Act 1992 ss 58 and 59 that 'commercial participators have written agreements with charities setting out the terms under which money is paid to charity and the way in which it reaches the charity'. There is no doubt, however, that the requirement for these formal commercial participators' agreements has made life more complex since, as in a typical affinity card deal, where there are transactions between the charity and the sponsor, such agreements will have to be in place with all parties. Any attempt to short-circuit this procedure could lead to an attack on grounds of trading if only the charity is party to the transactions. In another way, however, it is quite helpful in analysing the nature of the transactions to decide whether trading or some other taxable activity is in point.

18.41   The solution to the problem of sponsorship being considered as trading for income tax or corporation tax purposes and making taxable supplies for VAT purposes may, therefore, be to use a trading subsidiary company. Wherever possible, pure trading deals should be routed through the trading subsidiary. A mixed transaction should be split into its commercial and philanthropic component parts, the commercial element being routed through the trading subsidiary, and the philanthropic element being paid direct to the charity, making use of available tax reliefs including the Gift Aid provisions. Obviously, purely philanthropic gifts should go straight to the charity, again using Gift Aid where necessary.

18.42   Where there are complex sophisticated sponsorship and promotional deals, it may be that the only safe way to proceed is to agree the VAT and income and corporation tax treatment in advance, in principle with HMRC. This can cause charity fundraisers and commercial sponsors some frustration at the time it takes to reach agreement, but the risk of making expensive mistakes should not be underestimated. Even a simple decision, correct in principle, to route a sponsorship deal through a trading subsidiary can give rise to problems if the subsidiary does not have the necessary legal rights to exploit the name or logo of its charitable parent.

18.43   Care also needs to be taken where joint ventures or activities are concerned. Ideally, joint ventures constituted as such are to be avoided, as they may require separate VAT registration, and it is often more beneficial from a tax point of view if a commercial organisation takes all responsibility for VAT-related matters. Detailed planning advice needs to be taken in advance on both the VAT and direct tax implications of each sponsorship promotion.

Chapter 19

Tax incentives to donors

1 General proposition

19.1   There is no general relief from tax granted to a taxpayer who makes a gift to charity. However, a number of major and specific reliefs have been used and developed over the years, culminating in the Gift Aid scheme.

2 Deeds of covenant

19.2   Prior to the Finance Act 2000 (FA 2000), a deed of covenant could be used to make tax-efficient donations to charities. Covenants can be made by individuals or by companies, as explained in Chapter 18. Although still possible to make, and binding in law, their tax effect has now been subsumed within Gift Aid. It is likely that charities will still be happy for people to enter into deeds of covenant, as they result in a long-term obligation for the donor to give. However, a Gift Aid declaration can be adapted to allow for long-term support but they are not legally binding. Deeds of covenant can, and should, for the purposes of tax efficiency, be drawn up to be 'Gift Aid compliant'.

19.3   A covenanted payment to a charity had to:

● be made under a legally binding obligation;

● have a quality of recurrence (although the amounts might differ); and

● be pure income profit in the hands of the recipient charity.

'Pure income profit' meant that the donor gave the amount on the same basis that a pure donation is made; they did not receive, or expect to receive, any service or other supply in return for their gift. Although the amounts payable over the term of the covenant might differ, they had to be calculated on a consistent basis. Except for the legally binding obligation rule, Gift Aid payments are made on the same principles, with minor relaxations in respect of benefits provided to donors.

19.4   The 'pure income profit' rule was breached in only two ways in the case of covenanted subscriptions to membership charities:

(a)   by Inland Revenue concession where certain minimal benefits were allowed; and

(b)   by the Finance Act 1989 (FA 1989) s 59, which allowed a charity to reclaim tax on a covenant whilst providing benefits to the covenantor if the sole or main purpose of the charity was the preservation of property or the conservation of wildlife, and the only benefit provided was that of free or reduced admission to view that property or wildlife.

FA 1989 s 59 was abolished by FA 2000, but similar provisions on rights of admission to charity property are included in the extended Gift Aid legislation now included in the Income Tax Act 2007 (ITA 2007) s 420. See details in **19.17** below.

Documentation

19.5   Required documentation under the Gift Aid scheme is much simpler than covenant documentation. Deeds of covenant stated whether the annual amount payable was net or gross of basic rate income tax, with individual donors usually using net covenants. Gross covenants were usually used by companies.

19.6   Whether expressed net or gross, an individual donor was deemed to have deducted tax from the covenant, and only paid the net amount to the charity. Companies always had to withhold income tax from the covenanted donations and pay over the tax to the Inland Revenue. In each case, charity then claimed repayment from the Inland Revenue.

19.7   The ability to make payments to charity under a deed of covenant was not restricted to individuals, or the subsidiary company of a charity as mentioned in Chapter 18.

3   Donations to charity: Gift Aid

19.8   The Gift Aid scheme was introduced in 1990. Prior to FA 2000, the minimum donation to qualify for the scheme was £250. FA 2000 made some significant changes to the Gift Aid scheme and there is no longer a minimum limit for giving under the system. The Gift Aid scheme can be used by individuals as well as companies, and replaced the deed of covenant system, for donations by individuals made or due after 6 April 2000, and by companies after 1 April 2000. However, some confusion often arises in practice as donations from individuals are deemed to be made net of basic rate tax and company donations are made gross, although both are referred to as Gift Aid donations. A charity must clearly identify and exclude corporate donations when reclaiming tax under Gift Aid. It is wondered whether the confusion and errors in charity tax reclaims could be avoided by introducing different terminology for corporate donations.

19.9   It is now possible to make Gift Aid donations over the telephone or the Internet, as it is not necessary for the donor to sign a paper declaration. However, it is still incumbent upon charities to provide written notification to the donor of the circumstances of their donation (see **19.30** regarding Gift Aid declarations).

19.10   Although the certification requirements have been simplified from those in force before FA 2000, there has been pressure from the sector to simplify Gift Aid further to encourage Gift Aid donations and reduce administrative burdens for charities. In the Budget 2007, the Chancellor announced that the government planned to consider proposals to increase the take up of Gift Aid. The review of Gift Aid has been undergoing detailed consultation for the last two years, but positive changes have been introduced such as the new 'Yellow Card' system for HMRC Gift Aid audits and the aggregation of small donations on the tax reclaim form.

Lower rate and higher rate taxpayers

19.11   Gift Aid donations from individual taxpayers are deemed to be net of basic rate tax. Tax relief is now available on Gift Aid payments from individuals paying income tax at a rate below the basic rate and relief is also available to payments by donors paying capital gains tax. Donors are merely required to pay an amount of income tax and/or CGT equal to the basic rate tax reclaimed on their donations. Notional tax credits on dividends received are treated as tax paid for this purpose. The basic rate band of the donor for the year of donation is increased by the grossed-up amount. This means that a higher rate taxpayer gets higher rate tax relief on the grossed-up amount of the donation. However, current Gift Aid legislation does not provide for further relief on the introduction of additional levels of higher rate tax, as a further level (50% rate tax) has been proposed for the tax year from 5 April 2010.

19.12   Entitlement to personal reliefs is restricted, where necessary, to ensure that income tax or capital gains tax, equal to the tax 'deducted' from the donation and reclaimed by the charity, is actually paid. In addition to this restriction, ITA 2007 s 424 will treat the individual liable for the surplus tax where tax charged to the individual is lower than the tax deducted from the donation.

In 2009/10 Mr X earned income of £80,000. Tax of £21,930 was deducted under PAYE.

	£
Income	80,000
Personal allowance	6,475
Taxable income	73,525

Mr X made a Gift Aid donation of £,16,000 (net) to a local animal sanctuary, which received a tax refund of £4,000. The charity also receives *transitional relief* of £512.82. *Transitional Relief* is available from 6 April 2008 to 5 April 2011 and was introduced to compensate for the drop in basic rate tax from 22% to 20%.

19.13 *Tax incentives to donors*

Mr X's tax position is therefore:

	£
Taxable income	73,525
Basic rate band (37,400 × 20%)	7,480
Basic rate withheld on donation (16,000 net × 100/80 = 20,,000) × 20%	4,000
Higher rate liability (73,525 − 37,400 − 20,000) × 40%	6,450
Total tax payable	17,930
Difference from tax under PAYE	4,000

The charity therefore receives £16,000 + £4,000 tax refund, equalling £20,000 plus £512.82 transitional relief.

Mr X pays £400 less tax than he would do if he did not make the donation. The effect on his income is therefore £16,000 − £4,000, making an equivalent net payment of £12,000.

If Mr X is prepared for his equivalent net payment to be the £16,000 originally donated, his net donation should be £21,333. This grosses up to £26,667 added to his basic rate tax band, and results in a higher rate tax saving of £5,333. The effect on his income is therefore £21,333 − £5,333, which equals an equivalent net payment of £16,000.

This means that the charity receives the net donation of £21,333 plus a tax refund with transitional relief of £6,017. Thus the charity receives £6,837.18 more than under the original calculation with Mr X still only reducing his income by £16,000 when all the tax reliefs unwind.

19.13   FA 2002 s 98 made provision that Gift Aid donations made in a particular year can be treated as having been made in the previous tax year if an election is made. The election must be made to HMRC on or before the date the donor files his tax return for that previous year and, in any event, by 31 January following the end of that year for tax returns filed on line or 31 October for a paper return. This rule applies to donations made on or after 6 April 2003.

19.14   This mirrors an extension of Gift Aid introduced by FA 2000 s 40 in respect of donations made by companies which are wholly owned by charities after 1 April 2000. Provided the payment is made within nine months of the year-end, it can be treated as having been made in the previous accounting period. This rule, developed from earlier legislation dealing with profit-shedding deeds of covenant by trading subsidiaries of charities, enables a charity trading subsidiary to tailor the donation to the taxable profit of the subsidiary (see **18.24–18.27**). From 1 April 2006, legislation clearly defines that the extension applies to companies which are wholly owned by one or more charities.

19.15   From 6 April 2004, taxpayers are able to make a Gift Aid payment out of their tax repayment. They can elect for a charity to receive all or part of a tax repayment and make a Gift Aid declaration on the tax return itself. The charity must be on a list published on the HMRC website and charities are asked to put themselves forward if they wish to be on the list. The payment will be made automatically to the charity by the HMRC, but only one charity can be named in the return.

Some basic rules

19.16   Gift Aid donations must be by way of payment of a sum of money. They cannot be made by loan waiver or debt conversion, or in kind. Subject to the exceptions noted at **19.17** below, they must be outright payments to charity and cannot be in return for some service or product.

Benefits to donors

19.17   Although, in principle, donations should be pure gifts, a limited amount of benefits are allowed to be provided to donors. An acknowledgement of a donation is permissible provided it does not amount to commercial advertising (this is also a concern from a VAT point of view, and is discussed in Chapter 20). The free or reduced-price admission to view charity property is also allowed to the donor and his or her family, provided that any member of the public could make such a donation. HMRC perceived some abuse of this provision and, in FA 2006 further conditions were introduced which at the same time broadened the spread of relief to more charities from 6 April 2006. Benefits of admission are ignored where:

- the donation grants an annual right of admission to the donor (including the donor's family); or

- the donation giving right of admission to the donor (including the donor's family) exceeds the usual cost of admission to the public by 10% or more.

The second option appears to be less popular, as although a higher-rate taxpayer can benefit more from the increased donation rather than the usual admission fee, it is difficult to convey this message in practice at the time of admission. A donation for annual admission must provide either free or a reduced rate of admission but not a mixture of the two and an individual who chooses to make the donation but not to apply Gift Aid must also be entitled to the same free/reduced annual admission charges. The relaxation of the rules for benefits is limited to admission and does not extend to other benefits received as a consequence of making a donation.

19.18   Aside from these two specific allowances mentioned above, there is a sliding scale of the monetary value of benefits. For donations made from 6 April 2007:

Donation	Maximum benefit allowed
£0–100	25% value of donation
£101–1,000	£25
£1,000+	5% value of donation up to a maximum of £500 *(was 2.5% and £250 for donations before 6 April 2007)*

Where the benefits received are regular but cover a period of less than 12 months, they should be grossed up to 'annualise' the amount of benefit received, and the limits applied as above. This would apply, for example, where a donation resulted in six 'free' copies of a monthly publication. The relevant limit would be that which applied to the 'annualised' donation (in this case, the donation would be doubled to find the limit). The annualised amount of benefit received would be the value of the benefit if received continuously over the year (again, in this case, double the value of the benefit actually received). Ignoring the annualisation, the total value of all benefits received by a donor from the same charity in a tax year must not exceed £500 for donations, from 6 April 2007, to qualify as Gift Aid.

19.19   Valuing donor benefits can be difficult. HMRC interpretation is that it is the value to the recipient which is the measure of the benefit. For example, consideration in the form of a third party benefit or discount may cost the charity nothing to provide but there will still be a benefit to the recipient. Where something is sold to the public generally, the value will be the sale price; where it is not sold, some form of cost analysis may be needed. HMRC guidance suggests that in valuing benefits given in return for life membership of a charity, the estimated value of benefits for the first ten years should be calculated. Conversely, where the benefit consists of literature describing the work or objects of the charity, HMRC will accept that the benefit value for this purpose is nil even though there may be a cover price. In relation to discounts offered by the charity, HMRC will take into account the take up of the discount in considering the value.

19.20   An interesting possibility with regard to the rules on donor benefit is the possibility of making a 'split payment'. Where the value of the benefit would exceed the limits for donor benefits, the donor may specify that part of his or her payment is treated as payment for the benefit and the balance as a donation. Provided this is done before or at the time of making the donation, the donation element may still qualify for Gift Aid if it passes all the other requirements.

Some common examples

19.21   Charities will often seek to claim Gift Aid on purchases made in a charity auction. Purchases will often fail the benefits test and charities will need to carefully consider split payments. Where an item is not available commercially, the value of the benefit will be a price paid at auction and Gift Aid will not be available, particularly where items have been enhanced, for example an item of clothing worn or signed by a celebrity. HMRC will require supporters to be made aware of the commercial value of an item before the auction starts, if the excess payment is to qualify as Gift Aid.

19.22   HMRC may accept that voluntary parental contributions to charitable schools or charities associated may qualify for Gift Aid, provided the usual conditions are satisfied. HMRC have stated that where separate fees are charged at a level enabling the school to provide education without the need for further support or there are no/nominal fees but the school has sufficient alternative funding, there will be no benefit as a consequence of donations to charitable educational trusts from persons connected with the pupil. They also point out that where donations are aimed at subsidising an educational school trip, the value of the benefits provided will almost certainly disqualify the donation from Gift Aid.

19.23   In some circumstances, membership subscriptions can be paid by way of Gift Aid, if they do no more than secure membership of the society and do not give entitlement to personal use of any facilities or services provided by the charity. Strict criteria are set out on the HMRC website in its *Detailed Guidance for Charities*.

19.24   One area where Gift Aid can play an important part is in adventure/ challenge fund-raising events. Typically, participants are asked to pay a non-refundable participation fee and to guarantee to raise sponsorship of a minimum amount from friends, relatives, etc. The charity bears the cost of the event itself. Whilst the participant cannot claim Gift Aid for their deposit/entry fee, and persons connected with them cannot obtain Gift Aid for their sponsorship (because of the benefits the participant receives), unconnected sponsors can claim Gift Aid. Charity literature and sponsorship forms should make it clear that sponsors connected with the participant cannot Gift Aid their donations. For this purpose, 'connected' means a spouse, relative or lineal descendant, or the spouse of a relative. It also includes a company under the control of the participant or anyone connected with them.

19.25   Where volunteers incur expenditure on behalf of a charity and wish to forgo reimbursement, particular care needs to be taken if they wish to claim Gift Aid on the amount forgone. On the basis that Gift Aid must be a payment of a sum of money, HMRC will insist on the expenses first being paid to the volunteer and then paid back to the charity under Gift Aid. They will require a clear audit trail of the two separate transactions.

19.26   A significant relaxation to the above rules on Gift Aid appeared in the HMRC guidance notes in August 2007, '*3.51 Claiming Gift Aid when goods are sold by, and the proceeds gifted to, charities*'. In summary, as an alternative to donating goods to charity, a '*supporter*' can enter into an agreement where the charity (or its subsidiary company) sells their goods on behalf of the supporter who may then donate all or part of the proceeds to the charity under Gift Aid. HMRC will allow a default agreement for the proceeds to be retained by the charity as a Gift Aid donation, where the supporter has been notified of the sale proceeds and has not responded within a set reasonable period of at least 21 days. This must be made clear to the supporter before goods are sold. Interestingly, HMRC have relaxed the rule on a physical transfer of a sum of money but it is still required for volunteers' expenses donated and Gift Aid payments from subsidiary companies. The agency arrangement may impact on the charity's VAT recovery. The sale of donated goods is zero-rated but if items are sold by a charity as agent this activity could be non-business and the charity may need to consider charging a commission which will have direct tax implications as non-primary purpose trading income. HMRC may accept a nominal commission charge which is waived if the proceeds are then donated to the charity. HMRC are willing to discuss any proposals before implementation.

Gift Aid declarations

19.27   Whether a one-off donation or series of payments, Gift Aid declarations will be required from individuals. A charity will need a declaration before it can reclaim tax on gifts from individuals. No declaration is required in respect of company donations because a company's Gift Aid payments are made gross and there is no tax to reclaim.

19.28   In relation to the Gift Aid reclaims, HMRC adopt a system of 'pay now, check later'. Charity Gift Aid records are subject to random audits by HMRC. Gift Aid record-keeping requirements are stringent and at all times charities are responsible keeping a clear audit trail from the Gift Aid declaration to the amount of any tax repayment claim. HMRC audits are based on a sample period, often six months, in which they look to establish an 'error rate' where for example Gift Aid declarations are missing or incorrectly completed, and seek to apply this to a longer period going back up to six years. HMRC will now allow charities to go back and 'repair' errors by for instance requesting new declarations from donors where they are missing or invalid.

19.29   Declarations may be given at any time, whether before, at the time of, or after the gift concerned. They may be phrased to cover just one or a series of donations, and can be made in writing or orally. A written declaration by an individual must contain the following details:

- the donor's full name (HMRC will accept as a minimum an initial and surname) and home address;
- the name of the recipient charity;
- a description of the donation;
- a declaration that the donations are to be treated as Gift Aid donations;
- identify which donation(s) are to be covered by the declaration. This may simply say 'all donations I make from this date until further notice' or 'all donations I have made since …'; and
- there should be a note explaining that the donor must pay tax equal to the tax recoverable by the charity.

Curiously enough, there is no requirement for the declaration to be signed. Charities can design their own declaration, provided the above details are all present.

19.30   Where a declaration is made orally, for example, in a telephone response to a television appeal, the charity has to keep an audible recording and/or send the donor a written record of the oral declaration, showing:

- all the details provided by the donor (name, address, etc);
- a note explaining that the donor must pay sufficient tax to match the charity's reclaim;

- a note of the donor's right to cancel the donation within 30 days; and

- the date of the declaration and the date of the written record.

19.31   As discussed, Gift Aid records will be subject to HMRC audit, and a clear audit trail needs to be maintained in the charity's records. These records may be computerised, but as a bare minimum they should comprise:

- a Gift Aid declaration;

- copies of written records of oral declarations;

- correspondence with donors;

- bank statements and paying-in records; and

- accounting records showing receipts.

The records should be retained for six years minimum.

19.32   Charities are free to design their own Gift Aid declarations or sponsorship forms, but there are model forms on the HMRC Detailed Guidance website.

4   Payroll giving

19.33   The payroll giving scheme allows employees to give to charities through their payroll before the deduction of income tax (but after the deduction of National Insurance). As from 6 April 2000 there is no annual limit on payroll giving. It is not compulsory for an employer to run the scheme although the government provided cash incentives towards set up for small to medium-sized businesses which ceased in 2006; however, administration costs incurred by the employer are deductible for tax. The scheme can also apply to pension income where a company or personal pension provider is enrolled in the scheme.

19.34   The conditions for operating such a scheme are as follows:

- payments must be made through an agent, which must pay over the amounts deducted to the charity, or charities, of each individual employee's choice;

- the agent must be a charity approved by HMRC to operate the scheme; and

- sums deducted can only be so withheld by the employer at the request of the employee (this is a voluntary employee-driven scheme, not a compulsory employer-driven scheme).

19.35   Although a useful tax incentive for an employee, it can be administratively demanding for the employer. The cost of the administration is often incorporated by the agency as a handling charge from the employees' donations. Alternatively, the employers or even charities will meet the costs.

19.36 Such a scheme can only come into operation if both employer and employees agree to operate a machinery by which:

- the employer contracts with an approved agency;
- the employer makes the deductions requested by each individual employee and gives tax relief under a 'net pay' arrangement of applying PAYE;
- entry into the scheme is entirely voluntary on the part of each individual employee; and
- the amounts deducted are paid to an agency which distributes the money exactly in accordance with the wishes of each employee.

19.37 Approved agencies also have a significant administrative workload in that they must:

- be charities themselves;
- act in accordance with the wishes of each individual employee;
- take care gifts only go to bona fide charities;
- ensure that proper records are kept and returns made to HMRC; and
- distribute the gifts within 60 days, and ensure that no refunds can be made.

19.38 It is possible for an agency to be set up by an employer but these will be separate registered charities and as such subject to general charity regulation.

5 Business gifts

19.39 Donations to charity by businesses are not, (unless made under the Gift Aid scheme, or of qualifying shares and securities) normally deductible for tax purposes unless they are wholly and exclusively for trade purposes. For example, a butcher's gift of meat to the old people's home he supplies throughout the year could be said to be protecting and improving his customer relationships. The gift must be reasonable in amount and either boost the goodwill of the business or encourage staff morale.

19.40 Normally the Income Tax (Trading and Other Income) Act 2005 (ITTOIA 2005) s 45 disallows business gifts and entertaining, except where any gift is less than £50 in value and carries a conspicuous advert for the donor. However, ITTOIA 2005 s 47 (and the Corporation Tax Act 2009 (CTA 2009) s 1300) specifically permits a deduction for gifts to charity provided that they fall within the general Schedule D 'wholly and exclusively' rule. ESC B7 effectively extends this relief in relation to gifts to bodies without charitable status. This is provided that the gift is allowable under normal Schedule D rules and made to a body or association established for educational, cultural, religious, recreational or benevolent purposes which is local in relation to the donor's business activities. The gifts must not be connected with, or restricted to persons connected with, the donor.

19.41 The tax treatment of trading stock donated to charities is set out in ITTOIA 2005 s 108 and CTA 2009 s 105. Provided that the stock was originally manufactured or purchased for sale, later donation to charity in the course of trade will not cause the cost to be disallowed for tax purposes, nor lead HMRC to attribute any deemed market value sale proceeds. Market value would normally be imputed where stock is disposed of otherwise than in the course of a trade. HMRC have given the example of surplus sandwiches and other perishable goods being given to charities for the homeless as being made in the course of a trade, since the donation is the most commercially effective way of disposing of stock which would otherwise become unsaleable. The relief extends to trading stock or assets used in business which are donated to designated educational establishments. The relief applies where the stock or assets would qualify as machinery or plant in the hands of the educational establishment, eg computers or laboratory equipment. The Finance Act 2002 introduced relief for gifts of medical supplies and equipment but there is no requirement for the gift to be made to a UK charity. Items of plant and machinery do not give rise to a balancing charge for a business if given to a charity, a designated educational establishment or other exempt body.

6 Employee secondments and donated salaries

19.42 One way in which a growing number of employers have been helping charities is by seconding staff or management to charities to help them with the organisation or the establishment of a project. The employer continues to pay the seconded employee's salary and associated costs, eg pension and National Insurance. Under normal rules this expenditure, while the employee is working for the charity, is not deductible. ITTOIA 2005 s 70 and CTA 2009 s 70 contain legislation to permit the employer to continue obtaining a tax deduction in such circumstances, providing that the employee secondment is of a temporary nature. Temporary is not defined in the legislation and so takes its normal meaning. It follows that the charity and the employer must intend, at the very least, that the arrangement in relation to that particular employee will be for a limited period of time.

19.43 Some individuals, usually in religious orders, donate their services to their charitable trust or order. This may include services for which they are paid a salary, for example teaching or nursing. As individuals they would, after deducting personal allowances, obtain no tax relief for the gift of their services to charity. The solution is for the individual concerned to gift their income, including any salary, to the charity under the Gift Aid scheme. In theory they should always withhold income tax from their payment, but in practice the PAYE district issues a no-tax coding so that the charity receives the gross salary direct.

7 Interest-free loans

19.44 Interest-free loans can be a very simple and straightforward way of providing a charity with income. The cost to the lender is usually only the net after-tax income he would have derived, while the charity, being exempt on the income generated by the deposit, receives the gross amount.

19.45 Technically, the provision of such an interest-free loan can be caught by the revocable settlement provisions in ITTOIA 2005 s 624, which if imposed would tax the lender on the income received by the charity. The legislation does not apply to a company lending money. However, HMRC do not seek to invoke this legislation in respect of tax-free loans to charities, provided that:

- the loan is in cash;

- there are no arrangements as to how the loan should be invested or the income therefrom repaid;

- the loan will be repaid in cash and not by transfer of any assets; and

- the loan is not part of any wider arrangement.

8 Gifts of capital assets

19.46 The normal CGT treatment for the gift of a chargeable asset is that the giver is deemed to have disposed of the asset for market value at the time of the gifting. However, TCGA 1992 s 257 amends these rules where gifts of chargeable assets are made to charities. It treats them as being for such consideration that neither gain nor loss arises on the disposal. This relief only applies to gifts of chargeable assets. It does not extend to the sale by the donor of assets where the proceeds are then given to charity.

19.47 If a donor has an asset, or assets, which they wish to use to benefit a charity, they should consider whether it is more beneficial to give the assets direct to the charity or for the donor to realise the asset and then donate the proceeds. In order to determine this, the donor should estimate his total income tax and capital gains tax for the year.

19.48 If the asset is realised by the donor and a gain arises, there will be a liability to CGT (subject to annual exemptions, etc). The amount available for the charity will then be the sale proceeds less the amount of CGT. If this amount is paid to the charity under Gift Aid, it will be deemed to be net of basic rate tax, which the charity can then recover.

19.49 If the donor does not have sufficient tax liability to cover any relief due under the Gift Aid provisions, they should also gift the asset directly to the charity, thereby avoiding any complications of their tax position.

9 Gifts of securities and shares and land

19.50 FA 2000 s 43 introduced relief for gifts of certain shares or securities. Where such securities or shares are gifted to a charity or sold to a charity for less than their value, the donor receives a deduction from income or profit on the difference between the value of the shares and the consideration received. The deduction claimed can also include incidental costs of disposal, eg broker's fees.

19.51 Eligible shares and securities are those registered on a recognised stock exchange, units in authorised unit trusts, shares in open-ended investment companies, and some holdings in foreign collective investment schemes. They also specifically include shares and securities traded on the Alternative Investment Market, PLUS and overseas stock exchanges recognised by HMRC. The ability for donors of shares to claim relief on the full market value of the shares at the date of gift is a significant incentive to charitable giving both by successful entrepreneurs floating their companies and those people with large investment portfolios on which significant capital gains have been accrued.

19.52 The relief for gifts of shares and securities to charity was extended to gifts of UK-situated land by the Finance Act 2002 s 97. In the case of land, the charity must furnish the donor with a certificate specifying the description of the qualifying interest in the land, the date of disposal and stating that the charity has acquired the relevant interest. Donating a part share in land or property will not qualify for the relief. The donor must give away the whole of his or her beneficial interest in the asset and where the donor only has a part share, all joint owners must dispose of their interest to qualify for the relief. The donor cannot gift a house and continue to live there or have right of use over the property. The grant of a lease for a term of absolute years will qualify for the relief.

10   Inheritance tax

19.53 All transfers of value to charity, whether lifetime gifts or legacies on death, are exempt from IHT provided the gift is absolute. The exemption will be lost if the gift is dependent upon a condition which is not satisfied within 12 months of transfer. It will also be lost if the gift is defeasible (capable of being annulled or made void) or takes effect only after the termination of another interest. The exemption is also disallowed by IHTA 1984 s 23(4) if the donor, their spouse or other connected person retains any interest in the property given.

19.54 Where an individual wishes to leave money to charity in their will, great care is needed in the drafting. This is especially important where other bequests bring about a liability to tax and a residue is left to charity. Unless the will is drafted so that the other specific bequests bear their own tax, the tax thereon will be payable out of, and thus reduce, the residue available to the charity.

Chapter 20

Charities and VAT

1 General framework

20.1 Charities have no general relief from Value Added Tax (VAT), and the supremacy of EU law over domestic legislation limits the ability of the Treasury to alter the VAT regime in any significant way.

20.2 VAT law is shaped by EC Directive 2006/112 (formerly the Sixth Directive), with which domestic VAT law must be compatible, whereas charity law throughout the EU differs from state to state. Although the Directive requires certain supplies to be exempt from VAT, and limits some of these exemptions to charities or other non-profit making bodies, it does not mandate any specific VAT treatment for charities. There is, thus, a degree of responsibility left to domestic legislation, albeit within the parameters laid down by the Directive.

20.3 To prevent distortion of competition, VAT legislation is designed to avoid any unfair advantage resulting to one supplier over another. For this reason, where charities undertake activities that bring them into direct competition with commercial entities, they are subject to the same rules for VAT purposes as those commercial entities. A general relief for charities would be anti-competitive.

20.4 There is provision in Annex III of the Directive for the supply of goods and services by certain organisations engaged in welfare or social security work to be subject to reduced rates of VAT, as long as they are not otherwise exempt. This is not a requirement on member states, and at the time of writing, the UK has not adopted this measure.

20.5 A supply by a charity, therefore, will be exempt, standard-rated, zero-rated, outside the scope of VAT or subject to any other reduced rate of VAT currently available in the UK.

The Scope of VAT

20.6 VAT is charged on the supply by a 'taxable person' of goods or services in the course of a business, including 'all forms of supply, but not anything done otherwise than for a consideration'. A taxable person is someone who is, or is required to be, registered for VAT (see **20.176**). Being 'in business' for

VAT purposes does not require a person to have a profit motive; a loss-making or subsidised activity can be a business as much as a commercial concern. The exemption from direct tax for primary purpose trading does not equate to a blanket VAT exemption.

20.7 'Consideration' can be a difficult concept to pin down. Many charities now receive funding under contract, with 'key performance indicators' and targets to be met. It is important to remember that it is the nature of the activity, not the wording of the associated documentation (although this can be illuminating), that is determinative for VAT purposes. If there is a clear and direct link or 'nexus' between the activity to be undertaken and the money to be received, this will constitute a supply made in return for consideration.

20.8 The taxability of grants, subsidies or general funding is a complex issue. Generally speaking, receiving restricted funding does not in itself mean that a supply is being made, and HM Revenue & Customs (HMRC) accept that 'good housekeeping' requires funding bodies, particularly grant-making charities and public bodies, to receive reports on how their money has been spent. However, if funding is given with a contractual obligation placed upon the recipient to do something in return for that funding, this will be a supply, a business activity, and within the scope of VAT. Where the line is drawn is often a matter of extremely fine judgement.

20.9 HMRC will often refer charities to the published 'business test' to assist in this, but unfortunately this is of little help in distinguishing between non-business grants and business consideration, as it focuses on differentiating between activities carried on for business and pleasure, rather than the activities of the charity sector. For example, the test implies that a business is carried on if an activity is 'a serious undertaking earnestly pursued', which for a charity should describe all of its activities, whether business or non-business. If referred to the business test by HMRC, therefore, a charity would be advised to seek specialist professional assistance instead of simply responding to the listed questions, as it is perfectly possible for a non-business project to 'tick all the boxes' of the business test if its inherent weaknesses, and other relevant information relating to the project, are not pointed out.

20.10 When faced with a funding agreement and trying to determine if this is a contract for services (business) or a grant agreement (non-business), there can be no checklist for resolving the issue. The following aspects of a project may however be of assistance.

- 'Ownership' of the project – if the funding body develops the idea for a project and then seeks a 'subcontractor' to deliver it, this implies that the subcontractor will be making supplies to the funder. Conversely, if a charity develops a project and approaches a funder seeking their support, particularly if they approach several potential funders for the same project, this is more likely (although not definitively) to result in a grant.

- Costing of the project – if a charity is seeking funding to meet only a part of the expected costs, and meeting the remainder out of own resources or match funding, this implies that they are seeking a grant. Given the current focus on charities seeking 'full cost recovery' for government-funded projects, however, the converse does not necessarily mean that a business activity will result. Seeking to make a surplus on a contract would, however, strongly imply that this is a business activity.

- 'Tendering' – if a funder invites bids under a competitive tender for a specific project, particularly if this is open also to non-charitable organisations, this implies that a business relationship will result. Conversely, if a funder has a pot of money available and invites 'bids' from applicants proposing a range of projects, this is more likely (again, not definitively) to result in a grant.

- Intellectual property – many grant agreements include provision for IP to be shared in a non-commercial way (under terms such as 'worldwide non-exclusive royalty-free licence') which can be interpreted as simply 'good housekeeping', as above. The vesting of valuable IP solely in the funder for later commercial exploitation would, however, strongly imply that a supply is taking place.

20.11   Being 'within the scope of VAT' does not necessarily mean that VAT needs to be charged. Business activities may be exempt from VAT, or they may be subject to a reduced rate. As one of the reduced rates operated in the UK is a 0% rate, this means that a supply may be taxable without tax actually being charged. This is beneficial when VAT recovery is considered (see **20.20**).

20.12   Some exemptions and zero rates apply across the board, but charities do benefit from measures specific to the sector. These are contained in the Value Added Tax Act 1994 (VATA 1994) as follows:

Exempt:	Schedule 9	Group 6 (Education)
		Group 7 (Health and Welfare)
		Group 9 (Membership Subscriptions)
		Group 10 (Sports Services)
		Group 12 (Fundraising Events)
		Group 13 (Cultural Services)
Zero-rated:	Schedule 8	Group 4 (Purchase of Aids for Blind People)
		Group 12 (Purchase and supply of Aids for the Handicapped)
		Group 15 (Sales of Donated Goods and purchase of Advertising and 'relevant goods')

20.13   A reduced rate of 5% also exists, which serves to reduce VAT bills on residential and other accommodation, the most pertinent measures for charities being:

Reduced rate:	Schedule 7A	Group 1 (Domestic Fuel and Power)
		Group 2 (Energy Saving Materials)
		Group 6 (Qualifying Conversions)

Exemption

20.14   Exempt supplies must not be confused with zero-rated supplies or activities outside the scope of VAT (non-business). Many types of supplies typically made by charities are exempt as these follow from the Directive exemptions for activities in the public interest. While exemption means that VAT is not charged on the value of the supplies, it severely restricts the charity's ability to recover VAT on its inputs (see **20.20**), as VAT is only recoverable on costs which can be attributed to taxable supplies.

20.15   Some exempt supplies, such as financial services or land, are exempt no matter who provides them, but others are only exempt under special circumstances, usually contingent on the provider being an 'eligible body' for the purposes of that supply. The qualifying criteria for eligibility differ from group to group, and so charities should not assume that their activities will automatically be exempt.

Exempt supplies are dealt with in detail at section 5 (**20.126–20.159**).

The zero rate

20.16   The benefit of the zero rate as opposed to exemption is that VAT on costs attributable to taxable supplies is recoverable. Zero-rating applies to several types of supply made by charities, such as the sale of donated goods. It can also apply to supplies to charities, in which case it may also be called 'VAT relief'.

20.17   As exceptions to the normal rule that VAT is due at the standard rate, the zero-rating provisions are very narrowly drawn, and contained in some of the most complex parts of the legislation. These supplies are discussed at greater length in the sections on property (section 3 (**20.58–20.115**)) and specific reliefs (section 4 (**20.116–20.158**)).

20.18   Zero-rating is not available in every member state of the EU, and is only available in the UK during such time as the transitional arrangements and derogations allowed by the Directive continue.

20.19   The scope of the reduced rate may change as the European Union becomes more harmonised. At present, the 5% rate applies to some supplies connected to residential and charity property, which are discussed in section 3 (**20.58–20.115**).

2   VAT recovery

20.20   Although charities are treated as any other taxpayer when it comes to VAT compliance, they are in a significantly different position from most commercial concerns in that not all of their activities are in the sphere of business. This restricts their ability to recover VAT on costs even before having to take exempt supplies into account. Certain activities, like making grants or providing services free of charge, are not business activities and so are outside the scope of VAT.

20.21   A charity can undertake activities under three headings: 'non-business'; 'business-exempt'; or 'business-taxable supplies'. Input tax recovery is restricted to VAT incurred in the course of making taxable supplies, and so a two-stage calculation process is required to establish recovery where a charity is active in all three areas and incurs VAT that is not wholly and directly attributable:

(a)   business/non-business apportionment – splits the VAT incurred on all activities between business (ie exempt or taxable supplies) and non-business (ie outside the scope);

(b)   partial exemption calculation – calculates the proportion of input tax (VAT attributable to business activities) which is recoverable (attributable to taxable supplies) and that which is irrecoverable (attributable to exempt supplies).

Examples of this are given later.

20.22   Charities should always seek to ring fence VAT that is directly attributable to either non-business or business activities, or to taxable or exempt supplies. Only VAT that cannot be directly attributed is subject to apportionment, whether by means of a business/non-business apportionment or a partial exemption method. This VAT is often referred to as 'overhead' or 'pot' VAT.

20.23   Following the *Church of England Children's Society v HM Revenue & Customs* [2005] EWHC 1692, VAT on the cost of generating non-business donations can be seen not as attributable to a non-business activity (generating the income stream) but to the activities that the income goes to support.

20.24   Thus, if the donations raised only support activities that generate taxable income, the VAT on the fundraising costs can be recovered in full. If the donations support only exempt or non-business activities, the VAT is irrecoverable. If it supports all the activities of a charity and these involve some taxable activities, it is pot VAT and eligible for partial recovery.

Business/non-business apportionment

20.25   The first stage in the calculation process is to determine what proportion of VAT incurred can be attributed to the carrying on of business activities.

20.26   Tax on inputs relating wholly to business activities, both exempt and taxable, is called input tax, and is carried forward to the partial exemption calculation. Tax on inputs relating wholly to non-business activities is not 'input tax' within the strict meaning of VATA 1994, and is not recoverable. Where tax is incurred on inputs which relate to both business and non-business activities, an apportionment must take place to determine the proportion which can fairly and reasonably be attributed to business activities.

20.27 Here it is very important to differentiate between non-business income (such as donations) and non-business activities (free provision supported only by non-business income or own resources). Following the *Children's Society* case mentioned above, simply receiving non-business income does not in itself require restriction of VAT recovery; only carrying on a non-business activity requires this.

20.28 For example, a charity may be set up to run a religious bookshop. While it may receive donations and grants, if all its activities involve making a charge (selling books and other items), it will be wholly business and will not need a business/non-business apportionment.

20.29 Conversely, if the charity also runs a crèche and does not charge fees for this, covering the relevant costs from investment income and donations, this is 'free' and a non-business activity. VAT on the relevant direct costs will be irrecoverable, and VAT on overheads relating both to this activity and the business of the bookshop will be subject to business/non-business apportionment.

20.30 There is no default 'standard method' for performing this attribution; HMRC will not normally confirm their acceptance of a business/non-business method in a binding way. However, it is usually advisable to notify any proposed method to HMRC for their comments, to minimise the risk that the method will be challenged later. Any method proposed to HMRC will need to produce a 'fair and reasonable' result.

20.31 Possible bases for attribution include the proportion of business income to total income, floor space used wholly for business purposes over total floor space, or staff numbers used wholly for business purposes over total staff numbers. Given that charities will often be receiving significant amounts of income from donations, it may be desirable to look at methods other than the income-based approach, although is may be possible to agree a method that excludes unrestricted non-business income. Alternatively one can consider a cost-based method.

20.32 As the point of a business/non-business apportionment is to establish a proper attribution of costs to business and non-business activities, it may seem most appropriate to use cost to determine this. However, one must consider the correct approach – compare:

1   Business costs
     Business and Non-business costs

2   Business costs
     Total costs

20.33 The second of these approaches would include the overhead costs that the ratio aims to apportion. This can be criticised firstly for being a circular calculation and secondly for effectively treating overheads as wholly non-business in the calculation. Without further practical reasons for adopting the first approach and excluding overhead costs, however, neither argument will cut much ice with HMRC, who stress that 'we are concerned with achieving a fair and reasonable result, not with the mathematical purity of calculations'.

Example 1

20.34   For example, Charity X has several areas of activity. It solicits restricted donations to support its non-business activities (free summer schools), runs an independent school, and publishes books. VAT on inputs relating wholly to its business activities, the publication of books and the running of the school, is carried forward to the partial exemption calculation. VAT suffered on inputs relating wholly to the summer schools is not carried through. VAT not wholly relating to either activity needs apportioning.

- The income from donations for the summer schools is £100,000.

- School fees are £150,000.

- Income from selling books is £50,000.

Therefore, if apportionment were to be done on an **income-based method**, the calculation would be:

VAT to be apportioned $\times \dfrac{(150k + 50k)}{(150k + 50k + 100k)} = $ 67% VAT through to partial exemption calculation

Floor space

20.35   All the activities are carried on at one site. The fundraising office is very small, taking up only 10m^2. The school takes up 300m^2, and the printing press takes up 190m^2. If the apportionment were to be based on floor space, therefore, the calculation would be:

VAT to be apportioned $\times \dfrac{(300 + 190)}{(300 + 190 + 10)} = $ 98% VAT through to partial exemption calculation

20.36   However, HMRC could argue that as the summer schools take place in the main school area, this 300m^2 is not 'wholly business' and this may need to be allowed for, perhaps on the basis of time. For example, if the school has three terms of 14 weeks for fee-paying students, an eight-week period in which it holds the summer schools and shuts for one week at Christmas and one week at Easter, one could calculate the 'business floor space' (excluding the Christmas and Easter breaks when the building is not used at all) as:

$$300m^2 \times \frac{42}{50} = 252m^2$$

The result for the business/non-business method would then be:

VAT to be apportioned $\times \dfrac{(252 + 190)}{(300 + 190 + 10)} = $ 88% VAT through to partial exemption calculation

Staff numbers

20.37   Alternatively, staff numbers could be used. The fundraising team consists of six people working full-time. There are 30 members of staff at the school and 14 working the printing press. The calculation on this basis would therefore be:

VAT to be apportioned $\times \dfrac{(30 + 14)}{(30 + 14 + 6)} = $ 88% VAT through to partial exemption calculation

20.38 Again, if the school staff also work in the summer schools, they may also need to be 'pre-apportioned' based on, for example, the time spent on each activity. Using the same time figures as above, this would mean 'business school staff' of:

$$30 \times \frac{42}{50} = 25$$

And a resulting business/non-business calculation of:

VAT to be apportioned $\times \dfrac{(25 + 14)}{(30 + 14 + 6)} = $ 78% VAT through to partial exemption calculation

20.39 One can see from these calculations that the basis of apportionment can significantly affect the amount of VAT which is carried through to the partial exemption calculation. The charity must take a view on which method gives the most fair and reasonable result, and put this to HMRC to seek their views.

Partial exemption

20.40 The input tax wholly related to business activities and the proportion of VAT on overheads attributed to business activities by the business/non-business apportionment is carried forward to the next stage in the calculation process, the partial exemption calculation.

20.41 It must now be determined what input tax relates to taxable supplies and what to exempt supplies. That which is wholly related to the making of taxable supplies is recoverable in full. That which is wholly related to the making of exempt supplies is irrecoverable. This is called direct attribution, and all traders are required to directly attribute as much of their input tax as possible. Only where VAT cannot be directly attributed is a partial exemption apportionment required for the resultant overhead costs.

20.42 There is a standard method for apportioning such overhead or 'pot' input tax. This applies the ratio of taxable supplies to total business supplies to the pot input tax. An 'on account' calculation is required each quarter followed by an annual adjustment calculation which adjusts the sum of the four quarters to actual figures over the year. The annual adjustment is normally performed in the quarter after the end of the VAT tax year to which it relates. In April 2009 HMRC announced two optional simplifications to the standard method. The first is that the recovery rate for the previous year can be used as a provisional rate for the current year and secondly, the annual adjustment can be carried out in the last period in the VAT tax year.

20.43   If a charity wishes to use a non-standard method of apportioning their pot input tax (for example, one based on cost, floor space, staff numbers or any other criteria not matching the standard method), they can propose their alternative method to HMRC for approval as a special method. This method must produce a 'fair and reasonable' result if its use is to be approved, and must be accompanied by a declaration by the charity that this is the case, and that 'reasonable steps' have been taken to ensure that the person signing the declaration 'is in possession of all relevant information'. If this is not the case, or the declaration is made inappropriately, HMRC have the power to backdate changes to the agreed method, rather than having the power only to require changes from a current date. It may be difficult for larger charities, particularly those with regional offices or branches in other countries, to make this declaration; the signatory must ensure that they have been fully briefed on all the activities carried on to be able to sustain supportive arguments for the use of the proposed method in every case.

20.44   The sale of capital goods (assets used for the purposes of the business) and incidental supplies of land, such as the renting out of property, are excluded from partial exemption calculations, although if the supply is taxable, all wholly attributed input tax can of course be recovered. This measure aims to prevent distortion of recovery. If a special method is agreed, HMRC may also seek to exclude some other activities from the calculation in an attempt to reach the most 'fair and reasonable' result. Whether or not hiring out space etc is 'incidental' may also require agreement with HMRC.

Example 2

20.45   Charity X, therefore, has brought forward the VAT wholly related to business activities and that attributed to business activities using whichever method was settled upon and notified to HMRC. They now need to calculate their partial exemption method, which will let them know how much input tax incurred is actually recoverable.

20.46   The two business activities of Charity X are the running of the school (an exempt activity) and the printing and selling of books (a zero-rated taxable activity). The input tax which can be directly attributed to the running of the school is not recoverable. That which is directly attributed to the running of the printing press is fully recoverable. The 'pot', as before, can be apportioned in several different ways.

20.47   The standard method takes the taxable income of Charity X and compares it with the total business income. This method does not require HMRC approval, although they are allowed to direct the use of another method if they deem it necessary for 'the protection of the Revenue'. As before, income from school fees is £150,000, and from the printing press, £50,000. The standard method calculation would therefore be:

$$\text{Input tax} \times \frac{50,000}{(150,000 + 50,000)} = 25\% \text{ VAT recoverable}$$

Floor space

20.48 Alternatively, Charity X could propose a special method. As before, the floor space of the school is 300m², and that of the printing press is 190m². The calculation based on floor space would therefore be:

$$\text{Input tax} \times \frac{190}{300 + 190} = 39\% \text{ input tax recoverable}$$

However, if the floor space must be apportioned to take account of non-business use, the result would be:

$$\text{Input tax} \times \frac{190}{252 + 190} = 43\% \text{ input tax recoverable}$$

Staff numbers

20.49 Another special method to propose could be based on staff numbers. As before, 30 members of staff work in the school and 14 in the printing press. The calculation would therefore be:

$$\text{Input tax} \times \frac{14}{30 + 14} = 32\% \text{ input tax recoverable}$$

However, if the school staff need to be apportioned to take account of their involvement in the non-business activities, the result would be:

$$\text{Input tax} \times \frac{14}{25 + 14} = 36\% \text{ input tax recoverable}$$

20.50 As with the business/non-business method of apportionment, the basis of the partial exemption calculation can make a significant difference to the actual amounts recoverable by a charity. If the bulk of overhead VAT will go through both methods, it is worth considering the cumulative effect. Combined business/non-business and partial exemption methods are not currently allowed, but this is currently under consultation (and some older methods may cover both aspects, although the passage of time since this was possible suggests that such methods would warrant review). The calculations above can be summarised as follows:

Basis	Without 'pre-apportionment'			With 'pre-apportionment'		
	Business %	Taxable %	Cumulative %	Business %	Taxable %	Cumulative %
Income	67%	25%	16.75%	*Not applicable*		
Floor space	98%	39%	38.22%	88%	43%	37.84%
Staff	88%	32%	28.16%	78%	36%	28.08%

20.51 While Charity X might prefer to base their calculations on floor space, therefore, HMRC would need to be convinced that such a recovery rate would produce a fair and reasonable result before it would be advisable to use such a method.

De minimis limits

20.52   Low levels of exempt input tax, ie VAT directly attributable to exempt activities added to the exempt proportion of overhead input tax, can be recovered if it meets specific criteria. These are that the amount of exempt input tax is less than £625 per month on average and less than 50% of total input tax incurred. Both tests must be met for the exempt VAT to be recovered, and the calculations should be done both quarterly on a provisional basis and then adjusted for the full year's figures when the annual adjustment is calculated (see **20.42**).

Over-ride provisions

20.53   Two measures exist aimed at ensuring that VAT recovery is fair and reasonable and preventing distortions from arising. Both of these measures apply only to partial exemption calculations.

20.54   The standard method over-ride requires traders to adjust their VAT recovery where the standard method gives a result that is substantially different from one based on the use of the purchases in question. This requires traders to adjust their VAT recovery where the standard method gives a result that is substantially different from one based on the use of the purchases in question. How one is to calculate a 'use percentage' is not clear, and the basis of any such calculation should be agreed with HMRC. 'Substantially different' is defined as being different by £50,000 or more, or 50% or more of overhead input tax (being not less than £25,000).

20.55   Differences could arise where high levels of taxable income are received from supplies that do not 'consume' commensurate amounts of inputs; for example, if VAT on the refurbishment of head office is recovered as per the partial exemption method, whereas the bulk of the taxable activities of a charity are carried on at other sites, such as shops. The over-ride requires an adjustment to reflect the actual level of taxable activity carried on at head office, if this exceeds the above limits. This provision only applies to the standard method, although HMRC may require similar measures to be included in any special method proposed to them.

20.56   Secondly, a special method over-ride exists, which, unlike the standard method over-ride, which seeks to adjust recovery within the framework of an existing partial exemption method, aims to replace an 'unsuitable' special method for an interim period while a replacement is developed. If the difficulty of establishing what is a fair and reasonable apportionment is the primary reason why a method can take time to be prepared, it is not clear how a fair and reasonable 'interim method' can be imposed at a moment's notice. In light of this, the claim that this will prevent businesses from being disadvantaged seems disingenuous. However, the over-ride is meant to prevent taxpayers from deliberately delaying developing and agreeing a new method in order to retain the existing method as long as possible. Normally, unless there is significant disagreement with HMRC, new methods can be back-dated to have effect from the beginning of the current accounting period.

Example 3

20.57   The end result of this process can be summarised as follows:

- the Trustees of Charity X have decided to use staff numbers to calculate business/non-business apportionment, and have agreed to 'pre-apportion' these based on time, so the business percentage is 78%;

- they have decided to use the standard method of partial exemption, which gives a taxable percentage of 25%; and

- they then have to consider whether the standard method over-ride applies.

Business/non-business apportionment:

- VAT directly attributable to non-business activities is £1,500 – this is not recoverable;

- VAT directly attributable to business activities is £39,500 – this is carried forward to the partial exemption calculation; and

- overhead VAT is £14,500 – the percentage resulting from using staff numbers to perform the apportionment is 78%, so £11,310 is carried forward to the partial exemption calculation.

Partial exemption method:

- of the £39,500 VAT directly attributable to business activities, £1,500 is directly attributable to exempt supplies – this is not recoverable;

- of the £39,500 VAT directly attributable to business activities, £1,000 is directly attributable to taxable supplies – this is recoverable in full;

- therefore, of the £39,500 VAT directly attributable to business activities, the remaining £37,000 is overhead input tax;

- the £11,310 VAT attributed to business activities by the business/non-business apportionment is also overhead input tax;

- the total overhead input tax is therefore £37,000 + £11,310 = £48,310 – the standard method of partial exemption gives a recovery rate of 25%, which means that £12,077.50 is attributed to taxable supplies; and

- the total recoverable VAT without considering the standard method over-ride is therefore £1,000 + £12,077.50 = £13,077.50.

However:

Standard method over-ride:

- of the £37,000 that was directly attributable to business activities but treated as an overhead in the partial exemption method, £35,000 related to the construction of a new hall;

- the VAT on the hall was put into the 'pot' as it contains a small bookshop in the foyer, but it is otherwise used by the school for exempt educational purposes (the hall is not used by the summer schools so there is no non-business use);

- the charity therefore needs to consider the difference between the amount recovered under the partial exemption method (25%) and the amount recoverable based on use , for example based on the floor space taken up by the bookshop, say, 10% of the total;

- the amount recovered under the partial exemption method was £35,000 @ 25% = £8,750;

- the amount recoverable based on use is £35,000 @ 10% = £3,500;

- the difference between these two amounts is £5,250 – as this is below £50,000 and 25% of total input tax being at least £25,000, no adjustment is necessary.

However, if the hall involved a larger capital spend of £2 million plus £350,000 VAT (assuming a standard rate of 17½% for the purposes of longevity of this publication), the difference would be:

£350,000 × 25% = £87,500 (under the standard method)

£350,000 × 10% = £35,000 (under the use-based floorspace method)

Difference = £52,500

This is larger than £50,000 so is 'substantially different', and repayable to HMRC.

3   Property

20.58   Some of the most important reliefs available to charities relate to property and construction. Zero-rating applies to supplies in the course of construction of a new building, or the first sale of a major interest in a new building, provided the property in question is used for a relevant residential purpose or a relevant charitable purpose. A major interest is a freehold interest or a lease exceeding 21 years. Listed buildings are also eligible for VAT relief on some works of 'approved alteration' (see **20.84**), and the reduced rate can apply to conversion works in qualifying buildings (see **20.88**), some of which can be zero-rated on sale. It should be noted that these reliefs apply only to physical construction or conversion services and materials used; professional services such as those of architects, surveyors, or VAT advisors (!) are not eligible for relief where supplied separately (see **20.90**).

20.59   'Relevant purposes' are more narrowly drawn than might be expected from the terminology. Use for a relevant charitable purpose does not simply mean use by a charity; it means use by a charity *either* otherwise than in the course or furtherance of a business, *or* as 'a village hall or similarly in providing social or recreational facilities for a local community'. As mentioned previously, being 'in business' for VAT purposes is very different from commercial trading, and case law surrounding what constitutes a village hall is also very complex. This is explained in detail at **20.70**.

20.60   Use for a relevant residential purpose encompasses a wide but not unrestricted range of residential accommodation as well as dwellings, as detailed at **20.79**.

What is a building?

20.61 In order to qualify for zero-rating, structural requirements must first be met. Zero-rating applies to the construction of a new building, but the scope of this is restricted based upon the nature of the construction and its relationship with any existing buildings already on site.

20.62 The construction of a building does not include the conversion, reconstruction or alteration of an existing building (see **20.84** for rules relating to listed buildings). It does not include the enlargement or extension of an existing building, except to the extent that an additional dwelling or dwellings are created. Finally, it does not include the construction of an annexe to an existing building, unless it is used for a relevant charitable purpose, and meets specific structural criteria.

What is an annexe?

20.63 To qualify as a relevant charitable annexe, a new construction:

- must be capable of functioning independently from the existing building; and

- the only means of access, or, where there is more than one means of access, the main means of access, to the annexe is not via the existing building and vice versa.

20.64 In the case of *Grace Baptist Church v Customs and Excise Comrs* (1999) VAT Decision 16093, the Tribunal consulted the Shorter Oxford English Dictionary to aid in establishing the definition of an annexe, and, finding it to be 'a supplementary building or wing', pointed out that this meant that an annexe could be either a separate or a connected building, so long as it is a (lesser) building supplemental to another (greater) one. This approach was confirmed in *Cantrell (t/a Foxearth Lodge Nursing Home) v Customs & Excise Comrs* [2003] EWHC 404 (Ch), which, as a court case rather than a Tribunal decision, has the weight of precedent. The judgment included the following guidance:

> 'An annexe is an adjunct or an accessory to something else ... a supplementary structure, be it a room, a wing, or a separate building.'

20.65 However, HMRC state in their guidance (Notice 708) that for VAT purposes only an attached structure can be an annexe; freestanding buildings are to be treated as such whatever their function. This is because HMRC interprets the findings of the Tribunal and Court as meaning that an annexe is 'supplementary' in *structural* terms, not in relation to its function. Thus, only the degree of physical integration is relevant and this at most is 'tenuous'. Function is however relevant in that an annexe should be used for 'activities distinct from but associated with the activities carried out in the existing building'. The example used is of a residential hospice constructing an annexe to house a day-care facility. Thus, function must be distinct, but not necessarily subsidiary.

20.66 Problems have arisen where a new construction, while connected to an existing building, is structurally 'more important' such that the existing buildings end up as an 'adjunct or accessory' to the new building. In such cases, HMRC have been known to agree that despite the internal connection, the new construction is a new building, rather than an annexe, which therefore allows for zero-rating if use is for relevant residential purpose rather than relevant charitable purpose. This treatment would however depend entirely on the facts and on a case-by-case basis.

Certificates

20.67 Where buildings are to be used for relevant residential purpose or relevant charitable purpose, only the 'end user', ie the organisation that will operate the building, is eligible to claim relief; all earlier supplies in the chain are standard-rated. Thus, in order to benefit from the zero-rating or reduced rating on works of construction, approved alteration, or conversion, the charity must issue a certificate. In the case of construction services, the contractor should hold the certificate before zero-rating the work. By concession, HMRC allow a certificate to be issued after a supply has been made 'in genuine cases' (for example, where an invoice has been issued before the liability of the supply has been confirmed, which can take time if HMRC approval is needed), but in general terms certificates should not be issued on a retrospective basis.

20.68 Zero-rated disposals of property must also be supported by a certificate issued by the purchaser.

20.69 It is recommended that a charity confirms the eligibility for zero-rating or reduced-rating of the project in question before issuing a certificate, as a penalty equal to the difference between tax paid and tax due can result if a certificate is incorrectly issued, on top of also paying the correct amount of VAT.

A relevant charitable purpose

20.70 The difficulty of establishing use 'otherwise than in the course or furtherance of a business' was mentioned earlier; profit is not the benchmark of being in business. If a charity uses a building in connection with trading, fundraising events or other activities where supplies are made for a consideration, whether taxable or exempt, this is business use and prevents relief from applying unless it is de minimis.

20.71 HMRC now accept some business use as long as the non-business use exceeds 95% of the total use of the building. This can be calculated based on any method that is fair or reasonable. Historically, by concession which was withdrawn in June 2009 but can be applied to building started before 2010, HMRC would allow up to 10% business use measured on time used, or floor space or user numbers, although the latter two methods required HMRC approval, as does the application of the 'time used' method for a part, rather than the whole, of a building. The floor space and headcount methods cannot be applied to a part of a building.

20.72   This concession caused problems as the methods could not be combined and as any 'mixed' use was treated as non-qualifying. For example, if the floor space method is used by a school, it is of no relevance that a room is used only one hour per week for business lettings and the remainder of the time for non-business use; it is 'mixed purpose' and therefore non-qualifying floor space for the purposes of the calculation. Similarly, if the user-numbers basis is used, the charity cannot treat a pupil attending 40 hours per week for non-business education as 'worth more' than someone coming for one hour a week to a sports club and paying for that; both are 'one user' for the purposes of the calculation.

20.73   However, with the withdrawal of the concession, methods to determine business use can be mixed if they produce a fair result.

20.74   As an alternative to non-business use, use for a relevant charitable purpose also includes use as a village hall, which can be even more problematic. Although a degree of business use (hire charges etc) can be expected in such cases, Customs guidance on what constitutes a village hall or similar is regarded by many as being too narrow for practical application.

20.75   Customs and Excise consider that the ownership and management of the village hall is usually vested in local trustees drawn from representatives of local groups who use the facilities of the hall, ie that it is operated by a specific 'village hall' charity, rather than covering buildings used by charities with broader aims, or focusing on a particular group or groups in the local community. While the inclusion of 'or similarly' may avoid this condition having to be met in every case, HMRC's view on the use of such a building is equally restrictive; it should be 'the traditional, small, multi-purpose community hall and does not extend to all recreational facilities to the community'.

20.76   The key case is that of Jubilee Hall (*Jubilee Hall Recreation Centre Ltd v Customs and Excise Comrs* [1999] STC 381), a building used by a charity to provide recreational facilities in Covent Garden. The Court of Appeal held that it was not a village hall 'or similar', on the grounds that it was a commercial concern on a scale which could not reasonably be equated to that of 'a village hall'. It was also held to be of an overly specialised nature. The *Jubilee Hall* case was joined with that of *St Dunstan's Educational Foundation*, a fee-paying school that allowed community use of its facilities when not needed by the school. This also failed to convince the Court that it was similar to a village hall, and this element of the judgment has been used by HMRC to resist arguments that, for example, new City Academies are village halls, despite the fact that their funding agreements contain the requirement that they allow community use of their facilities.

20.77   However, in another case, *Bennachie Leisure Centre Association v Customs and Excise Comrs* (1996) VAT Decision 14276, the Tribunal allowed zero-rating of a property on the grounds that, although a similar kind of establishment to Jubilee Hall, membership of the leisure centre was automatic within a certain geographical area, and that area, in the Scottish highlands, was easier to define as a 'local community' than the neighbourhood of Covent

Garden. Similarly, in *Southwick Community Association v Customs & Excise Comrs* (2002) VAT Decision 17601, the Tribunal held that occupation of the majority of the building by three theatre/opera companies did not prevent zero-rating, as all parties were charities seeking only to cover their costs.

20.78   When considering this point, it should be remembered that the Court of Appeal decision in *Jubilee Hall/St Dunstans* is binding on all lower courts, whereas the Tribunal decisions in *Bennachie* and *Southwick* are not. The decision in *Jubilee Hall* can only be departed from where the facts are significantly different. Therefore, where business activities are carried on, to qualify as being relevant charitable seems to be restricted to the multipurpose, small-scale properties envisaged in published guidance (HMRC Internal Guidance Volume V1-8A section 15.7).

A relevant residential purpose

20.79   Buildings which qualify as being used for a relevant residential purpose are:

(a)   a home or other institutions providing residential accommodation for children;

(b)   a home or other institutions providing residential accommodation with personal care for persons in need of personal care by reason of old age, disablement, past or present dependence on alcohol or drugs or past or present mental disorder;

(c)   a hospice;

(d)   residential accommodation for students or school pupils;

(e)   residential accommodation for members of the armed forces;

(f)   a monastery, nunnery or similar establishment; or

(g)   an institution which is the sole or main residence of at least 90% of its residents

except use as a hospital, prison or similar establishment or an hotel, inn or similar establishment.

These buildings can be split into two broad categories:

● 'residential accommodation', including (d) and (e), which need not constitute a totality of the relevant institution – ie a university with pre-existing student accommodation can build a new block and benefit from the zero-rate; and

● 'institutions', being the other types of building listed, where what is constructed should form the totality of the institution.

20.80   Assistance in defining the type of buildings that are included is provided by both precedent and guidance. A hospice, for example, may include a variety of activities including day care and outreach or 'hospice at home' services, and the management of fundraising, but the zero-rating for relevant residential use applies only to residential hospice care, note 3 being interpreted in the context of 'relevant residential' (although the funding situation of the hospice sector means that as non-residential care services are normally funded by grants and own resources, the zero-rate for relevant charitable purposes can often apply).

20.81 Where a line is drawn between the type of home specified in note 3(b) and a hospital 'or similar institution' was the subject of *Hospital of St John and St Elizabeth* Tribunal 19141 (2005), in which it was found that the institution in question, while having some qualified nursing staff and regular visits from doctors and consultant psychiatrists, provided for its residents, who were dementia sufferers, care rather than treatment, and so to provide them with 'a home for life and to maximise the quality of their life through social interaction with other residents, parties, concerts and other activities and through therapy to enhance mobility and independence'. Thus it was a home rather than a hospital 'or similar'.

20.82 Following two Tribunal cases, *Urdd Gobaith Cymru v Customs and Excise Comrs* (1997) VAT Decision 14881, and *Denman College v Customs and Excise Comrs* (1998) VAT Decision 15513, residential accommodation for students or school pupils can apply to accommodation for short-term courses, not just that used for full-time students.

20.83 Please note that annexes can only be zero-rated when used for a relevant charitable purpose; use for a relevant residential purpose is not sufficient. This means that annexes used for a relevant residential purpose will not be eligible for zero-rating unless they are also used for a relevant charitable purpose.

Listed buildings

20.84 Although works of alteration cannot normally be zero-rated, 'approved alterations' of protected buildings may be eligible for relief. A protected building is a listed building used for a relevant residential purpose or a relevant charitable purpose. Approved alterations are works that alter the fabric of a protected building, which require and receive listed building consent; repairs and maintenance are specifically excluded. Here, VAT law and planning policy are in some disagreement; VAT law requires structural change to achieve zero-rating, while for obvious reasons, listed building consent is more likely to require like-for-like replacements and discourage knocking down walls or relocating windows. In addition, listed building consent is now more likely to be granted on the basis of a 'package' of works rather than line-by-line, so it should not be assumed that all works in a project granted consent will automatically qualify for zero-rating; the nature of each item of work will be key.

20.85 In addition, zero-rating applies to the first grant of a major interest in a substantially reconstructed protected building. A building is substantially reconstructed if either:

- at least 60% of the cost of the reconstruction relates to approved alterations; or

- the reconstruction retains no more than the external walls, and other external features of architectural or historical interest.

20.86   Certificates must also be issued in connection with reliefs for listed buildings, as explained in **20.44**.

Listed places of worship

20.87   A relief is available in the form of a grant scheme to cover the VAT cost of works of repairs and maintenance to listed places of worship. The grant scheme was originally introduced as an interim measure while the EU looked at the question of reduced rates more generally, but this process is taking longer than the government expected, and the scheme is still operational. It may be that in the future it has to be rescinded if it constitutes 'state aid', but for now the 'LPW Scheme' is a valuable relief for the faith community, and further details are available from the Department for Culture, Media and Sport.

The reduced rate

20.88   The 5% reduced rate applies to certain residential conversions, some of which may be of benefit to charities. As well as 'changed number of dwellings conversions', the reduced rate also applies to 'special residential conversions', where a building is converted from a dwelling or non-residential use to use for a relevant residential purpose. This could include converting a house into a children's home or a convent. It does not, however, apply to the conversion of one type of relevant residential building to another. Again, relief applies only to physical works and materials, not to professional fees, and a certificate is needed to confirm eligibility for the 5% rate.

20.89   The reduced rate applies also to supplies of domestic fuel and power, which includes fuel and power used in buildings used for a relevant residential purpose or by a charity for non-business purposes. Such supplies are also exempt from the Climate Change Levy. The installation of energy-saving materials (insulation, heating controls, solar panels etc) in such buildings is also charged to VAT at 5%.

Design and Build

20.90   As professional fees are excluded from relief in their own right, some charities choose to use design and build structures whereby a single entity engages the design team as well as the building contractor(s), to make a single (zero-rated) supply of the construction of a building, thus removing the VAT cost that would otherwise arise on professional fees. In principle this can also apply to works of approved alteration and qualifying conversions.

20.91   However, this must be a fixed-price contract and as such careful planning is needed to ensure that a design and build structure will give rise to an overall saving; commercial contractors will normally charge a premium for taking on the risk associated with professional fees, and if a subsidiary is used, a contingency amount should be built into the price for the same reason, and any relevant additional compliance requirements also met. These could include VAT registration, compliance with the Construction Industry Scheme, and consideration of the direct tax position of the subsidiary if the contract extends over a year-end, as this could give rise to a need to pay up a deemed profit by Gift Aid, before the work is completed, to remove a tax charge.

Apportionment

20.92   Where a building will be used partly for a relevant purpose and part for a non-qualifying purpose, works can be apportioned between zero-rated and standard rated items, and while this has not been transposed into the law on protected buildings, this is recognised as a drafting error and an apportionment can also take place for alterations to a part of a listed building used for a relevant purpose.

Building materials

20.93   Finally, relief applies to building materials used in the course of construction, approved alteration, or conversion, but only to those incorporated into the site. These are defined as those materials 'ordinarily incorporated by builders in any building of that description' but there are statutory exclusions, being:

- furniture other that fitted kitchens;

- electrical or gas appliances other than to provide heat, ventilation, air cooling, air purification or dust extraction, burglar alarms, fire alarms and fire safety equipment, and alarm call systems, lifts or hoists;

- carpets and carpeting material.

The vexed question of what is or is not furniture, and the liability of other items that may be incorporated into a building, is detailed in Notice 708.

Change of use

20.94   There are several measures which adjust VAT reliefs and recovery to reflect changes in use of buildings. VATA 1994 Sch 10 aims to 'clawback' VAT relieved on the construction of new buildings, and is explained at **20.95**. The Capital Goods Scheme and other regulations can adjust the recovery of VAT charged, as detailed at **20.99** and **20.109**.

Schedule 10 clawback

20.95   Where a building, zero-rated as used for a qualifying purpose, is used within ten years of completion for a non-qualifying purpose, provisions exist within VATA 1994 Sch 10 to charge the VAT at standard rate. This applies both to grants of an interest in a building and to change in use by the occupier.

20.96   Where a grant is made of the building, and it is not used for a quali-fying purpose after the grant, the grant is deemed to be taxable. There is no loss to the vendor, as output tax being due on the grant validates recovery of input tax on the acquisition, which would have been charged had zero-rating not applied. However, it does mean that the person being granted the interest will be charged VAT, and may also be required to include the asset within the Capital Goods Scheme (see **20.99**). Also, if the parties are connected, the pro-visions of VATA 1994 Sch 6 operate to allow HMRC to assess for output VAT on the open market value of the supply.

20.97   Where use is changed without an interest being granted, this will be more problematic for the person owning the building in question. If use ceases to be qualifying, they must account for VAT on the amount originally paid and previously zero-rated, calculated on the basis of how many years of qualify-ing use have been completed. For example, if a building has been used for six years for a relevant qualifying purpose, on a change in use to a non-qualifying purpose, 40% of the VAT originally relieved will be payable to HMRC. The occupant may also need to include the asset within the Capital Goods Scheme, although this is not clear, and it would also need to be confirmed if the scheme runs from the date of the initial acquisition or only from the later date of the change of use 'self-supply'.

20.98   However, largely as a result of the problems faced by City Academies trying to obtain zero-rating before their capital projects were brought back under direct government control as part of the Building Schools for the Future programme, Schedule 10 clawback now only applies where there was an inten-tion at the outset that use would change within the ten-year-period.

Capital Goods Scheme

20.99   The Scheme applies to interests in property worth over £250,000 where VAT was incurred and computers worth over £50,000 plus VAT. In the case of computers, and interests in land which have less than ten years to run, the Scheme applies for five years, otherwise the Scheme applies for ten years. Land interests constituting capital items for this purpose include a freehold or leasehold interest acquired, or an alteration, extension or refurbishment of a property.

20.100   The Capital Goods Scheme ensures that input tax recovery fairly reflects the use made of the capital item by adjusting recovery over the relevant period of time. The charity recovers VAT at the recovery rate appropriate at the time of acquisition, and thereafter makes adjustments to reflect any change in recovery rates.

Example 4

20.101   If the VAT incurred on refurbishing a building is £70,000, and the recovery rate in the year of refurbishment is 50%, £35,000 can be recovered in that year. If the scheme runs for ten years, then £7,000 is eligible for adjustment in each of the nine following years.

20.102 If in the second year of the scheme, the recovery rate rises to 60%, this is an increase of 10% on the initial recovery, and an additional £700 (10% of £7,000) can be recovered.

20.103 If in the third year, the recovery rate is 45%, this is a decrease of 5% against original recovery, and £350 must be repaid to HMRC.

20.104 In each subsequent year, a similar calculation is performed, comparing the current recovery rate with the original recovery rate.

20.105 The treatment of the disposal of a capital item within the time frame of the scheme will also affect recovery. If the disposal is taxable, the recovery rate for each year thereafter is 100%, but if it is exempt, the recovery rate is nil. The difference between the original recovery rate and the rate applicable on disposal is applied to the combined 'tenths' eligible for the years remaining until the scheme runs out.

Example 5

20.106 If we assume that the original recovery rate was 50%, and that the VAT incurred was £100,000, then the amount liable to be adjusted in each year is £10,000.

If the building is disposed of after six years, the result where VAT is charged would be:

$$4 \times £10,000 @ (100\% - 50\%) = £20,000$$

to recover on disposal

This would be recoverable only where the VAT charged on disposal exceeds this aggregate final adjustment.

Where VAT is not charged, the result would be:

$$4 \times £10,000 @ (0\% - 50\%) = £20,000$$

to be repaid to HMRC

20.107 However, where the total amount of VAT recovered on a capital item, including in all scheme periods, is less than the VAT charged on the subsequent supply, 'save as the Commissioners may otherwise allow', the VAT recovered can be adjusted to be equal to that charged on the later supply. If the supply on is taxable but this results in a lower amount of output tax than input tax, it may be possible to agree that no adjustment is necessary if this is for 'legitimate reasons', ie a downturn in the property market, need for a quick sale, etc. An exempt supply of a capital item, on the other hand, could require repayment in full of all VAT recovered, although this will be for negotiation with HMRC.

Lennartz

20.108   Where VAT is incurred on a building that will be used partly for private purposes, there is the option to use the *Lennartz* mechanism whereby the VAT on the non-business element can initially be recovered in full, following which VAT is due on the deemed supply of the building for non-business purposes over time. The repayment period, effective from 1 November 2007, is ten years to bring it in line with the Capital Goods Scheme (previously the period was capped at 20 years in line with the duration of the option to tax). However, recent concerns have thrown into doubt whether a charity can have private use and now business use will not qualify as 'private'. Extreme care needs to be taken if trying to apply *Lennartz*.

Clawback and payback under regulations

20.109   Where goods or services are acquired that are not capital items, there is still the possibility of adjustment of recovery to reflect use under clawback provisions set out in VAT Regulations 1995, SI 1995/2518, reg 108. This applies to any supply, not just those connected to land. It provides for repayment of input VAT recovered on the basis of an intention to make taxable supplies where actual use within six years of the initial deduction is exempt. There are also 'payback' provisions in reg 109, where items purchased with a view to making exempt supplies are later used in the course of taxable activities. In both cases, similar measures apply to adjust recovery where intended use and actual use change from full or no recovery to partial recovery, and vice versa. The provisions apply only where intention changes before any use is made of the item, not where there is, for example, actual taxable use followed by a change to exempt use.

The option to tax

20.110   The holding of property for investment purposes is an issue for some charities. Whereas dividend income is outside the scope of VAT (non-business), and interest and income from dealing in shares is exempt, rental income can be taxable or exempt depending upon circumstance or choice. The renting of residential accommodation is always exempt from VAT, but if a charity holds investments in the form of commercial property, they have the option to elect to waive exemption from VAT. The sale of freehold commercial property less than three years old is standard-rated by statute, but otherwise the grant of an interest in land is exempt unless an option is taken.

20.111   The option to tax, or election to waive exemption, enables supplies of property to be treated instead as taxable. The charity is then able to recover the VAT that is attributable to the property, such as maintenance, utilities and other services. HMRC must be notified when an election has taken place and, where exempt supplies have previously been made of the property, their permission must normally be granted in writing before an election can be made.

20.112   The option to tax may be of benefit if a charity refurbishes an investment property prior to seeking new tenants. By opting, the VAT on the refurbishment will be recoverable. However, as exempt supplies have previously been made, HMRC's permission will be needed, and they may seek to restrict recovery of VAT incurred prior to the option being taken. It is vital, therefore, to consider the VAT implications right from the beginning of any such project in order to avoid an unnecessary VAT cost.

20.113   The legislation governing the option to tax contains significant anti-avoidance provisions to prevent the option being used to gain inappropriate recovery. Unfortunately, as with other anti-avoidance measures, many innocent parties can be caught. The measures act to 'disapply' an option where a person developing land expects or intends that it will become exempt land.

20.114   Exempt land is land used by the developer, the person financing the development, or a party connected to either of them, otherwise than 'wholly or substantially wholly for eligible purposes', meaning at least 80% for eligible purposes. 'Eligible purposes' means, in effect, making taxable supplies. This prevents parent charities from using subsidiary companies to develop land and recover VAT, for example, where the eventual use will be exempt healthcare or education.

20.115   The option cannot apply to dwellings, or buildings to be used for relevant residential purposes, except in very specific circumstances and with the agreement of all parties, or to buildings to be used for a relevant charitable purpose, except as an office.

4   Specific reliefs – zero-rating

20.116   As well as the reliefs available in relation to property, zero-rating can also apply to other goods and services purchased by charities and some supplies made by them. In the case of purchases, a charity must issue a certificate to its supplier to confirm that relief is appropriate. Some supplies are zero-rated regardless of the identity of the supplier or purchaser, such as printed matter (books, magazines and leaflets), but the following are those supplies where zero-rating is specific to the charitable sector.

Zero-rating of advertising services

20.117   The relief applies to 'a right to promulgate an advertisement by means of a medium of communication with the public', and supplies of services (and closely-related goods) in the design or production of such an advertisement. This applies equally to advertisements for fundraising, campaigning or recruitment purposes, and includes advertising online. It does not, however, include services relating to a charity's own website, whether design, hosting, maintenance or other costs.

20.118   As relief requires that the advertisement is 'communicated with the public', this does not apply where any persons who are reached by whatever particular medium used have been selected, which includes being selected by address or at random. This means that 'mailshots' and door-to-door leafleting are now outside the statutory relief, unless this is by means of leaflets or other items qualifying as zero-rated printed matter in their own right. However, by concession, certain goods used in connection with the collection of donations are zero-rated by concession (Extra-Statutory Concession 3.3). This applies to lapel stickers and similar low-cost, low-value items given in acknowledgement of unspecified donations, although any item sold for a price will remain standard rated. It also covers the purchase of specialised collecting tins and buckets used in the solicitation of cash donations, and certain printed matter used in mailshots that would not necessarily fall within the statutory relief for printed matter. This includes pre-printed appeal letters, envelopes for returning donations, and outer envelopes, providing both types of envelopes are over-printed with a reference to the appeal request, as well as collecting and stewardship envelopes used in door-to-door collections or available from churches or other places of worship.

20.119   The relief also only applies to services and goods of producing an advertisement which are bought in; any inputs used 'in-house' by a charity to produce their own adverts do not qualify. This means that engaging an independent advertising company to prepare the necessary advertisements, in the course of which they will engage subcontractors such as printers, designers etc, will be zero-rated. However, if a charity uses its own advertising department and uses the same subcontractors for the work that the independent company uses, their charges will be standard-rated.

Supplies to benefit disabled persons

20.120   Zero-rating applies to goods for the use of blind or handicapped people, or the supply of adapting or maintaining such goods. 'Handicapped' in VAT law means chronically sick or disabled. HMRC recognise that this is now not a term in general use and that it may cause offence, and do try to be sensitive to the particular circumstances of the persons or organisations with whom they are dealing. 'Disability' includes mental disability, and those who are blind, partially-sighted or who suffer from acute hearing loss can also qualify; a condition must have a significant detrimental effect on the ability of the individual to carry out day-to-day activities. Those who are frail simply because of old age are not considered to be 'handicapped', however, per precedent 'where the physical condition of the person in question is so impaired on account of old age or as the result of a chronic condition that he or she cannot get about without a wheelchair or a walking aid', he or she can, in the ordinary and accepted sense of the term, be said to be 'disabled'.

20.121   The goods covered include medical and surgical appliances, chair or stair lifts, hoists and vehicles designed solely for use by the disabled. HMRC guidance (Notice 701/7) contains guidance on specific items, and many suppliers will have agreed the liability of their products, but if in doubt, an approach should be made before zero-rating is claimed.

20.122 Relief also applies to works relating to disabled access to buildings, such as the construction of ramps, the installation of lifts and the provision of toilet facilities suitable for disabled users. Lifts must be installed either in a residence or day centre for disabled persons, although it is not necessary for all users of the building to be disabled. It is no longer accepted that educational establishments qualify for relief unless the lift is in residential accommodation. Relevant goods are also eligible for relief, which include medical and other equipment supplied to a charity providing medical care, or undertaking research, and the supply of vehicles adapted for the carriage of wheelchair users.

20.123 Relief also applies to medical equipment ('relevant goods') used by charities engaged in caring for disabled persons, and guidance (Notice 701/6) again covers the specific items that can be purchased without VAT, and by which institutions and organisations.

Donated goods

20.124 Charity shops provide a much-needed source of revenue for the sector, and charity auctions are also a popular way to raise funds. Both of these activities can benefit from zero-rating where the goods sold have been donated. An additional benefit is that the relief is extended to 'profits-to-charity-persons' as well as charities themselves. A profits-to-charity-person is a person who has agreed in writing to transfer the profits from a sale to a charity, or whose profits are otherwise payable to a charity. Therefore a charity's subsidiary company can be used to make supplies without suffering adverse VAT consequences.

20.125 If goods require renovation before sale, VAT is due on an apportioned amount. HMRC usually recognise that VAT need only be charged on an amount reflecting the cost of renovation, including any replaced elements. For example, if a bike is donated that needs a new chain, and a new chain is purchased for £8 + VAT, the bike is then sold on for £20 in total, the output tax to be accounted for will be calculated as follows:

Standard-rated element (17½% rate)	£8.00
VAT on standard-rated element	£1.40
Zero-rated element	£10.60
Total selling price	£20.00

5 Exemptions

20.126 Exempt supplies are business supplies not subject to VAT, but with the disadvantage that the supplier cannot recover VAT on attributable costs. As exempt supplies are normally supplied to individuals, and are for the public benefit (healthcare, education, cultural services), many charities are active in these areas and need to be aware of the VAT implications. This is one area where the nature of the supplier, as much as the nature of the supply, is crucial to the VAT liability of the supplies being made. Exemptions for certain activities in the public interest are mandatory, but some may be extended to 'bodies other than those governed by public law', provided they satisfy at least one of four specified conditions. Member states allowing this extension of exemption may require one or all of the conditions to be met by suppliers. The conditions allowed that the UK applies to different groups include:

- that the body is not systematically aiming to make a profit;

- that it is managed and administered on a voluntary basis; and

- that: 'exemption of the services concerned shall not be likely to create distortions of competition such as to place at a disadvantage commercial enterprises liable to value added tax.'

20.127 This results in the various requirements for 'eligible bodies' in several of the exempt groups in UK VAT law, specified where relevant.

Health and welfare services

20.128 Exemption applies inter alia to medical or surgical care or treatment in a hospital or state-regulated institution such as a registered nursing home. The provision of otherwise zero-rated supplies, such as surgical appliances or medicinal products, in the course of an exempt supply of healthcare is normally also exempt, but this does not apply if the institution is run by a charity. Thus charities can zero-rate certain supplies to in-patients or residents in qualifying institutions, providing this is not connected to any contract with a non-charitable body (for example, an NHS Trust cannot use a charity as 'purchasing agent' for goods and achieve zero-rating that it would not normally be able to achieve).

20.129 From 1 May 2007, the exemption for supplies by qualified healthcare professionals was amended to bring it in line with the exemption for supplies by institutions; this now requires that their services 'consist in medical care' rather than being medico-legal or other services not being 'hands-on care'. This may impact on the cost of research or other health-related services bought in by charities that does not consist in medical care.

20.130 Exemption applies to welfare services supplied by charities, which means:

- the provision of care, treatment or instruction designed to promote the physical or mental welfare of elderly, sick, distressed or disabled persons;

- the care or protection of children and young persons; or

- the provision of spiritual welfare by a religious institution as part of a course of instruction or a retreat, not being a course or a retreat designed primarily to provide recreation or a holiday.

20.131 'Care' of elderly or sick persons includes personal care services such as bathing, feeding or dressing, as well as 'routine domestic tasks' such as cooking and cleaning where the recipient has been assessed as being unable to carry out the tasks safely, adequately, or without significant pain or discomfort.

20.132 Unhelpfully, 'distressed' is not defined in the legislation, although guidance states that this could include circumstances such as severe pain, anguish or financial straits, depending upon the context. The definition of 'distressed' is particularly important given that welfare services are not only eligible for exemption, but that in certain circumstances, if provided by a charity, they are able to be treated as non-business activities by concession. These circumstances are that the services be provided to 'distressed persons for the relief of their distress', and that they are provided 'substantially below cost'. HMRC define this as meaning that activities must be subsidised by at least 15% from sources other than fees.

20.133 The difference between services being exempt from VAT and outside the scope of VAT may not appear to be important, as attributable VAT on costs is not recoverable by a charity in either event. However, as zero-rating of construction services can depend upon a charity using these for non-business purposes (see **20.58**), this concession can result in significant savings for charities undertaking building projects.

20.134 The care or protection of children and young persons is not limited to protecting them from physical harm, but also includes the improvement of a child's well-being and protection against 'malign influences'. However, HMRC draw their understanding of this activity somewhat more narrowly than is set down in the law, as they normally require children and young persons to be 'in need of protection' in order for the services to be exempt.

20.135 In *Parents and Children Together v Customs & Excise Comrs* (2001) VAT Decision 17283, a charity officially accredited to undertake inter-country adoption work assessed prospective parents. The VAT Tribunal found that these services were not eligible for exemption as they were not directly connected with the protection of children, as a prospective adoptive child would normally only be identified after a certificate was issued to parents. Any charity undertaking work in the child protection field should therefore be very careful if any activities do not involve a particular child.

20.136 In relation to spiritual welfare, charities involved in the provision of retreats often do not require retreatants to pay a fixed amount, and if only donations are solicited, this is not a business activity. Amounts received will only constitute consideration, and the services provided constitute a supply, if the amounts are required of the retreatant in order to receive those services. Interestingly, one can identify a focus on the motives of supplier and persons to whom the supply is made (those that pay), leaving out those of the recipient of the actual services; the *Evangelical Movement of Wales (2004 V018556)* concerned organised holidays for children that included a spiritual element, but also canoeing, abseiling, and social events. This was held to be exempt as the provision of spiritual welfare as the supplier and parents were focused on the spiritual benefits to the children of undertaking such activities in the particular environment, and saw this as simply a practical way to get children 'on retreat', disregarding the opinion of the children who may have considered themselves to be 'on holiday'.

20.137   As HMRC internal guidance perceptively points out, spiritual welfare 'can be a difficult concept to grasp not least because there are no visible indicators that the recipient has a need for [it]'. However, while guided retreats for groups or individuals are accepted to be spiritual welfare by HMRC, if a charity is providing the opportunity for retreats for private reflection, or silent retreats, this may not qualify. Some element of guidance must be present for exemption to apply.

20.138   Charities providing basic residential accommodation in a retreat house, without providing a structured retreat may be informed by HMRC that they are making supplies of 'bed & breakfast', which is a taxable supply. However inappropriate this may sound, guidance will continue to be determinative of what falls within the exemption, unless a VAT Tribunal decision causes them to rethink their position, or an appeal to a higher court sets a precedent.

Education

20.139   Education is exempt from VAT where the supplier is an 'eligible body'. This includes schools, colleges and universities, as well as a body that:

'is precluded from distributing and does not distribute any profit it makes; and applies any profits made ... to the continuance or improvement of such [educational] supplies'.

The onus of proving that one is not making a profit for VAT purposes is on the charity, and is not automatically accepted by HMRC, who are becoming stricter in their application of the second requirement: if a surplus is made on such activities, it must be ploughed back into educational supplies for exemption to be allowed.

20.140   Education includes one-off seminars or symposia as well as more traditional 'training courses'. It also applies to 'vocational training', which can be for paid or voluntary work. Exemption also applies to supplies of research, but only where both supplier and recipient are eligible bodies. This is an area of the law ruled upon by the *European Court of Justice in EC v Germany* (2002) Case C-287/00, where research was held to be outside the definition of 'education' that can be exempt under EU law. Despite the clear nature of the ruling, this issue remains 'under consultation', with HMRC careful to point out that research is often grant-funded (and therefore non-business) and that supplies to non-eligible bodies, or supplies of consultancy work, are outside the exemption in any event.

Sports services

20.141   The exemption of sports services also relies on the supplier being an 'eligible body', the requirements for which mirror those of the education exemption, with any profits arising needing to be reapplied to similar supplies, with a significant addition. An eligible body for the sports services exemption must be not subject to 'commercial influence'. While the application of this requirement is less stringent when applied to charities, it is still a complex area, resulting from anti-avoidance measures taken to prevent essentially commercial concerns from benefiting from exemption by effectively removing 'profit' by means of a P&L deduction for (over-)charges for rent, salary or other services provided by connected persons.

20.142 Exemption can only apply to services supplied to individuals, and if a membership scheme is operated, supplies to non-members will be taxable. Only sports services are included; charges for saunas, health suites, catering, parking and other ancillary supplies are not covered. In the *Highland Council (2007 CSIH 36)*, there was an inclusive fee for a range of activities, and the appellant sought to apportion the fee between taxable and exempt elements. The court held that the whole fee was taxable as payment for the right to access a variety of services. However, the Council is not a charity, and local authorities cannot be eligible bodies in this group, so the exempt elements of the 'package' fell within the education group (swimming lessons) rather than the sports services group. Those charities charging an all-in fee for access to their facilities are therefore in a different position as their 'packages' could include supplies exempt under group 10. This is understood to be the subject of a separate appeal at the time of writing.

Cultural services

20.143 'Eligible bodies' are also defined differently for the exemption for cultural services. Such services are rights of admission to museums, galleries, art exhibitions, zoos or theatrical, musical or choreographic performances 'of a cultural nature'. Again, the body must be non-profit making, and reapply any profits to the continuance or improvement of the facilities made available, but there is an added requirement in that it must be 'managed and administered on a voluntary basis by persons who have no direct or indirect financial interest in its activities'.

20.144 This used to be interpreted as meaning that all persons involved in management had to be unpaid volunteers, but following *Customs & Excise Comrs v London Zoological Society* (2002) Case C-267/00, this was held to be too narrow.

20.145 It is now accepted that bodies are eligible for exemption where the 'decisions of last resort' are taken by unpaid persons, allowing salaried staff to undertake day-to-day management decisions without endangering exemption.

20.146 Following further cases, including *Longborough Festival Opera (C3/2006/0369)* and *Bournemouth Symphony Orchestra (C3/2005/1681)*, HMRC now accept that a financial interest is only problematic where it is actual, not potential, and if a payment is received. Exemption will therefore be endangered only if payment is above market rates and linked to the recipient's participation as trustee.

Membership subscriptions

20.147 Subscriptions to non-profit making bodies with objects in the public domain are, subject to certain limitations, exempt from VAT, where those objects are of a political, religious, patriotic, philosophical, philanthropic or civic nature. There is no requirement for the body to be a registered charity, and certain other non-profit-making bodies (such as trade unions and professional associations) can also benefit from exemption.

20.148 The exemption is limited, however, to benefits that are available without any further payment being required and so, if members are offered discounts on later supplies to be paid for separately, this can constitute a taxable supply. Similarly, exemption does not apply to granting members rights of admission to any premises, event or performance for free where non-members are charged for admission, unless this admission would be exempt anyway (for example, under the cultural services group, see **20.143**). Supplies of printed matter such as magazines and newsletters can also be zero-rated, although it must be remembered that if publications are provided in 'soft-copy' format, this is not eligible for zero-rating.

20.149 As a result, and as provided for by Extra Statutory Concession 3.35, subscription income may need apportionment between exempt, zero- and standard-rated benefits, which can be a complex procedure. There is no set way of apportioning subscriptions, but all benefits provided must be reflected in the calculation; it is not possible to claim full zero-rating if any other non-printed matter benefit, however ephemeral, is provided. In *Royal College of Anaesthetists (2004 V18632)*, members' rights to vote on management issues and use a designatory suffix were considered to be valuable benefits for members, requiring an apportionment. As such apportionments will impact upon the amount of VAT payable and any income-based VAT recovery method, it is important to agree with HMRC the basis on which this will be carried out, and review both the principle of the method and the figures used to calculate it, on a regular basis.

Fundraising events

20.150 Qualifying fundraising events are exempt from VAT. A qualifying event is an event whose primary purpose is raising money and which is promoted as such. Social events which make incidental profits do not qualify, nor do regular or continuous activities such as the running of a shop. Examples of events that could qualify include balls, dances, performances, fêtes, exhibitions or auctions.

20.151 This is one area in which indirect and direct tax exemptions are now co-ordinated, as an event meeting the requirements for VAT exemption automatically qualifies for exemption from income tax and corporation tax.

20.152 The exemption applies to the admission fees, sale of programmes and advertising therein, sponsorship specifically for the event and goods sold there by the charity. However, the relief only applies to the 'outputs' of the event, not the inputs. VAT on any purchases will, therefore, be charged as normal and irrecoverable if the event is wholly exempt. The exception to this is where donated goods are sold at a charity auction, which sales will be zero-rated supplies (see **20.124**), but admission tickets etc in relation to such events will remain exempt if meeting the other criteria. It should be noted that only donated *goods* are eligible for zero-rating, so the auction of services such as weekends away or meals out will remain exempt.

20.153 Events can also be exempt when held by a charity's subsidiary company, or by non-profit making bodies that qualify under the cultural services, sports services or membership subscription exemptions (see **20.143**, **20.141** and **20.147**).

20.154 A charity is now allowed to hold up to 15 events of the same kind at the same location in a financial year and exempt them from VAT, pro-rated if a financial year is for a period of less or more than a calendar year. A significant point to be aware of is that if the 15-event limit is exceeded, *all* the events will be taxable at the standard rate, not just those which exceed the limit. This means that if a charity mistakenly exceeds the limit, they will have to retrospectively account for VAT on the income of the previous events, thus reducing their income. VAT would, therefore, be due not only on ticket sales and sales of goods at the event, but also on advertising and sponsorship income received. If this happens, the only silver lining is the recovery of VAT on costs as attributable to taxable supplies.

20.155 Small-scale events, such as coffee mornings and jumble sales, which are deemed not to pose the risk of distortion of trade, can be excluded from the 15 annual events, provided that the gross weekly takings do not exceed £1,000.

20.156 Although 'location' is not defined, a prudent reading would be that it applies to a catchment area or local population rather than to a specific building or site. Customs' view is that 'location' is the geographical area within which an activity takes place. Thus, for an event that uses 'general use premises', such as a field or community hall, the location would be the area in which the field or hall is sited, rather than being the particular field or hall.

20.157 The 'anti-competition' clause in the exemption states that the exemption does not apply to any supply that would be likely to create distortions of competition where similar activities are carried on by commercial concerns unable to qualify for the exemption. Customs say that this clause will only be used where there is 'potential to distort the relief', which would appear to mean that it will only be invoked where the relief is being actively exploited and charitable status misused. However, the clause remains in the legislation, and charities planning events should take note of any similar events happening near them in case this clause could be invoked.

20.158 Finally, an example of the gradual modernisation of VAT law is that exemption also applies to events accessed wholly or partly by means of electronic communications. This means that 'web-cast' events are able to qualify for exemption, provided that their primary purpose is to raise funds, and they are promoted as such.

20.159   If accommodation is provided as part of an event, this can only be exempt where it does not exceed two nights, whether or not consecutive, and this accommodation must be incidental to the event. Any supply falling within the Tour Operators' Margin Scheme is excluded, which means any bought in accommodation. Fundraising events carried on abroad are not eligible for exemption as the exemption is UK-specific. The Tour Operators' Margin Scheme and other issues relating to overseas events are discussed at **20.173**.

6   Other supplies

20.160   The following is limited to the VAT implications of other activities, as the direct tax implications are dealt with in Chapter 18.

20.161   Many charities enter into sponsorship, consultancy and commission agreements in an attempt to increase revenue, but these will have unexpected VAT implications for the unwary. Charities should be particularly aware of the danger of entering into contracts that are silent on the issue of VAT or which are stated to be 'VAT-inclusive'. This means that if a charity is making taxable supplies under such a contract, VAT must be accounted for to Customs and Excise out of the amount stated in the contract, rather than in addition to it. Under a standard rated of 17½%, this means an effective reduction of 15% of income, and a reduction of 13% under the 15% standard rate effective from 1 December 2008 to the planned end-date at the time of writing, 31 December 2009.

Sponsorship

20.162   While 'donation' sponsorship income such as that received from people undertaking sponsored walks or other independent fundraising drives is outside the scope of VAT, commercial sponsorship, for which the sponsor receives recognition that constitutes advertising or promotion, is taxable. Income that is a freely given donation, and is only recognised with a simple acknowledgement, may in normal circumstances be treated as non-business, but if a sponsor's logo is displayed, or their name is attached to a product or publication, this will be a taxable supply.

20.163   The advertising relief discussed at **20.117** applies if the advertising services are supplied by another charity, so if you receive advertising income from another charity, this can be zero-rated if it meets all the conditions.

Commission income

20.164   Affinity credit card schemes involve an 'affinity group' providing a credit card company with a variety of services, such as the introduction of clients, product development, marketing and promotion etc. None of these fall within the exemption for financial services, unless the charity undertakes 'work preparatory to the conclusion of contracts', and so the fees or commissions receivable by a charity entering into such an arrangement are in principle taxable. The financial services exemption only covers intermediary services by a person acting in an intermediary capacity, but this requires that the charity acts in a brokering capacity between suppliers and individual supporters, rather than the supporter base as a whole. As credit card companies will not normally be able to recover this VAT, they may stipulate that such payments are inclusive of VAT, which will mean that the output tax due will be due out of the monies received. By concession, if there are two contracts a proportion of the money can be treated as a donation. Normally, arrangements will include access to a database, endorsement by the charity, and reciprocal logo displays; in such a case, there can be two agreements, one for standard rated marketing services, valued as at least 20% of any initial 'per card' fee, and one for using the charity's name and logo, for the balance of the initial fee and any subsequent fees for use of the card, which can be treated as non-business income.

20.165 Commissions received from insurance companies (for example, where a charity promotes a particular insurance plan to members), may be covered by the exemption for insurance intermediary services, which are framed slightly differently in the law. In such cases, bringing together an insurer and a person seeking insurance can be exempt, although this does not extend to promotional or advertising services. This means that if a charity receives a flat fee for advertising a particular insurer's products, this will be a taxable supply, but if they receive a commission based on how many people they 'introduce' to the insurer, this could benefit from exemption. Insurance companies, like credit card companies, would not normally be able to recover this VAT, and so care should be taken when reviewing any agreement.

20.166 It is likely that any other type of commission payments received by a charity will constitute consideration for the making of a taxable supply, and this can also have adverse consequences for direct tax purposes.

Royalties

20.167 Charitable trusts or foundations set up with the aim of preserving the works or memory of individuals should be aware that royalty payments constitute consideration for taxable supplies. The supply made in such cases is the grant of the right to make use of the charity's intellectual property, be it the written word, a picture or piece of music etc. As it is common practice for persons paying royalties to 'self-bill' under special rules, it is important for a charity to inform them that VAT is due, especially if VAT registration occurs after the relationship with them has begun. This would, in most circumstances, be an essential part of the royalty agreement.

20.168 Where royalties are paid by a taxable body in another country, the 'supply' of the royalty by the charity is in the country where the other body belongs. This means that if the recipient is within the EU and using the supply for the purpose of their business, the charity does not charge VAT, and the recipient has to account for VAT in their country using the reverse charge mechanism. This will require the submission of quarterly EC Sales Lists specifying the VAT number of the customer and the amount charged. If the recipient is outside the EU, VAT-free treatment applies whether the recipient is in business or not.

20.169 However, as such supplies are deemed to be supplied outside the UK, they cannot be included within the partial exemption calculation of the supplier if the standard method is used, although all directly attributable input tax can be recovered. Charities with substantial overseas royalty income should therefore consider agreeing a special method to take full account of this activity.

20.170 Royalties supplied to a non-taxable person in another EU member state will be subject to VAT at the standard rate and, as the place of supply is the UK, such supplies can be included in the partial exemption method.

Sale of goods

20.171 The sale of donated goods is discussed at **20.124**. The sale by a charity of bought-in or manufactured goods is treated like any other commercial concern, with zero-rating only allowed for goods eligible for relief in themselves, such as books, magazines or children's clothes. The sale of Christmas cards, gifts and adult clothing, therefore, will be a taxable supply.

20.172 The export of goods is a zero-rated supply. To be an export, goods must go to a destination outside the EU. In 'VAT speak', selling goods to a recipient in another member state of the EU is a 'despatch' and the liability of this will depend upon the status of the recipient. If they are in business and can provide a valid VAT number from another member state, the charity does not charge VAT on the sale and should include the net value in Box 8 of their VAT return. The customer will account for VAT on their VAT return in their home country. If the EU customer is an individual, however, the charity should charge VAT as they would to a UK customer, unless the distance selling threshold (either 35,000 or 70,000 per annum in each country) is breached, in which case the charity may have to register for VAT in that other country.

Overseas fundraising and other challenge events

20.173 Many charities undertake fundraising events overseas, such as walking the Great Wall of China or hiking the Inca Trail. Such events do not qualify for the exemption available for domestic events detailed at **20.150**. Instead, where travel and accommodation are arranged for volunteers, and the charity acts as principal, they fall within the Tour Operators Margin Scheme or 'TOMS'. This scheme aims to prevent the need for tour operators or anybody organising overseas travel from having to register for VAT in every country where they arrange accommodation or other services. Instead, they are required to account for VAT in the UK on the margin between their direct costs and the consideration charged. The direct costs will be the cost of the bought-in services that are then on-supplied, such as plane fares and accommodation charges. Once the margin has been calculated, VAT is accounted for out of this amount. For events taking place within the EU, VAT is due at the standard rate. For events taking place outside the EU, the applicable rate is 0%. The taxable margin will be included in any income-based VAT recovery method.

20.174 However, most charities will engage a commercial tour operator to arrange overseas events, and HMRC take the view that only the operator can use TOMS. Therefore, any consideration payable to the charity will be instead standard rated as an 'introduction' or arrangement fee. This would apply to registration fees or non-refundable deposits, but also to any minimum donation required of volunteers. This means that if someone has to raise £2,000 to take part, the consideration is £2,000, even if they actually raise £3,000; any additional money raised is a freely given donation and outside the scope of VAT. Thus, many charities suggest a 'target' for donations without making this an absolute requirement.

20.175 The same principle applies to UK events falling outside the exemption, such as organising participation in an event organised by somebody else. A good example is the London Marathon; this is not organised by a charity, and so any charity getting a team together to run should be aware that any required payment they charge to participants is standard rated. If places are sold (or minimum donations required), this means that the VAT on buying places can be recovered, even if the 'sale price' is below the purchase price.

7 Administration of VAT

Registration

20.176 When considering VAT, the first issue a charity must confront is whether it has to be registered. Registration is mandatory once the threshold of taxable supplies is exceeded. From 1 May 2009, the limit is £68,000, among the highest in the EU, and this allows charities making taxable supplies at a limited level to function outside the VAT regime, although they will not get any credit for input tax incurred. Only taxable supplies, at the standard or zero rates, count towards turnover for the purposes of the registration threshold. Whether or not a profit is made on these supplies is irrelevant; it is on the level of turnover, not profit, that the threshold is established. The value of non-business activities, such as income from donations and grants, does not count towards turnover.

20.177 The registration threshold also applies to the value of certain services bought in from overseas suppliers. In this case, the UK trader purchasing the service is treated as if it had supplied the services, and the value of these contributes towards taxable turnover. The services in question are those contained in VATA 1994 Sch 5, which are supplied where received (as for royalties, see **20.167**). Schedule 5 includes:

- transfers and assignments of copyright, patents, licences and trademarks;
- advertising services;

- consultancy services, including those of engineers, lawyers and accountants, data processing and the provision of information, but excluding any services relating to land;

- the acceptance of an obligation to refrain from pursuing any business activity, or pursuing any transfers or assignments of copyright, patents, licences and trademarks;

- banking, financial and insurance services;

- supplies of staff;

- letting on hire of goods (except means of transport); and

- telecommunications services, radio and television broadcasting services, and electronically supplied services.

From 1 January 2010 a change in rules means that with the exemption of certain services (lunch related, or services supplied where performed) that all services are caught under the reverse charge when bought in by a charity that is in 'business' even if the services are used for a non-business purpose.

Therefore, any trader purchasing supplies of this nature from suppliers outside the UK must add the value of these supplies to any other taxable turnover they may have to determine whether the registration threshold of £68,000 is exceeded.

20.178   The registration threshold also applies for persons who make acquisitions of goods from other EU member states. This is to prevent traders from buying in goods or equipment from a member state with a lower VAT rate than that applicable in the UK in order to reduce costs.

20.179   There are many traps for charities that may result in an unexpected liability to register, including receiving 'funding' for what are in fact taxable services. A common pitfall is where a charity recharges staff and other costs to its subsidiary; as the supply of staff is a taxable supply, unless joint contracts of employment exist and the charity acts as paymaster, such a move would render the charity liable to register for VAT if in excess of the threshold.

20.180   If supplies are made below the registration threshold, registration can be voluntary, but only if HMRC are satisfied that the registrant intends to make taxable supplies. A charity making no supplies (with no 'business activities') is not eligible to register.

20.181   The registration test can apply either prospectively or retrospectively. The prospective test applies when taxable supplies in the next 30 days alone will exceed the threshold, for example if a charity signs a contract under which it will receive a tranche of funding on a specified date. The charity must notify HMRC as soon as it has a reasonable expectation that the threshold will be breached in the next 30 days, and will be registered from that date of expectation.

20.182   The retrospective test applies when taxable turnover in a rolling 12-month period exceeds the limit; the charity must notify HMRC within 30 days of the end of the month in which the threshold is exceeded and will be registered from the notification date. Only if HMRC can be satisfied that turnover will then fall below the deregistration threshold (currently £66,000 from 1 May 2009) can a charity be excepted from registration (this does not apply to the prospective test). Alternatively if the majority of supplies made are zero-rated, exemption from registration may be possible. In both cases, it is necessary to notify HMRC at the correct time and agree this with them.

20.183 Once registered, a charity is responsible for accounting for VAT in the same way as any other registered entity. Returns are typically required to be rendered every three months, but can be allowed or directed to be submitted monthly. Charities can take advantage of a number of special schemes if they meet the relevant criteria.

20.184 The **annual accounting scheme** is available to businesses that regularly pay tax to HMRC and have annual taxable turnover of £1,350,000 or less. The scheme is optional, but if they wish to join the scheme, a trader need only submit one return each year. They still have to make payments on account, based on their estimated liability for the year. Customs makes the estimation on the basis of past performance of the business and any information provided about the business' future prospects.

20.185 The **cash accounting scheme** permits businesses with an annual taxable turnover of less than £1,350,000 to account for VAT by reference to payments made and received, rather than invoice dates. The VAT account of a trader using the cash accounting scheme must also reference amounts to dates of payments, not dates of invoices. The main advantages of the scheme are automatic bad debt relief and the deferral of time for payment where extended credit is given.

20.186 The **flat rate scheme** allows a trader to account for VAT as a flat rate percentage of relevant turnover. The percentages vary depending upon the nature of the trader's activities. Input tax is only recoverable on capital assets with a VAT-inclusive value exceeding £2,000, which is treated as being used wholly for taxable purposes. The scheme is restricted to traders whose annual taxable turnover does not exceed £150,000 and whose total turnover (including the value of exempt and non-business income) does not exceed £187,500 a year.

20.187 The scheme may suit small charities, and a significant benefit that may be particularly attractive to the charity sector is that there is no need to account for input tax deductions, except on capital assets as above, which means that no VAT recovery methods would be needed.

Group registration

20.188 Corporate bodies are able to apply for group registration, under which they are treated as a single taxable entity, so any charges between group members are ignored for VAT purposes. Any corporate body under common control can apply to join the group (although this currently excludes non-UK entities) This means that only one VAT number is held by all the members, and one member (the 'representative member'), is responsible for rendering returns for the whole group. Supplies made by any member are deemed to be made by the representative member. Thresholds, output tax and input tax apply to the group as a whole, not to individual entities, and VAT recovery calculations will need to be done on a group basis, so a special method may be advisable.

20.189   The rules relating to group registration have been substantially amended because of systemic abuse in the past. Accordingly, HMRC have powers to refuse any applications relating to group treatment, to mandate that a group dissolves, that specific members leave or join, or that a group be formed, as they deem necessary for the protection of the Revenue.

20.190   When applying to form a group, all members must declare the likely level of turnover or income from taxable, exempt and non-business sources, and the level of intra-group charges envisaged. Detailed proposals must be made for any VAT recovery method to be used.

20.191   The nature of the liability of a VAT group may cause special problems for charities, in that every group member is jointly and severally liable for the VAT due and the obligations of the group. It may be beyond the authority of trustees to bring the VAT liabilities of a trading subsidiary onto the parent charity, and legal advice should always be sought if a group registration is under discussion.

The four-year cap and correcting errors

20.192   If a trader has made a mistake on a VAT return, this can only be corrected within four years. If a mistake is found that will cost a charity money, it must still be disclosed, as voluntarily correcting such errors will normally avoid the imposition of a penalty, whereas failing to do so would constitute fraud if deliberate non-disclosure had occurred. HMRC have the power to assess going back 20 years if fraud is involved. The Finance Act 2008 included provision for the three-year period to be changed to a four-year period, and to broaden the circumstances in which the 20-year period can apply (where a person deliberately causes, or participates in a transaction knowingly resulting in, a 'loss of VAT'). These provisions were brought into force with a transitional period between 1 April 2009 and 1 April 2010. All VAT returns submitted after 1 April 2010 are capped at four years.

20.193   For return periods beginning before 1 July 2008, errors discovered in any one accounting period with a net effect of less than £2,000 can be corrected on the VAT return for the period of discovery without fear of penalty. For return periods beginning on or after 1 July 2008, the limit is the greater of £10,000 or 1% of turnover, capped at £50,000. If the errors found exceed the relevant limit, separate notification, called a voluntary disclosure, is necessary, and interest will be charged. HMRC may refuse to accept voluntary disclosures submitted after notification of a VAT visit has been received, if they believe that the error was only disclosed to prevent it being discovered at the visit, which could result in a penalty.

20.194 The three-year cap was introduced in 1996 for overpaid VAT and 1997 for input tax claims, replacing the previous six-year limit. As both measures involved a degree of retrospective application, several appeals challenged the legality of the changes. HMRC attempted to remedy the situation with an 'administrative transitional regime' but this was not sufficient and after the judgment of the House of Lords in *Fleming/Condé Nast* [2008] UKHL 2, HMRC accept that, where a right to a refund had accrued as at 6 December 1996, the three-year cap does not apply. It will, however, still be applied for any right accruing after that date.

Penalties

20.195 Where an error is disclosed, interest will be charged. The applicable rates follow those set by the Bank of England's Monetary Policy Committee and from 6 December 2008 the rate for amounts owing to HMRC is 5.5%. The rate for amounts due from HMRC due to their error is 2% from that date. Any further changes in rate can be see at www.hmrc.gov.uk.

20.196 If returns or payments are rendered late or not at all, or HMRC believe that they are incorrect, they can issue an assessment. Assessments are subject to the four-year cap (see **20.192**), unless fraud is a factor, in which case the limit is 20 years.

20.197 Surcharge liability notices will be issued when returns or payments are late or missing, requiring punctual compliance for the following 12 months, known as the surcharge period. If a second return or payment is defaulted on within that period, the trader will be liable to a penalty of 2% of the tax due on that return, and the surcharge period will be extended for another 12 months. The penalties rise per defaulted return or payment within the surcharge period, to 5%, 10% and, finally, 15%. If no VAT is due a fixed penalty of £30 may be assessed.

20.198 If a return is inaccurate, a misdeclaration penalty may be imposed. From 1 April 2008 the regime has been changed in an attempt to coordinate the penalties relating to the various taxes managed by HMRC. For VAT returns to be filed on or after 1 April 2009, therefore, the penalty depends on the potential lost revenue arising from the error. No penalty will be charged for mistakes made on returns where reasonable care was taken, providing these are amended promptly once identified. If not amended promptly, if a 'careless' error is made, or if an understated assessment is not amended, the penalty can be up to 30% of the potential lost revenue. For errors that are 'deliberate but not concealed', the penalty can be up to 70%, and for errors that are 'deliberate and concealed', it can be up to 100%.

20.199 In this case:

- 'careless' means a failure by the taxpayer to take reasonable care;

- 'deliberate but not concealed' means that despite making a deliberate error, the taxpayer did not make arrangements to conceal it;

- 'deliberate and concealed' means that the taxpayer makes arrangements to conceal a deliberate error, for example by submitting false evidence to support an inaccurate figure.

Thus, inadvertently entering an inaccurate figure onto an accounting system would seem to be careless at most. Deliberately doing so but not taking any other steps would lay one open to the 70% penalty, while altering an invoice to support a deliberately falsified figure would cause the 100% penalty to apply. In all cases the penalty can be mitigated if the taxpayer cooperates with HMRC.

20.200   Penalties can also be imposed if an entity does not register when it is supposed to. This is not subject to the four-year cap and could technically be backdated to 1 April 1973, the date on which VAT was introduced in the UK! The penalty for failure to register depends upon how late the liability is notified to Customs and Excise.

- Where registration is no more than 9 months late, it is an amount equal to 5% of the net VAT liability between the date registration was due and the date notification was made.

- Where registration is between 9 and 18 months late, the penalty is 10% of net tax due.

- Where registration is more than 18 months late, the penalty is fixed at 15% of net tax due.

20.201   Charities do not receive any dispensation from the penalty regime. The only mitigation available to them is that available to all traders, that is the possibility of satisfying HMRC that there was a 'reasonable excuse'. Statute specifies that this does not include insufficiency of funds, or reliance on another person, and in addition, ignorance of VAT law is not usually accepted as a reasonable excuse. It is therefore imperative that a charity seeks to confirm the liability of its activities, makes sure that any liability to register is made at the correct time, and takes reasonable care in recording its VAT accounts.

Rulings and Tribunals

20.202   Charities may be proportionately more likely to seek rulings from HMRC than other traders, as they tend to be active in areas governed by complex rules, such as the zero-rating of property or whether or not they qualify as an eligible body for the purposes of exempting the services they provide. If HMRC issue an assessment or a ruling with which a charity disagrees, they can be asked to reconsider their decision in light of further facts or arguments provided. If their view is still in opposition to that of the charity and their advisers, an appeal can be lodged with the VAT Tribunal.

20.203   It is regrettable that those least able to afford advice are those that most need it. Even so, the cost of making an appeal must be taken into account before any precipitate action is taken, and counsel's opinion may be very valuable in establishing whether a charity has a viable case to take forward. Taxpayers are entitled to represent themselves before a Tribunal but the complex nature of many of the matters a charity may wish to appeal often require professional representation.

20.204 Tribunal cases are only binding upon the parties involved and do not set precedents, but they have in the past caused HMRC to change their interpretation of areas of the law, for example in relation to the zero-rating of student accommodation and the liability of routine domestic tasks. Tribunal decisions may be appealed to the High Court and beyond, all the way to the European Court of Justice, and in the higher courts, judgments do set precedents. The *London Zoo*, *Longborough* and *Bournemouth* cases that had such significant repercussions upon the cultural services exemption (see **20.144**) are good examples. However, there are many, many cases that are lost or which fall because the charity does not have the resources to proceed. The situation is far from satisfactory since it results in undue weight being applied, in practice, to HMRC's opinions.

8 Miscellaneous

Investment management

20.205 Where charities hold investments, fund administration is another headache from a VAT point of view, as income-bearing assets in a varied portfolio may differ markedly in their treatment. As already mentioned, interest is exempt and dividend income is outside the scope of VAT, and investment property can be either exempt or taxable, depending on the availability and desirability of the option to tax (see **20.110**). Dealings in money, shares or other securities are, in the main, exempt from VAT. These different treatments will affect the extent to which any VAT on costs is recoverable.

20.206 On the cost side of managing a portfolio, fund management services are exempt from VAT when supplied by insurers but taxable when supplied by other providers, unless falling within a specific exemption. The management of OEICs, Authorised Unit Trusts and closed-ended investment undertakings, such as investment trust companies (ITCs), is exempt whereas that of other holdings is taxable. Following the judgment of the ECJ in *Morgan Fleming Claverhouse Investment Trust plc* (2007) C-363/05 ITCs were added to the list of 'exempt funds' for management purposes and so charities that have been charged VAT on the management of such funds in the past may be eligible for a refund. Certain recognised overseas funds may also now be eligible for exemption. The new rules remain contentious, despite HMRC's claims to have established a 'level VAT playing field for all similar collective investment undertakings which compete in the UK market under comparable conditions' and charities with queries should consider taking advice and approaching their fund managers,

Conflicts with direct tax

20.207 The non-complementary nature of the UK tax system means that an approach that seems to maximise revenue from a direct tax point of view might leave a charity open to unfortunate VAT consequences. Similarly, the best approach to take for VAT might have disadvantageous consequences when direct tax implications are considered. Expert advice on all aspects of administering a charitable trust, fund or investment portfolio should be taken before any method is set in stone. This advice extends to all fundraising activities.

20.208 An example of the unhelpful nature of the interaction of direct and indirect taxes is where a person makes a donation to a charity. HMRC allows for a de minimis limit on reciprocal supplies made to the donor which can be disregarded under the Gift Aid Scheme; HMRC makes no such allowances. For a donation to be outside the scope of VAT, it has to be a 'true' donation where the donor receives nothing in return.

9 Conclusion

20.209 VAT legislation is complex and the areas in which charities tend to be active are significantly more complicated than most. VAT recovery methods, the liability of activities, the apportionment of membership subscriptions and the particular difficulties attendant upon the VAT reliefs available for property, all require charities to be up-to-date with both their activities and the prevailing law.

20.210 At 15% during 2009 and 17.5% thereafter, VAT is a tax which can take a significant slice from income or capital otherwise meant for charitable purposes, and it is estimated that irrecoverable VAT alone costs the sector in excess of £500 million a year. While positive regard to the impact of VAT and to its management and administration will not guarantee no VAT charge, it will ensure that net costs are kept to a minimum and that the funds available for charitable activities are maximised.

Useful addresses

Association of Chief Executives of Voluntary Organisations	1 New Oxford Street London WC1A 1NU 0845 345 8481 www.acevo.org.uk
Buzzacott LLP	12 New Fetter lane London EC4A 1AG 020 7556 1200 www.buzzacott.co.uk
Charities Advisory Trust	Radius Works Back Lane Hampstead London NW3 1HL 020 7794 9835 www.charitiesadvisorytrust.co.uk
Charities Aid Foundation	Kings Hill West Malling Kent ME19 4TA 01732 520000 www.cafonline.org
COIF Charities Investment Fund	St Alphage House 2 Fore Street London EC2Y 5AQ 020 7588 1815
Charity Commission	
– London office	30 Millbank London SW1P 4DU
– Taunton office	Woodfield House Tangier Taunton Somerset TA1 4BL

Useful addresses

– Liverpool office	Charity Commission Direct PO Box 1227 Liverpool L69 3UG 0845 3000 218 www.charity-commission.gov.uk
Charity Finance Directors Group	3rd Floor Downstream Building, 1 London Bridge, London SE1 9BG 0845 345 3192 www.cfdg.org.uk
Directory of Social Change	Directory of Social Change 24 Stephenson Way London NW1 2DP 020 7391 4800 www.dsc.org.uk
Gambling Commission	Gambling Commission Victoria Square House Victoria Square Birmingham B2 4BP 0121 230 6666 www.gamblingcommission.gov.uk
Institute of Fundraising	Park Place 12 Lawn Lane London SW8 1UD 020 7840 1000 www.institute-of-fundraising.org.uk
Legislation Monitoring Service for Charities	Church House Great Smith Street London SW1P 3AZ 020 7222 1265 www.lmsconline.org
National Housing Federation	Lion Court 25 Procter Street London WC1V 6NY 020 7067 1010 www.housing.org.uk

Office of the Scottish Charity Registrar	2nd Floor Quadrant House 9 Riverside Drive Dundee DD1 4NY 01382 220446 www.oscr.org.uk
Scottish Federation of Housing Associations	Pegasus House 375 West George Street Glasgow G2 4LW 0141 332 8113 www.sfha.co.uk
HM Revenue & Customs	HMRC Charities St Johns House Merton Road Liverpool L75 1BB 08453 020 203 www.hmrc.gov.uk/charities
Interchange	Interchange Unit Cabinet Office Admiralty Arch Room 1.6c The Mall London SW1A 2WH 020 7276 1581 www.interchange.gov.uk
National Council for Voluntary Organisations	Regent's Wharf 8 All Saints Street London N1 9RL 020 7713 6161 www.ncvo-vol.org.uk
Northern Ireland Council for Voluntary Action	61 Duncairn Gardens Belfast BT15 2GB 028 9087 7777 www.nicva.org
Official Custodian for Charities	Care of the Charity Commission
Scottish Council for Community and Voluntary Organisations	The Mansfield Traquair Centre 15 Mansfield Place Edinburgh EH3 6BB 0131 556 3882 www.scvo.org.uk

Useful addresses

Wales Council for Voluntary Action

Baltic House
Mount Stuart Square
Cardiff Bay
Cardiff CF10 5FH
029 20431700
www.wcva.org.uk

Charity Commission Publications

CC1	Charity Commission Publications	May 2009
CC3	The Essential Trustee: what you need to know	Feb 2008
CC3a	The Essential Trustee: An introduction	Jan 2007
CC5a, CC5b and CC5c	See Registration Application Pack	April 2008
CC7	Ex Gratia Payments by Charities	Dec 2001
CC8	Internal Financial Controls for Charities	Dec 2003
CC8	A self checklist for charities	
CC9	Speaking Out - Campaigning and Political Activity by Charities See also our guidance update on Charities and Political Donations	Mar 2008
CC10	Hallmarks of an Effective Charity	July 2008
CC11	Trustee expenses and payments	June 2008
CC12	Managing Financial Difficulties and Insolvency in Charities	Sept 2004
CC13	The Official Custodian for Charities' Land Holding Service	Sept 2004
CC14	Investment of Charitable Funds: Basic Principles See also detailed guidance on investments	Dec 2004
CC15	Charity Reporting and Accounting: The essentials	May 2007
CC15a	Charity Reporting and Accounting: The essentials April 2008	April 2008
CC15b	Charity Reporting and Accounting: The essentials April 2009	April 2009
CC16	Receipts and Payments Accounts Pack (based on SORP 2005)	April 2009
CC17	Accrual Accounts Pack (based on SORP 2005)	April 2009
CC18	Use of Church Halls for Village Hall and Other Charitable Purposes	July 2001
CC19	Charities' Reserves	Mar 2008
CC20	Charities and Fundraising	April 2008
CC20a	Charities and Fundraising - A summary	Mar 2002
CC21	Registering as a Charity	April 2008

CC22	Choosing and Preparing a Governing Document	April 2008
CC23	Exempt Charities	April 2008
CC24	Users on Board: Beneficiaries who become trustees	Mar 2000
CC27	Providing Alcohol on Charity Premises	Nov 2002
CC28	Sales, leases, transfers or mortgages: What trustees need to know about disposing of charity land	May 2009
CC30	Finding New Trustees - What charities need to know We are amending part F of this guidance to reflect the recent introduction of parts of the Vetting and Barring Scheme. You can find guidance on the Scheme at www.isa-gov.org.uk/PDF/VBS_Guidance.Pdf	Oct 2007
CC31	Independent Examination of Charity Accounts: Trustees' Guide	April 2009
CC32	Independent Examination of Charity Accounts: Examiners' Guide	April 2009
CC33	Acquiring Land	Apr 2001
CC34	Collaborative Working and Mergers Also, see Collaborative Working and Mergers Resources	July 2008
CC35	Trustees, trading and tax	April 2007
CC36	Changing your Charity's Governing Document	Nov 2008
CC37	Charities and Public Service Delivery – An Introduction and Overview	Feb 2007
CC40	Disaster Appeals	Jan 2002
CC42	Appointing Nominees and Custodians: Guidance under s.19(4) of the Trustee Act 2000	Feb 2001
CC43	Incorporation of Charity Trustees	July 2002
CC47	Complaints about Charities	June 2008
CC48	Charities and Meetings	May 2003
CC49	Charities and Insurance	Feb 2007
CC63a	Independent Examination of Charity accounts – 2007	Feb 2007
Accounting & Reporting by Charities: Statement of Recommended Practice (SORP 2005)		Mar 2005

A Balancing Act: New perspectives on the charity/beneficiary relationship	Feb 2009
A snapshot of charities in Wales	Jan 2009
Cause for Complaint? How charities manage complaints about their services	May 2006
Cause for Complaint? How charities manage complaints about their services Annex A – E	May 2006
Charities and Commercial Partners	July 2002
Charities and Commercial Partners – Annex A, B & C	July 2002

Charities' awareness, understanding and attitudes towards the public benefit requirements	Dec 2009
Charities working in the field of human rights	Dec 2007
Charity Reporting and Accounting - taking stock and future reform	Dec 2009
Charity Reserves	Mar 2003
Charity Reserves – Annex A, B, C & D	Mar 2003
Charity Reserves: Key Findings	Mar 2003
Collaborative Working and Mergers Also, see Collaborative Working and Mergers Resources	Apr 2003
Collaborative Working and Mergers: Annex A, B, C & D	Apr 2003
Collaborative Working and Mergers: Summary	Mar 2003
Firm Foundations: A snapshot of how trusts and foundations are responding to the economic downturn in 2009	Aug 2009
Going Green: Charities and Environmental Responsibility	Dec 2008
In their own words	Dec 2006
In their own words Annex A – E	Dec 2006
Membership Charities	Mar 2004
Membership Charities: Annex A, B, C & D	Mar 2004
Milestones: Managing key events in the life of a charity	Dec 2003
Milestones: Managing key events in the life of a charity: Annex A, B, C, D & E	Dec 2003
Milestones: Summary	Dec 2003
Membership Charities: Summary	Mar 2004
Small Charities and Reserves	June 2003
Stand and deliver: the future for charities delivering public services	Feb 2007
Start as you mean to go on: Trustee Recruitment and Induction	July 2005
Start as you mean to go on: Trustee Recruitment and Induction Annex A, B, C, D & E	July 2005
Tell It Like It Is	Nov 2006
The Regeneration Game	Oct 2006
Transparency and Accountability	June 2004
Transparency and Accountability: Annex A, B, C & D	June 2004
Trustee Recruitment, Selection and Induction	Mar 2002
Trustee Recruitment, Selection and Induction Annexes	Mar 2002
Village Halls and Community Centres	Dec 2004
Village Halls and Community Centres: Annex A, B, C & D	Dec 2004
Village Halls and Community Centres: Summary	Dec 2004

Charity Commission definition of gross income and total expenditure

FROM CHARITY COMMISSION GUIDANCE NOTE ON COMPLETION OF THE ANNUAL UPDATE 2007

Definition of gross income

This is the total recorded income of the charity in all unrestricted and restricted income funds, but not resources received as capital (endowment) funds, nor capital gains in an income fund.

You should calculate income before deduction of any costs or expenses. The calculation of income should include:

- voluntary income from donations (including any related gift-aid tax reclaims), grants, gifts and legacies (see Note 1 below);

- gross proceeds from fund-raising and other trading activities undertaken for generating funds;

- investment income (including interest, dividends, related tax reclaims and rents);

- gross proceeds from the sale of goods or services in furtherance of the charity's objectives; and

- the amount of any expendable endowment spent or transferred to income funds and, where a charity operates a total return approach to investment of capital funds, the amount of any unapplied total return allocated or transferred to income funds during the year (see Note 2 below).

The calculation should exclude the following from income:

- receipt of a loan by the charity;

- loan repayments to the charity;

- proceeds, gains or profits on the sale or disposal of investments and functional fixed assets; and

- actuarial gains on any defined benefit pension scheme.

Note 1: Any gifts or donations that the donor expects the charity will or may keep for investment or ongoing use are capital (endowment), and should be excluded.

Note 2: Any allocation of unapplied total return will only affect endowed charities that have obtained a consent order from the Charity Commission to operate a total return approach to investments.

Definition of total expenditure

You should give the gross expenditure in all funds including capital (endowment).

You should include in expenditure:

- costs of generating funds, including fund-raising, trading activities, investment property costs and investment management fees;

- charitable expenditure in furtherance of the objects of the charity including:

    - grants and donations payable;

    - support costs; and

    - governance and management and administration costs of the charity.

Exclude from expenditure:

- granting of a loan;

- repayment of a loan;

- purchase of investments and functional fixed assets;

- losses on disposal of investments and functional fixed assets; and

- actuarial losses on any defined benefit pension scheme.

Stages of an audit

The work of an auditor can be broken down into four main stages, as follows:

(a)   defining and agreeing terms of audit engagement;

(b)   planning, controlling and recording audit work;

(c)   obtaining appropriate audit evidence from audit work; and

(d)   reporting and expressing audit opinion on accounts.

The stages of an audit, set out above, reflect the basic objectives and general principles of auditing standards. In undertaking an audit, auditors:

(a)   carry out procedures designed to obtain sufficient and appropriate audit evidence in order to determine with reasonable confidence whether the accounts are free of material mis-statement;

(b)   evaluate the overall presentation of the accounts in order to determine that they have been prepared in accordance with relevant legislation and accounting standards;

(c)   issue a report containing a clear expression of their opinion on the accounts (ISA (UK and Ireland) 700).

In expressing an opinion on a set of accounts, auditors provide a level of assurance that is reasonable in the circumstances of the work being carried out but, being based on a combination of facts and professional judgement, cannot be an absolute level of assurance or 'correct'.

In carrying out an audit, auditors are required to comply with the ethical guidance of their relevant professional bodies. Ethical principles, which underlie an auditor's responsibilities, include those of integrity, objectivity, independence and confidentiality, in addition to the basic expectation of professional competence and due care.

Agree engagement terms

It is important that the client charity and the auditors agree on the terms of engagement and that these terms are recorded in writing (ISA (UK and Ireland) 210). An engagement letter documents and confirms:

(a)   client's acceptance of the auditor's appointment;

(b)   respective responsibilities of those charged with governance (ie the trustees or directors) and of the auditors, including any statutory responsibilities;

(c)   scope of the audit engagement; and

(d)   the form of any report required of the auditor.

Terms of engagement must be agreed, in writing, at the outset of any audit appointment. Thereafter, both parties should regularly review the terms of engagement to ensure that they remain relevant and appropriate, and any updating should be confirmed in writing.

It is important that all trustees of the charity should be aware of, and agree, the terms of engagement, giving a detailed description of the audit work to be undertaken. Where day-to-day running of a charity is delegated to executive staff, those executives, for example the chief executive, should be aware of the terms of the auditor's engagement.

Matters that need particular reference within the letter of engagement may include:

(a)   auditor's responsibility in relation to other services and where these are covered by a separate engagement letter;

(b)   the respective responsibilities of trustees and auditors, with respect to fraud and other irregularities and to the consideration of laws or regulations that may materially affect the accounts, or conduct of the charity's business or operations;

(c)   the scope of the charity's accounts, including the identification and accounting treatment of branches, or connected entities (SORP);

(d)   the legislative framework under which the financial statements are prepared and the audit is conducted*; and

(e)   the statutory duty to report to the charity regulators any matters of which auditors become aware that may be of material significance to the respective regulators.

* At present the Charities Accounts (Scotland) Regulations 2006 also include the Trustees' Annual Report within the statement of accounts which is subject to audit. To address this unintended effect of the Regulations, the APB understands that the Scottish Government intends to amend the Regulations in order to remove any disparity with other UK jurisdictions.

Auditors ceasing office

Where an auditor appointed by charity trustees or under the Charities Act 1993 section 43A(2) or (3)(a), for any reason, ceases to hold office, he must send to the charity trustees a statement of any circumstances in connection with his ceasing to hold office, which he considers should be brought to their attention, or if he considers that there are no such circumstances, a statement is required that there are none. It is the auditor's responsibility to send a copy of the statement outlining circumstances of ceasing to hold office (but not a statement of no such circumstances) to the Charity Commissioners.

For charitable companies the auditor should also refer to sections 519–525 of the Companies Act 2006.

Appendix 5

Dispensations from audit or examination requirements

1   Reg 34(1) empowers the Commission in certain circumstances to dispense with the requirements of section 34(2) or (3) of the 1993 Act in the case of a particular charity. These circumstances include:

(a)   where the Commission is satisfied that the accounts of the charity concerned are required to be audited in accordance with any statutory provision contained in or having effect under an Act of Parliament which imposes requirements which, in the opinion of the Commission, are sufficiently similar to the requirements of section 43(2) for those requirements to be dispensed with; or

(b)   where the Commission is satisfied that the accounts of the charity concerned have been audited by the Comptroller and Auditor General or the Auditor General for Wales.

2   Reg 34(2) and (4) empower the Commission in certain circumstances to dispense with the requirements of section 43(2) or (3) of the 1993 Act in the case of a particular financial year of a charity. These circumstances include:

(a)   where the Commission is satisfied that the accounts of the charity concerned for the financial year in question have been, or will be, audited or examined in accordance with requirements or arrangements which, in the opinion of the Commission, are sufficiently similar to the relevant requirements of section 43 of the 1993 Act

applicable to that financial year of that charity for those requirements to be dispensed with; or

(b)   where the Commission considers that, although the financial year
in question of the charity concerned is one to which section 43(2)
of the 1993 Act applies, there are exceptional circumstances which
justify the examination of the accounts by an independent examiner instead of their audit in accordance with that subsection; or

(c)   where the Commission is satisfied that the group accounts of
the parent charity concerned for the financial year in question
have been, or will be, audited in accordance with requirements
or arrangements which, in the opinion of the Commission, are
sufficiently similar to the requirements of paragraph 6(4)(a) of
Schedule 5A for those requirements to be dispensed with.

3   Reg 34(3) empowers the Commission in certain circumstances to dispense with the requirements of paragraph 6(4)(a) of Schedule 5A of the
1993 Act in the case of a particular charity. These circumstances include:

(a)   where the Commission is satisfied that the group accounts of the
parent charity concerned are required to be audited in accordance
with any statutory provision contained in or having effect under an
Act of Parliament which imposes requirements which, in the opinion of the Commission, are sufficiently similar to the requirements
of paragraph 6(4)(a) of Schedule 5A for those requirements to be
dispensed with; or

(b)   where the Commission is satisfied that the group accounts of the
parent charity concerned have been audited by the Comptroller
and Auditor General of the Auditor General for Wales.

4   The Commission must make it a condition of a dispensation granted
under this regulation that the charity trustees send to the Commission
any report made to the trustees with respect to the accounts of that charity for the relevant financial year of which it requests a copy.

5   The Commission must make it a condition of a dispensation granted
under paragraph (2)(b) that the charity trustees comply with the requirements of section 43(3) of the 1993 Act as if they were able to make and
had in fact made an election under that section that the accounts of the
charity for the relevant financial year be examined by an independent
examiner.

6   The Commission may revoke a dispensation granted under this regulation if the charity trustees fail to comply with a condition imposed under
paragraph 4 or 5 above.

The duty of auditors to report matters of material significance to the Charity Commission and OSCR

Introduction

The Charity Commission and OSCR value the objectivity and independence that auditors bring to their work and the assurance that the audit process provides makes an important contribution to maintaining public trust and confidence in charities. Auditors in both England and Wales and Scotland have a common statutory duty to report matters of material significance to charity regulators. This important duty will be a key contribution to the ability of charity regulators to take timely action and so they have agreed a common list of matters of material significance to assist the auditor in reporting important matters on a timely basis. The sooner the charity regulators are made aware of a matter the sooner it can be considered and, where appropriate, regulatory action taken to protect a charity, its beneficiaries and its charitable assets.

Guidance

The Charities Act 1993 section 44, as amended by the Charities Act 2006, places a duty on the auditors of both a non-company charity and a company charity to report matters of 'material significance' to the Commissioners. Section 46 of the Charities and Trustee Investment (Scotland) Act 2005 places a similar duty on auditors of Scottish charities to report matters of 'material significance' to OSCR.

The duty to report arises where the auditor, in the course of their audit, identifies a matter, which relates to the activities or affairs of the charity or of any connected institution or body, and which the auditor has reasonable cause to believe is likely to be of material significance for the purposes of the exercise by the Commission of its functions under section 8 or 18 of the Charities Act 1993 or the exercise by OSCR of its functions under sections 28, 30 or 31 of the Charities and Trustee Investment (Scotland) Act 2005.

Subject to compliance with money laundering legislation regarding 'tipping off', in the circumstances leading to a right or duty to report, the auditor is entitled to communicate to charity regulators in good faith information or opinions relating to the business or affairs of the entity or any associated body without contravening the duty of confidence owed to the entity. In addition, in England

and Wales, the Charities Act 1993 provides additional statutory protection for the auditor as no duty, for example confidentiality, is regarded as contravened merely because of any information or opinion contained in the report.

The reporting of a matter of material significance is a separate report from the auditor's report on the accounts. The Charities Act 1993 and the Charities and Trustee Investment (Scotland) Act 2005 require the report to be made immediately the matter comes to the auditor's attention and in England and Wales the Charities Act 1993 requires that this is done in writing. There is no requirement under Scottish law for a report to be made in writing but it is recommended to do so.

It is not part of the reporting duty to require auditors to perform any additional scrutiny work as a result of the statutory duty nor are they required specifically to seek out reportable matters. Auditors do however include procedures within their planning processes to ensure that members of the audit team have sufficient understanding (in the context of their role) to enable them to identify situations which may give reasonable cause to believe that a matter should be reported to the regulator. Where a matter comes to light relating to a previous financial year which would give rise to a duty to report, then the auditor should still make a report.

In order to recognise whether a situation is likely to be of material significance to a regulator's function an understanding is needed of those matters which either due to their nature or potential financial impact are likely to require evaluation and, where appropriate, investigation by the regulator.

Both the Charity Commission and OSCR will always consider the following to be of material significance and hence reportable:

- matters suggesting dishonesty or fraud involving a significant loss of, or a major risk to, charitable funds or assets;

- failure(s) of internal controls, including failure(s) in charity governance, that resulted in a significant loss or misappropriation of charitable funds, or which leads to significant charitable funds being put at major risk;

- matters leading to the knowledge or suspicion that the charity or charitable funds have been used for money laundering or such funds are the proceeds of serious organised crime or that the charity is a conduit for criminal activity;

- matters leading to the belief or suspicion that the charity, its trustees, employees or assets, have been involved in or used to support terrorism or proscribed organisations in the UK or outside of the UK;

- evidence suggesting that in the way the charity carries out its work relating to the care and welfare of beneficiaries, the charity's beneficiaries have been or were put at significant risk of abuse or mistreatment;

- significant or recurring breach(es) of either a legislative requirement or of the charity's trusts;

- a deliberate or significant breach of an order or direction made by a charity regulator under statutory powers including suspending a charity trustee, prohibiting a particular transaction or activity or granting consent on particular terms involving significant charitable assets or liabilities; and

- the notification on ceasing to hold office or resigning from office, of those matters reported to the charity's trustees.

These matters are considered central to the integrity of a charity and as such will require evaluation and where appropriate investigation by the regulators. The Charity Commission and OSCR consider all such reports to have a very high intelligence value. Both take a risk based and proportionate approach to inquiry work when deciding to open an inquiry. The duty to report applies to the auditor who must make a report whether or not the matter has already been notified to other regulators or agencies and whether or not the trustees have already advised the charity regulators, for example, by making a serious incident report to the Charity Commission.

Matters which the Charity Commission and OSCR have indicated are likely to be of material significance are set out on the charity regulators' websites. Other sources of information include:

- the Charity Commission's Directions and guidance for independent examinations;

- Annual Returns (in Scotland, Supplementary Monitoring Returns[1]) which signpost a number of the areas that the relevant regulator considers significant; and

- in England and Wales, any serious incident report made by the trustees to the Charity Commission.

The list of 'serious incidents' is principally concerned with serious criminal or unlawful activity, or very serious incidents concerning a charity that may affect its funds, property, beneficiaries or reputation. Some of the incidents listed may not actually be criminal activity, but do flag up a risk of potential criminal activity or other risks, which if realised, would have a serious detrimental impact on the charity.

There is no serious incident reporting requirement placed on trustees in Scotland.

Where auditors make a report, they may not have all the information but should be prepared to provide as much as possible about the matter(s) they are reporting.

The auditor's right to report to charity regulators under the Charities Act 1993 and the Charity and Trustee Investment (Scotland) Act 2005

The auditor also has a broad discretionary right to report matters that they believe may be relevant to the work of the charity regulators but they are not under a duty to report such matters.

The Charity Commission and OSCR consider such reports to have considerable intelligence value and welcome these submissions. Given the broad discretion permitted it is not appropriate to list instances for reporting but the auditor may usefully review matters which were not considered material relating to the statutory duty and matters upon which trustees are requested to provide additional information as part of the annual return process.

Matters falling within this discretionary category are likely to be indicative of significant risks to charitable funds or their proper application and would therefore normally be relevant to the work of the regulators. Where such a matter arises, the auditor may discuss the matter with the trustees to identify whether it remains a matter of concern and whether the trustees have taken or are taking action which can reasonably be expected to remedy or mitigate the effect on the current or future years.

Although the auditor enjoys a discretion as to whether to make a report of a matter relevant to the work of the Charity Commission and OSCR, it is recommended that auditors document any relevant matters identified in the course of the audit and document the basis of any decision not to report a matter falling within this discretionary category.

Ceasing to hold office

In addition to the duty to report matters of material significance, Regulations under the Charities Act 1993 and the Charities and Trustee Investment (Scotland) Act 2005 provide that 'Where an auditor appointed by charity trustees ceases for any reason to hold office he shall send to the charity trustees a statement of any circumstances connected with his ceasing to hold office which he considers should be brought to their attention or, if he considers that there are no such circumstances, a statement that there are none; and the auditor shall send a copy of any statement sent to the charity trustees under this paragraph (except a statement that there are no such circumstances) to ...' the Charity Commission and/or OSCR.

Matters that may require consideration in relation to this duty include:

- disagreement over opinions expressed or to be expressed in an auditors' report;
- disagreement over any disclosure made or to be made to the Commission in respect of a matter of material significance;
- disagreement over any accounting policy, assumption, financial judgment or disclosure made in the accounts or in the preparation of the accounts;
- concerns over any matter which is believed to give rise to a material risk of a loss of charitable funds; and
- lack of co-operation or obstruction in the context of an audit.

Cross Border Charities

Where a charity registered in England & Wales also operates in Scotland it will need to be registered with OSCR as well as the Charity Commission. For such cross border charities neither regulator is considered to be the principal regulator and both will have an interest in receiving reports. The auditor should therefore make a report to both regulators who will determine which regulator takes forward the issues raised by the report.

Reporting gateways

To ensure that reports are handled efficiently and immediately, auditors should make reports to the regulators as follows:

- To the Charity Commission by e-mail – whistleblowing@charity commission.gsi.gov.uk

- To OSCR by e-mail – info@oscr.org.uk

Within the body of the e-mail, or in an attachment thereto, the following information should be provided:

- the auditor's name and contact address, telephone number and/or e-mail address;

- the charity's name and registration number (if applicable);

- whether the auditor is reporting a matter of material significance, or is exercising his right to report;

- a description of the matter giving rise to concern and the information available on the matter reported, where possible providing an estimate of the financial implications;

- where the trustees are attempting to deal with the situation, a brief description of any steps being taken by the trustees of which the auditor has been made aware;

- if the report concerns terrorist, money laundering or criminal activity confirmation that the auditor has already notified the Serious Organised Crime Agency and/or the Police as appropriate;

- if the report concerns the abuse of vulnerable beneficiaries details of whether the auditor has contacted the Police or Social Services.

In England and Wales the Charities Act 1993 requires the report to be in writing and therefore a hard copy of any report made orally should also be forwarded to:

Charity Commission Direct
PO Box 1227
Liverpool
L69 3UG

In Scotland, there is no legislative requirement to make the report in writing, but it is recommended that a written report or record of any verbal report is forwarded to:

OSCR
Quadrant House
9 Riverside Drive
Dundee
DD1 4NY

1   Completed by charities with gross income over £25,000.

Model Gift Aid declaration

Gift Aid declaration

giftaid it

Name of charity or CASC _____

Please treat

☐ The enclosed gift of £ _____ as a Gift Aid donation; **OR**

☐ All gifts of money that I make today and in the future as Gift Aid donations; **OR**

☐ All gifts of money that I have made in the past 6 years and all future gifts of money that I make from the date of this declaration as Gift Aid donations.

✓ *Please tick the appropriate box*

You must pay an amount of Income Tax and/or Capital Gains Tax for each tax year (6 April one year to 5 April the next) that is at least equal to the amount of tax that the charity or Community Amateur Sports Club will reclaim on your gifts for that tax year.

Donor's details

Title _____ Initial(s) _____ Surname _____

Home address _____

_____

_____

Postcode _____ Date _____

Signature _____

Please notify the charity or CASC if you:

1. Want to cancel this declaration.
2. Change your name or home address.
3. No longer pay sufficient tax on your income and/or capital gains.

Tax claimed by the charity or CASC

- The charity or CASC will reclaim 28p of tax on every £1 you gave up to 5 April 2008.
- The charity or CASC will reclaim 25p of tax on every £1 you give on or after 6 April 2008.
- The Government will pay to the charity or CASC an additional 3p on every £1 you give between 6 April 2008 and 5 April 2011. This transitional relief for the charity or CASC does not affect your personal tax position.

If you pay income tax at the higher rate, you must include all your Gift Aid donations on your Self Assessment tax return if you want to receive the additional tax relief due to you.

Sponsorship and Gift Aid declaration

Sponsorship and Gift Aid declaration form

giftaid it

Please sponsor me _____

To (event) _____

In aid of _____

We, who have given our names and addresses below and have ticked the box headed 'Gift Aid?' (✓)', want the charity or CASC named above to reclaim tax on the donation detailed below given on the date shown. We understand that each of us must pay an amount of income tax or capital gains tax at least equal to the tax reclaimed by the charity or CASC on the donation

Full name (First name and surname)	Home address Not your work address (this is essential for Gift Aid)	Postcode	Amount £	Date paid	Gift Aid? (✓)
			Total donations received £		
			Total Gift Aid donation £		

Remember: Full name + Home address + Postcode + ✓ – *giftaid it*

425

Trust and estate charities form

HM Revenue & Customs

TRUST AND ESTATE CHARITIES

Fill in these boxes first

Name of trust

Name of charity, if different

Tax reference

If you want help, look up the box numbers in the Notes on Trust and Estate Charities.

Claim to exemption

- Charity repayment reference **7.1**

- Charity Commission Registration Number or Scottish Charity Number **7.2**

If the trust is a charity are you claiming exemption from tax on all or part of your income and gains? **YES**

Have all income and gains that you are claiming to be exempt from tax been, or are they to be, applied for charitable purposes? **YES**

Return period

- Are you returning information for the **year ended 5 April 2009**? **YES**

- If not, what period does this Return cover?

Period begins **7.3** / / and ends **7.4** / /

- Are accounts to be enclosed with the Return? **YES**

- If 'No', explain why **7.5**

Repayments

Income Tax

- Amount already claimed on form R68 - *see Notes on page TCHN1* **7.6** £

- Total repayment/payment due **7.8** £

and

- further repayment/payment due **7.10** £

or

- amounts overclaimed **7.12** £

Boxes 7.7, 7.9, 7.11 and 7.13 are not in use

Has the amount in box 7.10 been included in any repayment claim on form R68? **YES**

Income on which you are claiming exemption

Non-exempt amounts should be entered in the appropriate parts of the Tax Return.

- Total turnover from exempt trading activities **7.14** £
- Investment income **7.15** £
- UK land and buildings income **7.16** £
- Gift Aid **7.17** £
- Other charities **7.18** £
- Legacies **7.19** £
- Gifts of shares or securities received **7.20** £
- Gifts of real property received **7.20A** £
- Other sources **7.21** £

SA907

HMRC 12/08 net

TRUST AND ESTATE TAX RETURN ■ CHARITIES: PAGE TCH1

continued over

426

Expenses as included in the charity accounts

- Trading costs **7.22** £ [   ]
- UK land and buildings **7.23** £ [   ]
- All general administration costs **7.24** £ [   ]
- All grants and donations made in the UK **7.25** £ [   ]
- All grants and donations made outside the UK **7.26** £ [   ]
- Others (not entered elsewhere on the Return) **7.27** £ [   ]

Assets

	Disposals in year	Held at 5 April 2009
• Tangible fixed assets	**7.28** £	**7.29** £
• UK investments (excluding controlled companies)	**7.30** £	**7.31** £
• Shares in, and loans to, controlled companies	**7.32** £	**7.33** £
• Overseas investments	**7.34** £	**7.35** £
• Loans and non-trade debtors		**7.36** £
• Other current assets		**7.37** £

- Were all investments qualifying investments, and were loans made qualifying loans, within s558 and s561 ITA 2007? *Please see Notes on page TCHN2*   **YES**

- Value of any non-qualifying investments and loans **7.38** £ [   ]

- Number of subsidiary or associated companies the charity controlled at 5 April 2009 **7.39** [   ]

Claim

I claim exemption from tax

7.40

Signature   Date

Print name in
full here

Status or capacity in which you are signing

7.41

7.42 *Additional information*

TRUST AND ESTATE TAX RETURN ■ CHARITIES: PAGE TCH2

Appendix 10

Company tax return form: charity supplementary pages

HM Revenue & Customs

Company Tax Return form - Supplementary Pages
Charities and Community Amateur Sports Clubs (CASCs)
CT600E (2006) Version 2
for accounting periods ending on or after 1 July 1999

Company information

Company name

Tax reference as shown on the CT603

Period covered by these Supplementary Pages (*cannot exceed 12 months*)
from (*dd/mm/yyyy*)   to (*dd/mm/yyyy*)

You need to complete these Supplementary Pages if

the charity/CASC claims exemption from tax on all or any part of its income and gains.

Important points

- These Supplementary Pages will form the charity's/CASC's claim to exemption from tax on the basis that its income and gains have been applied for charitable or qualifying purposes only.
- Please use the notes on page 2 to help you complete this form.
- Please enter whole figures or '0' where appropriate.
- How often you are asked to make a return will depend on the extent and nature of your activities.
- These Pages, when completed, form part of the company's return.
- These Pages set out the information we need and provide a standard format.
- These Pages are covered by the Declaration you sign on the back page of form *CT600*.
- The warning shown on form *CT600* about prosecution, and the advice about late and incorrect returns and late payment of tax, also apply to these Pages.

Claims to exemption

This section should be completed in all cases

Charity/CASC repayment reference

Charity Commission Registration number, or Scottish Charity number (if applicable)

Put an 'X' in the relevant box if during the period covered by these Supplementary Pages:

- the company was a charity/CASC and is claiming exemption from all tax on all or part of its income and gains.

- all income and gains are exempt from tax and have been, or will be, applied for charitable or qualifying purposes only.

If the company was a charity/CASC but had no income or gains in the period, then put an 'X' in the first box 'claiming exemption from all tax' above.

or

- some of the income and gains may not be exempt or have not been applied for charitable or qualifying purposes only, and I have completed form *CT600*.
See the note on Restrictions of relief for non-qualifying expenditure on page 2.

I claim exemption from tax

Signature

Date (*dd/mm/yyyy*)

Name (*in capitals*)

Status

Except where a liquidator or administrator has been appointed, any person who is authorised to do so may sign on behalf of the company. For CASCs the treasurer should sign. A photocopy of a signature is not acceptable.

HMRC 08/06

CT600E (2006) Version 2

Page 2

Notes

Repayments boxes E1/E1a, E2/E2b and E1a - E4d

Transitional relief only applies on qualifying distributions made on or after 6 April 1999 and before 6 April 2004. The time limit for claims is 2 years after the end of the charity's accounting period in which the distribution was made.

In boxes E1/E1a:

- Enter the amount of income tax and transitional relief claimed on forms *R68(2000)* or *R68(CASC)* for the period covered by these Pages.
- This should relate only to income arising in the period.
- Do not include amounts claimed for earlier periods.

In Box E2/E2b enter the total amount due for income received in the period on which a charity/CASC can claim.

CASCs should leave boxes E1a to E4d blank.

Trading income box E5

Enter details of the turnover of trades, the profits of which will be exempted by

a)   S505(1)(e) ICTA 1988, S46 FA 2000 or ESC C4 (for charities), or

b)   Schedule 18, Paragraph 4, FA 2002 (for CASCs).

If the charity/CASC has carried on a trade during the return period which falls outside the exemption, complete the *Company Tax Calculation* on form *CT600*. Do not include in the calculation sources of income which are otherwise exempt from tax. Also, complete the *About this return* section on page 1 and *Declaration* on the back page of form *CT600*.

Gifts boxes E11 and E12

Include in box E11 the value of any gifts of shares or securities received under S587B ICTA 1988.

Include in box E12 the value of any gifts of real property received under S587B/S587C ICTA 1988.

Other sources box E13

Enter details in box E13 of income received from sources other than those included in the boxes above where the income is exempt from tax in the hands of a charity/CASC. This will include Case VI income exempted by S505(1)(c)(iic) ICTA 1988.

Investments and loans within Sch 20 ICTA 1988 box E26 charities only

Qualifying investments and loans, for the purposes of S506 ICTA 1988, are specified in Parts I and II of Sch 20 ICTA 1988.

Charities can make claims to HM Revenue & Customs for any loan or other investment not specified in Sch 20 but made for the benefit of the charity and not for avoidance of tax, to be accepted as qualifying.

Put an 'X' in box E26 only if all investments and loans are qualifying investments and loans:

- automatically, because they are specified in Sch 20, or
- because the charity has either claimed (with this return or separately) that they are under Paragraphs 9 or 10 of Sch 20 ICTA 1988, or is prepared to do so on request.

For a claim for qualifying status to succeed, the loan or investment must be made for the benefit of the charity and not for the avoidance of tax (whether by the charity or any other person). Claims should be in writing and specify

- the nature of the item (loans, or shares for example)
- the amount
- the period
- whether the claim is under Paragraph 9 or 10.

It is helpful if a claim includes full details, for example the terms of a loan.

Investments and loans made outside Sch 20 ICTA 1988 box E27 charities only

If the charity has made any investments or loans which do not fall within Schedule 20 ICTA 1988, and no claim is being made with this return, enter the total of such loans or investments in box E27.

Restrictions of relief for non-qualifying expenditure

Relief under S505(1) ICTA 1988 and S256 TCGA 1992 may not be available to some charities.

The charity should attach a calculation of restriction of relief under S505(3) ICTA 1988 and send it with this return. If you need help with this calculation please telephone our helpline on **08453 020203** or email **charities@hmrc.gov.uk**

Where a CASC has incurred non-qualifying expenditure its exemptions from tax may need to be restricted. The CASC should include a calculation of the restriction of relief under Schedule 18, Paragraph 8 FA 2002 with this return. If you need help with this calculation please telephone our helpline on **08453 020203** or email **charities@hmrc.gov.uk**

Further guidance

Further guidance on the reliefs available to charities and CASCs is available on our website at **www.hmrc.gov.uk/charities**

CT600E (2006) Version 2

Company tax return form: charity supplementary pages

Repayments

Enter details of repayments of Income Tax/payments of Transitional Relief for income arising during the period covered by these Supplementary Pages

		Income Tax	Transitional Relief *Charities only*
E1/E1a	Amount already claimed for period using form R68(2000) or R68(CASC)	E1 £	E1a £
E2/E2b	Total repayment/payment due	E2 £	E2b £
and either			
E3/E3c	Further repayment/payment due *Where E2/E2b is more than E1/E1a*	E3 £	E3c £
or			
E4/E4d	Amounts overclaimed for period *Where E1/E1a is more than E2/E2b*	E4 £	E4d £

If any of the amounts in boxes E3/E3c have been included in any repayment/payment claim on form R68(2000) or R68(CASC) put an 'X' in this box. ☐

Information required

Enter details of any income received from the following sources, claimed as exempt from tax in the hands of the charity/CASC. Enter the figure included in the charity's/CASC's accounts for the period covered by this return
Do not include amounts which are not taxable. Non-exempt amounts should be entered on form CT600 in the appropriate boxes.

Type of income	Amount
E5 Enter total turnover from exempt trading activities	E5 £
E6 Investment income - exclude any amounts included on form *CT600*	E6 £
E7 UK land and buildings - exclude any amounts included on form *CT600*	E7 £
E8 Deed of covenant - exclude any amounts included on form *CT600*	E8 £
E9 Gift Aid or Millennium Gift Aid - exclude any amounts included on form *CT600*	E9 £
E10 Other charities - exclude any amounts included on form *CT600*	E10 £
E11 Gifts of shares or securities received	E11 £
E12 Gifts of real property received	E12 £
E13 Other sources	E13 £

Enter details of expenditure as shown in the charity's/CASC's accounts for the period covered by these Supplementary Pages

Type of expenditure	Amount
E14 Trading costs in relation to exempt activities (in box E5)	E14 £
E15 UK land and buildings in relation to exempt activities (in box E7)	E15 £
E16 All general administration costs	E16 £
E17 All grants and donations made within the UK	E17 £
E18 All grants and donations made outside the UK	E18 £
E19 Other expenditure not included above, or not used in calculating figures entered on the form *CT600*	E19 £

continued on page 4

CT600E (2006) Version 2

430

Company tax return form: charity supplementary pages

continued from page 3

Charity/CASC Assets	Disposals in period (total consideration received)	Held at the end of the period (use accounts figures)
E20/E20a Tangible fixed assets	E20 £	E20a £
E21/E21b UK investments (excluding controlled companies)	E21 £	E21b £
E22/E22c Shares in, and loans to, controlled companies	E22 £	E22d £
E23/E23d Overseas investments	E23 £	E23d £
E24e Loans and non-trade debtors		E24e £
E25f Other current assets		E25f £
E26 Qualifying investments and loans. *Applies to charities only. See note on Page 2*		E26
E27 Value of any non-qualifying investments and loans. *Applies to charities only*		E27 £
E28 Number of subsidiary or associated companies the charity controls at the end of the period. *Exclude companies that were dormant throughout the period*		E28

What to do when you have completed these Supplementary Pages

Follow the advice shown under 'What to do when you have completed the return' on page 23 of the *Guide*.

431

Index

Accounting for separate
  funds   5.11–5.22
  classification   5.13
  consistency   5.21
  definition   5.20
  fund accounting   5.18
  funds of charity   5.15–5.17
  funds structure   5.18
  reconciliation of funds   5.19

Accounting policies   5.1–5.48
  associates   5.44–5.48
  basis of accounting   5.10
  basis of apportioning costs 5.10
  branches   5.23–5.27
    connected charity
      distinguished   5.26
    consolidation   5.25, 5.27
    definition   5.23
    practical problems   5.27
    Westminster Roman Catholic
      Diocesan Trust   5.27, 5.30
  connected charities   5.28–5.32
    definition   5.28
    disclosure   5.31, 5.32
    "umbrella organisation"   5.29
    Westminster Roman Catholic
      Diocesan Trust   5.30
  consolidation   5.33–5.43
    corporate hierarchy, and 5.33
    disclosure requirements 5.37
    objectives of subsidiaries 5.40,
                                 5.41
    Statement of Financial
      Activities, and   5.39
  disclosure   5.10
  fixed asset investments   5.10
  fund accounting   5.10
  gifts in kind   5.10
  incoming resources   5.10
  joint arrangements   5.44–5.48
  joint ventures   5.44–5.48
  leased assets   5.10
  liquid resources   5.10
  matters to be considered   5.9
  non-aggregated activities   5.5

Accounting policies – *contd*
  notes on   13.4–13.12
  pension costs   5.10
  resources expended   5.10
  scope of accountability   5.3
  tangible fixed assets   5.10

Accounting requirements   3.1–3.22
  Charities Act 1993   3.3,3.4
    accounts   3.3,3.4
    reports   3.3,3.4
    returns   3.3,3.4
  Companies Act 2006   3.5–3.8
    accounting principles   3.8
    adequate accounting records 3.8
    approval of accounts   3.8
    audit reports   3.8
    directors' report, content and
      requirements   3.8
    format of accounts   3.8
    group accounts   3.8
    notes to accounts-disclosures 3.8
    preparing company accounts 3.8
    publication of non-statutory
      account   3.8
    signature of accounts   3.8
    true and fair view   3.8
  SORP *see* SORP
  summary information
    return   3.21,3.22

Accounts structure   5.1–5.48

Advantages of charitable
  status   1.33–13.7

Associates
  accounting policies   5.44–5.48

Audit   16.1–16.81
  advantages   16.80
  APB Practice Note   16.55–16.57
  applicable accounting
    framework   16.36
  auditing standards   16.54
  auditor, appointment of   16.25
  auditor, ceasing office   App 5
  auditors' remuneration 13.92–13.94
    disclosure   13.92–13.94
  benefit of   16.45

Audit – *contd*
 contractual requirements of
  auditor   16.69–16.79
 core elements   16.37–16.39
 duty of auditors to report
  matters   App 6
 independent examination,
  and   16.72–16.79
 ISAs   16.34, 16.58–16.64
 meaning of   16/34–16.43
 objective of   16.35
 opinion   16.43
 opinion on grant funding   16.70
 responsbilities of trustees and
  auditors   16.41–16.43
 stages of   App 4
 statement of trustees'
  responsibilties   16.43
 threshold   16.3, 16.4
Balance sheet presentation   9.1–9.30
 analysis of net assets between
  funds   9.21
 British Red Cross   9.8
 "comparing apples and pears" 9.10
 current assets   9.26–9.28
 designated funds   9.21
 disclosure of funds in
  deficit   9.15–9.17
 endowment funds   9.21
 fixed assets   9.22–9.25
 format   9.3
 free reserves   9.18
 functions   9.4
 fund accounting   9.12
 funds (group)   9.21
 funds (group and parent
  charity)   9.21
 funds (parent charity)   9.21
 grouping of funds   9.11–9.21
 guidelines   9.1–9.10
 liabilities   9.29, 9.30
 measurement principles   9.9
 purpose   9.2
 reserves policy   9.21
 restricted funds   9.17, 9.21
 simplicity, need for   9.14
 spread of assets and
  liabilities   9.6, 9.7
 transfer between funds   9.21
Benefits in kind   17.88, 17.89
Betting duty   17.91
Branches
 accounting policies   5.23–5.27
British Red Cross
 organisation   2.30

Building
 meaning   20.61, 20.62
Business gifts   19.39–19.41
Business rates   17.82
Capital assets
 gifts of   19.46–19.49
Capital gains tax   17.36–17.38
Cash flow statements   12.1–12.31
 balance sheet total, definition 12.9
 cash, definition   12.21, 12.22
 categoriies of inflows and
  outflows of cash   12.17,12.18
 consolidated   12.29
 disclosure requirements   12.10–12.20
 endowment fund
  movements   12.29–12.31
 exemptions   12.5
 gross income, meaning   12.8
 investment income   12.23–12.25
 nature of   12.10–12.20
 object of   12.10–12.20
 primary statement, as   12.6
 problem area   12.23–12.31
 reconciliation between 'operating
  profit' and cash flow from
  operating activities   12.19,12.20
 requirement for   12.1–12.9
 threshold   12.3, 12.4
 treatment of cash held as
  part of investment
  portfolio   12.26–12.28
Charitable incorporated
 organisation (CIO)   1.49–1.52
Charitable purposes   1.7–1.17
 Charities Act 2006   1.11
 definition   1.7,1.8
 effectiveness   1.76
 expansion   1.13
 guiding principles   1.74
 infringement   1.16
 jurisdiction   1.75
 reasons for change   1.9,1.10
Charity
 definition   1.1–1.6, 1.12
 two-stage test for new
  registrations   1.14
Charity Commission   1.63–1.76
 duty of auditors to report
  matters to   App 6
 functions   1.65
 gross income, definition   App 3
 monitoring role   1.69
 objectives   1.64
 powers   1.66
 publicatiions   App 2

Charity Commission – *contd*
  registration of new charities   1.68
  structure   1.63
  total expenditure, definition   App 3
Charity shops, income from
  notes   13.30–13.36
Commitments   11.15–11.22,
    13.121–13.123
  accounting policies   11.20
  constructive obligation 11.16, 11.17
  creditors: amounts falling due
    within one year   11.20
  designated funds   11.20
  different grades of obligation 11.18
  grant   11.20
  notes   13.121–13.123
Common Investment Funds
  (CIFs)   1.73, 15.55–15.57
Company limited by
  guarantee   1.45–14.8
Company tax return form
  charity supplementary pages App 10
Concessionary loans
  notes   13.50, 13.51
Connected charities
  accounting policies   5.28–5.32
  notes   13.18–13.21
Constitution   1.38–1.62
Contingent assets and liabilities 11.21,
    11.22, 13.127–13.130
  notes   13.127–13.130
Corporation tax   17.3–17.35
  annual payments   17.20, 17.21
  anti–avoidance   17.30–17.33
  claiming relief   17.34, 17.35
  Community Amateur Sports
    Clubs   17.94–17.96
  contemplative orders   17.28, 17.29
  exemptions   17.11–17.27
  fundraising events   17.25, 17.26
  interest   17.19
  land transactions   17.22–17.24
  small trades   17.12–17.16
  trading activities   17.17, 17.18
Council tax   17.83–17.87
Cross-border charities   15.34–15.45
  accounts   15.38
  annual returns   15.38
  branches   15.38
  charity test   15.38
  enquiries   15.38
  investigations   15.38
  monitoring returns   15.38
  registration   15.36, 15.40–15.45
  Scottish registration numbers 15.38

Cross-border charities – *contd*
  terminology   15.38
Current assets   11.1–11.3
Debtors   11.4–11.11
  analysis   11.4
  conditions, and   11.9–11.10
  grants   11.5, 11.6
  legacies   11.11
Deeds of covenant   19.2–19.7
  conditions   19.3
  documentation   19.5–19.7
  "pure income profit" rule   19.4
Disclosures   13.1–13.136
    see also Notes
Donated salaries   19.42, 19.43
Employee secondments   19.42, 19.43
Employees, emoluments
  of   13.83–13.91
  banding of   13.91
  part-time employees   13.50
  specific disclosure   13.85–13.87
  total emoluments,
    definition   13.88, 13.89
  volunteers   13.50
Ex gratia payments   13.107–13.110
  disclosure   13.107–13.110
Exempt charities   15.8–15.16
  regulations   15.9
  umbrella organisations   15.12
External scrunity   16.1–16.81
  forms of   16.11–16.14
  independent examination *see*
    Independent examination
  independent examiner,
    appointment of   16.27–16.33
  level of   16.15–16.24
    cross border charities 16.23, 16.24
    England and Wales   16.15–16.19
    Scotland   16.20–16.22
  source of
    requirements   16.11–16.14
  sources of legislation   16.6
  whistle blowing   16.65–16.68
Fixed assets   10.1–10.72,
    13.111–13.120
  accounting policies   10.31
  analysis   13.118
  classes   10.4
  depreciation   10.43–10.51
    categories of fixed assets 10.46
    exclusion from   10.45
    residual values   10.49
    very significant assets   10.47
  depreciation charge   10.52–10.59
  heritage assets   10.21–10.34

Fixed assets – *contd*
impairment | 10.52–10.59
initial valuation | 10.16–10.20
investments | 10.60–10.72
  analysis of assets | 10.65–10.69
  guidelines | 10.60, 10.61
  programme related | 10.70–10.72
  valuation | 10.62–10.64
meaning | 10.3
notes | 13.111–13.120
overview | 10.1–10.4
recognition | 10.16–10.20
relevant accounting
  standards | 10.5–10.15
  impairment | 10.10
  intangible assets | 10.5, 10.6
  investments | 10.11–10.13
  tangible assets | 10.7–10.9
revaluations | 10.35–10.42
  land and buildings | 10.37
  tangible fixed assets | 10.40–10.42
value in use, concept of | 10.56
Friendly society | 1.58
Funds' statement and movements
notes | 13.13–13.17
Gift Aid | 18.26–18.29, 19.8–19.32
basic rules | 19.16
benefits to donors | 19.17–19.20
declarations | 19.27–19.32, App 8
examples | 19.21–19.26
lower rate and higher rate
  taxpayers | 19.11–19.15
model declaration | App 7
Grants payable | 13.39–13.49
definition | 13.40
disclosure requirements | 13.41
individuals, to | 13.47
institutions, to | 13.44–13.46
specific disclosure
  requirements | 13.43
Guarantees | 13.124–13.126
disclosure | 13.124–13.126
Heritage assets | 10.21–10.34
definition | 10.24, 10.25
depreciation | 10.30
disclosure requirements | 10.31
exemption form
  captitalisation | 10.27, 10.28
group and foundation | 10.31
revised rules, effect | 10.32–10.34
Income and expenditure,
  detail of
notes | 13.37–13.38
Income tax | 17.3–17.35

Incoming resources | 7.1–7.84
activities for generating
  funds | 7.56–7.59
  definition | 7.56
  trading activity, as | 7.56–7.59
cash collections | 7.53–7.55
categorisation | 7.3
charitable activites, from | 7.63–7.66
  scope of | 7.65
contractual arrangements | 7.24–7.33
  level of entitlement | 7.30
  long-term contracts | 7.29
  performance-related grants | 7.27, 7.28, 7.31–7.33
disclosure | 7.7–7.9
donated services and
  facilities | 7.48–7.52
  "intangible income" | 7.49
  volunteers' time | 7.50–7.52
funds received as agent | 7.74, 7.75
gains and losses on fixed assets for
  charity use | 7.76–7.78
gains and losses on investment
  assets | 7.79–7.72
gifts in kind | 7.45–7.47
  basis of recognising | 7.45
  circumstances surrounding | 7.47
  Oxfam | 7.47
  value of | 7.47
grants and donations
  receivable | 7.10–7.23
  evidence of entitlement | 7.10
  matched funding, and | 7.15–7.16
  pre-conditions as to timing
    of use | 7.18–7.22
  pre-conditions on use | 7.13–7.17
  restricted grants for purchase
    of fixed asset | 7.23
  Royal College of Psychiatrists
    2006 accounts | 7.21
  Samaritans | 7.12
guidelines | 7.1–7.6
investment income | 7.60–7.62
legacies | 7.37–7.44
  assessing amount | 7.39
  assurances from trustees | 7.40
  impact of | 7.41, 7.42
  monitoring | 7.37
  notification of legal
    entitlement to | 7.43
Marie Curie Cancer Care | 7.84
recognition | 7.7–7.9
tax recoverable | 7.83, 7.84
trading activities | 7.67–7.73
  charity shops | 7.73

Incoming resources – *contd*
  trading activities – *contd*
    operational income   7.67–7.71
    voluntary income   7.34–7.36
Independent examination
  audit, and   16.72–16.79
  examiners' remuneration   13.92–13.94
    disclosure   13.92–13.94
    meaning   16.47–16.53
Indemnity insurance   13.79–13.82
  disclosure   13.79–13.82
Industrial and provident society   1.58
Inheritance tax   17.79–17.81, 19.53, 19.54
  annual payments   17.20, 17.21
  anti-avoidance   17.30–17.33
  claiming relief   17.34, 17.35
  contemplative orders   17.28, 17.29
  exemptions   17.11–17.27
  fundraising events   17.25, 17.26
  interest   17.19
  land transactions   17.22–17.24
  reliefs   17.4
  self-assessment   17.6, 17.7
  tax returns   17.8–17.10
Interest-free loans   19.44, 19.45
Irish charities   15.1–15.57, 15.46–15.54
  changes in law   15.46
  Charities Act 2009   15.49
Joint arrangements
  accounting policies   5.44–5.48
Land
  gifts of   19.50–19.52
Landfill tax   17.92, 17.93
Liabilities   11.12–11.14
Loan liabilities   11.23, 11.24, 13.131–13.136
  notes   13.131–13.136
  present value of assets   13.136
  security given on behalf of
    others   13.135
Management structure
  trustees' responsibilities   2.32–2.36
Netting off
  notes   13.26–13.29
Northern Ireland   15.51–15.54
Notes   13.1–13.136
    see also Disclosures
  accounting policies   13.4–13.12
  charity shops, income
    from   13.30–13.36
  concessionary loans   13.50, 13.51
  connected charities   13.18–13.21

Notes – *contd*
  contingent assets and
    liabilities   13.127–13.130
  fixed assets   13.111–13.120
  funds' structure and
    movements   13.13–13.17
  grants payable   13.39–13.49
  income and expenditure,
    detail of   13.37–13.38
  loan liabilities   13.131–13.136
  netting off   13.26–13.29
  subsidiary undertakings   13.22–13.25
  support costs   13.52–13.62
Official Custodian for Charities   1.70, 1.71, 1.72
OSCR
  duty of aufitors to report
    matters to   App 6
Payroll giving   19.33–19.38
Pensions   13.95–13.106
  disclosure   13.95–13.106
  funded schemes   13.97
Provisions   13.121–13.123
  notes   13.121–13.123
Public benefit   1.18–1.32
  new test   1.18–1.32
  principles   1.18–1.32
Related parties
  meaning   13.65–13.71
Remuneration of trustees   2.50–2.55
  conditions   2.51
  expenses   2.53, 2.54
Resources expended   8.1–8.71
  analysis   8.4–8.6
  categories   8.2
  charitable activities   8.4, 8.22–8.28
    analysis   8.23
    definition   8.22
    disclosure of support costs   8.25
    one activity   8.26
  constructive obligations   8.59–8.66
  contractual arrangements   8.56–8.58
  costs of generating funds   8.4, 8.10–8.21
  costs of generating voluntary
    income   8.11–8.16
  costs of goods sold   8.17–8.19
  definition   8.1
  fundraising trading   8.17–8.19
  governance costs   8.4, 8.41–8.44
    CFDG Consultation exercise   8.44
    defintion   8.41
  grant-making   8.29–8.40
    analysis   8.31, 8.33
    current practice   8.39, 8.40

Resources expended – *contd*
  grant-making – *contd*
    definition   8.29
    further details   8.34
    grants to institutions   8.36, 8.37
    individual   8.32
    individuals, grants to   8.38, 8.39
    support costs   8.30
  grants payable   8.59–8.66
  investment management
    costs   8.20, 8.21
  recognition-basic principles   8.7–8.9
  revised categorisation   8.5
  support costs   8.45–8.54
    administration costs   8.54
    allocation of costs   8.47–8.52
    bases for cost apportionment 8.49
    disclosure   8.46
    educational criteria   8.50, 8.51
    management costs   8.54
  VAT   8.67–8.71
Royal Charter   1.59, 1.60
Scheme of Charity Commission   1.53
Scottish charities   15.1–15.57
  accounts   15.18–15.33
  audit   15.27
  external scrutiny   15.25–15.28
  independent examination   15.26
  annual return   15.29
  monitoring return   15.30, 15.31
  Office of the Scottish Charity
    Regulator   15.17
Securities
  gifts of   19.50–19.52
Shares
  gifts of   19.50–19.52
SORP   3.9–3.20
  "negative franking"   3.12
  purpose of charity's annual report
    and accounts   3.16
  status   3.11
Sponsorship
  declaration   App 8
  tax implications   18.33–18.43
Stamp duty   17.90
Statement of Financial
  Activities   6.1–6.46
  acquired operations   6.46
  adaptation of formats   6.31–6.33
  Age Concern   6.40
  basic construction   6.5–6.27
  benefits of   6.3
  Catholic Marriage Care Limited 6.8
  Church Housing Trust   6.40
  discontinued operations   6.46

Statement of Financial Activities –
  contd
  examples   6.4
  net movement of funds   6.26, 6.27
  overall objectives   6.2
  post balance sheet events,
    discontinued activities   6.46
  purpose   6.1–6.4
  reconciliation of funds   6.28–6.30
  reconciliation schedule,
    workings   6.44
  St Albans Diocesan Board of
    Finance   6.44
  summary income and expenditure
    account   6.34–6.45
    adapting statement   6.38–6.40
    Butterfly Conservation   6.45
    problem   6.37
    purpose   6.42
    requirements   6.43
    St. Albans Diocesan Board of
      Finance   6.45
  Table reference A – incoming
    resources   6.11, 6.12
  Table reference B – resources
    expanded   6.13–6.16
  Table reference C – gross transfers
    between funds   6.17–6.21
  Table reference D – other recognised
    gains and losses   6.22–6.25
  Terence Higgins Trust   6.4
  Women's Therapy Centre   6.4
Subsidiary undertakings
  notes   13.22–13.25
Summarised accounts   14.1–14.25
  adaptation of accounts   14.22, 14.23
  characteristics   14.6
  charts   14.16–14.19
  contents   14.2
  cross-border charities   15.34–15.45
    see also Cross-border
        charities
  diagrams   14.16–14.19
  faults to be avoided   14.20
  financial review   14.13–14.15
  how information shown 14.10–14.25
  legislative requirements   14.9
  omissions   14.21
  proof-reading   14.24, 14.25
  purpose of   14.5
  SORP, and   14.9
  summarised financial
    statements   14.11, 14.12
Summary Information
  Return   3.21, 3.22

Support costs   13.52–13.62
  actual usage of common
    services   13.59
  apportionment   13.53
  disclosure   13.52–13.62
  disclosure of basis used   13.60
  floor space   13.57
  time spent   13.58
Tax exemptions   17.1–17.96
  accumulating income   17.53–17.61
  application for charitable
    purposes   17.39–17.61
  non-charitable expenditure   17.41,
                              17.62.17–77
    chargeable accounting periods
    from 22 March
    2006   17.62–17.67
    chageable accounting periods
    starting before 22 March
    2006   17.68–17.77
  payments to overseas body   17.42
  qualifying investments   17.43–17.47
  qualifying loans   17.43–17.47
  transactions with substantial
    donors   17.48–17.52
Tax incentives to donors   19.1–19.54
Trading activities   1.17 18.1–18.43
  deeds of covenant *see Deeds of*
    covenant
  Gift Aid   18.26–18.29
  profit-shedding   18.21–18.25
  small traders   18.11–18.13
  sponsorship   18.33–18.43
  tax, and   18.1–18.43
  tax exemption   18.4–18.10
  trading subsidiary   18.14–18.20
  VAT implications   18.30–18.32
Trust and estate charities form   App 9
Trustee indemnity insurance 2.41–2.43
Trustees' report   4.1–4.38
  achievements   4.24
  activities   4.20–4.23
  basic concept   4.4
  basic requirement   4.7
  charitable companies   4.8
  contents   4.9
  Coram   4.34
  duty to prepare   4.1–4.9
  essentials   4.29
  features   4.5
  financial review   4.25, 4.26
  funds held as custodian trustee on
    behalf of others   4.28
  governance   4.18
  illustrations   4.38

Trustees' report – *contd*
  management   4.18
  narrative information   4.14–4.38
  objectives   4.20–4.23
  performance   4.24
  plans for future periods   4.27
  public benefit   4.17
  purpose   4.1
  reference and administrative
    details of charity, trustees
    and advisors   4.10–4.23
  responsibility for preparing 4.6
  SCIE's board of trustees   4.19
  statement of responsibilities 4.36
  structure   4.18, 4.35
  target audience   4.32
  trustee induction and training 4.19
  Trust of St Benedict's Abbey
    Ealing   4.23
  Wandsworth Women's Aid   4.19
Trustees' responsibilities   2.1–2.55
  annual report   2.28
  compliance   2.7–2.11
  conflicts of interest   2.15
  constitution   2.37, 2.38
  delegation of powers   2.23–2.25
  insurance   2.39–2.45
    classes of risk   2.40
  investments   2.17–2.22
    duty of care   2.21
  legal responsibilities   2.1–2.25
  maintenance of property   2.16
  management structure   2.32–2.36
  overall   2.5, 2.6
  prudence   2.12–2.20
  reporting duties   2.46–2.49
  scope   2.26–2.31
Trustees, transactions with 13.62–13.78
  deemed material   13.74
  definitions   13.63
  disclosure   13.73
  material   13.64
  related parties   13.65–13.71
  related party transactions   13.72
Trusts   1.39–1.44
Unincorporated association   1.54–15.7
Useful addresses   App 1
Value added tax   17.78, 20.1–20.210
  administration   20.176–20.204
  annual accounting scheme   20.184
  business/non-business
    apportionment   20.25–20.36
  'business test'   20.9
  cash accounting scheme   20.185
  challenge events   20.173–20.175

Value added tax – *contd*
    charity activities   20.21
    commission income   20.164–20.166
    complexity of   20.209
    'consideration'   20.7
    correcting errors   20.192–20.194
    costs   20.210
    de minimis limits   20.52
    direct tax, conflicts with   20.207, 20.208
    exemptions   20.14, 20.15, 20.126–20.159
        cultural services   20.143–20.146
        education   20.139, 20.140
        fundraising events   20.150–20.159
        health and welfare services   20.128–20.138
        membership subscriptions   20.147–20.149
        sports services   20.141, 20.142
    flat rate scheme   20.186
    floor space   20.48
    four-year cap   20.192–20.194
    funding agreement, and   20.10
    general framework   20.1–20.19
    group registration   20.188–20.191
    investment management   20.205, 20.206
    over-ride provisions   20.53–20.57
    overseas fundraising   20.173–20.175
    partial exemption   20.40–20.47
    penalties   20.195–20.201
    property   20.58–20.115
        annexe, meaning   20.63–20.66
        apportionment   20.92
        building, meaning   20.61, 20.62
        building materials   20.93
        capital goods scheme   20.99, 20.100

Value added tax – *contd*
    property – *contd*
        certificates   20.67–20.69
        change of use   20.94
        clawback and payback under regulations   20.109
        design and build   20.90, 20.91
        Lennartz   20.108
        listed buildings   20.84–20.86
        listed places of worship   20.87
        option to tax   20.110–20.115
        reduced rate   20.88, 20.89
        relevant charitable purpose   20.70–20.78
        relevant residential purpose   20.79–20.83
        Schedule 10 clawback   20.95–20.98
    recovery   20.20–20.57
    registration   20.176–20.187
    royalties   20.167–20.170
    rulings   20.202–20.204
    sale of goods   20.171, 20.172
    scope   20.6–20.13
    specific reliefs   20.116–20.125
    sponsorship   20.162, 20.163
    staff numbers   20.37–20.39, 20.49–20.51
    trading activities   18.30–18.32
    tribunals   20.202–20.204
    zero rate   20.16–20.19, 20.116–20.125
        advertising services   20.117–20.119
        donated goods   20.124, 20.125
        supplies to benefit disabled persons   20.120–20.123
Whistle blowing   16.65–16.68